The Macmillan
Good English
Handbook

In memory of the flame and the poetry of

Susan Fleetwood

The Macmillan Good English Handbook

COMPILED BY

Godfrey Howard

MACMILLAN

First published 1997 by Macmillan

an imprint of Macmillan Publishers Ltd
25 Eccleston Place, London SW1W 9NF
Basingstoke and Oxford

Associated companies throughout the world

ISBN 0 333 64806 4

3 5 7 9 8 6 4 2

A CIP catalogue record for this book is available from
the British Library.

Typeset by Parker Typesetting Service, Leicester
Printed and bound in Great Britain by
Mackays of Chatham plc, Chatham, Kent

Notes on use

Everyone feels uncertain at times about the use of English. An up-to-date dictionary is essential for checking the spelling and meaning of words, but there are thousands of grammatical and other linguistic questions that dictionaries do not answer. This handbook fills that gap.

It is the first guide to the use of English compiled and designed to flip open while you're in the middle of writing a sentence, and offer an immediate clear-cut answer to a doubtful point of grammar, how to use a particular word, or which word to choose.

There is much more freedom now in the way we can use English. But a language cannot survive without order. The entries in this book maintain a balance between orthodox grammar and what is out of touch with the language on the brink of the 21st century.

For some people, an entry may err on the side of permissiveness: others may consider the occasional rule too prescriptive. But this is a handbook for the linguistic fast lanes of the 1990s, and the aim in every entry is to offer reliable guidance without the clutter of ifs and buts.

The authority for every RULE and RECOMMENDATION rests on a consensus of novelists, playwrights, editors, broadcasters and others who care about the English language.

Entries

● RULE(S)

set out what is generally regarded as correct English. To depart from these would usually be marked down as sub-standard.

● RECOMMENDATION(S)

sum up what many good writers and speakers accept as good up-to-date usage. Some people may be uneasy about certain recommendations, but serious users of the language have to decide at what point a departure from traditional usage has become standard English.

● OPTION(S)

offer alternatives that are equally acceptable. You can choose which one suits you, so long as you are consistent.

● CAUTION(S)

are warnings to be on guard against common mistakes, or a risk of misunderstanding.

Pronunciation

The simple system of phonetics, used for pronunciation of difficult words, can be read at sight. *Stressed syllables* are in capitals: 'CONjugal'.

Bold Type

Bold type in an entry tells you there is a separate entry under that heading.

Symbols

There are only three easy symbols to remember:

✓ Where there are OPTIONS (or choices in a RECOMMENDATION or a RULE), a tick marks the one preferred.

[!] This is a warning that some people might dispute a RECOMMENDATION or an OPTION. But many good writers go along with it, and if you do the same you will be in good company.

$ AMERICAN ENGLISH.

Acknowledgements

More than a hundred writers, broadcasters, editors, journalists, lecturers and other dedicated users of English contributed advice, suggestions and points of view. My thanks to them all for their time and patience in helping to sustain balance and good sense in the entries in this handbook. And it would all have been lonely and unrelieved without the support from my wife, Françoise Legrand, who shared every word of this book, and the backup from Chris Stewart, commissioning editor at Macmillan, Doreen Montgomery, my literary agent, and from my daughter's translation service, *Lesley Howard Languages*.

A

a/an

● RULES

1 The basic rule is well known – *a* before a consonant, *an* before a vowel: *a* woman; *an* egg.

2 Use *an* before the few words beginning with an 'h' which is *not sounded*: *an* hour; *an* honest broker; *an* honour.

3 Use *a* before words beginning with the vowels 'u' or 'eu' which are pronounced 'yoo': *a* union; *a* European.

4 Use *a* before the vowel 'o' pronounced as 'w': *a* one-night stand; *a* one-in-a-million chance.

5 Use *an* before 8, 80, 800, etc: *an* £8 million contract; *an* 80-year-old man.

6 Use *an* before abbreviations that begin with a vowel sound: *an* FRS; *an* EU citizen.

abbreviations

● RECOMMENDATION

Leave out stops in abbreviations, as nowadays it looks laboured to put them in, and unnecessary stops hold up the flow of the eye across a sentence. This includes:

numbers: 2nd; 3rd; 10th

metric measurements: 100km; 10cm; 75ml (see also **metric measurements**)

counties: Bucks; Oxon; Glos

days and months: Mon; Wed; Feb; Sept

time and dates: 9am; 7pm; 500 BC; AD 300

points of the compass: NW; SE; NE

titles: Mr; Ms; St (St Paul's Cathedral)

initials: HG Wells; GBS (George Bernard Shaw); M & S (Marks and Spencer)

shortcuts: co-op; demo; recap; repro

● RULES FOR THE PLURAL OF ABBREVIATIONS

1 Most are formed simply by adding *-s*: MPs; QCs; demos

2 In a few cases a letter is doubled: MS (manuscript), MSS (manuscripts); p7 (page 7), pp7–9 (pages 7–9)

● RULES FOR THE ORDER OF ABBREVIATIONS AFTER NAMES

Appointments on behalf of the Queen come first, followed by honours, then membership of learned societies, then degrees followed by professional qualifications, and finally MP (Member of Parliament): Henry Brown QC, CBE, FRS, MA, FRIBA, MP

- RULES FOR ACRONYMS (abbreviations pronounced as words)

  It is usually better to keep these in capital letters: UNESCO; ASLEF; CD-ROM (but *Aids* [**a**cquired **i**mmuno-**d**eficiency **s**yndrome] is more usual now than AIDS).

  NOTE A few acronyms lose their initial capital letter and are treated as ordinary words: *laser* (**l**ight **a**mplification by **s**timulated **e**mission of **r**adiation); *quango* (**qu**asi-**a**utonomous **n**on-**g**overnmental **o**rganisation).

- CAUTIONS

1 Abbreviations are justified when they are shortcuts (NATO is quicker to take in than *North Atlantic Treaty Organisation*). There's not much point in using an abbreviation for a term that's less than say six letters: prefer *April* to *Apr*; *Road* to *Rd* (unless it's a tightly-spaced caption or table).

2 Do not mystify readers by using abbreviations that are not understood by most people: OMOV (one member one vote); aka (also known as); EBU (European Broadcasting Union).

  When an obscure abbreviation occurs several times in the same text, write it in full the first time, followed by the abbreviation in brackets: Society for the Prevention and Relief of Cancer (SPRC). This leaves the way clear after that to use the abbreviation on its own.

3 Some shortcuts are conversational and are out of place in serious writing: fridge; telly; wellies.

$ Most stops are kept firmly in place: U.S.; U.S.A.; P.T. (Pacific Time); L.A. (Los Angeles). But stops are dropped in acronyms: NASA (National Aeronautics and Space Administration); NATO (North Atlantic Treaty Organisation).

ability / capacity

- RECOMMENDATIONS

1 Write 'the ability *to* . . .'; 'the capacity *for* . . .'.

2 Use *ability* for an acquired skill: 'her ability to speak several languages'.

3 Use *capacity* for an inborn talent: 'her capacity for learning languages'.

-able / -eable

- RULES

1 When a verb ends in a *silent -e*, drop the *e*, except after *c* or *g*: drive, *drivable*; but renoun*c*e; *renounceable*; chan*g*e, *changeable*.

2 With verbs of more than one syllable ending in a consonant followed by *-y*, change *y* to *i*: deny, *deniable*; rely, *reliable*.

- OPTION

  There are a few words where *able / eable* are alternatives: *movable* ✓, *moveable*; *ratable* ✓, *rateable*.

-able / -ible

  There is no reliable rule to tell you whether a descriptive word is formed from a verb by adding *-able* or *-ible*. Is it *accessible* or *accessable, responsible* or *responsable*? Because it is more usual, the most common mistake is to use *-able* instead of *-ible* (*accessible* and *responsible* are correct).

NOTES

1 Recent formations are more likely to be *-able*: clubbable; unbeatable; unget-at-able.

2 There are fewer *-ible* words, so it's worth noting the more common ones: accessible; admissible; audible; collapsible; compatible; comprehensible; contemptible; credible; defensible; destructible; divisible (but dividable); edible; eligible; fallible; feasible; flexible; forcible; gullible; indelible; intelligible; irresistible; legible; negligible; perceptible; permissible; plausible; possible; responsible; reversible; sensible; susceptible; tangible; visible.

● RULE

When in doubt, look it up in a dictionary.

abnormal / subnormal

● RULE

Abnormal is *different* from normal. *Subnormal* is *below* normal.

● CAUTION

When these words are used about people, they can have a pathological sense. Unless this is intended, it's gentler to substitute *not normal* or *below normal.*

NOTE *Above normal* is also available, and further up the scale, *supernormal* (one word), to describe someone or something greatly above normal.

about / around / round

● RECOMMENDATIONS

1 *Around* and *round* are usually interchangeable: 'she looked *round* ✓ (or *around*) the room'.

2 Mechanical things go *round*: 'the wheels are going round'.

3 Prefer *round about* to *around about*: '*round about* 20 people'. ('*About* 20 people' is preferable in writing, as *round about* is more conversational.)

4 For an approximate time, all three words can be used: 'it was *about* ✓ (or *around* or *round*) 7 o'clock'.

$ *round* is preferred: 'it was round midnight'.

(in the) **absence** (of)

● RECOMMENDATION

Avoid this long-winded expression: '*in the absence of* more details, we cannot deal with this matter'. *Without* does the same job and does it in one word instead of four: 'without more details . . .'.

absorb / adsorb

● RULE

Absorb is the everyday word for a sponge soaking up water, for example, or for the way we take in information. *Adsorb* is mostly restricted to chemistry, usually for a condensation of gases that forms a thin film.

abstract (pronunciation)

● RULES

1 'ABstract' (stress on the *first* syllable) is the *noun*, meaning a summary: 'this is an "ABstract" of what was said'. 'ABstract' is also the *descriptive word*, meaning theoretical, not practical: 'this is an "ABstract" question, with no relevance to everyday problems'.

2 'abSTRACT'(stress on the *second* syllable) is the *verb*, meaning to remove or take out: 'abSTRACT' papers from a file.

abstract nouns

Abstract nouns represent states and concepts: factor; poverty; situation; truth. They tend to diffuse the directness of a statement: 'Our *perception* of the *situation* is that economic *factors* require the continued *application* of the high-interest rate *discipline*.'

● RECOMMENDATION

When you want to lay it on the line and make sentences clear and immediate, use as few abstract nouns as possible: 'The way we see it, interest rates have to stay high.'

absurd / ridiculous

● RECOMMENDATION

Treat *absurd* as the more serious word for something separated from normal reason and common sense, sometimes deliberately cutting across rational life to present an oblique view of the human situation. Keep *ridiculous* as a lighter more everyday word for something that is silly: 'it's absurd to say people are happy because they are poor'; 'it's ridiculous to judge a painting by its frame'.

abysmal / abyssal

● RULE

1 Although both words relate to depth, *abysmal* is the only one that extends the meaning to qualities and conditions: abysmal ignorance; abysmal poverty.

2 *Abyssal* is now mostly confined to oceanography, usually for depths below 300 fathoms (a fathom is six feet or 1.829 metres).

● CAUTION

One *b* in both words.

academic

● CAUTION

If you use *academic* in the old sense of scholarly, you will probably be misunderstood, unless it's in an educational context. As a descriptive word, *academic* now often means 'theoretical; up in the clouds': 'his approach is *academic*' would usually be taken to mean 'it is out of touch with the real world'.

NOTE This does not apply to *academic* as a *noun*, which is the standard non-judgemental term for anyone teaching at a university or a college of higher education.

accent / accentuate / highlight

● RECOMMENDATIONS

1 Use *accent* to mean stressing a syllable or a word in speech.
2 Use *accentuate* in a general, visual or musical context to mean emphasising something or making it stand out: accentuate a point by banging the table; accentuate the whiteness of a dress with a jet-black belt.
3 *Highlight* is the more modern word meaning the same as *accentuate*, but is better restricted to *visual* emphasis: 'the whiteness of the dress is highlighted by a black belt'. *Highlight* is also the wordprocessing term for selecting part of the text. And hairdressers (and their customers) prefer to *highlight* hair rather than *dye* it (even if it does come to the same thing).

● CAUTION

The past form of *highlight* is *highlighted* (never 'highlit').

accents

Some accents still persist in English for words of foreign origin. Here are the more common accents:

Acute accent (´) When used in English, it is mostly in French words, where it changes the sound of *e* (*café*), and also in Spanish names to indicate stress: *Málaga* (PRON 'MALaga').

Cedilla The squiggle under *ç* to indicate an *s* sound: *Françoise*; *façade*.

Circumflex (^) Mostly found over *â* and *ô* in words of French origin: *pâté*; *rôle*.

Diaeresis See *umlaut* (below).

Grave accent (`) (PRON 'grahv') Mostly found in French and Italian words, where it modifies vowel sounds (or indicates a different meaning): *première*.

Tilde (˜) (PRON 'TILde(r)') Mostly familiar in Spanish words over *ñ* to indicate a *ny* sound (as in 'onion'): *señor*. (Also found in Portuguese over *ã* and *õ* to indicate a nasal pronunciation.)

Umlaut or *diaeresis* (PRON 'OOMlowt', 'dye-EHR-re(r)sis') These are terms for two dots over a vowel. In German words it is called an *umlaut*: *Düsseldorf*; *Dürrenmatt*. For English words, the term is *diaeresis*, and it is used to show that a vowel is pronounced separately: *naïve* (PRON 'nye-EEV'); *Chloë* (PRON 'CLOH-ee').

● RECOMMENDATION

In English, when in doubt leave accents out. The tendency now is to drop accents on many words of foreign origin: *role*; *cafe*; *premiere* (instead of *rôle*, *café*, *première*). [!] (Even in France, there is a proposal to phase out accents on a number of words.)

accentuate / highlight / accent

See **accent** . . .

accessory / accessary

● RECOMMENDATION

Use *accessory* for all meanings of the word, whether it's for someone involved in a crime without actually committing it, or something additional or extra, such as a radio fitted to a car.

$ Only one spelling: *accessory*.

accidentally

● CAUTION

Avoid the common mistake of spelling it 'accidently'. And in speech give it *five* syllables: 'ac-si-DENT-e(r)-ly'.

accommodate / accommodation

● CAUTIONS

1 Avoid jargon ('alternative accommodation' instead of 'another home') and pomposity ('Do you have any accommodation?' instead of 'Do you have a room?').
2 Always -*cc*- and -*mm*-.

account / invoice / statement / bill

● RECOMMENDATIONS

1 *Account* and *bill* are interchangeable general terms for a note showing how much you have to pay for goods or services (*bill* is down-to-earth, *account* more upmarket).
2 *Invoice* is more precise: a detailed note setting out lists of goods or services, with prices alongside, VAT (if applicable) and any discounts.
3 *Statement* is short for 'statement of account', and should itemise all invoices submitted during a period, cheques received, credits allowed, so that the final figure is the remaining sum due. (*Bank statement* is a record of transactions in a bank account.)
$ Although *bill* is also used for a note of charges for goods, the first meaning is usually for a banknote, such as a *ten-dollar bill*. A bill for a meal in a restaurant is a *check*.

accountable / responsible

● RECOMMENDATIONS

1 Treat *accountable* as the more solemn word, meaning that a person can be called to

account for something they have done: 'you are accountable for the crime you have committed'.

2 Although *responsible* means much the same, it should generally be used as a lighter word: 'he is responsible for not having done the washing-up'.

3 Use *accountable* only in relation to *people*, while *responsible* can be used for *people* or *things*: 'heavy rain is responsible for the delay'.

accursed (pronunciation)
● OPTION
Pronunciation with *two* or *three* syllables is acceptable: 'a-CURSED' or 'a-CUR-sed'✓.

acknowledgement / acknowledgment
● RECOMMENDATIONS
1 Both spellings are used, but choose *acknowledgement*. (Compare *abridgement*, *amazement*: when -*ment* is added to words ending in a silent -*e*, the -*e* usually stays.)

2 It is good plain English to 'receive a letter' rather than to 'acknowledge receipt of it', which is old-fashioned business jargon.

acoustics *is / are*
● RULE
When it's a science, it's *singular*: 'acoustics *is* an interesting subject'. When it's the qualities in a hall it's *plural*: 'the acoustics of the new concert hall *are* good'.

acquiesce / agree
● RECOMMENDATIONS
1 To *acquiesce* in something carries with it the implication that you've agreed simply by saying nothing to object: 'everyone kept quiet so it was assumed they acquiesced in the suggestion'.

2 To *agree* to something is more wholehearted, since it implies you've said so in one way or another: 'everyone agreed by putting up their hands'.
● OPTION
You can acquiesce *in* ✓ or *to* something (but not 'with').

acquire
● RECOMMENDATION
It is unnecessarily grand to *acquire* something, when you can *buy* it, *win* it or *get* it.

acre
● RULE
A statutory acre in Britain and the US is 4840 square yards.

● CAUTION

In Scotland and Ireland, as well as in some English counties, other measurements may still be referred to (a Scottish acre can be approx 1.27 and an Irish acre 1.62 statutory English acres).

NOTE Metric land measurements: *hectare* (PRON 'HECtaire') equals 100 *ares* (PRON 'ahrz'), equivalent to 2.471 acres. 3 hectares, 7 ares, for example, is expressed as 3ha 7a.

acronyms

See **abbreviations**

act / action

● RULES

1   An *act* is a thing that is done, immediate and complete: an act of kindness; an act of war.

2   An *action* is the process of *carrying out* an act: go into action; killed in action; the action taken by the Bank of England to counter a fall in the value of the pound.

activate / motivate

● RECOMMENDATIONS

1   Use **activate** for *things* (it is used in chemistry and physics for the bringing about of a reaction).

2   Use **motivate** for *people*, when someone is encouraged to do something: a salesforce is motivated to go out and get orders.

active / passive voice

These are grammatical terms. *Active* voice is when a noun relates to the verb directly: 'the dog bit the man'; 'the woman opened the door'. *Passive* voice is when sentences are turned round: 'the man was bitten by the dog'; 'the door was opened by the woman'.

● RECOMMENDATION

The *passive* voice is less out in the open, and can even seem evasive: compare 'it was already known that . . .' with 'we already knew . . .'. When you want to lay something on the line, use the *active* voice.

actor / actress

● RECOMMENDATIONS

1   Follow the present trend which is to use *actor* as the unisex word for both sexes. [!]

2   Where it is necessary to specify a woman, there's no choice but to use *actress* ✓ or *woman actor*.

● CAUTION

Feminists dislike *actress* and 'woman actor', because they feel it implies that the standard is male. But it is sometimes unavoidable: 'She won the award for Actress of the Year and her husband won the award for Actor of the Year.'

acute accent

See **accents**

AD / BC

● RULES

1 AD is necessary only for dates near the traditional date of Christ's birth, such as AD 100, or when BC (*before Christ*) dates come into the context: 'between 200 BC and AD 200'.

2 Because AD stands for *anno Domini* (in the year of the Lord), it should come *before* the year: AD 200 (in the year of the Lord 200).

NOTE Exceptions are dates, such as 'the fifth century AD', where it is customary to place AD *after* the date.

3 BC always comes *after* the date: 1500 BC.

4 A space should be left between AD / BC and the date: AD 200, 2000 BC.

NOTE Followers of other religions sometimes use CE instead of AD for the Christian era date system: CE 200. But CE does not appear often and many people wouldn't know what it means, so it cannot be recommended.

adaptor / adapter

● RECOMMENDATION

Use *adaptor* for *all* meanings of the word, whether it's a person who adapts a book for another medium, or an electrical or mechanical device used to adapt equipment.

addenda / addendums

● RULE

The Latin plural is the only correct form: one *addend**um**,* two or more *addend**a**.*

address (verb)

See **deal with / address**

addresses

● RECOMMENDATION

Follow the present style, which is to leave out *all* punctuation. The Post Office requests that the postcode should be given a line to itself, to help sorting machines:

Macmillan Reference Books
25 Eccleston Place
London
SW1W 9NF

adequate / sufficient / enough

See **enough** . . .

adjacent / adjoining / next to

See **next to** . . .

adjectives

See **grammatical terms**

adjoining / adjacent / next to

See **next to** . . .

adjudge / adjudicate / judge

See **judge** . . .

administrate / administer

● RECOMMENDATIONS

1 *Administrate* is the usual word in business contexts, meaning to look after the running of an organisation: administrate an accounts department.

2 *Administer* is better left to law and religion: administer justice; administer the rites of a sacrament.

admissible / admissable

● RULE

Admissible. See also **-able / -ible.**

admission / admittance

● RECOMMENDATIONS

1 You apply for *admission* to a club or a society.

2 It's an *admission* when you own up to something.

3 To enter a building, such as a museum, you ask for *admission* or *admittance*. They both mean 'Can I come in?' But it's *admission* to a hospital.

4 It's *no admittance* rather than *no admission*.

adsorb / absorb

See **absorb** . . .

adverbs

See **grammatical terms**

adverse / averse

● RULES

1 If you are *adverse* to something you are against it, its *adversary*: 'he is adverse to her getting married'.

2 If you are *averse* to something, you have a strong distaste for it, an *aversion* for it: 'she is averse to marriage'.

advocate / counsel / barrister

See **barrister** . . .

ae / oe

● OPTION

In a few words, and the number is increasing, dictionaries now allow the simple *e* as an alternative to *ae* or *oe*: *encyclopedia* ✓or *encyclopaedia*; *medieval* ✓or *mediaeval*; *primeval* ✓or *primaeval* .

● CAUTION

For the time being there are still a number of words where it is considered wrong to replace *ae* or *oe* by *e*: *archaeology*; *gynaecology*; *diarrhoea*; *aesthetic*.

● RECOMMENDATION

When in doubt check with an up-to-date dictionary. Where alternative spellings are shown, use the *e* spelling, rather than *ae* or *oe* (see examples under OPTION above).

\$ In nearly all words, *e* replaces *ae* and *oe*: *archeology, gynecology, diarrhea, esthetic.*

aerobic / anaerobic

● RECOMMENDATIONS

1 The biological use of **aerobic** (to describe micro-organisms that thrive on oxygen) has given way in general use to *aerobic* as a descriptive word for exercise (*aerobics*) sustained long enough to increase the body's oxygen intake and lower the rate of heartbeat at rest.

2 Although some fitness experts use **anaerobic** for a bodily state where more oxygen is required than is taken in, the word is better restricted to biology (*anaerobic* describes organisms that live without oxygen).

aerodrome / airport / airfield

See **airfield** . . .

aeroplane / airplane / aircraft

See **aircraft** . . .

aerospace / airspace

● RULES

1 *Aerospace* includes both the earth's atmosphere and outer space. A journey in *aerospace* could cover a quick hop over to Brussels or a voyage to the moon.

2 *Airspace* is subject to international law. It is the air or earth's atmosphere above a country, and comes under its sovereignty.

   NOTE Part of *aerospace* comes within a country's domain but the part in outer space, beyond the earth's atmosphere, does not.

affect / effect

● RULES

1 As a *verb*, *effect* means to accomplish something or to make something happen: 'the bonus scheme effected a big increase in productivity'.

2 As a *verb*, *affect* means to have an influence on something or somebody: 'outside work has been affected by the weather'.

3 As a *noun*, *effect* is always the word when you want to say the result, outcome or influence: 'the bonus scheme had a big effect on productivity'. (The noun *affect* is limited to a specialised clinical term in psychology, used for an emotion or desire.)

   NOTE A *knock-on effect* is a secondary effect that follows on: 'the knock-on effect of high interest rates is bigger wage settlements'.

affinity *between / with / to / for*

● RULE

   Keep to *affinity* **between** and *affinity* **with**: 'there's an affinity *between* us'; 'I have an affinity *with* her'.

aficionado

● RECOMMENDATION

   Use *aficionado* for both sexes: *she* or *he* is an *aficionado* of . . . ('aficionada' is the feminine word in Spanish, but not generally used in English).

● CAUTIONS

1 The plural is *aficionados* (never '-oes').

2 One -*f*- (the association with 'affection' sometimes leads to the mistake of -*ff*-).

aforementioned / aforesaid

● RECOMMENDATION

   A solicitor might write about the *aforementioned* or *aforesaid* lease, deed or whatever, in order to be precise. For the rest of us, outside legal contexts, we're better off saying 'the lease' or 'the deed' or, if it's clear what we mean, simply 'it'.

Afro-

● RULE

Afro- is the recognised abbreviation of 'African': *Afro-American*; *Afro-Caribbean*. *Afro-* is descriptive in the same way as *Anglo-*, and has no racist connotations.

after / after-

After is a common prefix, sometimes with a hyphen sometimes without.

● RECOMMENDATIONS

Hyphenate: after-care; after-effect; after-hours; after-sales; after-taste. Treat as *one* word: afterbirth; afterglow; afterlife; aftermath; aftershave; afterthought.

after / afterwards / in the wake of

● RECOMMENDATIONS

1 In writing, *after**wards*** is preferable to indicate a sequence of events: 'she made three telephone calls, and went to bed immediately afterwards'.

2 When we indicate how much time has elapsed, *after* or *after**wards*** ✓ are alternatives: 'she telephoned him three days *after* (or *afterwards*)'.

3 *In the wake of* suggests that something takes place, not only *after* an earlier event, but as an outcome of it: 'a committee of enquiry was set up in the wake of the minister's resignation'.

$ *Afterward* (without an *-s*). 'A quarter *after* 7' is the American way of saying 'a quarter past 7'.

-age (pronunciation)

● RULE

Unlike French, stress in English is on the *first* syllable of the word (not on *-age*): 'BARRage'; 'DRESSage'; 'GARage' (see also **garage**); 'MASSage'; 'MIRage'.

NOTE *Montage* and *collage* are thought of as French words, which puts the stress on the *-age* syllable: 'montAGE'; 'collAGE'.

$ Stress is on the *-age* syllable: 'garAGE'.

age / era / period

● RECOMMENDATIONS

1 *Age* is best for a truly long period (it is the basic division of time in archaeology: the Stone Age; the Iron Age).

2 *Era* is preferable when it's a period of time given some unity by cultural or historical circumstances: the Victorian era; the era of silent films.

3 *Period* can cover centuries (the period between Shakespeare and Dickens) or a few minutes (a ten-minute rest period).

ageism

In the 1990s *ageism* takes its place alongside *racism* and *sexism*. It is used for discrimination against someone because they are 'old'.

● CAUTION

The word 'old' is indeterminate: for a fighter pilot, it could be over 35, for a statesman, over 80, for a philosopher, over . . . ?

agenda / agendum

● RULE

The Latin 'agend*um*' for the singular is no longer in use in English. It is one *agenda*, two or more *agendas*.

aggravate / aggravation

● RECOMMENDATION

Two meanings can now be accepted. The standard meaning is to make a bad situation worse: 'the dispute was aggravated by the chairman's ultimatum'. A second meaning is now in general use. This uses *aggravate* to mean annoy or irritate [!]: 'the loud background music aggravated him'. Both meanings also apply to the noun *aggravation*.

agnostic / atheist

● RECOMMENDATION

Although the distinction is not always clear-cut, use *agnostic* for someone who has an open mind about the existence of God, and *atheist* for someone who rejects altogether the concept of a divinity.

agree / acquiesce

See **acquiesce** . . .

Aids / AIDS

See **abbreviations** (ACRONYMS)

ain't / aren't

See **aren't** . . .

aircraft / aeroplane / airplane

● RULES

1 *Aeroplane* is British, *airplane* is American.
2 *Aircraft* is the RAF term. It is both singular and plural (one aircraft, a flight of ten aircraft). *Aircraft* also includes helicopters.

● RECOMMENDATION

In British English, use *aircraft* in all contexts (*aeroplane* is an old-fashioned word).

$ See RULE 1 above.

airfield / airport / aerodrome

● RECOMMENDATION

Use *airfield* for a landing place with limited facilities for take-off and maintenance, and *airport* for a complex of runways and buildings with full facilities for passengers and customs. *Aerodrome* is an old-fashioned word, and belongs mostly in pre-World War II contexts.

à la . . .

● RULE

Although *la* is feminine in French, the expression *à la* can be used about a man or a woman: 'a glamorous 60–year-old *à la* Elizabeth Taylor'; 'exploit pension funds *à la* Robert Maxwell'.

alas

● RECOMMENDATION

Alas sounds archaic or melodramatic, so choose an alternative word: *unfortunately*; *sadly*; *tragically*; *disastrously*; *catastrophically* – according to how bad it is.

albeit / though / although

See **although** . . .

ale / beer

See **beer** . . .

alibi

● RULE

Alibi is correctly used when an accused person claims they were somewhere else at the time the offence was committed.

● CAUTION

Avoid using *alibi* simply to mean any excuse: 'he had a good excuse (not a 'good *alibi*') for being late for dinner'.

all alone

● RECOMMENDATION

Although *all* is unnecessary, since you are either alone or not alone, if you want to stress how lonely or frightened you are, *all alone* is valid, as Coleridge found in *The Ancient Mariner*: 'Alone, alone, all all alone . . .'.

allege / allegation

● CAUTION

When we read that someone is *alleged* to have done something, it means there is no proof, at least for the time being. But before you use *allege* or *allegation*, remember they are not neutral words. For many people they carry with them the connotation of guilt, which may be doing someone an injustice, because nothing has been proved.

alleluia / hallelujah

● RULE

Alleluia is the usual spelling in English for this Hebrew word meaning 'God be praised'.

NOTE An exception is the triumphant close to Part II of Handel's *Messiah*, which is always called the *Hallelujah Chorus*.

allied (pronunciation)

See **ally** . . .

all in / all-in / all in all

● RULES

1 When you feel *all in*, you're totally exhausted: there's no hyphen.
2 In industry, an *all-in* rate is a wage rate that includes bonuses and other extras. And this is extended to general use where an *all-in* price, an *all-in* rent . . . includes all charges. Used in this way it takes a hyphen, as it does in 'all-in wrestling'. See **hyphens** (RECOMMENDATION 4).
3 *All in all* does not take hyphens.

alliteration / assonance

● RULE

Alliteration is a run of words beginning with the same *consonantal* sound: 'I may marry Mary.' *Assonance* is a run of similar *vowel* sounds: 'The rain in Spain stays mainly in the plains.'

all of

● CAUTION

While *all of* is not wrong, use it with care, as it can seem clumsy. For the word *all* can stand on its own: 'you cannot fool *all* the people *all* the time' (rather than 'all *of* the people all *of* the time').

allow / allow *of*

● OPTION

Either will do: 'our agreement allows (or allows *of* ✓) two interpretations' ('. . . *allows of* ' is easier to take in).

all ready / already

● RULES

1 *All ready* can mean different things: 'we are all ready to leave' can mean that 'all of us' are ready, *or* 'we've now made all arrangements' (put our coats on, packed our bags, or whatever is required to be ready to leave).

2 *Already* relates to *time*, meaning that something has taken place, or up to a certain moment: 'we're already leaving'; 'by 7 o'clock we had already left'.

all right / alright

● RULE

All right ('alright' is usually considered substandard).

all that

● RECOMMENDATION

There's some argument about whether expressions, such as 'it's not as far as all that'; 'it's not as bad as all that' . . . , common in speech, are acceptable in writing. We can rephrase them as: 'it's not so far'; 'it's not so bad' . . . , but they do not mean quite the same, for *all that* suggests that whatever it is has been exaggerated. Written English and spoken English have become closer to each other, and there seems nothing wrong in writing as well as saying, 'they do not see each other *all that* often'.

all together / altogether

● RULES

1 *All together* relates to a number of things happening, or a number of people being somewhere or doing something *at the same time*: 'the women arrived all together'; 'All together now – let's sing!'

2 *Altogether* means totally, with nothing left out: 'he has had three wives altogether' (that is, a total of three wives). 'Three wives *all together*' would be polygamy, since it means three wives at the same time.

● CAUTION

Avoid 'in the altogether', a prudish way of saying *naked*.

allude / refer

● RECOMMENDATIONS

1 Use *allude* for mentioning someone or something indirectly: 'without giving his name, she alluded to a former lover'.

2 Use *refer* when it's more open and specific: 'she referred to John, who at one time had been her lover'.

ally (pronunciation)

● RULES

1 As a *noun*, the stress is on the *first* syllable: 'America was Britain's 'ALLy' during the war'.

2 As a *verb*, meaning linking things together, stress is on the *second* syllable: 'these two points of view 'aLLY' with each other'.

● OPTION

When things have been connected in the past, they can be 'ALLied'✓ or 'aLLIED'.

NOTE In military contexts, stress is always on the *first* syllable ('ALLied' forces).

almanac / almanack

● RECOMMENDATION

Almanac.

NOTE Exceptions are *Whitaker's Almanack* and *The Oxford Almanack.*

alphabetical order

● RECOMMENDATION

In a list, keep to strict alphabetical order, without taking into account capital letters, hyphens and spaces between words: data; databank; database; data flow chart; data *is* or *are*; data processing; Data Protection Act.

Alpine / alpine

● RULE

Use a capital A to relate *Alpine* specifically to the Alps in France, Italy, Switzerland and Austria: an Alpine ski resort.

● RECOMMENDATION

Use *alpine* in a general way for anything to do with high mountains anywhere: an alpine scene; alpine flowers.

already / all ready

See **all ready . . .**

alright / all right

See **all right . . .**

alter / change

● RECOMMENDATIONS

1 Use *alter* to suggest a relatively minor modification: alter a skirt by taking the waist in; alter a text by changing a word here and there.

2 Use *change* for something more significant: change the course of history; change a text by a lot of rewriting.

3 When the words seem more or less interchangeable, it's better to use *change*: change your mind (rather than *alter* it); change plans; change a colour scheme.

alternate / alternative

● RULES

1 *Altern**ate*** (and *alternately*) means to follow in turn: 'the forecast is for alternate rain and sunshine all day'.

2 *Altern**ative*** (and *alternatively*) suggests a choice, either one thing or others: 'you can come to lunch or alternatively for tea or dinner' (that is, choose lunch, tea or dinner, whichever you prefer).

alternative

● RULE

There is no need to restrict *alternative* to *one of two*: in present usage, we can have as many alternatives as we like.

NOTE The other meaning of *alternative* in the 1990s is for a less conventional, arguably a more enlightened approach: *alternative energy*; *alternative medicine*; *alternative living*.

although / though / albeit

● RECOMMENDATIONS

1 Mostly it doesn't matter whether you use **al***though* ✓ or *though*. Bear in mind that *though* is more conversational, **al***though* more literary. And there are a few instances where **al***though* cannot be used: 'he said he would pay, but he didn't *though*'; 'he spoke as *though* he would pay'.

2 *Albeit* has an old-fashioned ring to it, and the alternatives *though* and *although* are usually more direct: 'they eventually arrived, *although / though* (rather than *albeit*) too late for dinner'.

altogether / all together

See **all together . . .**

aluminium / aluminum

● RULE

*Alumin**ium*** (PRON 'aluMINyum').

$ *Alumin**um*** (PRON 'aLOOminum').

amateur

● CAUTION

Outside games or athletics, where *amateur* has a specific meaning, the word is often derogatory: *amateurish* dismisses someone as bungling and incompetent, and we hardly want a plumber or a surgeon to be an *amateur*.

● RECOMMENDATION

   PRON 'AMe(r)te(r)' (rather than 'AMe(r)ture').

$ PRON 'AMe(r)ture'.

ambassador / ambassadress

● RULES

1 Whatever they look like, an ambassador credited to the Court of Saint James should in a formal situation be addressed as *Your Excellency*, at least once in a conversation. Less formally they can be called simply *Ambassador*.

2 A woman should be called an *ambassador* (not 'ambassadress'). Nor should 'ambassadress' be used for an ambassador's wife (call her *Madam*).

ambience / ambiance

● RECOMMENDATIONS

1 Use *ambience* rather than the French form 'ambi*ance*'.

2 PRON 'AMbee-**e(r)**ns' (rather than 'AMbee-**ah**ns').

ambiguous

● CAUTION

   There is a tendency to consider *ambiguous* as derogatory. But *ambiguous* is not a synonym for 'vague' or 'indecisive'. *Ambiguous* tells us that a word or statement can have more than one meaning, which is in itself neither good nor bad: it depends on the circumstances, for to be ambiguous may sometimes be preferable to dogmatism or oversimplification.

amen (pronunciation)

● OPTION

   'AHmen' ✓ or 'AYmen'.

amend / emend

● RULES

1 *Amend* is the verb for making improvements or correcting errors in a piece of writing: 'he amended the letter to make it more friendly'.

2 *Emend* is a more limited word for removing *specific* things in a text: 'we shall emend the VAT return to omit zero-rated items'. *Emend* is also used for changes required for particular reasons: 'we shall emend the draft agreement to cover the new conditions'.

3 The corresponding *nouns* are *amend**ment*** and *emend**ation*** (PRON 'eemenDAY-shun').

America / the States / US / USA

● RECOMMENDATIONS

1   *America* is the generally accepted name for the USA. But at times it should be avoided, especially where there's a risk that *America* could be taken to include Canada and the countries of Central and South America.

2   *The States* is also commonly used, but is more conversational.

3   The *US* is all right in writing, but in speech the *United States* sounds better.

4   *USA* is standard for addresses. Other than that, *USA* is usually reserved for full-dress ceremonial use, one step less formal than *The United States of America.*

American

● RECOMMENDATION

We can accept, as dictionaries do, that the first meaning of the noun *American* is for a citizen of the United States (even though it could also apply to any inhabitant of the American continent). The same applies to *American* as a descriptive word: it is usually taken to cover specifically the United States and its people.

American English / Americanisms

● RECOMMENDATION

Describe the educated forms of the language used in the United States as *American English*, not as *Americanisms*. (In Britain, *Americanism* is usually taken to be a pejorative term, suggesting a debased form of the language.) See also **British English** . . .

amicable (pronunciation)

● RECOMMENDATION

Stress on the *first* syllable: 'AMicable'.

amid / amidst / amongst / among

See **among** . . .

amok / amuck

● RECOMMENDATION

While both spellings are correct, choose *amok*, which is more usual now. The meaning of this Malay word in English is running around, wrecking everything in sight ('run amok').

among / amongst / amid / amidst

All four words mean much the same.

● RECOMMENDATION

Prefer *among* in most contexts. *Amongst* is seen and heard less often now, while *amid* and *amidst*, although correct, are rather flowery words. The only everyday use for them is in relation to a background: 'he won the race *amid* (or *amidst*) roars of applause'. See also **between / among**.

among / between

See **between** . . .

amoral / immoral

● RULES

1 To be *amoral* is to be unaware of, or unable to accept, the concept of 'right' and 'wrong'. (This would be true of babies, for example, and could also apply to a psychopath.)

2 To be *immoral* you have to *do* something that society considers evil, dissolute or depraved.

● CAUTION

Use *immoral* with care, for all morals are not absolute, and can vary from one society to another, in different periods and in different circumstances. (For many people, for example, it is not immoral to kill in war, while others find it highly immoral.)

amount / number / quantity

● RULES

1 *Amount* or *quantity* is used when what is referred to is *singular*: an amount of money; a large quantity of food.

2 *Amount* is the word to use for money (as above), and when something is intangible: an amount of energy; any amount of time.

3 *Number* should always be used when what is referred to is *plural*: a number of words; a number of eggs.

● CAUTION

It's easy to go wrong with 'any amount of'; 'the right amount of'; 'a good amount of'; etc, and slip into 'any *amount* of eggs', 'the right *amount* of pages'; instead of 'any *number* of eggs'; 'the right *number* of pages' (see RULE 3 above).

ampersand (&)

Ampersand is the formal term for the *and* sign (&).

● RECOMMENDATIONS

1 The *and* sign should be used only in business names (Marks & Spencer), and should be avoided elsewhere ('men and women', rather than 'men & women'), except where space is limited.

2 Avoid the fast-food alternative for an ampersand, '*n* or '*n*' (steak 'n chips, ham 'n' eggs), with the exception of *rock 'n' roll*, where it is enshrined by custom.

amuck / amok

See **amok** . . .

an / a

See **a / an**

anaerobic / aerobic

See **aerobic** . . .

analgesic / painkiller / anodyne

● RECOMMENDATIONS

1 *Analgesic* (PRON 'analJEEZic') is the correct clinical term to cover a variety of drugs used to relieve pain. It can apply to drugs taken orally or by injection or inhalation.

2 *Painkiller* is an acceptable word in general rather than medical use, mostly for tablets that relieve pain.

3 While *anodyne* can also be used for pain-relieving drugs, remember it is more likely to be used pejoratively about something that is deliberately bland and unprovocative: 'the report is an anodyne, since it disturbs no one by glossing over the real issues'.

analogous (pronunciation)

● CAUTION

Because *analogy* is correctly pronounced 'e(r)NALe(r)jee', it is easy to slip into saying 'e(r)NALe(r)jus' for *analogous*. The *g* is hard, as in 'gate': 'e(r)NALe(r)**gus**'.

analogue / digital

These words describe two contrasting systems of showing numerical information.

● RULES

1 *Analogue* relates figures to other figures. Hence analogue instruments are most commonly based on a dial showing a range of figures, with a revolving pointer or pointers (the conventional clock with pointing hands is an example).

2 *Digital* instruments present numerical information in isolation, usually as numbers in a panel.

3 *Analog* is the spelling in America, and in computer language everywhere.

$ See RULE 3 above.

analyse / analyze

● RULE

Always *analyse*.

$ Always *analyze*.

anchovy (pronunciation)

● OPTION

> Stress on the *first* or *second* syllable is acceptable: 'ANchovy' ✓ or 'anCHOVy'.

and

> There are three common difficulties.

● RECOMMENDATIONS

1 Although some people dislike it, there is nothing wrong in *beginning* a sentence with *And*. Many good writers do when they want to create a feeling of continuity: 'And God saw the light, that it was good. And God called the light *Day*.' But avoid doing this too often or it becomes a mannerism.

2 When *and* comes in the middle of a sentence, precede it by a comma when what follows is a separate idea: 'She got out of bed, and decided to phone him.' But when what comes next flows on naturally, a comma gets in the way: 'After dinner, he stood up and raised his glass.' (No comma before 'and raised his glass'.)

3 In a list of items, when *and* precedes the final item, it is sometimes clearer to place a comma before *and*: 'there are courses in history, sociology, economics, and politics'. (If you omit the comma before 'and politics', 'economics and politics' could be taken as a combined subject.)

and / or

● RECOMMENDATIONS

1 On forms or specifications *and / or* has a place to explain that an item is a combination *or* an alternative: 'brass and / or steel screws'.

2 In letters and other forms of writing *and / or* is out of place, often unnecessary, sometimes making readers think twice about what is really meant. Try *and* or *or* on its own to see if that is satisfactory, or rewrite the sentence: 'brass or steel screws, or a combination of both may be used'.

and **sign (&)**

> See **ampersand**

Anglican / episcopalian

● RULE

> *Anglican* (spelt with a capital) or *episcopalian* (spelt with or without ✓ a capital) can mean the same, a member of or related to the Church of England, or one of the churches in communion with it. In America and Scotland and in some other countries, *episcopalian* is more likely to be used than *Anglican*, because the corresponding Church is called the Episcopal Church. (Episcopalian is government of the Church by bishops.)

Anglo-

● CAUTIONS

Anglo- sets all kinds of traps. Here are three to look out for:

1   In many contexts *Anglo-* can be used to cover the United Kingdom: 'an Anglo-French agreement'. In other contexts, *Anglo-* is limited to the English: 'an Anglo-Scots arrangement'; 'Anglo-Welsh relations'.

2   *Anglo-Irish* could refer to something that involves the United Kingdom and the Republic of Ireland, or it could refer to the English settler-rulers in Ireland, a highly charged part of Irish history.

3   *Anglo-Indian* can also mean two things: someone who is completely British and has lived much of their life in India, or someone of mixed British and Indian parentage.

● RECOMMENDATIONS

1   When in doubt, use *British-* ('a British-Irish agreement').

2   It is preferable to use *Anglo-Indian* for someone of mixed British and Indian descent, as that is how it would now generally be understood.

annex / annexe

● RULE

The *verb* is always *annex* (a country seeks to annex another country when it occupies its territory).

PRON 'aNEKS' (stress on the *second* syllable).

● RECOMMENDATION

Although either spelling exists for the *noun*, *annexe* is more usual: 'there's extra accommodation in the annexe'.

PRON 'ANeks' (stress on the *first* syllable).

$ *Annex* for both *noun* and *verb*.

annuity / pension

There is an overlap in the way these words are used, but it's better to keep them separate.

● RECOMMENDATIONS

1   Use *pension* for an income set up for someone who has retired from or has been invalided out of full-time employment.

2   Use *annuity* for an income purchased by putting down a lump sum. Although strictly speaking *annuity* suggests once a year, it can also be used for payments made monthly or even weekly.

anodyne / painkiller / analgesic

See **analgesic** . . .

Antarctic / Arctic

See **Arctic** . . .

ante- / anti-

● RULES

1 *Ante-* means *before*: an antenatal clinic; to antedate something is to backdate it.

2 *Anti-* means *against*: anticlockwise; antiseptic; antisocial.

3 PRON 'ANtee' for both words.

antennae / antennas

● RULES

1 *Antennae* (PRON 'anTENee') are the sensitised feelers on the heads of some insects (or, borrowing that idea, imaginary probes that some people believe they have to help them pick up what is going on).

2 *Antennas* are television or other aerials.

3 The *singular* form for both 1 and 2 is *antenna*.

anti- / ante-

See **ante-** . . .

anticipate / expect

● OPTIONS

1 Use *anticipate* only when the meaning is to estimate something in advance: 'a good driver anticipates what will happen next', and do not use it to mean 'expect'.

2 ✓ Use *anticipate* more or less interchangeably with *expect*: 'she *anticipates* (or *expects*) he will be here soon'. [!]

antisemitism / anti-Semitism

Both versions are correct.

● RECOMMENDATION

Use the form *antisemitism* (following the precedent of 'antichristian').

antiseptic / aseptic / sterile

All three words can be used about bandages, surgical instruments, etc that are free from germs or other micro-organisms. (In hospitals these words may be used in precise ways.)

● RECOMMENDATIONS

1 Use *aseptic* for things that are free from germs.

2 In the specific context of operating theatres, use *sterile* for the same meaning as 1 above.

3 Use *antiseptic* for products that destroy germs: antiseptic cream.

antisocial / unsociable / unsocial

● RECOMMENDATIONS

1   If you wake the neighbours with loud music, you are ***anti**social*, that is inconsiderate towards other people.

2   If you always refuse invitations to parties, you might be called ***un**sociable*, because you don't want to mix with other people.

3   ***Un**social* tends to be used for circumstances that exclude someone from normal social activities, as in '*unsocial* working hours'.

antithesis / converse / reverse / opposite

See **opposite** . . .

antonym / homonym / synonym

See **synonym** . . .

any / any *other*

● RECOMMENDATION

The word *other* is often unnecessary, and can be omitted: 'he is a better actor than *any* in the play' is just as clear as '. . . any *other* in the play'.

anymore / any more

● OPTIONS

1   You can make a distinction between *anymore* (*one* word) for time and *any more* (*two* words) for quantity: 'she doesn't work here anymore', but 'I don't have any more money'.

2   ✓ Use *any more* (two words) in all contexts.

\$ Usually follows OPTION 1 above.

anyone / any one

● RULE

Keep it as *one* word, unless it's one of a number: 'you can invite *anyone*'; 'you can do it in *any one* of six different ways'.

\$ Follows the same rule.

any *other* / any

See **any** . . .

any place / anywhere

See **anywhere** . . .

anytime / any time

● RULE

    Any time (*two* words).

$ *Anytime* (*one* word).

anyway / any way

● RECOMMENDATIONS

1 *Anyway* (*one* word) when it's an alternative to 'in any case': 'no matter how late it is, you can come here anyway'.

2 When it's a way of going somewhere, it's better as *two* words: 'you can go any way you like, on the motorway or along country roads'.

3 When it's a way of doing something, the choice of *one* or *two* words helps to avoid misunderstanding: 'you can do it *any way*' (*two* words) means in whichever way you like, but 'you can do it *anyway* (*one* word) could mean 'you can do it in any case'. In speech, this difference of meaning can be conveyed by the way you say the words, or by spelling it out: 'in whichever way you like' or 'in any case'.

$ Always *anyway* as *one* word ('anyways', often heard, is substandard).

anywhere / any place

● RECOMMENDATION

    Although *any place* sounds American, there's nothing wrong with using it, at least in conversation. In writing, *anywhere* is preferable.

$ *Any place* is more usual, but *anywhere* is also used.

apart from / *aside* from

● OPTION

    Use *apart* from ✓ or *aside* from, whichever comes naturally to you.

apartheid

● RECOMMENDATIONS

1 Because it is an Afrikaans word, associated with racial discrimination in South Africa, it avoids misunderstanding to use it only about the former regime in that country.

2 PRON 'aPAHThate' (the pronunciation used by Nelson Mandela).

apartment / flat

    See **flat** . . .

apostrophe

    Even experienced writers have to think twice at times over the use of apostrophes. The following keeps it as simple as possible.

● **RULES**

1 *Possession* If the noun is *singular* add 's: the *boy's* dog; the *woman's* hat. If it's *plural* , ending in -*s*, just add an apostrophe: the *boys'* dog (a dog belonging to two or more boys). If it's plural, *not* ending in -*s* , add 's: the *women's* husbands.

   PROBLEMS

   i *Names ending in -s* There is no reliable rule, only custom. In spite of the build-up of *ss*, *Charles's* office is more usual than *Charles'* office. In writing, it is usually the *Joneses'* house (the house belonging to the Jones family); the *Phillipses'* children. (When speaking we can relax and say 'the Jones' house'; 'the Phillips' children'.) See also **names ending in -s, -ch, sh.**

   NOTE It is *Jesus'* (never 'Jesus's') in speech and writing: Jesus' parables.

   ii With some names you have look up the correct form: St James's Street; Queen's College Oxford but Queens' College Cambridge; Lord's Cricket Ground but Earls Court; St John's Wood but All Souls College; Marks & Spencer's but Harrods.

   iii *Two names* Place the apostrophe after the *second* name only: 'Jack and Jill's party' (rather than 'Jack's and Jill's party').

   iv *Expressions such as 'ten years' experience'; 'a mile's distance'* Although these are not strictly possessives, the apostrophe should be included, as shown above.

   v *Drawn-out possessives* It's all right to *say* 'the woman I'm going to *marry's* name is Susan', but it doesn't work in writing. Rephrase it: 'the name of the woman I'm going to marry is Susan'.

   NOTE There is a tendency for apostrophes to be dropped in names of certain places and organisations: some pub-signs read 'The *Kings* Head', and it's '*Barclays* Bank'.

2 *Hers, yours, theirs, ours, its* never take an apostrophe, because they are already possessive.

3 Do not use an apostrophe for the plural of abbreviations: it's 'six MPs'; 'two QCs' (not 'six MP's'; 'two QC's'). Treat abbreviations like ordinary nouns, using an apostrophe only to show possession: the MP's husband; the QC's secretary (one secretary working for one QC); the QCs' secretary (one secretary working for two or more QCs).

4 Do not use an apostrophe after *years*, except to show something belongs to a particular year: 'the 1960s launched the miniskirt', but 'the 1960's miniskirt'.

5 An apostrophe marks omitted letters in contractions: *can't* (cannot); *you've* (you have); *they're* (they are). See **contracted forms.**

● **CAUTION**

   Distinguish between *its* (possessive) and *it's* (contraction for *it is*); *theirs* (possessive) and *there's* (contraction for *there is*): '*it's* easy to see why *its* owner is proud of it'; 'it is *theirs*, and *there's* no doubt about that'.

appal / appall

● RULE

Appal, appalling, appalled.

$ *Appall, appalling, appalled.*

appear *to*

● CAUTION

When *appear* is followed by *to*, look out for the risk of confusion: 'she *appeared to* answer the question' can mean two quite different things. It could mean she *arrived* to answer the question, or she *seemed* to answer it, with a suggestion that she had not really done so. In such cases, use either 'arrive' or 'seem', or other words that make the intended meaning clear.

appendixes / appendices

● RULE

Both the Latin plural *appendices* (PRON 'e(r)PENDe(r)seez') and the Anglicised plural *appendixes* ✓ are correct. But in anatomy it is always appendi*xes*.

applicable (pronunciation)

● OPTION

Stress on the *first* or *second* syllable is acceptable: 'APplicable' or 'apPLICable' ✓.

appoint / consult / engage / retain

● RULES

1   Accountants, advertising agents and management consultants are *appointed*.
2   Doctors and medical specialists are *consulted*.
3   Solicitors are *engaged*.
4   Barristers are *retained*.

appreciable

● RECOMMENDATION

Only use *appreciable* if you intend to be noncommittal ('an appreciable sum of money' is vague). Otherwise, choose a more positive word: a *vast* , *considerable, great* sum of money.

apprehend / comprehend

As well as other meanings, both ***appre****hend* and ***compre****hend* mean to understand something, but offer different nuances.

● RECOMMENDATIONS

1   Use *comprehend* to suggest a mental process: 'I have thought about it and comprehend how you are planning the campaign.'

2 Use *apprehend* to suggest becoming aware more by intuition: 'I apprehend why you are so concerned.'

a priori / prima facie

● RULES

1 An *a priori* conclusion (PRON 'ay- pryeAWrye') is a conjecture which assumes that because one thing is true, something else follows from it: if the roads are icy and there is an accident, you assume it was caused by a skid, which may not be true.

2 *Prima facie* (PRON 'pryme(r)-FAYshee') means 'at first sight'. A lawyer or the police may talk about a *prima facie* case, meaning there is a sufficient case to proceed with, based on what is known so far.

● RECOMMENDATION

If you want to avoid getting caught up in this, see if you can use a phrase with 'assume' or 'assumption' instead of *a priori*: 'because the roads were icy, we assume (instead of 'it is an *a priori* conclusion') the accident happened because of a skid'. And you can often substitute 'at first sight' or 'from what can be seen' for *prima facie*.

apropos / à propos

● RULES

1 *Apropos* is English, while *à propos* is French.

2 The proper meaning of *apropos* (PRON 'apre(r)POH' with stress on the last syllable) is 'to the point'; 'strictly relevant': 'your comment is apropos what we have been talking about'. It can also be used to mean 'with reference to' or 'concerning', when 'of' is often tagged on (but this is not necessary): 'apropos *of* the problem', or simply 'apropos the problem'.

● CAUTION

Don't let 'approve' mislead you: *apropos* has only one *p*.

apt / liable

● RULES

1 *Apt* suggests a tendency, not necessarily good or bad: 'he's apt to look in for a drink on the way home'.

2 *Liable* follows the meaning of 'liability', and suggests an undesirable tendency or a risk: 'he is liable to get drunk'; 'we are liable to lose money over this'.

Arab / Arabic / Arabian / Islamic

● RULES

1 *Arab* is the word for nearly everything concerning the inhabitants of the Middle East, and is generally applied to the countries that form the Arab League, including Morocco, Tunisia and Algeria: the Arab world; Arab traditions; Arab politics.

2 *Arabic* is reserved mostly now for the script, language and literature of the Arabs. Where *Arabic art* was used at one time, the expression now is *Arab* for secular art, or

Islamic for religious art. (*Islamic* relates to *Islam* [Arabic for 'submission'], that is to the religion established by the prophet Mohammed.)

3 *Arabian* belongs to mythology and to geographic references to parts of Arabia, the vast peninsula contained partly by the Red Sea in the West and the Persian Gulf in the East: Arabian Desert; Arabian Sea.

arabic / roman numerals

Arabic numerals are our standard numbers (1, 2, 3, 4 . . .). *Roman numerals* are I, II, III, IV . . . .

● OPTION

The terms can be spelt with an initial capital or a small letter: arabic ✓ or Arabic numerals, roman ✓ or Roman numerals.

See also **Roman / roman.**

arbitrarily (pronunciation)

● OPTION

Stress on the *first* or *third* syllable is acceptable: 'ARbitrarily'✓ or 'arbiTRARily'.

archaeology / archeology

● OPTION

Both spellings are now found in many dictionaries: arch*aeology* ✓ or arch*eology.*

$ arch*eology.*

archetype / prototype

These words are similar, and they are used in various ways. The following cover the most useful and generally understood meanings.

● RECOMMENDATIONS

1 Use ***archetype*** for the principal or primary pattern on which copies are based, but more in relation to institutions and principles than concrete objects: 'the House of Commons is the archetype of all representative assemblies'.

2 Use ***prototype*** for the first or trial model of a machine which can be tested and modified before going into production.

Arctic / Antarctic (pronunciation)

● CAUTION

Lightly pronounce the first *c* in both words: 'ARCtic'; 'anTARCtic'.

are (metric measure of land)

See **acre**

aren't / ain't

● RULE

Aren't is good English ('Well I'm here, aren't I?'), but *ain't* isn't (unless you're writing cockney dialogue: 'Fings ain't wot they used to be!').

Argentina / the Argentine

● RECOMMENDATIONS

1 *Argentina* (rather than 'the Argentine') for the name of the republic in South America.

2 *Argentinians* (rather than 'Argentines') for the people.

● RULE

It is the *Argentine Republic* (not the 'Argentinian Republic').

-arily (pronunciation)

The pronunciation of words ending in *-arily* presents a problem. They are formed from three-syllable words which have stress on the *first* syllable: 'MOmentary'; 'ORDinary'; 'VOLuntary'.

When *-y* is replaced by *-ily*, and the words become *four* syllables, keeping the stress on the *first* syllable leads to an awkward flight of unaccented syllables: 'MOmentarily'; 'ORDinarily'; 'VOLuntarily'.

● OPTIONS

1 Practise keeping the stress on the *first* syllable, until you can handle it comfortably.

2 Recast the sentence, using phrases such as 'for the moment'; 'in the ordinary way'; 'on a voluntary basis' (in place of 'momentarily', 'ordinarily', 'voluntarily').

3 ✓ Follow the American stress pattern, which shifts the stress to the *third* syllable: 'momenTARily'; 'ordiNARily'; 'volunTARily' [!].

$ See OPTION 3 above.

aristocrat (pronunciation)

● RULE

Stress the *first* syllable ('ARistocrat').

$ Stress on the *second* syllable ('aRIStocrat').

around / round / about

See **about** . . .

arouse / rouse

These are alternative forms with no difference in meaning.

● RECOMMENDATIONS

1 Use *rouse* for waking someone up: 'she roused him early that morning'.

2 Music is *rousing* rather than 'arousing'.

3 Use *arouse* as a lower-key alternative to 'excite': arouse curiosity or suspicion; sexually aroused.

artificial / synthetic / man-made

● RECOMMENDATIONS

1 Use *artificial* mostly for something that is an imitation of the real thing, even if it is made by hand with considerable skill: artificial flowers; artificial limbs.

2 Use *synthetic* to suggest production in factories using chemical compounds: synthetic leather; synthetic silk (the term 'art silk' is old-fashioned).

3 Avoid *man-made*, an advertising euphemism that seeks to sidestep the negative associations of *artificial* and *synthetic* (it means exactly the same thing).

as

This short word gives many problems. The following cover the more common difficulties:

● RECOMMENDATIONS

1 'You can do it as well as *I* ', 'she does it as well as *he*' . . . sound formal. Yet '. . . as well as *me*', '. . . as well as *him*' are sometimes considered ungrammatical, because 'can' is understood to follow ('. . . as well as *me* can' is clearly wrong). But '. . . as well as *me / him / her / us / them*' are used so often now by good writers and speakers, that the old grammatical objection is hardly relevant. Use 'you can do it as well as *me*' ✓, or more formally, if you prefer it, 'you can do it as well as *I can*'. Either can now be considered correct.

2 *as* or *like* 'She did it perfectly *like* she always does.' does not read as well as '. . . *as* she always does'. Although *like* for *as* is used by writers in the class of Iris Murdoch and Patrick White, it is still better to avoid it.

3 *equally as* The only thing wrong with this is that *as* is unnecessary and gets in the way: 'both restaurants are equally good' is better than '. . . equally *as* good'.

4 *as . . . as* or *so . . . as* Use whichever comes naturally: 'he is not *as* clever as she is' or '. . . *so* clever as she is' ✓.

● CAUTIONS

1 'She loves me as much as Helen' can have *two* meanings. It could mean 'she loves me as much as Helen loves me', or '. . . as much as she loves Helen'. When there's any risk of misunderstanding, spell out what you mean.

2 *as* or *while* It is all right to use *as* for *while*, but check the sentence for a risk of misunderstanding. '*As* they were shouting, he came into the room' could mean he came in *because* they were shouting, or *while* they were shouting.

as and when / if and when

● RECOMMENDATIONS

1 Don't slip into these trite combinations, unless it's really necessary – and that's not often.

2 Reserve *as and when* for something that is going to happen in stages: 'we'll warn you of regular increases in prices as and when they are unavoidable'.

3 Use *if* on its own when it's possible that something will happen, but not certain:

'we'll warn you if there's an increase in price' (implying that it may not happen).

4 Use *when* on its own where it's almost certain that something will happen sooner or later: 'we'll warn you when there's an increase in price' (implying that it's likely at some time).

5 Use *as* on its own to suggest something will happen because of circumstances: 'prices will be increased as the cost of raw materials go up'. (*If* or *when* could be used in this example, with the nuances described in **2** and **3** above.)

as a result of

● RECOMMENDATION

Nearly always the simple word *because* is better than *as a result of*: 'as a result of the increased price of petrol, we have to make extra charges for delivery' is laboured: 'because the price of petrol has gone up . . .' hits the nail squarely on the head.

aseptic / sterile / antiseptic

See **antiseptic** . . .

as follows / as follow

● RULE

As follows is an invariable expression independent of whether what comes before or after is *singular* or *plural*. 'The subjects discussed were as follows . . .'. Although 'subjects' is plural and a list of things may follow, it is always *as follows* (**never 'as follow'**).

as *from* / as of

● OPTION

Both phrases indicate a date or a time at which something, such as an increase in prices, comes into effect.

As of, the American equivalent of *as from* , has now passed into British English [!]: 'as *from* ✓ (or as *of*) 7 July, the new tax will be applied'.

● CAUTION

There is sometimes a doubt whether 'as *from* (or as *of*) 7 July' means from midnight 6 July or midnight 7 July, and in law there could be the onus of proving what was the intention. If there's any uncertainty, specify 'as from midnight 6 July' or 'as from and including 6 July'.

Asian / Asiatic

● RECOMMENDATION

Use *Asian* as the parallel to *European*, *African* . . . .

● CAUTIONS

1 *Asiatic* is now often regarded as a racist word, except in scientific or geographical contexts, such as The Royal Asiatic Society.

2   PRON 'AY**sh**e(r)n', 'ay**sh**eeAtic' (not 'AYzhe(r)n', 'ayzheeAtic', alternatives which are not liked).

Asian / Hindi / Hindu / Hindustani / Indian

See **Indian** . . .

aside from / *apart* from

See *apart* from . . .

as *of* / as *from*

See as *from* . . .

as possible

● RECOMMENDATION

Position *as possible* immediately after the noun or other word it refers to: 'we should give as much time as possible to develop these new ideas' puts more stress on 'time' than when *as possible* is separated ('we should give as much time to develop these new ideas as possible').

as regards

● RECOMMENDATION

Whenever possible, and that will be nearly always, replace the self-important phrase, *as regards*, by the simple word *about*. When you change, for example, '*as regards* your investments . . .' to '*about* your investments . . .', you strike a blow for good plain English.

assign / transfer

● RECOMMENDATIONS

1   Use *assign* for contractual transferring of rights or ownership: a lease is assigned to the person who purchases it.

2   Use *transfer* as a lighter word for passing over something to someone else: transferring a reservation.

assonance / alliteration

See **alliteration** . . .

assume / presume

The difference may be subtle, but it's useful.

● RULES

1   Use ***presume*** when it is a reasonable conclusion from the evidence: 'he presumes they are satisfied, because they have sent further orders'.

2   Use **assume** to express an opinion, without evidence one way or the other: 'he
    assumes they are satisfied, although we haven't heard yet'.

assurance / insurance

A technical distinction is made. *Insurance* is for an event that may never happen,
such as a burglary, accident or fire. *Assurance* pays out money against a certain event,
such as death (*life assurance*) or the expiry of a fixed number of years.

● RECOMMENDATION

Leave this distinction to insurance specialists, and in general use, use *insurance* right
across the board.

$ This follows RECOMMENDATION above.

assure / ensure / insure

● RULES

1   *Assure* means 'promise' or 'guarantee'.

2   *Ensure* means 'to make certain'.

3   *Insure* is restricted to financial protection through insurance (see **assurance /
    insurance**).
    This example sums it up: 'I **assure** you that I have **ensured** that you are fully **insured**.'

asterisk / star (*)

● OPTION

Either word can be used for this symbol (*). *Asterisk* ✓ is more usual in Britain, *star*
is used more in America.

  NOTE   The most common use of an asterisk is to direct the reader to a reference
at the bottom of the page. Another use is to cast a veil of typographical coyness over
words regarded as obscene (f**k, c**t).

● RECOMMENDATIONS

1   Where possible, avoid using an asterisk to mark a footnote. It sends readers to the
    bottom of the page, and they then have to find their place again in the text above.
    Sometimes the footnote can be included in the main text by inserting it in brackets;
    at other times, the reference may not be all that necessary anyway. Asterisks and
    corresponding footnotes are more justified in technical or academic texts.

2   As for using asterisks as a cover-up for *four-letter words,* it depends on the context
    and situation. There are double-standards, and in some circumstances there is a case
    for writing these words in full for all the world to see, which most dictionaries now
    do.

● CAUTION

If you do give such words full frontal exposure, look out for shockwaves, as they can
give great offence, if used without care. See also **four-letter words.**

asthma (pronunciation)

● RULE

'ASSme(r)'.

$ 'AZZma'.

astronaut / cosmonaut / spaceman

● RECOMMENDATIONS

1   Use **cosmo**naut only for space exploration by Russians. Otherwise **astro**naut is the general word.

2   *Spaceman* (and *spacewoman*) belong more to science fiction and journalism.

astronomical

● CAUTION

Astronomical compares something to the vastness of the universe, so anything it describes should be truly large (it's exaggerated to call a 10 per cent increase in prices *astronomical*).

astronomy / cosmology

● RULES

1   *Astronomy*, said to be the oldest exact science, is the study of the sun, moon, planets and stars.

2   *Cosmology* seeks to explain how the universe came into being.

NOTE Astronomers observe the stars and the planets: cosmologists are physicists and mathematicians, who seek to solve the riddle of the universe through equations.

atheist / agnostic

See **agnostic** . . .

athletics *is* / *are*

● RECOMMENDATION

Athletics *is*.

NOTE In Britain *athletics* covers track and field sports.

$ *Athletics* is used for any kind of sport.

atomic / nuclear

● RULE

Atomic physics deals with the structure of atoms: *nuclear physics* studies the central core of an atom, the nucleus, which contains most of the mass and the positive charge of energy.

● RECOMMENDATIONS

1   *Atomic* and *nuclear* are close enough in meaning for it not to matter much, outside

scientific contexts, which word is used. For most general purposes, *nuclear* has become the usual word.

2 PRON 'NEW-cleer' (*two* syllables, not three).

at this moment in time / at the end of the day

● RECOMMENDATION

There's no need to be afraid of using these expressions because it's fashionable to criticise them as pompous and pretentious. They do have a place at times where a cosmic or biblical tone is appropriate (Einstein used *at this moment in time* for cosmic exactitude).

● CAUTION

There should always be a good case for choosing *at this moment in time* or *at the end of the day* in place of the simple words *now* or *finally* (or *when it's all over*).

attitude / opinion / taste

● RECOMMENDATIONS

1 *Attitude* is based on personality, experience and prejudices. It can describe a knee-jerk reaction.

2 *Opinion* is not inborn but more a result of reflection, and should always imply some thought (a *considered opinion* suggests a good deal of thought).

3 *Taste* suggests our personal likes and dislikes.

● CAUTION

When we say something is in *good* or *bad taste*, it is less an objective comment than a narrow-minded observation reflecting what we feel is the right way to dress, decorate our homes and so on.

au courant / au fait

Both phrases are usually followed by *with*.

● RULES

1 *Au courant* means being up to date: 'she's au courant with the latest arrangements'.

2 *Au fait* means informed: 'she's au fait with the arrangements that have been made'.

● RECOMMENDATION

Why use French expressions when 'up to date' (for *au courant*) or 'know about' (for *au fait*) lays it neatly on the line?

Aussie

● RECOMMENDATION

Aussie, as a friendly name for anything to do with Australia, is all right in conversation, and Australians don't mind it. But it is out of place in formal contexts.

authentic / genuine / real

Although these words are often used interchangeably, here are three suggestions.

● RECOMMENDATIONS

1 *Authentic* is the strongest word, and may suggest proof: 'the signature shows beyond doubt this is an authentic Picasso'.

2 *Real* comes lower down the scale, and can be used about everyday things: real leather; real coffee.

3 *Genuine* comes somewhere between *authentic* and *real*: genuine pearls.

● CAUTIONS

1 Be restrained in the unnecessary use of *real* in front of pristine words, such as *crisis* and *truth*: 'this is a crisis'; 'this is the truth' (rather than '. . . a real crisis'; '. . . the real truth').

2 *Genuine* rhymes with 'feminine' (not with 'swine', unless you're trying to be funny, and even then it's a tired joke).

author / writer

See **writer** . . .

auto-

Auto-, from the Greek word for 'self', is a guide to the meaning of many words in English.

● RECOMMENDATION

Treat nearly all *auto-* formations as *one* word: *autoimmune*; *autopilot*; *autofocus*. Two exceptions are *auto-erotic* and *auto-suggestion*.

automated / automatic

● RECOMMENDATIONS

1 Use *automated* for things on a large scale, such as a factory controlled by computer technology.

2 Use *automatic* about modest appliances, such as a kettle that switches itself off when the water comes to the boil.

average / mean

● RECOMMENDATION

Average can have various meanings. With figures, use *average* as the term for the total of a number of figures divided by the number of figures involved: 'the average of the four figures 20, 30, 50, 100 is 50' (total of 200 divided by four).

● CAUTION

Unless you are a mathematician, avoid using *mean*. For there are different interpretations of *mean*, which need to be specified (*arithmetic mean, geometric mean*). These do not necessarily equate with *average*, so do not use the terms interchangeably.

averse / adverse

See **adverse** . . .

awake / wake

These are confusing words, even to the best of us.

● RECOMMENDATIONS

1 Use *wake* (or *wake up*) as the usual verb: 'Quiet! You'll wake the baby!'

2 '*Wake* me (up) at 7' is the usual way of putting it. ('*Awaken* me at 7' is all right but rather grand.)

3 For the past, *woken* or *woken up* are the most usual: 'he was woken (up) by the noise'. *Awakened* is also correct ('he was awakened by the noise') but more formal.

awhile / while

● OPTION

Either 'he remained there *awhile*' or '. . . for a *while*' ✓.

● CAUTION

'. . . for a while' (see OPTION above) is correct, but '. . . for awhile' is wrong, since *awhile* (as *one* word) already means '*for* a short time'.

a year / per annum

● RECOMMENDATIONS

1 In most contexts, it's better to use English than Latin, so use *a year* whenever possible: 'this takes place three times a year'. The main use of *per annum* is the abbreviated form *pa*, which is convenient after sums of money or annual percentages.

2 Leave a space between the figure (or the % sign) and *pa*: £10,000 pa; 10% pa.

See also **per.**

B

-babble / -spiel / -speak

We can attach these prefixes to a number of words to describe a specialised jargon or a way of speaking. For differences in meaning, see **-speak / -babble / -spiel**.

backlog

● CAUTION

Look out for the different meanings of *backlog* in Britain and America. In Britain it's bad to have a backlog, because it nearly always means a pile-up of work that hasn't been done, or orders a firm is behind with.

$ A *backlog* is a good thing, because it usually means something in reserve ('a backlog of orders' suggests there's enough work to keep the factory going).

backup / back-up / back up

● RULES

1 *Backup* as *one* word (sometimes with a hyphen but usually without), is the *noun*, meaning technical support in handling new equipment, or moral support for an argument or principle; or, in computer language, the copy of data kept on disks for security.

2 *Back up* as *two* words, is the *verb* for giving support (as above) or for making a copy of data in a computer.

backward / backwards

● RECOMMENDATIONS

1 When attached to a *verb*, use *backwards*: walk or look backwards; lean over backwards.

2 When attached to a *noun*, use *backward*: a backward look; a backward movement.

$ *Backward* is more usual in all contexts.

bacteria / microbe / virus / germ

See **germ** . . .

bad / badly

The correct grammatical distinction requires *bad* to be used with *nouns* ('the big bad wolf'), and *badly* with *verbs* ('he drove badly'). But this is not natural in all contexts.

● RECOMMENDATIONS

1 Use *bad* with the verb *feel*, when it's in relation to health: 'she feels very bad after the operation'. It can also be used about ordinary feelings, especially in conversation: 'he feels bad about being so late'. In writing, prefer *badly*, unless it's informal.

2 Use *badly* with most other verbs: 'I want it badly'; 'they didn't do so badly'. Maybe 'want it bad', 'didn't do so bad' would pass in casual conversation, but would be out of place in writing or a serious discussion.

bad taste

See **attitude** . . .

bail / bale

● RULES

1 Always *bale* when it's a bundle of hay or other things.
2 Always *bail* for the security against the provisional release of someone who is waiting trial.

● OPTIONS

1 *Bail* ✓ or *bale* out water from a boat.
2 *Bale* ✓ or *bail* out from an aircraft with a parachute.

balding

● CAUTION

As well as saying that a man is becoming bald, a statement of fact, *balding* carries with it a hint that he is showing his age and the stress of the job he is doing: 'this balding politician'.

ballgame

● RECOMMENDATION

The extended meaning of *ballgame* for a situation, project, circumstances . . . is a cliché: 'it's a whole new ballgame'; 'that's a different ballgame altogether'. Use one of the other words suggested above.

bank / public holiday

See **public holiday** . . .

barbaric / barbarous

● RULES

1 Use *barbaric* to describe something that is uncivilised or, by extension, brutal or cruel: 'it is a barbaric community with no laws'; 'his treatment of her is barbaric'.
2 Treat *barbarous* as an even more severe word that indicates extreme cruelty and harshness. An exception to this is in relation to literary style ('he writes barbarously').

● CAUTION

Although *barbaric* is occasionally used in a good sense, to mean unspoilt and primitive (especially about art), the meaning in RULE 1 above is predominant.

bar / *pie* **chart**

Bar and *pie* charts are part of the language of statistical presentations.

● RULES

1   A *bar chart* is a visual way of comparing different sets of figures, such as sales of competing products. Vertical rectangles (or bars), drawn to the same scale, are arranged side by side, so different values can be clearly related to each other.

2   A *pie chart* uses a circle representing a pie, divided up into slices showing how various parts make up the whole. For example, personal capital might have segments of different sizes showing what proportion should be in equities, building societies, etc, and what should be kept available for emergencies.

barely / **hardly** / **scarcely**

● CAUTION

These three words are already negative, so avoid a second negative creeping in: 'with*out* barely a sound, he left'; 'I could*n't* hardly hear him'; 'scarcely *no* one understood'. Those should be: 'with barely a sound . . .'; 'I could hardly . . .'; 'scarcely anyone . . .'. See also **double negatives.**

barrel / **cask**

Both are shaped like a cylinder, usually bulging in the middle, and they can both contain beer, wine or other liquid.

● RECOMMENDATIONS

1   A *barrel* should be made of wooden staves secured by metal hoops.

2   A *cask* can be made of wood, metal or plastic.

NOTE   Only a *barrel* can designate a specific measure of capacity (the price of crude oil is quoted by the *barrel*, measured as 159 litres).

barrister / **advocate** / **counsel**

● RULES

1   The usual word for a person admitted to plead at the Bar in England or Wales is *barrister*. The equivalent in Scotland is *advocate*.

2   The usual expression is 'to take *counsel's* opinion' (rather than '*barrister's* opinion'), although it means the same thing.

3   When a barrister is appointed to senior rank they become a Queen's *Counsel* (QC) or King's *Counsel* (KC).

$ The usual word for a *counsel* in a legal sense is *attorney*.

-based

● RULE

A hyphen should always be used when *-based* is added to the name of a city or a country where an organisation is located: 'a Swiss-based corporation'; 'the Brussels-based committee'; 'the London-based institute'. This indicates that the corporation, committee or institute may be international or, for that matter, British, American, Italian, etc, but happens to be located in a particular city or country.

bases (pronunciation)

● RULE

When *bases* is the plural of *base* it is pronounced 'BASE-*iz*'; when it is the plural of *basis*, it's 'BASE-*eez*'.

. . . basis . . .

● RECOMMENDATION

'On the basis of . . .'; 'on a something-or-other basis', and other such phrases using *basis* are roundabout expressions that are better avoided. Compare 'we shall charge on the basis of the amount of time the work takes' with 'we shall charge according to how much time it takes', or 'the new product is available on a strictly limited basis' with 'supplies of the new product are strictly limited'.

bathos / pathos

● RULES

1 *Bathos* (PRON 'BAYthos') is mostly used as a literary word, to describe a build-up to something that turns out to be trivial: 'I have something of the greatest importance to announce – a coffee-break!'

2 *Pathos* (PRON 'PAYthos') is also more likely to be used in literary contexts ('it is a novel full of pathos'). The everyday words with a similar meaning are 'pity' or 'sadness'.

baulk / balk

● OPTION

Although a distinction is sometimes made, both *baulk* ✓ and *balk* can be used for both *verb* and *noun*: a drawing-back from doing something is to *balk* ✓ or *baulk* at it; a squared wooden beam is a *baulk* ✓ or *balk*.

BC / AD

See AD . . .

bearskin / busby

● RULE

Bearskin is the proper word, the word used by regiments who wear these ceremonial furry hats. *Busby* is an informal word that should not be used in serious writing.

because

● CAUTIONS

1 In a negative sentence, *because* can be ambiguous: 'she didn't marry him because he was rich' could mean 'she married him, but not because he was rich', *or* 'because

he was rich, she did not marry him'. When necessary, rephrase the sentence (as suggested above) to avoid misunderstanding.

2   *Because* has a way of edging in when it is not required: 'the reason is *because* he is rich'; 'one value of power steering is *because* it makes parking easier'. Leave out *because* and those sentences work just as well, or even better: 'the reason is he is rich'; 'one value of power steering is it makes parking easier'.

beep / bleep
● RECOMMENDATION

Use *beep* for this edgy high-pitched sound that yelps at us from answering machines and other electronic equipment: 'Please speak after the *beep*.' (*Bleep* is the alternative word, used less often now.)

beer / ale
● RECOMMENDATION

Dictionaries disagree about the difference between *beer* and *ale,* and pubs are often equally undecided. It is better to stick to the everyday word – *beer* .

begrudge / grudge
● RECOMMENDATIONS

1   *Begrudge* is followed by a word that represents a person or something a person possesses: 'I begrudge him his success'; 'she begrudged John his happy marriage'.

2   *Grudge* is followed by a word that represents an action or a condition: 'I grudge paying so much money for dinner'; 'she grudged giving him dinner'.

beg the question
● RULE

Beg the question means to reach a conclusion on the basis of an unproved assumption: 'the plan will fail because of his misguided policies'. That *begs the question*, unless you have proved the policies are misguided.

● CAUTION

Beg the question is so often misunderstood that it is better not to use it, outside legal contexts. An alternative is 'That is unjustified unless . . .'. (see example above.)
See also **leading question**.

behalf
See **on behalf of . . .**

behove
● RULE

Behove must always be preceded by 'it': 'it behoves you to take care how you speak to me'; 'it ill behoves you to speak to me like that'.

● RECOMMENDATION

Behove is starchy, so consider putting it more simply: 'you should be careful how you speak to me'; 'you shouldn't speak to me like that'.

\$ It is spelt *behoove,* and pronounced that way.

beige / buff / fawn

They all mean a light brown colour.

● RECOMMENDATIONS

1 *Beige* is lighter and has a yellowish tinge, while *fawn* has a greyish tinge, the colour of a fawn.

2 Use *buff* for envelopes and for the colour of men's clothes. Use *beige* for the colour of women's clothes.

Beijing / Peking

● RECOMMENDATION

Use *Beijing* (PRON 'bayDJING') for the name of the capital of the People's Republic of China. (It is the name preferred by the Foreign Office and the BBC.)

belly / stomach

● RULE

Belly includes the outside of the body and the internal organs as well, whereas *stomach* refers to one specific internal organ.

● RECOMMENDATION

Use *belly,* except in specific medical contexts. In spite of what some people think, dictionaries do not classify *belly* as 'vulgar'.

benchmark / hallmark

● RULES

1 **Bench**mark is a standard or point of reference against which other things are measured, or as a criterion for assessing standards: 'this new computer has become the benchmark against which the performance of all other computers will be compared'; 'how much money you make is not a benchmark for success as a human being'.

2 **Hall**mark has three meanings:

   i The mark made on gold, silver or platinum that guarantees its standard of fineness.

   ii The characteristic feature that marks out a special quality in a person or a concept: the hallmark of genius; the hallmark of great art.

   iii The design or emblem that represents a company or a brand: 'the company uses a lion as its hallmark'. This use is now more or less superseded by the term **logo**.

bent

● CAUTION

Be wary of the slang use of *bent*, because it has two meanings. The older meaning is to be corrupt or dishonest. The second meaning, recognised by recent dictionaries, is to be homosexual. The second use is taking over, but should be avoided since it is offensive and prejudiced.

bent / bended (past form)

● RULE

The past form of the verb *bend* is *bent*, with one exception: we go down on our *bended* knees.

bereaved / bereft

● RULE

Bereaved is used about death. *Bereft* refers to being deprived, usually of an abstract quality, when it is followed by 'of' (bereft of hope; bereft of comfort). 'I shall be *bereft* when you are gone', means I shall miss you very much when you have gone away; 'I shall be *bereaved* when you are gone', means I shall have lost a relative or a friend when you are dead.

berserk (pronunciation)

● RECOMMENDATION

'berZURK' (second syllable rhyming with 'Turk').

beseeched / besought

See **besought** . . .

beside / besides

● RULES

1 *Beside* when it means alongside: 'I'll walk beside you'; 'put it beside me'; and if something is not relevant, it is 'beside the point'.

2 *Besides* when it means 'as well as': 'Besides paying for dinner, I paid for the taxi!'

besought / beseeched (past forms)

● OPTION

Besought ✓ or *beseeched*.

better

● CAUTION

Remember *better* compares one thing with another: 'this is better than that'. Do not write 'this restaurant serves a better quality of wine', unless you are comparing it to another restaurant (make it '. . . a good quality . . .').

between

● RULES

1 *Between* does *not* have to be limited to *two* persons or things: 'let us divide the bill between the six of us'.

2 *Between* is a choice between one thing *and* other things, not 'or' other things: 'we have to decide between going to Florence *and* (not 'or') going to Rome'.

between / among

● RULES

1 *Between* puts things alongside each other: 'there are differences between cats and dogs'. And *between* is the only word to show how one thing relates to a number of other things individually: 'there is an understanding between Britain, America and France'.

2 *Among* suggests in the middle of: 'put the cat among the pigeons'.
   See also **among / amongst; between.**

between you and *me / I*

   See **I / me** (RULE)

biannual / biennial / bimonthly / biweekly

● RULES

1 *Biannual* is twice a year.

2 *Biennial* is every two years.

● CAUTION

   Bimonthly and *biweekly* can be taken to mean either every two months, every two weeks, *or* twice a month, twice a week. So it is better to say what you mean: 'every two months'; 'twice a month'.

biased / biassed

● OPTION

   Either *biased* ✓ or *biassed* can be used for the past form of *bias*.

bicycle / cycle / bike

● RECOMMENDATION

   Bicycle has come to sound rather elderly, so use either *cycle* or *bike*. But remember that *bike* is also the most common word for a motor cycle, whereas *cycle* is usually assumed to mean a bicycle.

   NOTE Riders are *bikers* or *cyclists*.

bid / bade (past form)

● RECOMMENDATION

   Use *bid* as the past form of the verb (*bade* is old-fashioned, almost to the point of being obsolete): 'she bid him farewell'.

biennial / biannual / bimonthly / biweekly

See **biannual** . . .

bike / cycle / bicycle

See **bicycle** . . .

bill (British and American English)

● RULE

For Americans, *bill* means first of all a banknote, such as a *ten-dollar bill*. (In the States, when you want a bill for something you've bought, you ask for a *check*.) For British usage, see **account / invoice / statement / bill**.

bill / invoice / statement / account

See **account** . . .

billion / trillion

● RULE

Use *billion* for a *thousand million* (1,000,000,000); *trillion* for a *million million* (1,000,000,000,000).

● CAUTION

The former British use of *billion* for a *million million* and *trillion* for a *million million million* is no longer valid.

$ This follows the RULE above.

bimonthly / biweekly / biennial / biannual

See **biannual** . . .

bio-

This Greek prefix, for life or living organisms, guides us to the meaning of words: *biolinguistics* is the branch of linguistics that studies the conditions necessary for man to develop the use of language; *bioengineering* is the use of mechanical organs, such as an artificial kidney, to replace parts of the body that are not functioning; *biochemistry* is the science that deals with the chemical processes affecting substances present in living organisms; *biotechnology* develops therapeutic agents, such as human growth hormone, substances to counter Aids, cancers and other disorders, as well as biological processes in industry, such as the manufacture of packaged food and wine-making.

● RULE

The hyphen is now dropped between *bio-* and the following word, even when the latter begins with a vowel (*bioengineering*).

bitten/bit (past form)

● RULE

> *Bitten* is the past form of the verb: 'he's been *bitten*' (not 'bit').

biweekly/bimonthly/biennial/biannual

> See **biannual** . . .

black/blacken (verbs)

● RULES

1 *Black* is used for the actual colour: to black shoes; to black a grate.

2 *Blacken* is used less specifically to suggest that something has become dark or dirty: the sky blackens; the walls were blackened by smoke; a person's character can be blackened.

black/coloured

● RULE

> As a parallel to 'white', 'black' has replaced 'coloured' which should now be avoided. And it's spelt with a small letter, just as 'white' is, except in contexts such as Black rights.

● CAUTION

> How dark-skinned a person should be before they are *black,* is a sensitive question. In most contexts, it is better to use *black* for dark-skinned people of African descent.

blacken/black (verbs)

> See **black** . . .

blank cheque/carte blanche

● RULES

1 A *blank cheque* is a signed cheque with no sum of money written in. And there is a useful extension of meaning: if someone is allowed to spend as much money as they like on a project, they are 'given a blank cheque'.

2 Giving someone 'a blank cheque' can also mean giving them complete freedom of action in a situation. This is the same meaning as *carte blanche* (literally a blank sheet of paper), which is preferable in this sense, because it has only one meaning.

blasphemy/obscenity

● RULES

1 *Blasphemy* (and *blasphemous*) should be restricted to vulgar or coarse use of sacred words and names.

2 *Obscenity* is crude sexual language or pictures.

● CAUTION

Blasphemy and *obscenity* are far from clearly defined, so opinion varies, sometimes passionately, about what is blasphemous or obscene.

blatant / flagrant

● RECOMMENDATION

Generally, *blatant* and *flagrant* have become so similar in meaning that it is difficult to put a whisker between them: they can both be used for something glaringly wrong, with no attempt to hide it: 'a *blatant* (or *flagrant*) misuse of public money'.

NOTE A former use of *blatant*, to mean 'insistent noise', still survives, as in the description 'a blatant salesman', meaning that he wouldn't stop talking.

bleep / beep

See **beep** . . .

blessed / bless-ed (pronunciation)

● RECOMMENDATIONS

1   In church, *two* syllables: 'bless-ed'.
2   When it comes before a noun, *two* syllables: a 'bless-ed' event.
3   Otherwise, *one* syllable: he is blessed with good health.

blizzard / cyclone / gale / hurricane / tornado / typhoon

Storms have different names in different parts of the world.

● RULES

1   *Blizzard* is a strong wind and a snowstorm occurring at the same time, with a blinding effect (hence a *blinding blizzard*).
2   A *cyclone* is a centre of atmospheric low pressure caused by wind blowing in the same circular direction as the rotation of the Earth (anticlockwise in the northern, clockwise in the southern hemisphere). Cyclones give rise to violent winds in tropical areas.
3   A *hurricane* is a cyclonic storm where the wind reaches at least 122kph (approx 76mph). Although the word has been used about exceptionally high winds in Britain, *hurricane* is a term usually reserved for such storms around the Caribbean Sea and the Gulf of Mexico, which can affect the Florida peninsula.
4   Hurricanes, when they occur in the midwestern United States (and in some other parts of the world), are called *tornadoes*.
5   A *typhoon* is a word for a hurricane that occurs in the China Sea.
6   *Gale* is a general word for any high wind. (For meteorologists, a gale requires the wind to reach at least 50kph [approx 32mph].)

block / bloc

● RULE

Block is the standard spelling, except when used for an alliance of political parties or governments (the Eastern *bloc*).

block / hang-up / inhibition

All three words can be used for a psychological or emotional impediment that prevents someone doing something, or even thinking about it.

● RECOMMENDATION

Treat *hang-up* as the least formal, *block* as the standard everyday word, and *inhibition* more as a psychological term.

NOTE A hang-up for a writer is a *writer's block*.

blow up / blow-up

● RULE

You *blow up* (no hyphen) a photograph and the result is a *blow-up* (with a hyphen).

blush / flush

● RECOMMENDATIONS

1 Use *blush* more for women, especially young girls, and only for embarrassment.

2 Use *flush* for either sex, and for anger as well as embarrassment.

(the) **board** *is / are*

See **collective words**

boat / ship / vessel

● RULES

1 A *boat* is usually a small ship. But a fishing trawler, no matter how big, is a fishing *boat*; cross-Channel ferries are cross-Channel *boats*; yachts are sailing *boats*.

2 In the Royal Navy, almost anything afloat is HMS – Her Majesty's *Ship*, unless it is a boat launched from a ship. But submarines are *boats*.

● RECOMMENDATION

In doubt, fall back on *vessel*, which can be used for almost any boat or ship.

boatswain / bosun / bo'sun

All three spellings are used.

● RECOMMENDATION

Use *boatswain* and leave *bosun* and *bo'sun* to writers of stories about the sea.

● RULE

Only one pronunciation, whatever the spelling: 'BOHsun'.

bogey / bogy

● RULE

It's always *bogey* in golf (for a score of one stroke more than the scratch score for a hole).

● OPTION

It is *bogey* ✓ or *bogy* for an awkward circumstance or an evil spirit (*bogeyman* ✓ or *bogyman*).

bolero (pronunciation)

● RULES

1 For the Spanish dance, stress on the *second* syllable: 'boLEro' (hence the title of Ravel's composition has the stress on the *second* syllable, indicated by an acute accent: 'Boléro').

2 For the short open jacket, stress on the *first* syllable: 'BOLero'.

bona fide / bona fides

● RULES

1 *Bona fides* is a *singular* noun meaning genuine and with honest intentions. So 'their bona fides *is* unquestionable' is correct.

2 *Bona fide* describes something that has *bona fides*: 'a bona fide offer'; 'a bona fide scheme'.

● RECOMMENDATION

Outside contract law (where a *bona fide* contract has a legal meaning), use 'in good faith'; 'genuine'; 'sincere' (or some other expression): 'this proposition is in good faith' (rather than 'a bona fide proposition').

bonus / windfall

● RECOMMENDATIONS

1 Treat *bonus* as a more or less reasonable outcome of something: it can be extra payment to workers for achieving a production target, or a special dividend paid to shareholders because a company has done well.

2 Treat *windfall* as something that comes out of the blue, such as an unexpected legacy from an uncle you haven't seen for years. A company benefits from a *windfall profit* if an increase in tax enables it to sell goods, on which a lower rate of tax has been paid, at a higher price.

bordeaux / claret

● RULES

Although both terms can be used for wines from the Bordeaux region of France, *claret* is now a more elderly word. Use *bordeaux*, which is more or less the standard term in the wine trade.

● OPTION

For the wine, a small *b* or capital *B* can be used: *b*ordeaux ✓ or *B*ordeaux (see also **wines**).

born / borne

● RULES

1 *Born* is the word relating to giving birth: we are born into this world; born lucky; a born-again Christian.

2 *Borne* is the past form of the verb *bear*: we are borne by our mothers; it is too much to be borne; when an aircraft takes off, it is airborne.

borrow *from / of / off*

● RULE

Borrow *from* (not *of* or *off*): 'he borrowed money from his father'.

bosom / breast / chest

There are anatomical differences between these three words. But it is more custom that dictates their everyday use.

● RULES

1 *Bosom* and *breasts* are mainly for women, *breasts* for the milk-secreting organs, while *bosom* is used in relation to clothes (the bosom of a dress).

2 *Bosom* is used for both sexes as the centre of feeling (a bosom friend; the bosom of the family).

3 Men have *chests* rather than bosoms or breasts. (But tailors talk about the *breast pocket* on a man's jacket.)

4 Both sexes have *chest* colds, and get something off their *chests* (express their feelings or own up to something).

boss

● RECOMMENDATION

As a noun, *boss,* for the person in charge, can be regarded as standard written English. But *boss* as a *verb* (to boss someone around) is conversational.

$ *Boss* often has a negative aspect, especially when used for the boss of a union or of a political organisation.

bosun / bo'sun / boatswain

See **boatswain . . .**

both

● RULES

1 *Both* should be used about *two* things or people, so it is wrong to say 'both John,

Mary and Helen are coming to dinner'. To emphasise a number that is more than two, use 'all': 'John, Mary and Helen are all coming to dinner'.

2 *Both* can be used for 'each': 'there is a chemist on both sides of the street'. [!]

3 *Both* should be placed directly in front of the word it refers to: 'she loves both men and money' (not 'she both loves men and money').

● CAUTION

Look out for a confusion in meaning: 'both directors and their secretaries were at the meeting' could mean two directors plus their secretaries, or a number of directors with their secretaries. It has to be spelt out: 'the two directors and their secretaries . . .' or simply 'the directors and their secretaries . . .'.

boyfriend / girlfriend / partner

● RECOMMENDATIONS

1 If you want to use *boyfriend* or *girlfriend,* reserve them for a steady, often but not necessarily a sexual relationship. But many people now prefer the alternative word *partner,* the word used on some official forms to cover husband, wife or one of an unmarried couple living together.

2 A woman can be relaxed about using *girlfriend* for any woman friend, without it necessarily suggesting a sexual relationship. Nevertheless, many women prefer 'woman friend'. Cohabiting males usually prefer the word *partner.*

$ US census forms include *partner* as an official category.

boyish / girlish

● CAUTION

To use *boyish* about a man is on the whole complimentary, suggesting that he is youthful and charming; but to say a woman is *girlish* suggests she is silly and behaving in a way that is much younger than her age. *Girlie* is offensive, as it is patronising and used about pornographic photographs.

brackets ( ) [ ]

Brackets are useful for including a piece of background information, without holding up the flow of the sentence. The same job can be done by *commas* or *dashes,* with varying degrees of separation.

● RECOMMENDATIONS

1 *Commas,* you could say, mark off the least separation. (See also **commas**.)

2 *Dashes* come next up the scale, and are useful - when the fancy takes you – for a humorous or dramatic effect. (See also **dashes**.)

3 *Brackets* (which can be round or square) mark off a complete separation from the main sentence.

● RULES FOR BRACKETS AND PUNCTUATION

1 If the brackets come in the middle of a sentence, punctuation of the *main* sentence belongs *outside* the brackets: 'As he was late (over two hours), we had to wait for him.'

2   Even when the words in brackets form a complete sentence in the middle of the main sentence, it does not take an initial capital or closing stop: 'He arrived late (**this is what he told me later**), and left early.'

3   A sentence on its own in brackets, standing after the main sentence, is treated as an ordinary sentence, given an initial capital and ending with a stop: 'They made love that night. (It was a tradition on Saturdays.)' In that case there is no stop *after the closing bracket*.

4   When ellipses (a row of dots) come within brackets they do not double up as a stop, so one has to be added *after* the closing bracket: 'Any hard cheese can be used (cheddar, gruyère, gouda . . .).'

5   Exclamation marks and question marks *belonging to the words in brackets* come *within* the brackets, and do not affect punctuation outside: 'She believed his excuse (she is that kind of a woman!), and they spent a happy evening together.' 'He made a silly excuse, which she believed (how could she have been so stupid?), and they spent a happy evening together.'

6   Exclamation marks and question marks belonging to the *main* sentence stay *outside* the brackets: 'Would you like another glass (it's very good wine)?'

● CAUTION

Be careful about putting a long passage in brackets, or readers will lose the flow of the main sentence.

● RULES FOR USING SQUARE BRACKETS

1   To separate a comment by someone else inserted into a quotation: 'To be or not to be? [Indecision reigns supreme!] That is the question.' Round brackets in that example would suggest that the interpolation is part of the actual quotation.

2   To put brackets within other brackets: 'That quotation (the most famous of all Shakespeare's lines [who doesn't know it?], which begins Hamlet's soliloquy) describes a state we are all in at times.' But whenever possible, avoid brackets within brackets, as readers have to work hard to follow the sense.

$ The term *parentheses* is used for rounded brackets ( ), and *brackets* is reserved for the square kind [ ].

brandy / cognac

● RULE

Brandy is a spirit distilled from grapes or any other fruit (cherry brandy, apricot brandy . . .). For a brandy to be called *cognac* (PRON 'CONyak'), it must be made from *grapes* grown and distilled in the region round Cognac, a town in Charente in western France.

bravado / bravura

● RULES

1   *Bravado* is putting on a show of bravery or confidence, with the suggestion that there is a touch of swaggering about it.

2   *Bravura* is used more than anything else about a musician or a singer performing a difficult piece with showy virtuosity.

breakdown / break down

● RULE

As *one* word *breakdown* is the *noun*; as *two* words it's the *verb*: 'to *break down* sales by regions'.

● CAUTION

The two meanings of *breakdown* (as one word) can cause misunderstanding. One meaning is a total failure to function or to make progress: 'a nervous breakdown'; 'a breakdown of negotiations'. The other meaning is analysis or division into categories: 'a breakdown of sales'. But someone could get the wrong idea from 'a breakdown of the business' or 'a breakdown of hospital patients by sex'. In those examples 'analysis' or 'classification' is a better word.

breasts / chest / bosom

See **bosom** . . .

breath / breathe

● RULE

Breath is the *noun*, *breathe* the *verb*: 'take a deep breath and then breathe out'.

bright / brightly

● RULE

Although grammatically, 'the moon shines *brightly*' is correct, the poetic use of *bright* for *brightly* (as in Blake's line, 'Tiger! Tiger! burning bright . . .') is transferred to prose. So 'the moon shines bright'; 'the candle burns bright' and similar expressions are as acceptable as '. . . shines brightly'; '. . . burns brightly'.

Brit / Britisher / Briton

● RECOMMENDATIONS

1   *Brit* is a relaxed conversational abbreviation for a British person, and has no place in formal writing.
2   *Britisher* is more at home in American rather than British English.
3   *Briton* is rarely used except as *Ancient Briton* (a historical term for a native of southern Britain before the Roman conquest) or when singing *Rule Britannia!* Otherwise, *Briton* is a useful shorthand term in headlines: TWO BRITONS WIN GOLD MEDALS.
$ See RECOMMENDATION 2.

Britain / Great Britain / British Isles / United Kingdom

● RULES

1 *Britain* is short for *Great Britain*. Both names include England, Scotland and Wales, but exclude Northern Ireland, the Isle of Man and the Channel Islands.

2 *British Isles* is geographical, not political: it includes the *whole* of Ireland as well as all the adjacent islands, the Hebrides, Shetlands, Channel Islands, etc.

3 *United Kingdom* is political, short for the *United Kingdom of Great Britain and Northern Ireland*.

British / English

● RECOMMENDATION

Use *British* rather than *English* for anything relating to the United Kingdom.

● CAUTIONS

1 The habit of using *English* as synonymous with *British* could offend the Irish, Scottish or Welsh.

2 In everyday use, *British* can sometimes be ambiguous: it is used about the United Kingdom (as above), but also about Great Britain (see **Britain**), or about the British Commonwealth.

British English / *standard* English

● RULES

1 *British English* is the accepted term for the variety of more or less educated forms of the language used in the United Kingdom.

2 For the general consensus of what is considered correct English in the UK, *standard English* (*standard* with a small *s*) is the most suitable term.
   See also **Queen's English.**

$ **American English** is the term that corresponds to *British English*, with *General American* as the term used in linguistics to correspond to *standard English* in Britain.

Britisher / Briton / Brit

See **Brit** . . .

British Isles / Great Britain / United Kingdom / Britain

See **Britain** . . .

Briton / Britisher / Brit

See **Brit** . . .

broad / wide

They both mean that something is large from side to side.

- RECOMMENDATIONS

1 *Broad* is more general (a broad expanse) and a word that is used about people (broad shoulders; broad hips).

2 *Wide* is more specific and tangible: a wide pavement; a wide entrance; a board two metres wide.

3 A *broad* view of something is a general overall view, without focusing on detail; a *wide* view suggests taking as many other things as possible into account.

broadcast / broadcasted (past form)

- RECOMMENDATION

Broadcast is now the usual past form, and should be used in preference to *broadcasted*.

broadcast / telecast

- RECOMMENDATION

Although **broad**cast covers radio and television, it is more associated with radio. To avoid misunderstanding, use **tele**cast for television.

brusque (pronunciation)

- OPTIONS

Three pronunciations are acceptable: 'broohsk' ✓ (*oo* as in 'moon'); 'broosk' (*oo* as in 'foot'); 'brusk' (to rhyme with 'rusk').

buff / fawn / beige

See **beige** . . .

buffet

- RULES

1 *Buffet* can mean a sideboard, when it is pronounced 'BUFFay', or a serve-yourself meal, when it is pronounced 'BOOFFay'.

2 *Buffet* is also a *noun* meaning a blow, and the *verb* for giving a blow (both PRON 'BUFFett'). The *t* is not doubled in the other forms: buffeted, buffeting.

bulk / majority

- RECOMMENDATION

Use *bulk* for quantity, *majority* for numbers: 'the bulk of the work'; 'the majority of the workers'.

bullion / gold

- RULE

Bullion is gold in bulk form (usually bars), rather than gold coins or other objects, which are simply *gold*.

● RECOMMENDATION

Bullion can also be used for silver (and even other metals), and although it usually refers to gold, it is still better to use the term *gold bullion*.

bull's-eye / bullseye

● RULE

This expression means 'the eye of a bull', which is why it has to be written *bull's-eye*.

bureaux / bureaus

● RECOMMENDATIONS

1 It's old-fashioned to use *bureau* for a desk with drawers. Its use now is mostly governmental for an office or department dealing with specific business (Citizens' Advice Bureau).

2 Use *bureaux* for the plural (*bureaus*, while accepted by dictionaries, is less usual). Either way, PRON 'BYOORohz'.

$ *Bureau* is a chest of drawers, usually with a mirror fitted above. It is also used for a government department (Federal Bureau of Investigation). The usual plural form is *bureaus*.

burned / burnt (past form)

● RECOMMENDATIONS

1 Use *burnt* in sentences such as 'she burnt the letter'; 'the toast was burnt'.

2 *Burned* is preferable when it is describing *how* something is burning: 'the candle burned brightly'; 'the fire burned fiercely'.

busby / bearskin

See **bearskin** . . .

buses / busses

● RULE

Buses.

$ *Busses.*

business / trade

● RECOMMENDATIONS

1 *Business* has a general meaning covering everything to do with commercial activities from a multinational to a corner shop.

2 *Trade* is often used about wholesale and international dealings. For example, the *jewellery trade* suggests the overall market in jewellery, while a *jewellery business* suggests a high street shop.

businessman / businesswoman

● RECOMMENDATION

Avoid *businessperson* as a unisex word, and use *business people* for women and men in business.

but

● RECOMMENDATIONS

1 There is nothing wrong in *beginning* a sentence with the word *but*.

2 Should it be 'but *I / she / he*' or 'but *me / her / him*' ? See OPTIONS.

● OPTIONS

1 Complete the sentence, and see which fits in grammatically: 'Who can do it?' 'No one but *I* (can do it).'; 'Who could have written this?' 'No one but *she* (could have written this).' On the other hand, 'there's no one here but *her*', as the sentence is already complete.

2 ✓ Use 'but *me / her / him*' in all cases: 'Who can do it?' 'No one but *me*.'

● CAUTION

But is a double-edged word: it can put people on guard or it can encourage them. 'It's very good, but . . .' will produce a reaction of caution; 'It will be very difficult, but . . .', gives some hope. Be especially careful of 'Yes, but . . .', which often means *No*.

by / bye

● RULES

1 It's a *bye* in cricket (a run scored from a ball not hit), and in golf (remaining holes not played after the match is decided).

2 It's *by*-election; *by*-laws (with hyphens); *by*gone; *by*pass; *by*path; *by*road; *by*stander; *by*way; *by*word (without hyphens).

3 *By the bye* is the spelling for the expression meaning 'by the way'.

4 It is always *goodbye*.

$ *Goodby* is more usual than *goodbye*.

by / in comparison

See **comparison**

Byzantine

● RECOMMENDATIONS

1 Use *Byzantine* for religious art, especially the architecture of churches of the eastern Roman Empire, that makes use of the round arch dominating a cross of equal arms formed by the aisles in the church below. Also for the lavish stylised mosaics of the same period.

2 *Byzantine* can also be used to describe obscure or devious situations, especially political ones.

● OPTIONS

    PRON 'biZZANtyne'✓, 'BIZZantyne' or 'byeZANtyne'.

$ PRON 'BIZZanteen'.

C

caddie / caddy

● RULE

Caddie is someone who carries golf clubs for players on a golf course; *caddy* is a box for keeping tea.

café / restaurant

● RECOMMENDATIONS

1   The word *café* has come down in the world since the *café society* at the turn of the century, and cafés are now modest places serving teas, snacks or simple meals. (There are a few exceptions, such as the legendary Café Royal in London.) *Restaurant* is the standard word for places that serve full meals, and it is derogatory to call one of them a *café*.

2   For the acute accent over the *e* of *café*, see **accents** (RECOMMENDATION).

3   For the pronunciation of *restaurant*, see **restaurant**.

calculate

● CAUTION

The American use of *calculate* to mean 'suppose' is creeping into British English, and leading to ambiguity. In America 'I calculate the train will arrive at 5 o'clock' suggests 'I *expect* or *suppose* it will arrive then.' In Britain it could mean 'I have worked out from the timetable that it will arrive at that time.'

calendar / calender

● RULE

Calendar is the word for a chart showing the days, weeks and months of a year. *Calender* is a rare word for a machine used in paper-making.

cameo / intaglio

● RULE

An *intaglio* (PRON 'inTALLyoh', without sounding the *g*) is carved out, leaving a sunken image (seals are intaglios). A *cameo* is the other way round – it is carved in relief.

can / may

● RULES

1   *Can* expresses ability to do something: 'I can help you' means 'I know how to, or have permission to do so'.

2 *May* suggests possibility rather than certainty: 'I may help you' leaves it open one way or the other.

● RECOMMENDATION

Both *can* and *may* are used to express permission: 'you *can* (or *may*) go now' means it is in order for you to go. *May* is more formal, *can* more relaxed. 'You *may* proceed' has an official or condescending ring to it: 'You *can* go ahead' is more friendly.

● CAUTION

'I may help you' suggests possibility (as in RULE 2 above), but could also mean 'I have permission to help you'. In practice, the 'possibility' meaning would usually be assumed, but there is occasionally a risk of misunderstanding.

can / tin

● RECOMMENDATION

The words have become interchangeable, with *can* (the standard word in America) taking over: a can of soup; a can of beer.

$ *Tin* is not used for a container.

candelabra / candelabrum / chandelier

● RULES

1 *Candelabrum* is the *singular* word for a multi-branched candlestick: *candelabra* is the *plural* form.

2 *Candelabrum* (*candelabra* in the plural, as above) is the *standing* version: *chandelier* is the *suspended* kind.

3 The same words are used whether they hold candles or electric-light bulbs.

cannabis / marijuana / pot / grass / dope / hashish

● RULES

1 *Marijuana* for the preparation made into cigarettes.

2 *Cannabis* for the preparation that is eaten.

3 *Pot* and *grass* are popular slang names for marijuana rolled into cigarettes.

4 Avoid *dope*, loosely-used slang for any narcotic drug.

5 *Hashish* (from the Arabic name for powdered hemp leaves) should only be used in relation to the drug in Arab countries.

cannon / canon

● RULES

1 A *cannon* is a gun mounted on a carriage, mostly now as a relic on display.

2 In modern warfare, *cannon* is used only for automatic guns firing shells that are fitted to aircraft.

3 A *cannon* is the shot in billiards when a ball is made to *cannon* off two other balls in succession.

4 With one *n*, *canon* has a number of meanings: the most common are the title of a

priest appointed as a member of a cathedral ('a canon of Westminster'); a church decree that regulates practice ('the canons of the Church'); the list of works of an author ('the Shakespeare canon'); and a piece of music in which the same theme is taken up in successive parts.

can't

See **contracted forms**

canvas / canvass

● RULES

1   *Canvas* (rarely used as a *verb*) is the *noun* for the cotton or jute material.

2   *Canvass* (rarely used as a *noun*) is the *verb* for trying to win votes or orders, or to seek opinions.

3   In the art world, *canvas* is sometimes used for an oil painting (because it's painted on canvas). With that meaning, there are alternative plurals: *canvases* ✓ or *canvasses*.

capacity / ability

See **ability** . . .

capitalism / capitalist

● CAUTION

Although dictionaries define *capitalist* simply as someone who possesses capital and uses it in business, *capitalist* and *capitalism* are for many people abusive words for bosses who control the means of production. For this reason, capitalists prefer to be called *industrialists* or, where property is involved, *developers*.

capital letters

The style in the 1990s is to use fewer capital letters. The National Consumer Council advises 'Avoid too many capital letters in a sequence, as they are difficult to read.' There are few rules, but a number of firm recommendations.

● RULES

1   Among personages, *God* takes a capital, so does the *Pope*, and a particular king or queen (see RECOMMENDATION 1 below).

2   Be consistent: do not write 'the **F**oreign **S**ecretary' followed by 'the **h**ome **s**ecretary'.

● RECOMMENDATIONS

1   *Titles*   Use capitals to distinguish between the specific person and a group: 'the **B**ishop gave an address to the assembly of **b**ishops'; 'Edward Heath was the **P**rime **M**inister who took the UK into the Common Market, a decision endorsed by the **p**rime **m**inisters who succeeded him'; 'among the **q**ueens who were present was the **Q**ueen of the Netherlands'. Use a capital for the reigning monarch (in Britain, Queen Elizabeth is the **Q**ueen).

2   *Jobs* No capitals for titles: **b**ank **m**anager; **m**anaging **d**irector; **c**hief **e**xecutive; **c**hairman; **h**eadmaster; **c**ivil **s**ervant; **m**ember of **p**arliament.

3   No capitals for the four seasons: **s**pring; **s**ummer; **a**utumn; **w**inter.

4   *Acronyms* See **abbreviations**.

5   *Points of the compass in geographical names* Use capitals for established and political names or when defining a region: **N**orthern **I**reland; **S**outh **A**merica; unemployment in the **N**orth; the **W**est **C**ountry. But if you are driving **s**outh or exposed to a **n**orth wind, use small letters.

● CAUTION

Distinguish between **N**orthern **I**reland (the province) and **n**orthern **I**reland (the northern part of the country).

6   *History* Major historical events take a capital: the **R**enaissance (but 'a recent **r**enaissance'); the **R**evolution (French or Russian, but 'a **r**evolution in fashion'); the **L**ast **S**upper (the biblical event).

7   *Titles of books, plays, etc* Use a capital for the first and last words, and other important words but not for short words, such as *a, the, for, of, in*: *The Taming of the Shrew*; *A Man Born to be King*.

   NOTE Sometimes a writer chooses to give every word of a title an initial capital: *The War Of The Worlds*; *How Late It Was, How Late.*

8   *Standard names of things associated with countries* Use small letters: **f**rench windows; **v**enetian blinds; **i**ndian ink; **y**orkshire pudding.

9   *Proper names used in a general way* Use small letters: '**h**oover the carpet'; 'fill a thermos'; 'please **x**erox this'; 'put on your **w**ellingtons'.

10 For names of wines, see **wines**.

capital / corporal **punishment**

● RULES

1   *Capital punishment* is the death penalty.

2   *Corporal punishment* is usually a beating (although it could be any other punishment inflicted on the living body not intended to kill the person).

Capitol / capitol

● RULES

1   Use *Capitol* for: the temple of ancient Rome dedicated to Jupiter in 509 BC, and the building in Washington, DC where the US Congress meets.

2   Use *capitol* for the building in each state of the USA where the State legislature meets.

3   PRON Either way, the *to* is not stressed, and *capitol* is pronounced in the same way as 'capital': 'CAPite(r)l'.

● CAUTION

Do not confuse *Capitol / capitol* with 'capital'.

caption / subtitle

● RECOMMENDATIONS

1 *Subtitle* (as a *noun* or *verb*) for films: 'English subtitles on a foreign film'; 'he subtitled the film'.

2 *Caption* for photographs, diagrams, etc in print: 'the caption under the picture in the newspaper'.

   NOTE Operas performed in foreign languages sometimes have *surtitles*, that is titles above the stage for the audience to read.

3 *Caption* is also the word to use for a title printed *above* an illustration.

carefree / careless

● RULES

1 *Carefree* is a happy state, free from care or anxiety.

2 *Careless* at one time meant the same ('careless rapture'), but now *careless* is always used in a negative way, to mean 'not bothering; not giving a damn'.

carelessness / negligence

● RULES

1 *Negligence* puts the stress on not doing something that should have been done, and in law implies a culpable failure to perform a duty that is a legal responsibility.

2 *Carelessness* is a lighter word, usually suggesting sloppiness or someone not thinking about what they are doing.

carillon / peal

● RULES

1 When a bell or bells are rung it is a *peal*.

2 When it is a tune played on bells, or the effect of bells created on a keyboard instrument, such as an organ, it is a *carillon* (PRON 'kerRILLion').

caring / humanitarian

   Caring is the 1990's alternative word to *humanitarian,* describing a person or policy that promotes human welfare: a caring profession; a caring attitude.

● CAUTION

   Caring is often a vague word, corrupted by glib political use, without anyone defining what it means, or saying who is being taken care of.

carte blanche / blank cheque

   See **blank cheque** . . .

cartel / monopoly

● RULES

1 A *cartel* is a group of companies which carves up the market between them, manipulating prices, production and advertising.

2 A *monopoly* is when there is one organisation controlling production and the market.

cartridge / cassette

Both words are used for plastic boxes ready for immediate insertion into an appliance.

● RECOMMENDATIONS

1 *Cartridge* is the term for removable units in computers and ribbons in electronic typewriters.

2 *Cassette* is the term for film-boxes inserted into cameras and magnetic tapes for tape-recorders.

case (grammatical)

● RULES

Case defines the grammatical relationship of certain words in a sentence. Take this sentence: 'She sent him Mary's letter.' 'She' does the action and is in the *nominative* (or *subjective*) case; 'letter' is the object of the action and is in the *accusative* (or *objective*) case; 'him' is the recipient of the action and is in the *dative* case; 'Mary's' denotes possession and is in the *genitive* (or *possessive*) case.

cast / throw

See **throw** . . .

caster / castor

See **castor** . . .

Castilian / Catalan

● RULES

1 *Castilian* is another name for the official Spanish language, developed from the language spoken in Castile, the former kingdom in the central plateau of Spain.

2 *Catalan* is the language of Catalonia, the region of NE Spain bordering France.

castor / caster

● RULE

It is always *castor* oil.

● RECOMMENDATION

Although *caster* is an alternative, use *castor* for swivelled wheels on armchairs and sofas, and for white sugar more finely ground than granulated sugar.

Catalan / Castilian

See **Castilian . . .**

catalyst

● **RULE**

In everyday use, a *catalyst* is somebody (or something) who does or says very little but changes a situation or brings about an understanding, simply by being present or involved (a counsellor can act as a catalyst in a difficult marital situation). That is the proper extension of the use of the word in chemistry.

● **CAUTION**

It is wrong to use *catalyst* simply to mean making something happen: 'lack of planning was a catalyst in the failure of the project'. 'Factor' is the proper word in that context: '. . . was a factor . . .'.

catch-22

● **RULE**

Catch-22 is useful shorthand to describe a 'heads I lose – tails you win' situation. Suppose your boss asks you to come up with a brilliant new idea. You do just that, but then he asks 'How do we know it will work – we've never tried anything like it before?' That's a *catch-22*, because the characteristic is that the case for both sides is so reasonable, there's no way out.

● **CAUTION**

This expression, from the title of the novel by Joseph Heller, is often wrongly used to mean there is something dishonest with a proposition.

categorical / unconditional

Both words mean without conditions or reservations, but are better used in different contexts.

● **RECOMMENDATIONS**

1 *Categorical* fits with words, such as *refusal, statement, denial* (categorical refusal; categorical statement). It means there is no room for discussion or argument.

2 *Unconditional* is more at home in military contexts (unconditional surrender; unconditional withdrawal). It also belongs to agreements: an unconditional agreement is one with no ifs or buts.

Catholic / catholic

● **RULES**

1 *Catholic* with a capital *C* is religious, referring to the Roman Catholic religion and its adherents.

2 With a small *c*, *c*atholic is a secular word, meaning a wide range of tastes and interests.

cause / causation

● RULES

1   *Cause* is the general word for someone or something that makes an event occur.

2   *Causation* belongs more in medical contexts to describe why certain symptoms appear.

● CAUTION

Cause says it all, and there is no need to add 'because of', 'due to' or any other linking phrase: 'the cause of the government's defeat was *because of* the poll tax'. Leave out 'because of' and the sentence is sharper and more direct: 'the cause of the government's defeat was the poll tax'.

caustic / sarcastic

● RECOMMENDATIONS

1   In general use, relate *caustic* to caustic soda, which burns the skin on contact. Use it also about a comment that is particularly sharp and hurtful: 'his caustic remark made her wince with pain'.

2   Use *sarcastic* for a comment that is double-edged, achieving its effect by words clearly intended to mean the opposite to their meaning on the surface.

   EXAMPLE   If someone comes to stay for the weekend, bringing as an offering a packet of crisps, a *caustic* comment would be 'Thank you for nothing!'; a *sarcastic* one would be 'Thank you for being so *very* generous!'

cavalcade / motorcade

● RULES

1   **Caval**cade is a procession of horsemen or horse-drawn carriages. **Caval**cade can also be used for a sequence of connected historical events: 'a cavalcade of the Kings and Queens of England'.

2   **Motor**cade is a procession of cars or motor cycles.

caviare / caviar

● RULE

   Caviare.

$ *Caviar*.

cc

● RULE

   At the bottom of letters, the abbreviation *cc* indicates that copies of the letters have been sent to other people (cc John Brown, Mary Smith).

● RECOMMENDATION

   The letters *cc* stand for 'carbon copies', so are as out of date as carbon paper. Instead of *cc*, use: *copy* (or *copies*) to . . . .

CE **(Common Era)**

See AD

cease / discontinue / terminate / stop

See **stop** . . .

cedilla (ç)

See **accents**

ceiling

● CAUTION

If you are determined not to drop below a stated upper limit, do not say you are 'determined to stick to the ceiling'!

celibacy / chastity

The correct meaning of *celibacy* is the state of being unmarried, while *chastity* means abstention of sex.

● RECOMMENDATIONS

1   The distinction between the words has become so blurred that it is unreliable. It's best to follow general usage, and accept that *celibacy* (and *celibate*) means to most people abstention from sex.

2   *Chastity* (and *chaste*) are old-worldly, and are rarely used about a man. So they are better avoided, except in poetic or archaic contexts.

3   Because of the possibility of misunderstanding, it is usually better to use alternatives, such as 'unmarried' (for *celibate*); 'an unmarried state' (for *celibacy*); and 'abstains (or abstention) from sex', instead of *chaste* and *chastity*.

Celsius / centigrade

● RULE

They are both names for exactly the same temperature scale: water freezes at 0°, boils at 100°. They are both abbreviated with a capital *C* (20°C). Written in full, only *Celsius* (taken from the name of an astronomer) has a capital, while *centigrade* does not.

● RECOMMENDATION

Use *Celsius* (now officially adopted by the BBC).

Celt / Celtic / Gaelic / Gallic

There are no clear-cut definitions of *Celt, Celtic, Gaelic*.

● RECOMMENDATIONS

1   *Celt* can be used for the present-day Irish, Scottish, Welsh, Bretons, and for the people of Cornwall and the Isle of Man.

2   *Celtic* is the corresponding general descriptive word, and is the name of the group of
    languages that includes Breton, Cornish, Irish and Welsh.
3   Pronounce *Celt* and *Celtic* with a *k* (rather than an *s*) sound: 'kelt', 'KELtic' (an
    exception is the Scottish football team, *Celtic*, always pronounced '*S*ELtic').
4   *Gaelic* can be used in the same way as *Celtic*, but should be reserved for the *languages*
    of the Celts, especially the forms spoken in Ireland, Scotland and the Isle of Man
    (PRON 'GAYlic' but 'GALLic' in Scotland).

● RULE

    Gallic is a different word altogether. It describes anything that has a particularly
    French style, from the worldly way a Frenchman gestures ('a Gallic shrug') to the
    way Parisiennes walk ('a Gallic swing of the hips').

centigrade / Celsius

    See **Celsius** . . .

Century / century

● RULES

    Spell *century* with a small *c*: 21st *century;* 5th *century* BC. A capital *C* is preferable for
    the abbreviation: 17thC; 19thC.

ceremonial / ceremonious

● RULES

1   *Ceremonial* is used for pomp and splendour: 'a ceremonial occasion'; 'after the feast,
    there were ceremonial dances'.
2   *Ceremonious* is used about people and behaviour, and is not usually complimentary,
    as it suggests an exaggerated and fussy formality: 'before speaking, he gave a
    ceremonious bow'.

certain

● CAUTION

    Certain can mean *un*certain: 'she has a certain talent for cooking' could mean you
    might eat well – if you're lucky, *or* that you're bound to eat well. In speech, it's
    usually clear by the way someone says it: emphasis means *certain*, a slight hesitation
    implies *un*certain. In writing it is better to put your cards on the table: 'an
    undoubted talent'; 'a real talent' *or* 'a modest talent'; 'a limited talent'.

cervical (pronunciation)

    Cervical is most familiar in the phrase *cervical smear test*, a specimen taken from the
    neck (or cervix) of the womb, which is examined for early detection of cancer.

● OPTION

    PRON 'SERvicle'✓ or 'serVYcle'.

chagrin (pronunciation)

● OPTION

'SHAgrin'✓ or 'shaGREEN' (this alternative pronunciation confuses *chagrin* with a different word 'shagreen', a type of leather with a rough surface).

chairman / chairperson / the chair

● RECOMMENDATION

Follow the BBC lead and use *the chair* as the unisex term for a person chairing a meeting. But when it's the head of a company, use *chair**man** or chair**woman***. *Chair**person*** is a more laboured alternative.

chaise longue

● RULES

1   The plural is *chaises longues*.

2   The pronunciation of the plural form is 'shezzLONG' (final *s* not sounded).

chamois (pronunciation)

● RULE

When it is a goat antelope, it is 'SHAMwah'. The plural remains *chamois*, pronounced the same as the singular *or* with a final *z* sound: 'SHAMwahz'✓. When it's the soft leather for washing cars or windows, it's 'SHAMee'.

chandelier / candelabrum / candelabra

See **candelabra** . . .

change / alter

See **alter** . . .

character / personality / persona

● RECOMMENDATIONS

1   *Character* should apply to someone's mental, emotional and moral qualities that set the standards of their behaviour.

2   *Personality* describes the qualities a person projects outwards, their force, style, humour . . . .

3   A *persona* is a role acted out in real life, the impression a person seeks to make on the outside world.

characteristic / representative / symptomatic

Each of these words can describe something that fits into a pattern.

● RECOMMENDATIONS

1   *Characteristic* suggests that something is in keeping with other things manifested

previously: a novel is characteristic of a writer if it is in the same form and style as previous novels.

2 *Representative* adds the suggestion that things and qualities have appeared before: a novel is representative of a writer when it contains characters, turns of plot, etc, that have been used in previous novels.

3 *Symptomatic* should be used for examples of problems or difficulties that occur regularly in the same context: 'the character of Helen in the novel is symptomatic of the writer's failure to understand how a woman feels'.

● CAUTION

Symptomatic can relate to physical or mental indications of a disorder, so it should not be used about something good, as in 'this is symptomatic of his ability to handle a complex plot'. The word there should be *characteristic*.

charisma / charismatic

● CAUTION

These words are from a New Testament Greek word meaning the gift of grace, a quality conferred by God. They should not be tagged on lightly to anyone a little out of the ordinary, but should be reserved for some extraordinary quality that truly sets a person apart.

charter / hire

● RECOMMENDATIONS

1 *Charter* is used about a means of transport: ships are chartered; a charter flight is an aircraft chartered by a travel company.

2 *Hire* is used for people, objects and places: hiring a dance band; a hall; equipment. (Exceptions are taxis, which are 'for *hire*', and cars, which are *hired*.)

chastity / celibacy

See **celibacy** . . .

cheap / cheaply

● RECOMMENDATION

Cheap is conversational ('we must buy as cheap as we can'): *cheaply* is preferable in writing ('the goods were purchased as cheaply as possible').

● CAUTION

Cheap can often be taken to mean worthless and shoddy. When the context does not make it clear, add an extra phrase: 'we must buy as cheaply as we can, so long as the quality is first class'.

check / check *up on* / check *out* / checkout

● RECOMMENDATIONS

1   *Check* and *check up on* can both be used, with *check up on* possibly suggesting an extra careful check because there is doubt.

2   *Check out*, an American expression, is now equally at home in Britain, and is used for looking into something or somewhere, to see if it is suitable: 'check out the location to see if it can be used for the scene we want to shoot'.

3   *Check up* are separate words as a *verb* ('please check up on this'), but hyphenated as a *noun* ('he went to his doctor for a check-up').

4   *Checkout* (*one* word) is the counter in a supermarket where you pay, or as *checkout time*, the latest time you have to vacate a room in a hotel.

chemist / pharmacy

● OPTION

Chemist ✓ remains the usual everyday word, although many chemists now prefer *pharmacy*.

$ The usual word is *druggist*.

cherubs / cherubim (plural forms)

● RULE

The usual plural is *cherubs*. The plural *cherubim* (PRON 'CHERe(r)bim') is for an order of angels in a biblical context or in a painting.

chest / breast / bosom

See **bosom** . . .

chicory / endive

These are names for the elongated white salad vegetable with smooth tight leaves. *Chicory* was the usual British name, with *endive* sometimes used for a type of lettuce. *Endive* is the French name.

● RECOMMENDATION

As *endive* (PRON 'ENNdeeve'✓ or 'AHNdeeve') is taking over more and more in Britain, it makes sense to use it, especially as *chicory* is the word for the root of the vegetable, roasted and ground as a coffee substitute.

childish / childlike

● RULE

*Child**like*** is to have the natural innocence and openness of a child: *child**ish***, unless it is used about a child, is immature, spoilt and stupid.

Chinese / Chinamen

● RULE

Chinese is the only word to use now for the people of China.

● CAUTION

Chinamen is considered derogatory.

chiropodist (pronunciation)

● OPTION

Two pronunciations are heard: '***ki***ROPodist' ✓ and '***shi***ROPodist'. [!]

choosy / choosey

● RULE

Choosy.

chop / cutlet

● RULES

1 A *chop* is always *meat* (a slice cut from the ribs and left on the bone).

2 A *cutlet* is usually boneless, and can be meat or any other food (even a chopped nut mixture) formed into flat cakes for frying or grilling.

chord / cord

● RULES

1 *Chord* is the musical term, and *cord* is tightly twisted string.

2 It is vocal *cords* (because they are cord-like tissues in the larynx that vibrate to produce sounds).

Christian name / *forename* / *first* name

See ***first*** name . . .

Christmas / Xmas

● RECOMMENDATION

Use ***Christ***mas, and leave **X**mas to Christmas cards and tinsel displays in shop windows.

cinema / pictures / films

See **films** . . .

cinematic

● RECOMMENDATION

Cinematic is no longer used only about films. It can be applied to any narrative form, such as a novel or a play, or even a painting, using a style that has something in common with film realism or cutting from scene to scene.

cipher / cypher / code

See **code** . . .

circumflex (ˆ)

See **accents**

(*in / under* the) **circumstances**

● OPTION

It is all right to do something *under* ✓ or *in* the circumstances.

citation / quotation

See **quotation** . . .

cite / quote

See **quote** . . .

(the) **City**

The City is the accepted name for the *City of London*, the square mile that forms the old city, now the financial centre of Britain, containing the Bank of England and the Stock Exchange.

● CAUTION

The *c*ity of London is not the same as the *C*ity of London: the *City* is precisely defined, whereas the *city* is usually taken to include the expanse of Greater London.

city / town

The distinction between *city* and *town* is not always clear-cut, although strictly speaking, a *city* in Britain is established by royal charter.

● RECOMMENDATIONS

1 In general use, any large town can be called a *city*.
2 A *town* is distinctly larger than a village, and would be expected to have at least one important shopping street, a large church and at least a modest town hall plus a mayor and a town council. But there are borderline cases where it is uncertain whether a place is a village or a town.

  NOTE In some phrases, a *city* is called a *town*: people in the country visiting London go 'up to town', just as in New York you can be 'on the town'.
  See also (the) **City**.

$ Any important town is often called *The City* (with a capital *C*).

civil / human rights

● RULES

1 *Civil* rights are the rights of citizens under the law of the land.
2 *Human* rights go beyond the statute book to what is sometimes called *natural law*,

the rights of an individual as a human being. These rights include liberty, freedom from persecution and from imprisonment without trial, and economic and political rights.

claim

The proper meaning of *claim* is to assert a right, such as 'to claim compensation'. It has become extended to mean 'state' or 'contend': 'he claims that he was not there at the time'.

● CAUTION

In the extended meaning, *claim* may be seen to suggest doubt about what is claimed: 'he claims that he was not there at the time' (implying 'but I wonder . . .').

clandestine (pronunciation)

● OPTION

'clanDEStin'✓ or 'CLANdestyne'.

claret / bordeaux

See **bordeaux . . . ; wines**

clarinettist / clarinetist

● RULE

Clarinettist.

$ *Clarinetist.*

class

● RECOMMENDATIONS

1 *Working class* and *upper class* are uneasy terms in the 1990s, and are better avoided. The BBC use 'top social bracket' and 'lower income group', which are recommended as alternative terms for general use.

2 *Middle class* remains in general use but more as a term for a large section of society, rather than restricted, as it once was, to people in the professions.

3 In economic or marketing contexts, 'socio-economic groups' is the standard way of defining people's social prestige and financial position, starting with *A* at the top, down the scale to *D* at the bottom. Chief executives of public companies, judges, barristers, for example, would be described at being in 'socio-economic group A', with 'socio-economic group C' representing, more or less, the *middle class* as described in RECOMMENDATION 2 above. But this terminology should not be used outside marketing and statistical contexts.

classic / classical

● RECOMMENDATIONS

1 *Classic* is a descriptive word for the highest level of achievement in anything, an

outstanding or perfect example of its kind: a classic performance; a classic example; even a classic crime.

2 As this embodies the idea of timelessness, *classic* is used about things that transcend passing fashion: a classic black dress; a classic car.

3 *Classical* is the descriptive word for art and architecture, firstly for the art and architecture of ancient Greece and Rome. For later art, *classical* is used in two ways. The first is for art of any period that is inspired by the style and form of ancient classical art. The second makes a distinction between classical restraint and the expressive or emotional romantic approach, so that *classical* is opposed to *romantic*.

4 In musicology, *classical* can be treated as a chronological term, music from about 1750 up to the death of Beethoven (1827). But in general use, *classical music* is music of any period, including the 1990s, that is considered 'serious', rather than light and popular.

classics *is* / *are*

See -**ics**

classified

● CAUTION

Be careful of the term *classified information*. It could mean information divided into categories, but could also mean *classified* in its other sense: information that must not be published, because it could affect military, national or commercial security.

clean / cleanse

● RECOMMENDATIONS

1 *Clean* is the word we use most, to mean removing dirt: clean the floor or a wound, etc.

2 *Cleanse* can have a spiritual meaning, suggesting purification, and is usually followed by 'of': cleanse someone of their sins.

 NOTE By custom, a product that cleans the skin is a *cleansing* cream.

clear / clearly

● RULE

Clearly is the correct form: 'I can see clearly now'; 'Will you say it clearly?'

 NOTE One exception is the expression 'loud and clear': 'Will you say it loud and clear?'

clear / plain (about language)

● RECOMMENDATION

When used about language, *clear* and *plain* mean more or less the same. But *plain* implies simple and easy to understand ('plain English'), with *clear* suggesting free from obscurity or ambiguity, even though the language may not be all that simple.

clergy (forms of address)

● RULES

1   In the Church of England, *archbishops* are written to as: The Most Reverend and Rt Hon the Lord Archbishop of . . . . Letters begin *Dear Archbishop*. They are spoken to as *Your Grace*, or less formally as *Archbishop*.

2   *Bishops* are: The Right Reverend the Lord Bishop of . . . (the Bishop of London rates: The Right Reverend and Rt Hon the Lord Bishop of London). Letters begin *Dear Bishop*. They are spoken to as *My Lord* or *Bishop*.

3   Lower down the hierarchy: The Very Reverend the Dean of . . . , The Venerable the Archdeacon of . . . , The Reverend Canon John Brown. Letters begin *Dear Dean, Dear Archdeacon, Dear Canon*. They are spoken to as *Dean, Archdeacon, Canon*.

4   *Vicars* are: The Revd John Brown. Letters begin *Dear vicar* or *Dear Mr Brown*.

5   *Wives*, even of an archbishop, are simply *Mrs* . . . , and written to as *Dear Mrs* . . . .

6   *In the Roman Catholic Church:* His Eminence the Cardinal Archbishop of . . . , His Eminence Cardinal . . . . Letters begin *Your Eminence* or *My Lord Cardinal*. They are spoken to as *Your Eminence*, or less formally as *Cardinal*. Roman Catholic priests are: The Revd John Brown, written to as *Dear Father Brown*.

clerk (pronunciation)

● RULE

'clahk'.

$ PRON 'clerk' (to rhyme with 'jerk').

clever

● CAUTION

Look out for a misunderstanding over the meaning of *clever*: 'that's a clever idea' would probably be taken as a compliment, but 'that's *just* a clever idea' writes it off as having no real value.

cliché

Cliché comes from the French verb 'clicher', meaning to stereotype. In English it means a penny-in-the-slot expression, a word or phrase used too often by too many.

● RECOMMENDATION

Words and expressions do not start out as clichés, so how do we know when it happens to them? If you read or hear an expression half-a-dozen times in a week, if you find yourself using it three or more times a day, you probably have a *cliché* on your hands. (This does not apply, of course, to technical terms required as part of a job.)

client / customer / clientele

● RECOMMENDATIONS

1   *Client* is the grander word: solicitors, accountants, advertising agencies, insurance brokers, etc, all have clients.

2   *Customer* is more down-to-earth, so shops, plumbers and other tradesmen have customers.

3   *Clientele* is the most upmarket of all: couturiers and expensive dress-shops have clientele (PRON 'clee-on-TELL'). Some of them even grace it with a grave accent (*clientèle*), which is affected.

    NOTE Social workers refer to the people they deal with as *clients.*

climax (verb)

● RECOMMENDATION

It is better not to use *climax* as a *verb*, except in a sexual context (see NOTE below): 'this event brought the situation to a climax' (rather than 'this event climaxed the situation').

    NOTE The exception is using the verb *climax* to mean having a sexual orgasm.

$ *Climax* is freely used as a *verb* in all contexts.

climb *up* / climb *down*

● RECOMMENDATIONS

1   Although *up* is unnecessary (*climb* already points to an upward direction), *climb up* is acceptable, and sometimes useful for emphasising the effort: 'it was difficult for him to climb up six flights of stairs'.

2   *Climb down*, although illogical, is normal usage when it involves holding on with one's hands: 'he climbed down the drainpipe'.

clinic / hospital

● RECOMMENDATIONS

1   Use *hospital* most of the time, especially for hospitals that are part of the National Health Service.

2   *Clinic,* when used for a hospital, suggests that only private patients are admitted (the London Clinic). But see RECOMMENDATION 3 below.

3   *Clinic* can also be used for a building with consulting and treatment rooms, or where patients are given specialised advice (a fertility clinic). In this second sense a hospital may include several clinics for out-patients.

clinical

● RULE

Clinical distinguishes treating patients from detached academic study: a clinical psychologist works in a hospital; clinical medicine is concerned with the treatment of patients, as against research.

● CAUTION

Outside medicine, *clinical* can have a negative meaning, suggesting cold and unfeeling: 'a clinical way to look at a human tragedy'.

clock *in* / *on* / *off* / *out*

● RECOMMENDATION

Employees who record the time they start and finish work clock *in* or clock *on* for starting, and clock *off* or clock *out* for finishing. But in a general way, clock *in* and clock *off* are preferred as a way of saying what time you start and finish work: 'I clock in every morning at 8, and clock off about 4.'

close / shut

● RECOMMENDATION

In many cases it's a matter of custom whether *close* or *shut* is used. At other times it doesn't matter (we *shut* or *close* doors). If anything, *close* is perhaps more formal or polite, with *shut* more down-to-earth: a shop may be *shut*, but the sign on the door puts it more politely – CLOSED.

close proximity

● CAUTION

Close proximity is no more than a pedantic way of saying 'near'.

close scrutiny

● RECOMMENDATION

Although the word *close* is not really required (it is already implied in *scrutiny*), its justification is stressing the meaning of *scrutiny* as an intense examination of something.

closet

● RULES

1 In Britain, *closet* is no longer used for a cupboard, nor is *water-closet* used for a lavatory (although some older people might still use the abbreviation WC).

2 In the 1990s the most common use for *closet* is for something kept secret: 'the government's real intentions are now out of the closet'.

    NOTE *Closet gay* is used about a man who keep his homosexuality secret.

$ *Closet* is still in use for a small storage room or cupboard. It is also used as in RULE 2 above.

co / co-

● RECOMMENDATION

Most *co* words do not need a hyphen: cooperate, coordinate, copilot. To help with pronunciation, *co-author* and *co-star* retain hyphens, as does *co-opt*. And traditionally, a *co-op* shop keeps its hyphen.

$ The hyphen is dropped, even in words such as *coauthor* and *coopt*, but is retained for *co-star*.

coarse / common / vulgar

● RECOMMENDATION

The words *vulgar* and *common* have snobbish implications, and *coarse* is often preferable to describe unacceptable behaviour.

● CAUTION

These words, as comments on style and behaviour, can be subjective, suggesting that whatever it is does not conform to the way *we* would dress, speak or do something. See also **common / mutual**.

cock up / cock-up

● RECOMMENDATION

Cock-up, as a *noun* (with a hyphen), meaning a muddle or a mistake, or a verb (no hyphen), meaning to bungle something, is not usually considered vulgar. It is conversational, rather than literary, although the noun may at times find a place in writing [!]: 'the worst cock-up for Margaret Thatcher was the poll tax'.

$ The above usage is not familiar in America.

code / cipher / cypher

These words can all mean a secret way of writing or transmitting messages.

● RECOMMENDATIONS

1   Use *code* as the up-to-date word in data security and business: 'the code for a new product'. And *codes* belongs to computer language for ways of activating different features of a program.

2   *Cipher* is seldom used now for a secret language. Its more likely use is for a nonentity or something altogether inconsequential: 'he is a cipher in the organisation'. (The alternative spelling *cypher* is rare now.)

3   Use *decode* for breaking the code of a secret message.

4   Use *decipher* for interpreting something difficult to read, such as bad handwriting or a carving that is worn away, or for working out the meaning of something that is obscure: 'some political speeches are so involved that it's almost impossible to decipher what is meant'.

coed

● RECOMMENDATION

Coed, for a school ('my daughter goes to a coed'), is a dated word. Use 'coeducational school' or preferably 'mixed school'.

$ *Coeds* are women students, not the colleges.

cognac / brandy

See **brandy . . .**

cognoscente / cognoscenti

● RULE

Cognoscente is the *singular* word for someone in the know, especially about literary and cultural matters. It is more commonly used in the plural – *cognoscenti* (PRON 'konnye(r)-SHENtee' for both singular and plural).

collaborate / cooperate

Although the distinction is blurred at times, it's worth deciding which word to use.

● RECOMMENDATION

Collaborate suggests working together: 'collaborate on a book'. *Cooperate* is a more passive word for being helpful: 'cooperate with the police'.

● CAUTION

Although *collaborator* has an innocent meaning, describing a co-author, for example, it also has the sinister meaning of a traitor who cooperates with an enemy in occupation.

See also **collusion / cooperation**.

collage / montage

● RECOMMENDATIONS

1 Any combination of cut-outs, tear-offs, or three-dimensional objects, pasted on a backing can be called a *collage,* even if it is combined with the use of paint (the art-gallery term for that is 'mixed media').

2 *Montage* (or *photomontage*) is a collage made of fragments of photographs or other illustrations.

3 By extension, any assembly of words or music to form a composite whole can also be called a *montage.*

collateral / security

See **security** . . .

colleague

● RECOMMENDATION

Colleague is the only blanket word available for someone working in the same organisation. ('Fellow-worker' sounds Marxist, 'mate' is too chummy and belongs to plumbers, and 'associate' has other specific meanings.)

collective words

These are words, such as *board, company, committee, collection, family, orchestra,* that cover groups of separate people or things. The problem is whether to treat them as *singular* or *plural*.

● RECOMMENDATIONS

1 Whenever possible, treat these words as *singular:* 'the committee *is* having a meeting'.

2   When it is clearly about individual members, it is more natural to treat the words as *plural* : 'the board *are* having coffee'; 'the orchestra *are* travelling with *their* wives and husbands'.

● RULES

1   You cannot have it both ways: 'the committee *is* having a meeting, and will give *their* decision'. If you start off with *is,* it must be followed by '*its* decision'.

2   *Government* is treated as singular: 'the government *is* in crisis'.

3   When necessary, a collective word must be followed by *which* when it is *singular,* but *who* when it is *plural*: 'the board *which is* meeting . . .'; 'the orchestra *who are* having coffee . . .'.

college / school / university

The three words are used in different and confusing ways in Britain and America.

● RULES

1   When an American says 'I'm at *school*' it's generally the equivalent in Britain of 'I'm at *university*'.

2   'I'm at *college*' in Britain means a place of higher education other than a university. For an American it will often mean this too, but may also refer to a department within a university specialising in a particular subject.

3   While there are *colleges* in some British universities, a student at an Oxford college, for example, would not say 'I'm at *college*', but 'I'm at *university*'.

4   By long tradition, anyone studying art, whether in Britain or America, is at art *school*.

$ See RULES 1, 2 and 4 above.

colloquial / demotic

● RULE

Colloquial refers to conversational language, and *demotic* to the current everyday language in writing and speech. *Demotic* is used particularly about classical languages: demotic Greek is the language written and spoken in modern Greece, as against the language of classical Greek literature.

NOTE No one refers to *demotic* English (Shakespeare used the language of the people, not a classical form of English).

colloquial / informal / slang / non-standard

These terms are an attempt to draw a line between different kinds and standards of language. The following RULES include the usual abbreviations of the terms found in dictionaries.

● RULES

1   *Colloquial* (colloq) and *informal* (inf) mean the same, language freely used in relaxed conversation or casual writing, but not considered suitable for serious or formal writing.

2   *Slang* (sl) is on the fringe of linguistic respectability. It covers off-beat words and

phrases used by different groups, and is constantly changing.

3 *Non-standard* is a term for usage that would generally be considered uneducated.

● CAUTION

Decisions about these categories are often subjective. At best, the dividing lines keep moving: *colloquial* today may become standard English tomorrow, this year's *slang* can move up to *colloquial* next year. And *non-standard* can sometimes be a presumptuous umbrella term for anything a linguistic expert disapproves of.

● RECOMMENDATIONS

1 Because of radio and television, spoken English is lubricating the wheels of written English, leaving it more easygoing, and it is often impossible to decide whether certain words and phrases are conversational or suitable for serious writing. Do not try to be trendy, if that is not your style, but remember that an overcareful use of language can seem out of touch, even pompous. The best guide is not a dictionary, but the way good current writers and speakers are using words and expressions.

2 *Colloquial* and *informal* are lexicographers' terms, and *conversational English* is often preferable to describe words and expressions used in intelligent everyday conversation, but which might seem out of place in formal writing.

collusion / cooperation

● RULE

Do not use *collusion* in a good sense: 'the two scientists are working in collusion on the experiments'. The proper word there is *cooperation,* because *collusion* always means something dishonest: 'the directors were in collusion over falsifying the accounts'. See also **collaborate / cooperate.**

colon (:) / semicolon (;)

● RECOMMENDATIONS

A *semicolon* has a place:

1 As a heavy-duty comma. Take this sentence: 'There are few rules about punctuation; mostly it is a matter of recommendations.' A *comma* in the middle would do, but the two statements are better with a stronger separation.

2 In lists of names or things, a comma is usual between the items: 'In Oxford Street, there are many famous shops, such as Selfridges, John Lewis, Marks & Spencer, . . .'. But when required, a *semicolon* is available for a more definite separation, which may in some contexts make it easier for the reader: 'In Oxford Street, there are Selfridges, the first department store to be opened in Britain; John Lewis, part of the John Lewis Partnership; Marks & Spencer, perhaps the best loved of all stores; . . .'.

A *colon* has a place:

1 As a symbol for 'as follows', that is to lead on to a quotation, a list of things or a sequence of separate points. It should not be followed by a dash (:-).

2 When a statement follows on from or explains a preceding remark: 'It is a just war: naked aggression must not be allowed to triumph.'

3 To contrast two opposing statements, when it works like a gentle clash of cymbals: 'Sometimes I sit and think: sometimes I just sit!'

colony / dependent territory

● RECOMMENDATION

Colony is now an uneasy word, associated with imperialism and exploitation. Unless you intend to make this point, use *dependent territory*.

colossal / gigantic / huge / vast

● RECOMMENDATIONS

1 *Colossal* suggests classical grandeur as well as size ('the Colossus of Rhodes, a statue of the sun-god, was one of the wonders of the ancient world').

2 *Gigantic* carries with it a hint of the grotesque ('a gigantic birthday cake').

3 *Huge* is a more everyday word ('a huge breakfast').

4 *Vast* is more suitable for space or expanse ('the vast loneliness of the desert').

coloured / black

See **black** . . .

colour negative / transparency / diapositive

● RULES

1 A *colour transparency* is a positive image, on a transparent film base, with direct colour values, and is intended for projection on to a screen (although it can also be used for making colour prints).

NOTE An alternative technical term is *diapositive*.

2 A *colour negative* is a colour film image on photographic emulsion, in which colours and tones are reversed, so it is intended only for making prints.

combine (pronunciation)

● RULE

As a *verb*, the stress is on the *second* syllable: 'comBINE'. As a *noun*, it moves back to the *first* syllable: 'COMbine'. The exception is in agriculture: farmers 'COMbine' crops using a 'COMbine' harvester.

comedian / comedienne / comic

● RECOMMENDATIONS

1 Use *comedian* for an actor of either sex who plays comedy roles in plays or films.

2 Use *comic* (as a *noun*) for a performer of either sex who is more like a clown than an actor.

3 As noted in RECOMMENDATIONS 1 and 2 above, *comedian* and *comic* are unisex words, and for some people the feminine word, *comedienne* is a dated word for a woman actor who plays comedy roles (see also **actor / actress**).

comedy / humour

● RECOMMENDATIONS

1 *Comedy* suggests a funny situation in a play, a film, or in real life.
2 *Humour* is more abstract, the expression of comedy in literature, a painting, a situation, or a remark.

comic / comedienne / comedian

See **comedian** . . .

comic / comical

● RECOMMENDATIONS

1 *Comic* suggests something that is contrived to be funny, such as comic verse or a comic opera.
2 Comic*al* describes the funny side of life, comedy that happens inadvertently.

comma (,)

The style now is to use commas more sparingly.

● RECOMMENDATIONS

1 *Addresses and dates* Omit commas after house numbers and months: 10 Downing Street; 25 March 1946. See also **addresses.**
2 *Letters* Omit commas after *Dear Sir; Dear Lesley.* Also after *Yours sincerely* and other sign-offs at the end of letters.
3 *Items on a list* Use a comma to separate each item, except the *last but one* item and the *and* leading up to it: history, literature, politics and economics. But where there are descriptive words, include a comma before the *and*: Roman history, English literature, international politics, and economics. (Leaving out the comma after *politics* suggests that *international* also applies to 'economics'.)
4 *Commas before degrees, etc* When there are one or two abbreviations after a person's name, a comma isn't necessary after the name: John Brown QC, CBE. But when there are a string of honours, degrees, etc, a comma after the name is a useful separation: John Brown, QC, CBE, MA, MP.
5 *Commas between descriptive words* Where there are only two descriptive words, omit the comma between them: a well-written imaginative novel. Where there are a number of descriptive words, commas help your reader: a long, colourful, well-written, imaginative novel.
6 *When 'and' divides a sentence into two parts* See **and** (RECOMMENDATION 2).
7 *Commas round 'perhaps', 'of course', 'however', 'therefore'* The practice of sandwiching such words and phrases between commas now seems heavygoing, and in many cases the commas can be omitted. With *perhaps* and some other words, commas may be necessary to avoid misunderstanding. Take this sentence: 'I am going away, perhaps, with my wife.' Omit the comma *after* 'perhaps', and the sentence takes on a different meaning: 'I am going away, perhaps with my wife.' Omit *both* commas, and

you're not sure what the sentence means.

8   One of the best guides to whether a comma should go in is to read the sentence aloud. If it's just as easy to read and understand without a comma, it's usually safe to leave it out. But when there's any doubt, help the reader by including a comma.

● CAUTION

Before omitting commas, make sure the sentence doesn't convey the wrong meaning, or that it doesn't sound silly: 'Before eating, my wife, who had just come home, wanted a drink.' Leave out the comma after 'eating', and you invite a double-take.

commander / commandant

● RULES

1   *Commander* is a specific rank in the Royal Navy, the US Navy and the police.

2   *Commander* can also be used in all the services for an officer of any rank in charge of a unit or a military establishment.

3   *Commandant* is an alternative word for an officer of any rank in charge of a service establishment, rather than in the field.

commence / start

● RECOMMENDATION

Commence is a formal word, *start* an everyday word: proceedings or a ceremony might *commence*, but we *start* dinner; *start* work; *start* a fight.

comment / commentate

● RULES

1   'Would you please *comment* on this' means either would you explain it, or simply make a few remarks about it.

2   'Would you please *commentate* on this' means would you give a running commentary on something taking place.

commercial

● CAUTION

This word has a legitimate use relating to business and trade. But it often carries with it the suggestion of being more interested in profits than in quality and integrity: 'the commercial theatre'; 'too commercial'.

commission / committee

● RECOMMENDATIONS

1   Use *commission* for an authority that can take action. (*Commission* is the title used by governments for a body set up to deal with a problem, and given legal powers: the Commission for Racial Equality.)

2   Use *committee* to suggest a group of people limited to discussion and giving recommendations.

(the) **committee** *is* / *are*

See **collective words**

common / **joint**

● RECOMMENDATIONS

1 Use *joint* in law, finance and administration: joint bank accounts; joint ventures; joint mortgage.
2 Use *common* as the more friendly everyday word: common aim; common purpose; common point of view. See also **common** / **mutual.**

common / **mutual**

● RULES

1 *Mutual* means reciprocal, from one person to another: mutual love; mutual agreement.
2 *Common* means to share something: a common point of view; a common objective.

● CAUTION

Common also has the meaning of vulgar, or cheap and nasty, or ordinary and everyday. So there is a problem with expressions such as 'our common friend'. We can sidestep this by 'our friend in common', or 'our mutual friend', which in this context is an acceptable misuse of *mutual* (good enough for Charles Dickens, who called his novel *Our Mutual Friend*).

common / **vulgar** / **coarse**

See **coarse . . .**

Common Era (CE)

See AD

common *man* / **common** *woman*

● CAUTION

While *the common man* carries a suggestion of noble simplicity, *common woman* is disparaging.

commonsense / **common sense**

● RECOMMENDATION

When it's *descriptive*, it's better as *one* word: 'a commonsense approach'. When it's a *noun*, it's better as *two* words: 'the approach is common sense'.

communal / **commune** (pronunciation)

● RULES

1 With *communal* stress is on the *first* syllable: 'COMMunal'.
2 With *commune* as a *noun*, stress is on the *first* syllable: a 'COMMune'.

3   As a *verb*, stress is on the *second* syllable: 'commUNE' with nature.

\$ For *communal* stress is on the *second* syllable: 'comMUNal'. *Commune* follows RULES 2 and 3 above.

(a) **commune** / (a) **cooperative**

● RULES

1   A *cooperative* is a voluntary organisation sharing common facilities and arrangements, such as processing and packing machinery, purchasing and marketing, run by the owners or workers who share profits on an agreed basis.

2   A *commune* (PRON 'COMMune') is a way of living, rather than an economic arrangement, usually based on idealistic or religious convictions.

compact / **small** / **petite**

● RECOMMENDATIONS

1   Use *compact* to suggest convenience because of an efficient use of space: a compact camera.

2   Use *small* to refer to size only, without necessarily suggesting efficiency.

3   Use *petite* as a complimentary word about a small woman, suggesting well-proportioned rather than dumpy.

company / **firm**

● RULE

In a legal sense, a *company* is a business registered under the Companies Acts, in which case the name of the company is followed by 'Limited', 'Ltd' or 'plc' (public limited company). (See **Ltd** / **plc.**)

● RECOMMENDATIONS

1   *Company* can be used in a general way for any business, not necessarily a company in the legal sense, with at least a handful of employees.

2   *Firm* can be used for any small to medium business, whether it is a legally registered company or not, but it is out of place for really big companies, such as ICI, where *company* is the appropriate term.

(the) **company** *is* / *are*

See **collective words**

comparable (pronunciation)

● RULE

Stress the *first* syllable: 'COMperable'.

comparatively / **relatively**

● RECOMMENDATIONS

1   Both words should make or imply a comparison with something else: 'a

comparatively (or relatively) large amount was spent on television advertising'
implies a comparison with the amount spent in other media.

2 Avoid using *comparatively* or *relatively* without a comparison: 'he is comparatively
rich'; 'she is relatively happy'. Instead choose words, such as 'fairly', 'reasonably',
'more or less', whichever shade of meaning you intend: 'he is fairly rich'; 'she is
reasonably happy'.

compare / contrast

● RULES

1 *Compare* is an invitation to look for *similarities*: 'Shall I compare thee to a summer's
day?' (Shakespeare's sonnet).

2 *Contrast* points up differences: 'Contrast a summer's day in London with a
summer's day in the country.'
PRON *Contrast* as a *noun* has stress on the *first* syllable ('CONtrast'), but as a *verb*, on
the *second* syllable ('conTRAST').
See also **compare to / with**.

compare to / *with*

● OPTION

Compare *to* and compare *with* are interchangeable: 'he compared the flavour of the
wine *with* ✓ (or *to*) the taste of wild blackberries'.

● RULE

In negative contexts, use compare *with*: 'Beethoven cannot be compared *with* bebop.'

(by / in) **comparison**

● OPTION

There is no difference between *by* or *in* ✓ comparison, but it should always be
followed by *with* (not *to*): 'air transport is expensive *in* (or *by*) comparison *with* road
transport'.

(points of the) **compass**

See **abbreviations; capital letters** (RECOMMENDATION 5)

compel / impel

● RECOMMENDATION

Compel suggests external force, and *impel* suggests a force from within: 'the minister
was compelled to resign'; 'the minister felt impelled to object'.

compelling / compulsive

● RECOMMENDATIONS

1 *Compelling* is usually a good word: a compelling novel is one you cannot put down;
a compelling argument sweeps aside all objections.

2   *Compulsive* can carry the idea of an obsessional mental disorder: a compulsive gambler; a compulsive eater.

compilation (pronunciation)

● CAUTION

Do not let 'compile' lead to pronouncing the second syllable of *compilation* as 'pyle'. It rhymes with 'pill': 'comPILLation'.

complacent / complaisant

● RULE

Complacent (PRON 'comPLAYsnt') means smug and pleased with yourself: *complaisant* (PRON 'comPLAYznt') suggests an over-willingness to please other people.

complete

● RECOMMENDATIONS

1   Although *complete* describes an absolute quality, in some contexts it is acceptable to have degrees of completeness: 'this is the most complete account of what happened'.

2   Avoid saying that something is 'very complete', because that can never make sense.

complex / complicated

● RECOMMENDATIONS

1   *Complex* can be complimentary: 'a complex novel' suggests it offers insights at different levels.

2   *Complicated* can be a term of criticism, suggesting that something is mixed up and confused: 'a complicated novel' could suggest that the writer has not thought through his ideas properly.

compose / comprise / consist / include

● RULES

1   The three expressions *comprise, consist of, is composed of* all mean the same. You can write 'the orchestra consists of 60 musicians' or 'the orchestra is composed of 60 musicians' or 'the orchestra comprises 60 musicians' (*comprise* is not followed by 'of'). These three expressions must be followed by *all* the parts that make up the whole: it is wrong to say 'the orchestra *comprises* (*consists of* or *is composed of*) 20 violins', unless that is the *whole* orchestra. Otherwise use *include*: 'the orchestra includes 20 violins' refers to *part* of the orchestra.

2   There is a difference between consist *of* and consist *in*. Consist *of* describes what something is composed of: 'an omelette consists of eggs and whatever filling you choose to put in'. Consists *in* describes the essence of something: 'all enjoyment consists in undetected sinning' (George Bernard Shaw).

comprehend / apprehend

See **apprehend** . . .

comprise / consist / include / compose

See **compose** . . .

comptroller / controller

See **controller** . . .

compulsive / compelling

See **compelling** . . .

computer *science / technology*

● OPTION

The study of the operations and applications of computers can be called computer *science* or computer *technology* ✓.

conceal / hide

● RECOMMENDATIONS

1 *Conceal* is more formal, and is the better word for abstract qualities: 'she concealed her embarrassment'.

2 *Hide* is more down-to-earth: 'she hid the letter under the pillow'.

concensus / consensus

See **consensus** . . .

concerned

● CAUTION

Concerned can trap us into pompous roundabout expressions: 'as far as this matter is concerned'; 'this is important as far as our customers are concerned'; 'as far as I am concerned'. It is much more direct to write: 'about this matter'; 'this is important to our customers'; 'as for me'.

concert / recital

● RULE

A *concert* requires a number of musicians, whereas a *recital* is a performance by a soloist (a piano recital) or a small group, such as a quartet.

NOTE The exception is pop music: even if it's only one singer, it is a *concert*.

concerto / sonata

● RECOMMENDATIONS

1 Use *concerto* for a piece of music written for a virtuoso performance by a soloist, accompanied by an orchestra.

2 Use *sonata* for a composition for one instrument on its own, or for an instrument with a piano accompaniment.

● OPTION

The plural of sonata is straightforward: *sonatas*.

The plural of concerto has two forms: *concertos* ✓ and *concerti*.

conditional / dependent

● RECOMMENDATIONS

1 Use *conditional* when something is subject to requirements imposed: an order 'conditional on a delivery date' means that if the date is not met, the order could be cancelled.

2 Use *dependent* to suggest a connection with outside circumstances: a price can be quoted dependent on the cost of raw materials when the order is placed.

NOTE Both words are usually followed by 'on'.

condole / console

See **console** . . .

confidant / confidante / confident

● RULES

1 *Confidant* is a noun for someone you confide in. If it is a woman, it can be spelt *confidante*, but this isn't necessary.

PRON 'confiDANT' (stress on the *last* syllable) for both spellings.

2 *Confident* is the descriptive word meaning sure of yourself.

PRON 'CONfident' (stress on the *first* syllable).

confidential / secret / personal / private

● RECOMMENDATIONS

1 *Confidential* and *secret* should describe things not to be disclosed. *Confidential* is the usual word in business matters, the word you might put on an envelope or at the top of a letter. *Secret* is the more powerful word, the word used about information that could help an enemy or the competition, a word that might appear on the cover of a file. To say something is *secret* suggests that it should not be revealed to anyone, but you might feel free to share a *confidential* matter with others who are involved.

2 *Secret* is the word for intimate situations: lovers have secret meetings; people have secret longings.

3 *Personal* covers matters that an individual might not want others to know about.

And *Personal* is used on an envelope to indicate it should be opened only by the person it's addressed to.

4 *Private* is often used as an alternative to *personal*, when a matter is not intimate, but concerns only a few people.

NOTES

i *Private and confidential*, which sometimes appears on envelopes, is a belt-and-braces approach.

ii If you write to someone and mark the envelope *Confidential* or *Private*, a secretary might be entitled to open it. But if it is marked *Personal*, only the person named on the envelope really has that right.

conform *to* / *with*

● RECOMMENDATIONS

1 Use conform *to* when it relates to rules or what is usual or standard: 'we shall conform to government regulations'; 'the hotel conforms to good standards of accommodation'.

2 Use conform *with* in less specific contexts: 'the hotel conforms with what we were expecting'.

confront / face

● RECOMMENDATIONS

1 *Confront* suggests an aggressive or defiant attitude: 'we must confront the problem and fight back'; 'she will confront him with new evidence'.

2 *Face* is a more neutral word, and may mean no more than dealing with something: 'we must face the difficulties in the best way we can'; 'Let's face the music – and dance!'

NOTE When it comes to difficult situations or problems, the fashionable word now is *address* ('the company is addressing the problem of falling profit margins'). See also **deal with / address.**

congenital / hereditary / genetic

● RULES

1 *Congenital* means a condition that was *present at birth*. Such a condition may or may not be *hereditary*, that is an illness or weakness present in a person's family.

2 *Hereditary* can be a good or bad quality, a weakness, an illness, or a talent, inherited from blood relatives.

3 *Genetic* is the usual word now to describe a *hereditary* disease or weakness (genes are transmitted across generations).

congressman / congresswoman / representative / senator

● RECOMMENDATIONS

1 Dictionaries define *congressman* and *congresswoman* as a member of the US

Congress, which is unarguable. But in practice a member of the US upper house is nearly always called a *senator*, and *congressman* and *congresswoman* are used more for members of the lower house.

2 *Representative* is an alternative name for members of the lower house, and has the advantages of clearly not including senators, as well as being unisex.

3 The tendency is not to use initial capitals for these titles (see **capital letters**).

conjugal (pronunciation)
● RULE

Stress the *first* syllable: 'CONjoogle'.

conjunctions

See **grammatical terms**

connection

For RECOMMENDATIONS about the use of the phrases *in connection with* and *in this connection*, see **in connection with . . . .**

connection / connexion
● OPTION

Although *connection* ✓ and *connexion* are shown in dictionaries, *connexion* is rarely used.

connote / denote

Both words can relate to the meanings of words.

● RULE

Denote is the straightforward definition of a word: **connote** refers to other meanings associated with words, meanings that dictionaries may not have caught up with. For example, 'mankind' *denotes* the human race in general, but for some women, 'mankind' *connotes* sexism, suggesting that men are the primary sex (see **humankind / mankind**).

NOTE Both words are used in more general ways, *connote* to mean imply or suggest ('his failure connotes lack of experience'), and *denote* to mean an indication of something ('an arrow denotes the direction you should take').

consensus / concensus
● RULE

Consensus (*concensus* is not in dictionaries).

consensus of opinion
● CAUTION

Since *consensus* already means a general agreement about something, there is no need to add *of opinion*: 'the consensus is this is the best restaurant in town' (not 'the consensus of opinion is . . .').

consequent / consequential

● RECOMMENDATION

Consequent usually means as a *direct* result, while *consequential* implies an *indirect* result, and is mostly restricted to legal and insurance matters. For example, if there is a fire in a factory, there is a *consequent* loss because machinery is damaged or destroyed. There could also be a *consequential* loss, because production is interrupted. (*Consequential* can also mean significant or important: a consequential matter.)

conservation / preservation

● RECOMMENDATIONS

1 Use *conservation* to embrace a wider concept than **preservation**. *Conservation* takes in the planned efficient use of natural resources, so that life on earth can be sustained into the future. Used about art treasures, architecture or historic monuments, *conservation* carries with it the belief in a cultural heritage that belongs by right to generations to come.

2 Use **preservation** as the more everyday word for protecting things from deterioration and damage.

Conservative / conservative

● RULE

Conservative, with a capital *C*, relates to the Conservative Party: *conservative*, with a small *c*, is a descriptive word for moderate or traditional opinions and attitudes.

● CAUTION

Confusion may arise when we are speaking. The broadcaster, Sue MacGregor, interviewing someone, literally spelt out what she meant: 'You are not as conservative – with a *small c* – as your predecessor.' Be careful also when *beginning* a sentence: 'Conservative views are . . .' is ambiguous. If a political meaning is intended, you can either begin the sentence with *Tory* (see **Conservative / Tory**), or rephrase the opening: 'The views of Conservatives are . . .'.

Conservative / Tory

● RECOMMENDATION

For some people, *Tory* is an old-fashioned name, so prefer *Conservative* for the political party (but see CAUTION in previous entry).

$ In American history, a *Tory* was a colonist who remained loyal to England during the American Revolution.

conserve / preserve / jam

See jam . . .

consider / consider *as*

● RECOMMENDATION

There is a subtle difference between *consider* and *consider as*. Read these two statements: 'I consider Mary a friend'; 'I consider Mary *as* a friend'. The first means I believe Mary is a friend; the second could mean that, although Mary is not a friend, I behave to her as if she is one.

consist / comprise / include / compose

See compose . . .

consistent / persistent

● RULE

Consistent suggests unvarying, without change, which can be a good quality, whereas *persistent* is usually negative, often a calculated or relentless going-on that drives you mad.

consist *in* / of

See compose . . . (RULE 2)

console / condole

● RULES

1 *Console* is the word we usually want. It means to comfort and support: 'I tried to console her . . .'.

2 *Condole* is not used often. It means to express sympathy, and is always followed by 'with': 'I condoled with her on the loss of her child'.

consonant / vowel / letter

● RECOMMENDATION

When you refer, for example, to the consonants *b* or *d* or the vowels *a* or *i* , it should be an allusion to *speech sounds*. If you mean *written* characters, it is better to use the word *letters*.

consortia / consortiums

A *consortium* is a group of companies or individuals forming an association for a purpose.

● OPTION

Consortia ✓ or *consortiums* are alternative plural forms.

constrained / limited

● RECOMMENDATIONS

1 *Constrained* (and *constraints*) is not necessarily negative, as it suggests working within certain requirements, which may well be a creative challenge: 'architects are always constrained by a budget and the function of the building'.

2 *Limited* (and *limitations*) is more negative, since it implies a cramping of style and possibilities: 'it's a mean building, limited by a small budget and a poor site'.

3 *Limited* is often used to mean 'small' ('he has a limited income'), and there's nothing wrong with that. But the simple word 'small' usually makes the point more directly.

consult / consult *with*

● RECOMMENDATION

We can *consult* our lawyer, our doctor, or anyone else, without *with* getting in the way.

$ The usual form is consult *with*.

consult / engage / retain / appoint

See **appoint** . . .

consulting room / surgery

● RULE

Harley Street in London, the centre for medical specialists, uses the term *consulting room*. Doctors in general practice call their consulting rooms *surgeries* (medical practitioners in Britain have to qualify as surgeons).

NOTE MPs and social workers (who hardly know one end of a scalpel from the other) have presumptuously taken over the term *surgery* for the room where they see people with problems or complaints.

consummate (pronunciation)

● RULE

With the stress on the *second* syllable ('conSUMMut'), it means perfect or masterly: 'a consummate performance'. With the stress on the *first* syllable ('CONsyoomayt'), it means to make complete: a marriage is consummated by sexual intercourse.

contagious / infectious

● RULES

1 A **contag**ious disease can be caught only by direct *physical* contact with someone or something.

2 An **infect**ious disease is transmitted through micro-organisms in air or water.

contemplative / meditative / reflective

● RECOMMENDATIONS

1 *Contemplative* carries with it the idea of timelessness, a withdrawal to an inner state apart from the temporal world.

2 *Meditative* is more focused, a conscious directing of thought, sometimes as a spiritual exercise.

3 *Reflective* is nearer the surface: it suggests a thoughtful nature, a habit of mind, rather than a way of life, or could mean an approach to a specific matter (a reflective attitude towards a problem).

contemporary / modern

● CAUTION

Both words mean different things to different people and in different contexts. The RECOMMENDATIONS that follow are based on a consensus of a number of cultural historians, although not everyone will agree with them.

● RECOMMENDATIONS

1 With *contemporary,* be consistent in the way you use it. Perhaps the best thing is to relate *contemporary* to the 1990s, using it about style, fashion, art, architecture and ideas.

2 *Modern* is complex, with different meanings when it is connected with different subjects: in linguistics, *modern English* is usually taken to be the English language from about 1500 up to the present; *modern art* is usually seen as 20th-century art, starting with Picasso and Braque finding their way into cubism in the early 1900s; *modern architecture* in Britain is usually regarded as starting in the 1930s; *modern dance* is the abstract style of dance concerned more with social and psychological content than entertainment.

3 When we use *modern* in a general way, rather than in the specific contexts listed in RECOMMENDATION 2 above, we can hardly do better than relate *modern* to the 20th century as a whole.

4 When you want to be precise, avoid *contemporary* and *modern* altogether: 'the English language between the wars'; 'British art in the decade after World War I'; 'attitudes towards marriage in the 1990s'.

contemptible / contemptuous

● RULE

*Contemp**tible*** means *deserving* contempt, while *contemp**tuous*** means *feeling* contempt for somebody or for something they have done: 'the way he treats her is contemptible'; 'she is contemptuous of the way he treats her'.

content *by* / *with*

● RULE

As a verb, *content* is followed by *with* (not *by*): 'she contented herself with saying no more about it'.

● CAUTION

When other words come in between, it's easy to slip into using *by* when it should be *with*: 'she contented herself, at least for the time being, *with* saying no more about it' (not '. . . *by* saying no more . . .').

context / framework / setting

● RECOMMENDATIONS

1 *Context* is the flow of words that relates to other words in the same passage. If something is quoted *out of context*, it might have an altogether different meaning: 'I found it fascinating', splashed across a theatre poster, might have been lifted out of a review that said 'I found it fascinating to work out why *anybody* should come to see this play.'

2 A *framework* is the structure that supports something: 'this argument is within the framework of the agreed marketing plan'.

3 A *setting* is the surrounding scenery or the place and time against which something takes place: 'this is against the setting of a wide-ranging review of the subject'.

● CAUTION

All three words can be unnecessarily long-winded: 'this could only be possible *in the context* (or *within the framework* or *against the setting*) of a sound economic policy'. The writer simply means '. . . if there is a sound economic policy'.

(the) **continent / Europe**

See **Europe** . . .

continual / continuous

● RULE

Continual describes something that is going on all the time, but with interruptions, while *continuous* is going on all the time without interruptions: a bee can give a continuous buzz, but a dog is more likely to bark continually.

continuance / continuation / continuity

● RULES

1 *Continuance* is used about a state, circumstances or a condition: continuance after death; continuance of the same economic policy.

2 *Continuation* applies to an action, an event, an occurrence: continuation of the war; continuation of the takeover bid.

3 *Continuity* is the consistent flow of something that is in process of continuing: the continuity of a television programme is the way it holds together as a logical sequence.

continuous / continual

See **continual** . . .

contracted forms

I'm, I'll, you're, you'll, isn't, it's, can't, don't, he's, she's, they're . . . . We all use them in conversation, but some people hesitate to use them in writing.

● RECOMMENDATIONS

1   Written English and spoken English are much closer to each other, and when it seems laboured to write these forms out in full every time, the way is now open, even in quite formal writing, to use the contractions. [!]

2   When asking questions, 'is it not?', 'are you not?', etc tend to make the question more pointed than 'isn't it?', 'aren't you?': 'Those are the facts, are they not?'

● CAUTIONS

1   Remember that using contracted forms all the time seems too casual. Write them out in full from time to time, especially when it seems appropriate. Reading the sentence aloud is a good guide.

2   *I'd, you'd,* etc sound perfectly all right when we say them, but look a little odd in print, so don't use them as freely as the other contracted forms.

3   *Shan't* and *won't* are conversational forms, and have no place in writing, unless it's very informal, or recording dialogue.

4   Conversation is the only place for such extreme contractions as *would've, I'd've, Mary'll.* Even in informal writing, they look out of place, and are difficult to read.

contradiction / paradox

● RULES

1   A *contradiction* is two opposing statements, points of view or pieces of information that simply cannot both be true: 'it is a contradiction to say the business is doing well, and to give figures of falling sales and profits'.

2   A *paradox* is an *apparently* contradictory statement that contains a truth: 'the paradox she experiences is to feel lonely when surrounded by people'.

contrary (pronunciation)

● RULES

1   When it's a *noun,* as in 'on the contrary', stress the *first* syllable ('CONtrary').

2   As a *descriptive word,* the stress changes the meaning. A 'CONtrary' point of view is an opposite viewpoint: a 'conTRARY' point of view is an obstinate or perverse attitude ('Mary, Mary, quite conTRARY').

contrast / compare

See **compare** . . .

contribute (pronunciation)

● OPTION

Stress on the *second* syllable ('conTRIBute')✓ and the *first* syllable ('CONtribute') [!] are alternatives shown in most dictionaries.

$ 'conTRIBute'.

controller / comptroller

● RULE

*Comp*troller is an old-fashioned word, and survives only in some official titles. In all other contexts use *controller*.

controversy (pronunciation)

● OPTION

Stress on the *first* syllable ('CONtroversy')✓ or the *second* syllable ('conTROVersy') [!] are alternatives shown in most dictionaries.

$ 'CONtroversy'.

convenience

● RECOMMENDATION

Replace *at your convenience* by 'whenever it suits you', and *at your earliest convenience* by 'as soon as possible'.

conventional

● CAUTION

In general, *conventional* means conforming to what is generally accepted and expected, not necessarily a bad thing. But *conventional* is increasingly used for a dull stick-in-the-mud approach: 'it's a conventional book' suggests it has no original ideas.

converse / reverse / antithesis / opposite

See **opposite** . . .

convey

● CAUTION

Using *convey* instead of 'give', 'take', or 'pass on' carries formality to the edge of pompousness: 'Would you convey my suggestion to the minister?' Replace *convey* by *pass on*, and the sentence is more direct.

cooperate / collaborate

See **collaborate** . . .

cooperation / collusion
See **collusion** . . .

cooperative / commune
See **commune** . . .

cord / chord
See **chord** . . .

coronary / stroke / heart attack
● RULES

1   A *coronary* (stress on the *first* syllable: 'CORonery') is short for *coronary thrombosis*, called informally a *heart attack*. It is a blood clot in one of the arteries that supply blood to the heart.

2   A *stroke* is a blood clot in one of the arteries that supply blood to the brain, or a rupture of one of the blood vessels in the brain, which usually causes partial paralysis.

corporal / *capital* punishment
See *capital* punishment . . .

correspond *to* / *with*
● OPTION

There's no distinction between correspond *to* and correspond *with* ✓ (except when it's about writing letters, when it's always correspond *with*).

cosmology / astronomy
See **astronomy** . . .

cosmonaut / spaceman / astronaut
See **astronaut** . . .

cosmopolitan / international
● RECOMMENDATION

Cosmopolitan implies worldly, fashionable, sophisticated, rich, while *international* is political, cultural and economic: an *international* gathering suggests statesmen, business executives, scientists . . . , whereas a *cosmopolitan* gathering is less serious, more social and pleasure-seeking.

cost / cost *out*
● RECOMMENDATION

Cost *out* has become a sophisticated alternative to *cost*: a local builder will still *cost* a job, that is work out an estimate, but a chief executive might ask someone to *cost out* a project.

cost / price

● RECOMMENDATIONS

1 In general use, the *cost* and the *price* of something both mean how much do we pay for it. In business, the *cost* usually represents what something cost to produce, and the *price* how much it could be sold for.

2 *Cost* is usually preferred for services and abstractions, such as cost of living; cost of phone calls; the cost of war.

cost *out* / cost

See **cost . . .**

cosy

● CAUTION

It's all right to use *cosy* about a room or a house, but be careful about using it in a good sense about a person, since it can have the meaning of smug and self-satisfied: 'she's very cosy about marrying a rich man'.

$ The spelling is *cozy*.

couch / sofa / settee

● RECOMMENDATION

Use *couch* or *sofa* interchangeably, with one exception: a *sofa* always has a rest at *both* ends, while a *couch* can have a rest at both ends, or at *one* end only, making it easier to lie on.

● CAUTION

Settee has become a downmarket word.

could / might

● OPTION

It is pointless to make a distinction: in practice, 'the sun *might* shine tomorrow' ✓ and 'the sun *could* shine tomorrow' come to the same thing.

council / counsel

● RULES

1 *Council* can only be a *noun*, for an official body of people.

2 *Counsel*, as a *noun*, means advice, usually on something important, *or* a barrister (see **barrister / advocate / counsel**).

3 As a *verb, counsel* means the same as 'advise', but is more formal, and usually applied to a professional adviser.

4   A *counsel of perfection* is advice of the ideal thing to do in a situation, but implying
    that it's advice that is almost impossible to carry out.

(the) **council *is / are***

See **collective words**

councillor / counsellor

● RULES

1   A *councillor* is a member of a council, usually in local government.
2   A *counsellor* is someone who gives advice: marriage-guidance counsellor.

counsel / advocate / barrister

See **barrister . . .**

counsel / council

See **council . . .**

counsellor / councillor

See **councillor . . .**

(a) **couple *is / are***

● RECOMMENDATIONS

1   For people and objects, treat *a couple* as *plural*: 'a young couple *have* bought the
    house'; 'a couple of books *are* on the table'.
2   For units of time, treat *a couple* as *singular*: 'a couple of hours *has* past'; 'a couple of
    centuries *is* a long period'.

courage / fearlessness

● RECOMMENDATIONS

1   Treat *courage* as a quality that is acquired by refusing to let fear dictate actions and
    attitudes.
2   Treat *fearlessness* as a gift that is innate and inborn, not requiring conscious effort.
    See also **fearless / unafraid.**

creative / imaginative

● RECOMMENDATIONS

1   Use *creative* to encompass much more than *imaginative*: it is an amalgam of
    intellectual abilities combined with talent that brings forth a synthesis, something
    truly original ('God created the heaven and the earth').
2   Treat *imaginative* as a slighter word that can be used about lesser things, such as
    solutions to practical problems: 'that's an imaginative way to cook an omelette'.

credible / credulous

● RULES

1 Someone or something can be *credible*, that is you can believe them or it: 'she is so credible that he believes everything she says'.

2 Only a person can be *credulous*, too easily taken in: 'he is so credulous that he believes everything she says'.

credit / debit

● RULES

1 To *debit* a sum of money is to show it as a sum you owe, or as a sum taken off the balance in your bank account.

2 To *credit* a sum of money is to show it as a sum you have paid, or to add it to the balance in your bank account.

credulous / credible

See **credible** . . .

Creole / mulatto / half-caste

See **half-caste** . . .

Creole / pidgin

See **pidgin** . . .

crepe / crêpe

● RECOMMENDATION

Crepe (no circumflex) when it is the fine crinkled material: *crêpe* (with a circumflex) when it is a thin pancake.

PRON 'krayp' for both meanings.

crescendo

● RULE

Crescendo relates to *sound* or *noise*: 'the shouting reached a crescendo'.

● CAUTION

Do not extend the meaning to other things, such as 'the crescendo of his achievement' (use a word such as 'climax' or 'peak' instead).

crevasse / crevice

● RULES

1 A *crevasse* (PRON 'kre(r)VASSE') is an awesome opening with sheer drop in a glacier or in ice.

2 A *crevice* (PRON 'KREViss') is a narrow crack or split in a rock or wall.

criteria / criterions (plural forms)

● RULE

One *criterion*, two or more *criteria*.

criticism / critique / notice / review

See **review** . . .

cross-check / verify

● RECOMMENDATIONS

1 A *cross-check* (or *to cross-check* something) is checking a fact or result by using an alternative method: a simple example is to cross-check that 3 times 7 equals 21 by dividing 21 by 3.

2 *Verify* is more far-reaching: it is to establish the truth or correctness, often by research or a careful enquiry.

crossroads / crossroad

● OPTION

Crossroads ✓ and *crossroad* are alternative forms.

● RULE

The plural form *crossroads* is treated as *singular*: 'the crossroads *is* about a mile away'.

$ *Crossroad* is the standard form, and means a road that crosses another road, rather than the actual intersection.

(the) crowd *is* / *are*

See **collective words**

crude

● CAUTION

Look out for the double meaning of *crude*: 'this is a *crude* proposition' can mean it is still at a rough stage, not yet properly worked out, *or* that it is offensive and lacking in refinement. Where there could be a doubt, spell out which meaning is intended.

cubic / cubical

● RULES

1 For *measurements*, it is always *cubic*: a cubic yard; a cubic metre.

2 *Cubical* describes something shaped like a cube, although even in that sense, *cubic* is the more usual alternative: 'a cubic structure' (rather than 'a cubical structure').

culture

● RECOMMENDATION

Culture can have two meanings in everyday use: 'Australian culture' could mean the arts in Australia; or it could mean the pattern of behaviour, thoughts, institutions and the rest, that make up the Australian way of living. Where there is a risk of misunderstanding, use 'cultural scene' for the arts, and 'institutions', 'lifestyle' or 'attitudes' for other things.

cupfuls / cupsful

See -ful

curb / kerb

● RULES

1   It's *curb* for the *verb*, meaning to hold back or restrain, and also for the *noun* with that meaning ('to put a curb on spending').
2   It's *kerb* for the *noun*, meaning the edge of a pavement or path.
$ *Curb* for all meanings.

currently

● RECOMMENDATIONS

1   *Currently* has a place when something supersedes something that was going on previously: 'he is currently recommending fixed-interest investments' suggests that previously different investments were being recommended.
2   There is no good reason for saying 'I am *currently* working on a new book', instead of using the short and simple word 'now'.

curricula / curriculums

● OPTION

Both *curricula* ✓ and *curriculums* [!] are used as plural forms of *curriculum*.

cursed (pronunciation)

● RULE

Before a noun, it is *two* syllables: 'this is a *curs-ed* business'. *After* a noun, it is *one* syllable: 'the whole business is *cursed*'.

customer / clientele / client

See **client** . . .

cutback / cut back

● RULE

'There is a *cutback* in production' (*one* word for the *noun*), but 'production has been *cut back*' (*two* words when *cut* is a *verb*).

● RECOMMENDATION

Strictly speaking, *back* is unnecessary, since it's enough to say there is a *cut*, or that production has been *cut*. Yet *back* does have a value, since it stresses the negative aspect of a *cutback*.

cutlet / chop

See chop . . .

cutting edge

● RECOMMENDATION

Cutting edge is a useful, if fashionable, way of stressing that some development is right in the lead: 'the cutting edge of computer technology'.

CV / cv

● RECOMMENDATIONS

1 It is usual for the abbreviation *cv* (PRON 'seevee') to be used both in writing and speaking, rather than the expression in full: *curriculum vitae* (PRON 'kerRIKyoolum VEEtye').

2 Although it's an abbreviation, use small letters, rather than capitals: *cv*.

$ *Résumé* is the usual word for a cv.

cycle / bike / bicycle

See bicycle . . .

cyclone / gale / hurricane / tornado / typhoon / blizzard

See blizzard . . .

cypher / cipher / code

See code . . .

Cyrillic / Russian

● RULES

1 *Cyrillic* is the *alphabet* used in the Russian language (also in some other Slavonic languages).

2 *Russian* is the written and spoken language.

czar / tsar

See tsar . . .

D

dago

● CAUTION

Dago is an abusive and racist slang name for almost any foreigner, especially for Spaniards and Portuguese.

Dáil

● RULE

Dáil (PRON 'doyl') is the name of the elected assembly of the Republic of Ireland (*Dáil Eireann* in full).

daily / diurnal

● RECOMMENDATIONS

1 *Daily* is the usual word for the daily round of ordinary things that happen every day: daily papers; daily chores.

2 *Diurnal* has a place in science for cycles that occur at daily intervals, applied, for example, to animals active only in the daytime; plants that open during the day. In these contexts, *diurnal* is the opposite of 'nocturnal', used for the daytime period of an activity that continues during the night.

dais / rostrum / podium / platform

See **platform** . . .

Dame

● RULE

The title must always precede a woman's *first* name: Dame Judi Dench (never 'Dame Dench').

damn

● RULES

1 *Damn* becomes *dam* in *damfool* and *dammit* (these words are more conversational than written English).

2 In established phrases, such as 'to damn with faint praise', 'damning evidence', and in the theological use of *damn* as a condemnation, *damn* can be used even in formal writing.

dance / dancing

● RECOMMENDATION

Use *dance* for the art form, often choreographed, while *dancing* is usually a pastime. African *dance* is treating it as ethnic culture: African *dancing* is dancing in an African style. You learn *dancing* but you study *dance*.

dashes

● RECOMMENDATIONS

1 Use dashes, like an aside in the theatre, to mark off a detached comment from the flow of the sentence: 'I was leaving for the office – early that morning as it happens – when the telephone rang.'

2 A dash can lead to a follow-up: 'It was one of the kindest things you could have done – to ask me out to dinner that evening.'

3 A dash can gather up a list of thing and lead on to a general statement about them: 'Income tax, a mortgage, instalments on the car, renting a TV – by the time you've paid all those, there's not much left.'

4 A dash can replace a **colon** (:) before a follow-on statement or a list: 'Here are the things you need – a passport, airline ticket, money.' A colon would have done after 'need', but a dash is sharper, more energetic. (It is never necessary to use a colon and a dash [:-], as either does the job.)

5 Leave a space on each side of dashes (see examples above).

\$ Usually there's no space on either side of dashes.

See also **brackets**.

databank / database

● RECOMMENDATIONS

1 Use *databank* for a mass of information stored in a form accessible by a computer.

2 Use *database* for a scheme of organised information relating to a particular subject, usually but not essentially in computerised form.

3 Use *database* for a collection of texts relating to a particular writer or piece of linguistic or literary research.

data *is / are*

● RECOMMENDATION

Although *data* is the *plural* of *datum,* it is usual to treat it as a collective *singular* noun: 'this *is* all the data we need'; 'what data *is* available?'

PRON 'DAYta' (rather than 'DATTa' or 'DAHta').

data *protection / security*

● RULES

1 Data *protection* is concerned with protecting us against the wrong use of personal information stored on a computer. (There is a UK Data Protection Act 1984.)

2 Data *security* is concerned with computer crime, such as the manipulation of data maliciously or for fraudulent transfers of money.

date rape

● RECOMMENDATION

Date rape is a valid term now, to distinguish between violent rape by a stranger in a lonely place, and rape by a man a woman knows well, often in a social setting.

dates

● RECOMMENDATION

Write dates like this: 21 May 1997 (no *st* or *th*, and no *comma*).

● CAUTION

When a date is expressed entirely in figures, there could be a misunderstanding because of varying conventions in different countries: 7 5 1997 means 7 May 1997 in Britain, but in some countries, including America, it would be taken to mean 5 July 1997.

$ See CAUTION above.

daughters-in-law / daughter-in-laws

● RULE

Daughters-in-law.

De / de

● RULE

It is nearly always *de* in French names (Charles de Gaulle), but it may be *De* in some Italian names (Vittorio De Sica), in some Dutch names (Hugo De Vries), and in some English names (Geoffrey De Havilland).

de- / dis- words

● RECOMMENDATIONS

1 The *de-* prefix is useful when there's a need to emphasise that something is *undone*: *decontaminate*; *derestrict*; *deregulate*.

2 *Dis-* is an alternative to *de-*, sometimes because the word it is linked to begins with a vowel (*disown; disestablish; disunion; disallow*), sometimes because it sounds better (*displease; disservice; discourteous*), sometimes because of custom (*disrobe; disconnect; discontent*).

3 The tendency is to drop the hyphen in most *de-* and *dis-* words: *defrost; defuse; disuse; disorganise.* But use a hyphen where it helps the reader to take in a new formation (*de-computerise*), or when the next word begins with a capital (*de-Europeanise*).

4 If you find a need for a new *de-* or *dis-* word, check with an up-to-date dictionary to make sure that someone has not already thought of it, and has established the prefix.

If not, choose *de-* or *dis-*, whichever sounds better when attached to the word that follows.

● CAUTION

Avoid using or coining new *de-* or *dis-* words when a straightforward alternative exists: 'unlearn'; 'divorce'; 'legalise' are better than *de-educate; demarry; decriminalise.*

deadly / deathly

● RULES

1   Something that is *deadly* can kill you: 'a deadly poison'.
2   *Deathly* is used when something resembles death: 'a deathly silence' (as quiet as the grave); 'a deathly pallor'.
3   Only *deadly* can be used with an extended meaning to suggest that something kills you, in a manner of speaking: 'deadly bowling at cricket'; 'deadly dull'.

deadpan / dispassionate / impassive / poker-faced

● RECOMMENDATIONS

1   *Deadpan* describes someone's face as not showing any emotion or reaction, no matter how they feel. It may have a hint of American English about it, but British dictionaries treat it as standard English.
2   *Poker-faced* is the exact equivalent of *deadpan*, if anything slightly more American in tone, but generally regarded as standard British English.
3   *Impassive* also means not displaying emotion, but suggests that the person is unaffected by feelings, rather than concealing them.
4   *Dispassionate* does not suggest someone is cold and unfeeling, so much as calm and objective: 'he remained dispassionate about the accusation'.

deal with / address

● RECOMMENDATION

Address has become a fashionable word in politics and business: ministers talk about having to *address* an issue; chief executives *address* problems. It sounds self-important, but it is not as straightforward as *dealing with* whatever it is. See also **confront / face up to.**

Dear Sir / Madam

● RECOMMENDATIONS

1   *Dear Sir* or *Dear Madam* is now used mostly when the writer doesn't know the other person's name. Otherwise, *Dear Mrs Robinson, Dear Mr Russell* . . . is the usual way of beginning a letter in the 1990s.
2   *My dear Sir* now sounds Dickensian; *My dear Mr Russell* sounds patronising, although *My dear Mary* is affectionate.

● CAUTION

Some people prefer to avoid the formality of *Dear Mr* . . . by using the name in full:

Dear Godfrey Howard. This is all right in some situations, but it can backfire if it seems overfamiliar to the other person.

deathly / deadly

See **deadly** . . .

debacle

● RULE

Debacle takes in the combined meanings of a complete failure, a defeat, and a shambles when everything goes wrong: 'the vote was a debacle for the government'.

● RECOMMENDATION

It is unnecessary to use French accents (*débâcle*).

PRON is half anglicised: 'dayBAHke(r)l'.

debar / disbar

● RECOMMENDATIONS

1 *Debar* is to exclude someone, or prevent them doing something. It is usually followed by 'from': 'we shall debar her from serving on the local committee because she lives outside the area'.

2 *Disbar* is mostly used in the legal sense of taking away the right of barristers to practise, or expelling them from the Bar.

debatable / questionable

● RECOMMENDATIONS

1 *Debatable* suggests there are good arguments on both sides, so it keeps the door open by inviting discussion.

2 *Questionable* hints that something is untrue, or even dishonest. At best, it can be a tactful way of suggesting that something is wrong (but not as tactful as *debatable*).

debit / credit

See **credit** . . .

debug

● RULE

Debug has two separate meanings. In computer technology, *debug* is to locate an error in the system: in espionage, *debug* is to check a conference room or hotel bedroom for hidden microphones. (And there's no need to raise eyebrows over the word *debugger* – it is no more unwholesome than a computer program devised to trace errors.)

debut / début

● RECOMMENDATION

The acute accent over the *e* is unnecessary.

● OPTION

PRON 'DAY-byoo'✓ or 'DEBB-yoo'.

● RULE

Debuts is the plural form, with the *s* pronounced ('DAYbyooz').

decade (pronunciation)

● OPTION

Both 'DECade'✓ (stress on the *first* syllable) and 'deCADE' [!] (stress on the *second* syllable) are acceptable.

decent

● CAUTION

Decent is a loaded word. It often means doing 'the right thing', behaving 'in the right way'. But 'right' may mean conforming to our own standards. Look at *decent* carefully, to see if its meaning is relative only to a particular way of looking at life.

decidedly / decisively

● RULES

1 *Decidedly* is positively and without question. When we speak *decidedly* against something, there is no doubt that we are completely against it.

2 *Decisively* is settling something finally. When we speak *decisively* against something, it suggests that our arguments are conclusive.

decimal currency

● RECOMMENDATION

The accepted practice is to express sums less than a pound as: 25p; 50p (no stop after *p*). For sums over a pound, the *p* is usually dropped: £20.25; £35.50. This does not apply to *columns of figures*, where it is more practicable to show 25p; 50p as 0.25; 0.50.

decimate

● RECOMMENDATION

Although the original meaning (which some people still insist on) of *decimate* is to kill one in every ten, it is now established, through use, as meaning killing a large unspecified proportion. [!]

decipher / decode

See **code** . . . (RECOMMENDATIONS 3 and 4)

(*make* / *take* a) **decision**

● OPTION

You can either *make* ✓ or *take* a decision, since there's no rule about it, and it comes to the same thing.

decisively / **decidedly**

See **decidedly** . . .

decode / **decipher**

See **code** . . . (RECOMMENDATIONS 3 and 4)

decoy (pronunciation)

● RULE

As a *noun* for a person or object used to trap someone or an animal, stress the *first* syllable: 'DEEkoy'. As a *verb*, meaning to trap someone by using a decoy, stress the *second* syllable: 'deeKOY'.

deep sea / **high seas**

● RECOMMENDATION

In everyday use, *deep sea* is an indeterminate expression for the ocean in general. Although *high seas* can also be used in the same way, it does have a specific legal meaning, which is the open sea not subject to any country's jurisdiction.

defect (pronunciation)

● OPTION

As a *noun* the stress can be on the *first* syllable ('DEEfekt')✓, or the *second* ('diFEKT').

● RULE

The only pronunciation of the *verb* (for someone leaving a political party or a country to ally themselves with another) stresses the *second* syllable: 'diFEKT'.

defective / **deficient**

● RECOMMENDATIONS

1 Use *defective* for something that does not work properly, or when the *quality* falls short of what is necessary.

2 Use *deficient* when an essential part is missing, or the *quantity* is inadequate. (A *defective* supply of water, for example, suggests the water is polluted: a *deficient* supply means there is not enough.)

● OPTION

Referring to human senses, the words are often interchangeable: bad sight or hearing, for example, can be *defective* ✓ or *deficient*.

defence / defense

● RULE

Defence is English and *defense* is American. But wherever we are, we should use the American spelling for official US posts and institutions: the US Secretary of Defense; the US Department of Defense.

deficient / defective

See **defective** . . .

deficit / shortfall

● RECOMMENDATIONS

1 *Deficit* (PRON 'DEFicit') is the more official word (balance of payments deficit), and the word used in accountancy.

2 *Shortfall* is a more everyday word, used particularly when not enough money has been raised or is available for a specific purpose, or when production has not reached the target set.

definite / definitely

● CAUTION

The wrong spellings 'definate' and 'definately' are common mistakes.

definite / definitive

● RULE

Definite means clear-cut and unmistakable: *definitive* always suggests finality. For example, a *definite* offer is a positive firm offer, whereas a *definitive* offer is a final offer – not a penny more.

defuse / diffuse

● RULE

A bomb is *defused* (PRON 'diFYOOZD'): light or other things are *diffused* (PRON 'diFYOOSSD'), that is spread out widely.

NOTE Writing or speech can also be *diffuse*, when it is rambling and imprecise.

(to a) degree

● CAUTION

There can be confusion over the meaning. *To a degree* can be short for 'to the last degree': if someone has made you angry *to a degree,* it means you were furious. But *to a degree* can also be taken to mean 'up to a point': 'we can do it *to a degree*' suggests we can only go so far. When there is a doubt, specify *to the last degree* if you mean 'all the way', or *to some degree* if you mean 'just so far'.

deliver

● RECOMMENDATION

Deliver has the straightforward meaning, as in 'When can you deliver the car?' But the question 'Can you deliver?' can also have the sense of 'Will you be able to keep your promise?' This use (also expressed as 'Can you *deliver the goods*?') is well-established now, and available when you need the sharpshooting language of business or politics: 'Expansion plans are one thing, but will they deliver the promised increase in profits?'

deliverance / delivery

● RECOMMENDATION

*Deliver**ance*** belongs more to the pulpit ('deliverance from evil'), with *delivery* the down-to-earth word of the milk round.

delusion / illusion

● CAUTIONS

1 In practice it is not likely to matter much if you use these words interchangeably, but be careful: 'he has so many *delusions*' suggests he is wrong about many things, with the implication that this could do harm. 'He has so many *illusions*' *suggests he lives in cloud-cuckoo-land and is probably harmless.*

2 There is no point in saying that something is a *false* illusion, because all illusions are false.

de luxe

● RECOMMENDATION

De luxe has become so commercialised that it is often meaningless ('de luxe ice-cream'), so it's usually better avoided. Descriptive words, such as *luxurious, sumptuous, top-quality*, are more explicit.

● OPTION

PRON 'deLUKS'✓ or 'deLOOKS'.

demand *from / of / on*

● OPTION

We can demand something *from* ✓ or *of* someone: 'he demanded money *from* (or *of*) me'.

● RULE

When we *make* a demand, it is always followed by *on*: 'she makes too many demands on him'.

demanding

● CAUTION

The meaning can be uncertain. 'A demanding task' is clearly one that is difficult to carry out. But if a *person* is *demanding*, it can mean they are always thinking of themselves and what they want, or that it takes a lot of energy to deal with them, for one reason or another. We can distinguish between the two by alternatives, such as 'makes a lot of demands' or 'needs a lot of attention (or care)'.

demand *of* / *on* / *from*

See demand *from* . . .

demi- / hemi- / semi-

● RULES

1 All three prefixes mean 'half' (*semi-* and *demi-* are from Latin, *hemi-* from Greek).

2 *Demi-* is the least used: *demigod* – part god, part human (or more loosely, someone of exceptional beauty or authority); *demi-pension* – half-board (bedroom, breakfast and either lunch or dinner).

3 *Hemi-* is reserved mostly for scientific words, nearly always without a hyphen: *hemiplegia* (paralysis of one side of the body); *hemihydrate* (two molecules of substance to one molecule of water); *hemisphere.*

4 *Semi-* is the prefix used in most formations, sometimes with a hyphen (*semi-basement, semi-detached, semi-skilled*), but often without (*semicircle, semicolon, semitone*).

5 Nearly all later or new formations use *semi-,* usually with a hyphen: *semi-autobiographical, semi-independent, semi-invalid.*

Democrat / democrat

● RULE

With a capital *D*, a *Democrat* is a member of the Democratic Party, one of the two major political parties in the USA. With a small *d, democrat* can mean two things. One meaning is someone who believes in democracy: it can also be used for someone who believes in abolishing hereditary class distinction and the influence of wealth. (Many people who are democrats in the first sense are far from being democrats in the second.)

demonstrable (pronunciation)

● OPTION

Stress on the *second* or the *first* syllable is acceptable, but 'deMONstrable' ✓ is easier to say.

demotic / colloquial

See colloquial . . .

denims / jeans

● RECOMMENDATION

Both words are names of the material itself (*jean* was originally a cotton twill from Genoa, and *denim*, originally made in France, comes from *serge de Nîmes*). Nowadays *jeans* is the word for the trousers, and *denims* for shorts, jackets, skirts, etc, made from that kind of cloth.

denote / connote

See **connote** . . .

denouement / dénouement

● RECOMMENDATION

Although it's pronounced in a French manner ('dayNOOmah(n)'), it's gilding the lily to put an acute accent over the first *e*. Spell it *denouement*.

deny / refute / rebut

● RECOMMENDATIONS

1   *Refute* means that conclusive evidence has been produced to show that something is untrue: 'here are the facts that refute that statement'.

2   *Rebut* can be used to argue against something without necessarily disapproving it: 'I shall rebut that statement, and hope that you will agree with me.'

3   Neither *refute* nor *rebut* should be used instead of *deny*, that is simply for saying that something is not true: 'he refutes that statement, which he claims is a lie' (the proper word there is *denies*).

dependant / dependent

● RULE

It's this way round: you claim tax relief for a depend**a**nt, but the rate of relief may be depend**e**nt on your income.

dependence / dependency

● RULES

1   *Dependence* is the state of being dependent or reliant on someone or something.

2   The main use of *dependency* is for a territory that comes under the control of another country or of a larger administrative centre.

dependent / conditional

See **conditional** . . .

dependent territory / colony

See **colony** . . .

depend *on / upon*

● RECOMMENDATION

In conversation *on* or *upon* can often be omitted ('It depends what you think'), but in writing, follow *depend* by *on* or *upon* (depends *upon* is more formal): 'it depends *on* (or *upon*) what the minister considers advisable'.

depositary / depository / repository

● RULES

1 *Depositary* is a *person*, such as a trustee, to whom documents, money or anything else are entrusted.

2 *Depository* is a *place* where things, most commonly furniture, are stored.

3 **Repository** is either a *place*, a *person* or an *object*: furniture can be stored in a repository; someone can be a repository of information on a subject; a book can be a repository of wisdom; an urn a repository of someone's ashes.

● CAUTION

There's no such word as *repositary*.

depression / recession / slump / downturn

These four terms describe different degrees of reduction in business and economic activity.

● RECOMMENDATIONS

1 *Slump* should be used with extreme caution. It is reserved for a drastic and long-lasting cutback in trade and spending by consumers, with massive unemployment, a reminder of the soup kitchens of the 1930s.

2 A *depression* is not quite as severe as a *slump*, but still suggests a major economic setback.

3 A *recession* is a serious slowdown, although not as drastic as a *slump* or a *depression*. It is a technical term in economics, sometimes defined as a drop in national output for two consecutive three-monthly periods.

4 *Downturn* is a milder word, suggesting a temporary economic hiccup.

derisive / derisory

● OPTION

A comment or a remark can be either *derisive* ✓ or *derisory*, meaning scornful, suggesting that something is ridiculous.

● RULE

Only *derisory* is used about something that is absurdly small: pay-offers and financial settlements can be *derisory* (not *derisive*).

derivative

● CAUTION

Although *derivative* simply means that something comes from another source (it is also a mathematical term used in calculus), it is often derogatory in everyday language. This applies particularly when *derivative* is used about art, music, literature, or ideas in general, as it suggests that something is a shadow of an original concept.

descendant / descendent / descended

● RULES

1 *Descendant* is the *noun*: a son is a descendant of his mother and father.
2 *Descendent* is the *descriptive word*: a son is descendent from his father. This usage is rare, as the usual way of putting it is 'a son is *descended* from his father'.

description of / about

● RULE

A description is always *of* someone or something (not *about* them).

desert / dessert

● RULES

1 A *desert* is a sandy wasteland, and stress is on the *first* syllable ('DEZZert'). So we have *desert boots* (because they're the colour of sand); *desert rats* (the armoured division that fought in the North African desert).
2 When husbands and wives *desert* one another, stress is on the *second* syllable ('dezZERT').
3 Only after dinner, does the double -*ss*- appear, as a *dessert* is the sweet course (see also **dessert / pudding**).

designer

● CAUTION

Designer is a trendy cryptic word attached to almost anything that works hard at being new and different: designer jeans; designer stubble (the fashionable unshaven look); designer violence. In this descriptive sense, *designer* is so overworked, that it is better avoided and a more precise word used instead ('original', 'fashionable', 'specially designed', 'stylish').

desire / want / wish

● RECOMMENDATIONS

1 With a few exceptions, *desire* as a *verb* is formal to the point of being pompous: 'Does madam desire some more wine?'
2 *Wish* is more deferential than *want* : 'Do you wish for some more wine?' might be all right from a waiter in a grand restaurant, but in everyday contexts *want* is the usual word.

despatch / dispatch

See **dispatch** . . .

despite / despite *of* / *in* spite of

● OPTION

In spite of ✓ and *despite* mean the same, with *despite* as possibly more literary: '*in spite of* (or *despite*) his money, he never travels first class'.

● RULE

Despite *of* is wrong, for *despite* stands on its own: 'despite his money . . .'.

dessert / pudding

● RECOMMENDATION

Dessert has become almost a formal word for the sweet course at the end of a meal, and *pudding* has taken over, even in some grand restaurants. Although a *pudding* is properly a cooked dish, usually served hot (plum pudding; rice pudding), it is now often used for any dessert, even ice-cream.

desultory (pronunciation)

● RULE

Stress on the *first* syllable is the only accepted pronunciation: 'DEZultry' ('deZULtry' is substandard).

deteriorate / worsen

● RULE

Only what is good, such as fresh food, can *deteriorate*, and only what is bad can *worsen*. It's a mistake to say 'a bottle of wine will *worsen* if left near a radiator' (it will *deteriorate*).

● CAUTION

Deteriorate should be pronounced with its full *five* syllables ('dee-TEER-ree-er-rayht'), and it's careless to contract it to four ('dee-TEER-ree-ate').

determine / find out

● RECOMMENDATION

Determine, as an alternative to *find out,* should carry with it the idea of precision: 'we have to *determine* how production will be affected' suggests a detailed analysis, whereas 'we have to *find out* . . .' may mean that the problem should be looked into, perhaps in a more general way.

● CAUTION

In law, *determine* means 'to terminate; to end'. When an agreement is *determined,* it is brought to an end. Hesitate before applying this legal meaning in non-legal contexts, because many people will be uncertain of what is intended.

deterrence / deterrent

● RULES

1 Deterrence is always a *noun*: 'high unemployment is a deterrence to strike action'.

2 *Deterrent* can be either a *noun* or a *descriptive word*. But because *deterrent* has become the standard noun in defence matters (nuclear deterrent), it has taken over as the *noun* in other contexts, as well as being the usual *descriptive word*: 'deterrent measures prevented strike action'.

● CAUTION

Don't let *reference* lead to spelling dete**rr**ence or dete**rr**ent with *one r*.

detour (pronunciation)

● CAUTION

The pronunciation 'DAYtour' is out of date, and the standard pronunciation now is 'DEEtour'.

Deutschmark / Deutsche Mark

● OPTION

Either will do, but the tendency now is to write it as *one* word (Deutschmark) ✓, and say it with *two* syllables: 'DOYTCH-mahk'✓ (rather than three syllables: 'DOY-tcher-mahk').

develop

● CAUTION

Develop means something happening gradually, in stages: 'a situation can develop over years'; 'a town develops as the population increases'. Avoid the common mistake of 'develop suddenly' or 'develop overnight'. Instead use 'suddenly occurred' or 'just happened'.

developing / underdeveloped country

These are indeterminate terms for poor and primitive countries relying on agriculture, crafts and raw materials.

● CAUTION

Underdeveloped country is now regarded as a pejorative description, and the more euphemistic term *developing country* is used by the United Nations. In some cases, but not all, that suggests the process of changing over to an industrial base.

deviant / perverted

● CAUTIONS

1 The two words are now so associated with psychosexual problems, that it is better to use them only in that context. *Deviant* may or may not imply a degree of condemnation, but *perverted* is always censorious, and should only be used when that is intended.

2 A personal attitude often decides where the line is drawn between normal sexual behaviour and perverted practices. For example, some people would use *perverted*, and some would not, about oral sex.

diabolic / diabolical

● RECOMMENDATIONS

1 *Diabolic* has a theological flavour, used about the attributes of the devil himself.

2 *Diabolical* is more for human beings who behave like the devil: 'his treatment of her is diabolical'.

● CAUTION

To use *diabolic* and *diabolical* about food, the weather or anything else we're fed up with, is usual enough in conversation or casual writing, but should not cross the line into formal English.

diaeresis / umlaut

See **accents**

diagnosis / prognosis

● RULES

1 A doctor *diagnoses* a disease by discovering what is wrong with the patient, and the result is a **diagnosis**. A doctor's **prognosis** is his forecast of how the disease will develop. By extension, the *diagnosis* of a problem in business, or any other sphere, is finding out the cause. The *prognosis* might be that it will sort itself out, or that the business will go bankrupt.

2 The plurals are *diagnoses* and *prognoses* (last syllables pronounced 'seez').

dial (verb)

● RECOMMENDATION

The verb *dial*, in connection with telephones, has not been pensioned off. We still *dial* a number, even though we are punching out the numbers on a keypad.

dialect / patois

● RECOMMENDATIONS

1 Use *dialect* for a minority language belonging to a region, a language that has a literature and a linguistic tradition.

2 Use *patois* for a primitive, usually a peasant language with no literature, often a crude version of the language it is adapted from.

● CAUTION

A cultural value is now seen in preserving minority languages, and we should be careful not to use *dialect*, in particular, in a way that suggests it is an inferior language.

dialogue

● RULE

A *dialogue* is *any number* of people speaking together, not just *two* as is commonly supposed.

● CAUTION

The fashionable use of *dialogue* for an exchange of views is overdone: 'Can we have a dialogue about this?' instead of 'Can we talk about it?'

diapositive / transparency / colour negative

See **colour negative . . .**

dictate (pronunciation)

● RULE

The *noun* is stressed on the *first* syllable, the *verb* on the *second*: we follow the 'DICtates' of conscience, but 'dicTATE' letters.

dictionaries

We should be lost without dictionaries. They chart the vast wilderness of words in which we wander all our lives. But words in a dictionary are like do-not-touch exhibits in a museum. It is only when we use them that they come to life, and sometimes they take on a life of their own. The following is planned to help you get the most out of your dictionary, and to relate to it in the way that good users of English have learnt by long experience.

● RECOMMENDATIONS

1 Remember that dictionaries, like railway timetables, become out of date. English is on the move all the time. A new word or the new use of a word is not necessarily wrong just because it is not recorded in one dictionary. Look in your dictionary for the date of the last *new edition*. In the linguistic fast-lanes of the 1990s, five years is a reasonable bookshelf life for a dictionary.

2 Remember that the status of words changes. A word written down as *slang* at one time can move up over the years into standard English, suitable for use even in formal writing. During the transition period, dictionaries often disagree over whether a word has crossed over, and we have to make up our own minds, or better still take note of how good writers and speakers are using it. See also **colloquial / informal / slang / non-standard.**

3 Some dictionaries hedge certain entries with the qualification *disp,* short for *disputed,* or some other cautionary note to indicate there are people who reject a particular way a word is used or pronounced. As time goes by, not every *disp* label is still justified, for when most reasonable and experienced writers and speakers accept a usage as normal, the fact that a few linguistic Colonel Blimps still make a song and dance about it hardly warrants a *disp.*

4 Bear in mind that many meanings and the usage of words reflect in some way the

opinions of the editor of the dictionary, which is why good dictionaries can differ from one another. Treat entries in your dictionary as valuable guidelines, but not as tablets of stone. Editors' decisions are not always final: there are times when we – not our dictionary – can decide to have the last word.

● CAUTION

But before you depart from anything in a dictionary, make sure there are some good writers and speakers who take the same line as you do. Then at least you will be in good company.

didactic / pedantic

● RECOMMENDATIONS

1 Use **pedantic** to describe a scholastic nit-picker who fusses over academic principles, no matter how meaningless and out of touch they are.

2 Use **didactic** to describe someone who shows how much they know by constantly seeking to teach others, when it is neither called for nor asked for.

● CAUTION

While *didactic* is less derogatory than *pedantic*, neither word is a compliment.

didn't

See **contracted forms**

die *of* / *from*

● OPTION

We can die *of* ✓ or *from* an illness, old age . . . .

dietetics / nutrition

● RULES

1 *Dietetics* embraces the scientific study of both the food that is actually eaten, or should be eaten for a healthy diet. *Dietetics* is treated as *singular* ('dietetics *shows* that fruit and salads are good for you').

2 *Nutrition* is a branch of physiology that deals with the values of food and the way carbohydrates, fats, proteins, minerals, etc, are utilised by the body.

dietitian / dietician

● OPTION

Both spellings are used. Most dictionaries prefer *dietitian* ✓, putting *dietician* in brackets as an alternative.

differences / differentials

● RECOMMENDATION

It is unnecessary to use *differentials* simply because it sounds more important than *differences*: 'charges in the hotels relate to the differentials of amenities'. Why not *differences*?

● RULE

Differential is the standard term in industrial relations for established different levels of pay for different categories of jobs. As a descriptive word, it singles out this factor: '*differential* pay settlements' indicates more than '*different* pay settlements'. It links agreements specifically to levels of pay already established for different levels of skills.

different

● CAUTION

This word has a way of slipping in where it's not wanted: 'he has had three different wives'; 'she looked it up in six different books'. Leave out *different* in those sentences and nothing is lost.

different *from / to / than*

● OPTIONS

1 Put your money on different *from*, which is gilt-edged and irreproachable.

2 ✓ Use all three forms. Different *to* [!] has been used by good writers from George Eliot to Evelyn Waugh. Different *than* [!] has been used by writers in the class of Defoe, Coleridge, Trollope and Carlyle. (*Than* is particularly useful after *differently*: 'they do things differently in New York than in London'.)

differentials / differences

See **differences** . . .

differentiate / distinguish

● RECOMMENDATIONS

1 Choose *distinguish* as the verb in most contexts.

2 *Differentiate* can suggest a slight difference, and is usually followed by 'between': 'the colours are so similar that it's difficult to differentiate between them'.

3 Use *differentiate* in scientific contexts, such as differentiating between a number of botanical species.

differ *from / with*

● RECOMMENDATIONS

1 When people or things are not the same as each other, they differ *from*: 'Italian wines differ from French wines.'

2 When people hold different opinions, they differ *with* each other (differ *from* is also correct, but can be ambiguous – see CAUTION below).

● CAUTION

'She differs *from* her brother' could mean she is different from him, or that they hold different opinions. Make your meaning clear by adding either 'in some ways' (to mean different from each other), or 'over this', 'over some things' (to cover a difference of opinion).

diffuse / defuse

See **defuse** . . .

digest (pronunciation)

● RULE

The *noun* (meaning a synopsis of a book, article . . .) is stressed on the *first* syllable ('DIgest'). The *verb* is stressed on the *second* syllable: 'diGEST' food; 'diGEST' information.

digital / analogue

See **analogue** . . .

dilemma

● CAUTIONS

1 Do not use *dilemma* simply to mean any kind of indecision, as in 'we're in a dilemma over where to go for our holiday'. To be *in a dilemma* is to be faced by two unpleasant alternatives: 'she's in a dilemma over whether to pay the telephone bill or have the phone cut off'.

2 It's better to use *dilemma* about *two* unpleasant possibilities, not any number.

● RULE

To be *on the horns of a dilemma* means no more than *to be in a dilemma* (as in CAUTION 1 above), except perhaps that it emphasises even more the stress of the choice involved.

● OPTION

PRON 'diLEMMa' (first syllable rhymes with 'pill')✓ or 'dyeLEMMa'.

dimension (pronunciation)

PRON '*dye*MENshun'✓ or '*dim*MENshun'.

dinghy / dingy

● RULES

1 *Dinghy* (PRON 'DINgee' with a *g* as in 'get') is a small boat, especially one carried by a ship.

2 *Dingy* (PRON 'DINjee') describes something that looks dirty or drab.

diphtheria (pronunciation)

● OPTION

Some dictionaries allow the *p* to be pronounced ('DIPtheria') [!], others insist on an *f* sound ('DIFFtheria') ✓.

diphthong (pronunciation)

● CAUTION

Unlike *diphtheria*, where there is an OPTION (see **diphtheria**), the *p* must have an *f* sound: 'DIFFthong' (not 'DIPthong').

direct / direction / director / directory (pronunciation)

● OPTION

With all these words, you can pronounce the first syllable to rhyme with 'dye'✓ or with the first syllable of 'mirror'.

direct / directly

● CAUTION

'You can go *direct* to the river' means there is a more or less straight path there. 'You can go *directly* to the river' could mean the same thing, but it could also mean that you can go immediately. Where there is a risk of misunderstanding, replace *directly*, in the *second* sense, by 'at once', 'immediately', 'straightaway', 'without delay'.

direct / indirect object

This distinction is useful for understanding grammatical explanations.

● RULES

1   A *direct* object is someone or something directly in line with the action of a verb: 'he sent a letter'; 'she spoke the truth' (*letter* and *truth* are direct objects).

2   An *indirect* object is someone or something one stage removed: 'he sent a letter to Mary' (or 'he sent Mary a letter'); 'she spoke the truth to him' (*Mary* and *him* are indirect objects, while *letter* and *truth* remain direct objects).

direct / indirect speech

These are stylistic terms to describe two different ways of reporting what someone has said.

● RULES

1   *Direct* speech encloses within quotation marks the *actual words* that are said: 'Will you come to dinner?' he asked.

2   *Indirect* speech describes what has been said, without using the actual words that were spoken: 'He asked her if she would come to dinner.'

3   A question in *indirect* speech is not followed by a question mark: 'She asked him if he could stay to dinner.'

director / directory (pronunciation)

See **direct** . . .

dis- / de- words

See *de- / dis-* words

disability / inability

● RECOMMENDATIONS

1 Generally *disability* should be used about a physical or mental handicap, because in many contexts that is what people would assume is meant.

2 *Inability* is for someone unable to do something because they do not have the knowledge, the skill, the intelligence, or the resources. It should not be used for a physical or mental handicap.

disadvantage (verb)

● RECOMMENDATION

Disadvantage is normally a *noun*, but it can also be useful as a *verb* [!]. 'High interest rates should not be allowed to *disadvantage* business' is more direct than '. . . to put business at a disadvantage'.

disadvantaged (noun)

● RECOMMENDATION

Disadvantaged is a politically correct and evasive alternative word for the poor, suffering, maltreated, loveless. If you don't want to play that game, come out into the open and say what you mean.

disappointed *at* / *by* / *in* / *with*

● RULES

1 If it is a *person*, we can be disappointed *in* ✓ or *with* them, meaning a disappointment in what they are like or how they act: 'they are disappointed *in* (or *with*) their son'.

2 If we are disappointed *by* someone, it is because of something specific they have done or not done: 'she was disappointed by his late arrival'.

3 If it is an *object*, we are disappointed *with* it: 'he is disappointed with his new car'.

4 If it is a *result*, an *occurrence* or an *event*, we can be disappointed *by*, *in* or *with* it: 'they were disappointed *by* (or *in* ✓ or *with*) dinner' means they didn't like the food.

5 If they were disappointed *at* dinner, it means that something happened during dinner to disappoint them.

disapprove / disapprove *of*

● RULE

If someone disapproves *of* a plan, it means they don't like it, but if they *disapprove* a plan, they have turned it down. (Someone may disapprove *of* your plan but still let you go ahead with it, whereas if they *disapprove* your plan, it's a dead duck.)

disassociate / dissociate

See **dissociate** . . .

disastrous / disasterous

● RULE

Always *disastrous* ('disasterous' is an incorrect spelling). See also **-erous / -rous**.

disc / disk

● RULE

Disk should be used only in connection with *computers*. In other contexts, the spelling is disc: floppy dis**k**, but compact dis**c**.

$ Dis**k** in *all* contexts.

discernible / discernable

● RULE

Discern*i*ble is now the only accepted spelling.

disclose / reveal

● CAUTION

Although *disclose* and *reveal* mean no more than to make something known, they often carry the suggestion that it was hidden for dubious reasons. Unless that is intended, it's often better to use words, such as 'show', 'explain', 'announce', which are less likely to imply that anything undercover has been going on. Compare 'he explained his motives' with 'he revealed his motives'.

discontinue / cease / terminate / stop

See **stop** . . .

discount (pronunciation)

● RULES

1 The *noun* is stressed on the *first* syllable: when we buy something for less than the going rate, we get a 'DIScount'.

2 The *verb* is stressed on the *second* syllable, when it means to write something off as untrue or unimportant: 'we can disCOUNT that information as it has no bearing on the matter'.

● OPTION

When the verb means to reduce a price, it can be stressed on the *first* or the *second* syllable: 'she asked the shop to DIScount ✓ (or disCOUNT) the price'.

discover / identify

● RECOMMENDATION

'The problem was *discovered*' suggests it came to light more or less by chance: 'the problem was *identified*' suggests an effort was made to find or define it.

discover / invent

● RULE

We can only *discover* something that is already there, but unknown to us: it could be a star, an island, a writer. We *invent* something that did not exist before, such as a new piece of equipment.

● OPTION

When it's a concept, a technique, a new way of doing something, we can either discover✓ or invent it.

discrepancy / divergence

● RECOMMENDATIONS

1 Use *discrepancy* when things should agree but do not, especially when it concerns figures: 'a discrepancy in accounts'.

2 Use *divergence* about things that simply happen to be different, usually not in a marked way: 'a divergence of opinion'.

discrimination

● CAUTION

Discrimination can of course be a good word, describing the ability to distinguish between what is fine and the run-of-the-mill. But now the first meaning that comes into many people's minds is prejudice because of race, colour or sex. Be careful when using *discrimination* in a good sense to avoid misunderstanding.

NOTE A new expression has arisen: *positive discrimination* for preferential treatment given to certain groups of people.

disease / illness

The words are often interchangeable: 'she has an *illness* (or a *disease*)'.

● RECOMMENDATIONS

1 *Disease* is preferred for infection: we catch a disease from polluted water.

2 *Illness* is preferred for common diseases, such as a cold.

3 *Illness* is the word used about mental disorders: 'a mental illness'.

4 When the nature of an illness is specified, *disease* is usually the appropriate word: Parkinson's disease; heart disease; a rare eye disease.

● CAUTION

The descriptive word *diseased* means that someone has a disease, just as *ill* means they have an illness; but we should be careful how we use *diseased* since it has acquired a strong connotation of abnormality: 'he is diseased' sounds much more sinister than 'he is ill'. See also **contagious / infectious; ill / sick.**

disgusted *at / by / with*

● OPTIONS

1 We can be disgusted *at* or *by* ✓ things, or something that has happened.

2   If it is a person, we are disgusted *at* or *with* ✓ them.

disinterested / uninterested

● RULE

Disinterested means impartial, not taking sides: *uninterested* means having no interest in something. (A judge should be *disinterested*, but if he is *uninterested*, he might doze off because he's bored with the proceedings.)

● CAUTION

Both *disinterested* and *uninterested* are used so often to mean 'not interested', that we cannot rely on people understanding the distinction. Safer words to use now to indicate you are objective and not influenced by personal gain, are 'unbiased' or 'impartial'.

disk / disc

See **disc** . . .

dislike

● RULE

While we can like *to* go to the theatre, like *to* travel, and so on, we cannot dislike *to* do anything. The correct construction is '*dislike going* to the theatre'; '*dislike travelling*' (not 'dislike *to* go'; 'dislike *to* travel').

disoriented / disorientated

● OPTION

Both *disoriented* ✓ and *disorientated* are correct.

● CAUTION

The words have two meanings. One is to lose a sense of physical direction: 'the familiar landmarks had gone and she was *disoriented*, not knowing which road to take'. The other is to be confused or thrown off balance: 'she was *disorientated* by the bright lights and loud music'.

dispassionate / impassive / poker-faced / deadpan

See **deadpan** . . .

dispatch / despatch

● OPTION

Dispatch ✓ and *despatch* are alternative spellings.

PRON 'disPATCH' whatever the spelling.

dispute (pronunciation)

● RULE

Whether it's a *noun* or a *verb,* stress is on the *second* syllable: 'disPUTE'.

dissatisfied / unsatisfied

● RULE

Dissatisfied is a state of mind, when something has not come up to expectations: **un**satisfied is when there isn't enough, or a need has not been met. We are dissatisfied by a meal when the food is disappointing: we are unsatisfied when we are still hungry after it.

● CAUTION

Remember double s: dissatisfied.

dissociate / disassociate

● OPTION

Both dissociate ✓ and disassociate are correct, although the string of s sounds in disassociate is better avoided.

distil / distill

● RULE

Distil, distilling, distilled.

$ Distill, distilling, distilled.

distinct / distinctive

● RECOMMENDATIONS

1   When something is distinct, it is clear and pronounced: if a soap has a distinct smell of roses, that smell comes through strongly. If something is not distinct, it is uncertain.

2   When something is distinctive, it is characteristic of what it is: a soap with a distinctive smell of roses has a scent that seems to belong particularly to roses (rather than to any other flowers). If it is not distinctive, it is not truly characteristic of what it is supposed to be.

distrait / distraught

● RECOMMENDATIONS

1   If you are distrait (PRON 'disTRAY'), your mind is elsewhere, because you are worried about something.

2   Distraught (PRON 'disTRAWT') is a stronger word, suggesting extreme worry and agitation.

distribute (pronunciation)

● RULE

Stress the second syllable: 'disTRIBute'.

distrust / mistrust

● RECOMMENDATIONS

1 In most cases it doesn't matter whether *distrust* ✓ or *mistrust* is used, when it's about a person, an organisation, motives, intentions.

2 If it is about an ability, *mistrust* is preferable: 'I mistrust my ability to see this through'; 'I mistrust his understanding of the situation'.

diurnal / daily

See **daily** . . .

divergence / discrepancy

See **discrepancy** . . .

division of words

The division of a word, with part at the end of one line and the rest at the beginning of the next, is always a nuisance to readers. When it is unavoidable, disrupt the visual flow as little as possible.

● RECOMMENDATIONS

1 Keep *prefixes* and *suffixes* intact: *aero-* space; *atmo-* sphere; *bio-* degradable; *para-* military; *re-* invest; *xero-* graphy.

2 When consonants or vowels are pronounced as *one sound*, keep them together: de*bt-* ors; o*ph-* thalmology; wa*sh-* ability; b*eau-* tiful; s*ou-* venir.

3 The following endings can be carried over: -cial(ly) (ra- *cially*); -ing (develop- *ing*); -ism (commun- *ism*); -ist (activ- *ist*); -logy (psycho- *logy*); -logist (bio- *logist*).

● CAUTIONS

1 Words with similar beginnings do not necessarily break in the same place (this applies especially to names). Follow pronunciation and sense: *tran-* scend but *trans-* port; *Fre-* da but *Fred-* erick.

2 Look out for parts of words left in awkward isolation: *reap-* pear; the- *rapist*; *leg-* end.

3 It is inexcusable to divide a word at the bottom of a page and continue it at the top of the next.

divorcee / divorcé(e)

● RECOMMENDATION

Divorcé and *divorcée* are French masculine and feminine forms. In English, whether it's a man or a woman who is divorced, use the unisex word: *divorcee* (no accents).

Dockland / dockland

● RULES

1 With a capital D, *Dockland* is the development of office blocks and houses and flats replacing the slums of London's dockland.

2   With a small *d*, *dockland* is the area of wharves and warehouses near the docks of any
    city.
\$ *Waterfront* is the usual word for dockland.

doctor / physician
● RECOMMENDATIONS
1   Use *doctor* for a general practitioner.
2   Use *physician* for a medical specialist other than a surgeon.
● CAUTION
    A peculiar kind of inverted class-distinction makes it wrong to use *doctor* for
    someone with a post as a *surgeon* in a hospital: they are *Mr, Mrs, Miss* or *Ms.*

doesn't
    See **contracted forms**

dogged (pronunciation)
● RULES
1   As *one* syllable ('doggd'), it is the past form of the verb meaning to follow closely, in
    the way of a hunting dog: 'their every move was dogged by misfortune'.
2   As *two* syllables ('dogg-ed'), it is the descriptive word meaning determined or
    persistent: 'dogged pursuit'.

dogma
● CAUTION
    Although *dogma* is a valid term for the tenets of the Christian faith, and is used that
    way in theology, in almost any other context, *dogma* would be taken to mean
    something narrow and authoritarian: 'for directors of some companies, share-option
    schemes are a dogma'.

don't
    See **contracted forms**

doorkeeper / doorman / porter / janitor
    All four words can be used for a man posted near the door of a building to usher
    people in and prevent unauthorised persons from entering.
● RECOMMENDATIONS
1   *Door**man*** is more upmarket: the Ritz has a *door**man*** while a factory is more likely to
    have a *door**keeper***.
2   By tradition, the stage door of a theatre has a *door**keeper***.
3   Also by tradition, Oxford and Cambridge colleges and clubs in Pall Mall have *porters*.
4   *Janitor* is not heard often, and usually means the caretaker of a building.

dope / pot / grass / hashish / marijuana / cannabis

See **cannabis** . . .

dots (. . .)

A row of dots (traditionally three) is a linguistic device in a number of cases.

● RULES

1　Dots can be used in the middle of a quotation to show that some words are omitted from the original (see **quotation / citation** RULE 3).

2　Dots can be used as an alternative to 'etc': 'a variety of vegetables, such as carrots, peas, beans, spinach . . .'.

3　Dots can mark a longer pause than a dash, particularly in dialogue: 'Come up for a drink . . . don't worry there are no strings attached!'

4　If a word is considered obscene, dots can be used to draw a typographical veil over some of the letters: f . . . k, c . . . . See **four-letter words** (OPTION).

5　When a sentence ends with three dots, add a fourth dot to mark the final stop. But when the sentence ends in a *question mark*, that takes the place of the *fourth* dot: 'What vegetables do you need – carrots, turnips, onions . . . ?'

● CAUTION

An overgenerously dotted page is irritating to readers.

double negatives

● CAUTION

Most double negatives are considered uneducated: 'I did*n't* do *nothing*'; 'he do*n't* know *nothing* about it'. Those are obvious examples, but double negatives have a way of creeping in unnoticed: see **barely / hardly / scarcely** (negative words easily and mistakenly combined with a second negative).

● RECOMMENDATIONS

1　There are times when a double negative is useful to provide an in-between meaning: see **not in- / not un-**.

2　It comes naturally to follow 'I shouldn't wonder if . . .' and 'I shouldn't be surprised if . . .' by a second negative: 'I should*n't* be surprised if it did*n't* rain' should really be: 'I shouldn't be surprised if it did rain'. This is so common in speech, that it's fussing to object to it.

3　Two negatives can be deliberately used to make a statement less confrontational: 'I can't believe he's not lying' says in effect 'I believe he's lying'.

doubling final letter before *-ed* and *-ing*

For example, is it *developed, developing* or *developped, developping*?

● RULES

1　With words of more than one syllable, *not* stressed on the *last* syllable, the final consonant is not usually doubled (unless it is the letter *l*: see RULE 2): ballot – balloted, balloting; bracket – bracketed, bracketing; develop – developed, developing.

2   Most words ending in *l* double the *l*, wherever the stress falls: bedevil – bedevilled, bedevilling; cancel – cancelled, cancelling; rebel – rebelled, rebelling.

● CAUTIONS

1   Look out for **parallel**, the most common exception to RULE 2 above: paralleled, paralleling (also unparalleled).

2   See **focused / focussed**.

$ Most words ending in *l* do *not* double the *l* (as in RULE 2 above): traveling; canceling; labeling.

doubt *if / that / whether*

● OPTION

   Use *if* ✓, *that* or *whether* after *doubt*: 'I doubt *if* (or *that* or *whether*) she will marry him' (meaning it is possible she will but I don't think so).

● RULE

   In a *negative* statement, implying certainty, *that* always follows *doubt*: 'I don't doubt *that* she will marry him' (meaning I am sure she will).

$ 'Doubt *that*' is the usual form.

dour (pronunciation)

● RULE

   Dour (meaning severe or stern) should rhyme with 'moor', and not sound like 'dow-er'.

douse / dowse

● RECOMMENDATION

   Use *douse* as the spelling for the verb meaning to throw water over something ('douse a fire'). Some dictionaries show *dowse* as an alternative spelling, but this could lead to confusion, since *dowse* is the verb for water-divining, searching for hidden springs by holding a divining-rod, also known as a dowsing-rod.

down *to / up* to

● RECOMMENDATION

   Direction: Whether we're travelling north or south, we go *up* to London (perhaps because it's the capital).

● OPTION

   To express responsibility: The usual form is 'it's *up* to so-and-so to decide'. But it's become trendy to reverse it: 'it's *down* to you to decide'. So it's *up* ✓ (or *down*) to you to choose.

   NOTE   Oxbridge is a special case: to go *up* to Oxford or Cambridge is to enter the university.

downturn / slump / recession / depression

See **depression** . . .

dowse / douse

See **douse** . . .

doze / snooze

● RECOMMENDATION

Most dictionaries still regard *snooze* as informal usage, but the word has been in use since the 18th century, and it's all right to use either *doze* or *snooze* as a noun, meaning 'a short sleep', or as a verb: 'he *dozed* (or *snoozed*) after dinner'.

draft / draught

● RULES

1   We *draft* legal documents, treaties, letters or a plan for carrying out a project.

2   The legal document, treaty, etc, is a *draft*.

3   We drink *draught* beer and do not like sitting in a *draught*.

4   A *draftsman* or *draftswoman* draws up legal documents, but a *draughtsman* or *draughtswoman* does drawings.

\$ *Draft* is the usual spelling for all the above meanings. A game of *draughts* is a game of 'checkers'.

drank / drunk / drunken

● RULES

1   I *drink* today, I *drank* yesterday, and when I have *drunk* too much, I am *drunk*.

2   The main use of *drunken* is as a descriptive word: 'What shall we do with the drunken sailor?'

● CAUTION

Drunken suggests habitual drunkenness ('his drunken ways'), so unless this is intended, it's better to use *drunk*: 'the drunk sailors lurched back to their ship'.

draught / draft

See **draft** . . .

dreamt / dreamed

● OPTION

Either will do: 'I *dreamt* ✓ last night' or 'I *dreamed* last night'.

drier / dryer

● RECOMMENDATIONS

1   Use *dryer* for the noun: a hair-dryer.

2   Use *drier* for the descriptive word: 'sauvignon is a drier wine than most other white wines'.

$ This follows the above recommendations.

drily / dryly

● OPTION

We can say something *drily* ✓ or *dryly*.

drunk / drunken / drank

See **drank** . . .

dryer / drier

See **drier** . . .

due to / *owing* to

● OPTIONS

1   Keep to the grammatical rule. This lays down that *due to* must always be used in a descriptive sense: instead of saying 'due to illness he was absent', we must say 'his absence was due to illness', so that *due to* 'qualifies' the word *absence*. This principle is not easy for everyone to follow.

2   ✓ Use *due to* and *owing to* in exactly the same way: '*owing to* (or *due to*) illness he was absent'. [!]

3   If you are still worried about the whole business, fall back on 'because of', as no one can ever throw a grammar book at you for that: 'because of illness he was absent'.

duly

● RECOMMENDATION

At one time letters and people *duly* arrived, cheques were *duly* sent, matters *duly* dealt with. *Duly* did nothing in such sentences, except make them sound starchy and important.

dwarfs / dwarves

● OPTION

Most dictionaries show *dwarfs* ✓ and *dwarves* as alternative plural forms.

dynamics *is / are*

● RECOMMENDATION

Treat *dynamics* as *singular*, whether it is used about Newtonian mechanics, or about human action: 'the dynamics of this policy *is* . . .'.

dyslexic / dyslectic

● RECOMMENDATION

Use *dyslexic* as the *descriptive word* ('a dyslexic student') and *dyslectic* for the *noun* ('the student is a dyslectic').

E

-eable / -able

See **-able** . . .

each

● **RULES**

1 When *each* comes *before* the word it relates to, it is *singular*: 'each of them *has* . . .'; 'each of the players *was* . . .'.

2 When *each* comes *after* the word it relates to, it is *plural*: 'they each *were* . . .'; 'London and New York each *have* many good restaurants'.

3 *Each one* is always *singular*: 'each one of the women *is* . . .'.

each and every

● **RECOMMENDATION**

While *each* or *every* is sufficient on its own, when we want to make something doubly clear, extra emphasis doesn't do any harm: 'visitors have to pay an entrance fee *each and every* time they come here'. But most of the time choose either *each* or *every*, and reserve *each and every* for when you want to thump the table. This also applies to *over and above*.

each other / one another

● **RECOMMENDATION**

There is no justification for the old rule that *each other* refers to *two* persons or things, and *one another* to *more than two*: we can say 'they love each other' *or* 'they love one another'.

● **CAUTION**

The possessive is *each other's* (not *each others'*): 'we like each other's friends'.

earned / earnt

● **RULE**

With the verb 'learn', there is a choice for the past form (see **learned / learnt**), but with 'earn' there is only one possible past form: *earned*.

Earth / earth / world

● **RULE**

The *Earth* refers to our planet in everyday contexts, and we talk about other *worlds* in outer space.

● RECOMMENDATIONS

1 *Earth* (with a capital *E*) is more appropriate in connection with the environment, and in astronomical and religious contexts: 'the Earth's natural resources'; 'the Earth orbits the sun'; 'The Earth is the Lord's'. Otherwise *earth* is more usual.

2 *World* is appropriate for human activities, international affairs, and in geographical and political contexts: 'All the world's a stage' (*As You Like It*); 'different regions of the world'; 'the leaders of the world'.

3 *Earth* is the more poetic word, and then usually with a capital *E*: 'the ends of the Earth'; 'heaven on Earth'; 'At the round Earth's imagined corners' (John Donne).

4 *World* is more materialistic: 'workers of the world'; 'all the money in the world'; 'the way of the world'.

5 It is a useful distinction in some contexts to use *Earth* for the planet we occupy and *earth* for soil or the ground: 'the Earth is affected by global warming', but 'the seed is buried in the earth'. This does not apply to familiar phrases, such as 'What on *e*arth. . . ?'; 'You look like nothing on *e*arth!'

See also **in the world / on earth.**

East / east

See **North / north . . .**

Eastern / eastern

● RULES

1 With a capital *E*, *Eastern* is often used about the spiritual teachings of India, China and Japan: Eastern religions.

2 With a small *e*, *eastern* is used for general direction, instead of 'east': eastern France; the eastern shores of a lake.

3 A capital or a small letter is used for the half of the world that includes Europe, Asia, and Africa: the Eastern (or eastern ✓) hemisphere.

4 The time zones in the eastern United States, eastern Canada and eastern Australia are known in those countries as Eastern Time.

● CAUTION

In some contexts *Eastern* can be ambiguous, as it could refer to the Near, Middle or Far East: it is better to avoid expressions, such as 'Eastern politics' or 'Eastern attitudes', and to choose a more specific description.

eastward / eastwards / easterly

See **northward . . .**

eatable / edible

● RULE

Edible means safe to eat ('an edible mushroom'); *eatable* implies that the taste is good enough. (Something that is *edible* may not be *eatable*, if it is badly cooked.)

● CAUTION

Not everyone makes this distinction, so there is a risk of misunderstanding. The distinction should always be observed for *inedible* and *uneatable* (see **inedible/ uneatable**).

-eau

For the plural form of words with this ending, see **French words ending in -***eau***.

EC/EEC/EU (European Union)

See **EU . . .**

ecology/environment

● RECOMMENDATIONS

1   *Ecology* should relate surroundings to living organisms, hence *botanical ecology* (the effect of changes in the environment on plants); *human ecology* (ways in which people are affected by the physical world around them).
2   *Environment* is a much less specific term: 'we live in a nice environment' usually means no more than a pleasant road. Generally, *environment* should be used for the *green* issues on the political agenda, keeping *ecology* as the more scientific or academic term.

economic/economical

● RECOMMENDATIONS

1   When it's cheap at the price, or at least good value, use *economical,* especially about everyday things.
2   For bigger or more important projects, *economic* is the more suitable word for something that is worth the expenditure for the benefits or savings it will bring.
3   *Economic* relates to *economics*, the science of the production and distribution of wealth (an *economic summit* is a conference of heads of states on international economy).

NOTE   Although the distinction in RECOMMENDATIONS 1 and 2 above can also apply to **un**economic and **un**economical, these words are used mostly about everyday things.

● OPTION

There is a choice of pronunciation of the first *e*, either *ee* ('eekoNOMic')✓, or like the *e* in 'egg' ('eckoNOMic').

economics *is/are*

● RECOMMENDATIONS

1   When it is the name for an academic theory or refers to the academic subject, treat it as *singular,* since it relates to 'the science of economics': 'economics *does* not always provide a solution to a political problem'.

2 When it concerns practical applications, it is usually *plural*: 'the economics of running a business *are* complicated'.

ecstasy / extasy
● RULE

It is always *ecstasy* (*extasy* is no longer an alternative spelling).

-ed
● RULES

1 With a very few verbs, used as descriptive words, *-ed* is pronounced as a separate syllable. The most common ones are learn-*ed* ('my learn-*ed* friend') and blessed ('a bless-ed event'). See **blessed / bless-ed; learned / learnt.**

2 After a *t* sound, *-ed* is pronounced separately: fat-*ed*; rat-*ed*; slat-*ed*.

edible / eatable

See **eatable** . . .

editor / editress
● RULE

Editor is now the standard unisex term.

editorial / leader
● OPTION

Either word can be used for the central article expounding a newspaper's policy on an issue. But *leader* ✓, short for 'leading article' has taken over as the standard term.

$ *Editorial* remains the more usual word.

editress / editor

See **editor** . . .

EEC / EC / EU (European Union)

See **EU** . . .

effect / affect

See **affect** . . .

effeminate / effete / feminine / girlish
● RULES

1 A man who minces, gestures or speaks in a feminine way is *effeminate*, and the word is always uncomplimentary.

2 A woman is never called *effeminate*: if she behaves in an particularly coy manner, she might be called *girlish*, also uncomplimentary. If she displays attractive womanly

qualities, she is *feminine*, a word generally used admiringly about a woman, but if used about a man, means much the same as *effeminate*.

3 *Effete* is used mostly about men, rarely about women, to mean weak, ineffectual, lacking in virility.

● CAUTION

For some women, *feminine* can, in certain contexts, be a condescending sexist word, used by some men to write down women. Attitudes between the sexes are passing through a period of transition and we can no longer take for granted previously accepted usage of some words.

eg / ie

● RULES

1 *eg* (Latin *exempli gratia*) is shorthand for 'for example', and is preceded by a comma: 'there is a wide choice on the menu, eg steak, trout and chicken'.

2 *ie* (Latin *id est*), also preceded by a comma, is shorthand for 'that is': 'there are only three dishes on the menu, ie steak, trout and chicken'.

● RECOMMENDATION

There's no need to use stops with these abbreviations.
See also **ie / viz**.

egocentric / egoistic / egotistic

● RECOMMENDATION

While there are subtleties of difference in the meanings of these three words, they are now used interchangeably to describe people who are full of themselves, conceited and self-centred. *Egocentric* is taking over as the more usual word.

● OPTION

The first syllable of all three words can be pronounced *ee* ✓or *e* (as in *egg*).

Eire / Southern Ireland

See **Ireland . . .**

either

● RULES

1 If *both* words after *either* are *singular, either* is also *singular*: 'either pilot error or mechanical failure *was* to blame'.

2 If *either* of the words is *plural, either* becomes *plural*: 'either the flight controllers or pilot error *were* to blame'.

3 In other sentences, the verb takes its cue from the *second* word related to *either*: 'either he or I *am* to blame'; 'either she or you *are . . .*'.

● RECOMMENDATIONS

1   Place *either* immediately before the words it refers to: 'we shall go to either Paris or Rome' makes the point better than 'we shall either go . . .'.

2   There is no need to restrict *either* to *two* choices, as is sometimes maintained: 'it is available in either red, blue, green or yellow'.

3   In spite of what some grammar books say, there's nothing wrong in using *either* as an alternative to *each,* about pairs of things: 'at *either* (or *each*) end of the table'.

4   Although it's not wrong, there's no need to repeat *at, for, in* or *of,* when one of those words precedes *either*: 'candidates must be fluent in either French, (in) German or (in) Spanish' (the second and third *in* can be omitted: '. . . in either French, German or Spanish').

● OPTION

　　PRON 'EYEther'✓ or 'EEther'.

$ PRON 'EEther'.

elapse / lapse

● RULES

1   Time *elapses*, that is passes by.

2   Customs and traditions *lapse*, that is fall into disuse. And insurance policies *lapse* if you don't pay the premiums.

elder / older / eldest / oldest

● RECOMMENDATION

　　There used to be rules about when *elder* and *older* should be used, but in practice now, it is easier to forget *elder* and *eldest*, and simply use *older* for one of two: 'the *older* of two brothers' and *oldest* for when there are more than two: 'the *oldest* of the three brothers'.

elderly / old

● CAUTION

　　While it's all right to have an *old* car, *old* friends, *old* wine, etc, some people consider it more polite to call people *elderly:* an elderly woman; my elderly father.

elementary / simple

● CAUTION

　　Do not use *elementary* as a pretentious word for *simple.* When something is easy to understand or easy to do, *simple* is the right word to use. *Elementary* has a place to describe first or basic steps: elementary German lessons; elementary precautions.

elision

　　Elision is the linguistic term for leaving out a letter (usually a vowel), as in *can't, haven't, isn't.*

NOTE There is no rule about when elisions can be used. For guidance, see **contracted forms.**

ellipsis

Ellipsis is the term for the linguistic device of a row of dots (usually three) to show that some words have been omitted. See **dots** (. . .).

emend / amend

See **amend** . . .

emigrant / immigrant

● RULE

When people are leaving their country to live in another, they are *emigrants.* When they arrive in the new country, they are *immigrants.*

● CAUTION

Immigrant has *two m*s.

empathy / sympathy

● RULE

Empathy is entering, in one's imagination, into someone else's feelings, or into the mood and style of literature, music or a painting. *Sympathy* is similar, but embraces compassion for suffering or distress.

NOTE *Sympathetic* is the descriptive word corresponding to *sympathy. Empathetic* also exists to describe a feeling of empathy, but is rarely used.

enclave

● RULE

An *enclave* is not an area where people are held prisoner, but part of a territory of one State entirely surrounded by another State. It can also be used for the people themselves, who are socially or ethnically apart from the people surrounding them. The word implies isolation as against integration.

● OPTION

Enclave is a French word, and some people preserve the French sound in the first syllable: '**AHN**clave'. It is more usual now to give it an English sound: '**ENN**clave'✓.

enclose / inclose

● RECOMMENDATION

Enclose things with letters. *Inclose* as a variant of *enclose* is more or less obsolete.

encyclopaedia / encyclopedia

● OPTION

Most dictionaries show *encyclopaedia* and *encyclopedia* ✓ as alternative spellings, and do not agree on which is preferred. See also **ae / oe.**

$ *Encyclopedia.*

ended / ending
● RECOMMENDATION
When it's a period in the future, use *ending*: 'the tax year ending April next year'.
When it's a period in the past, use *ended*: 'the tax year ended last April'.

endive / chicory
See **chicory** . . .

engage / consult / retain / appoint
See **appoint** . . .

English / British
See **British** . . .

engraving / etching / print
● RULES
1 *Engraving* can cover a variety of processes used for reproduction, such as woodcuts
   and linocuts. But in practice, an *engraving* is usually taken to mean a reproduction
   made from a metal plate, with the design incised by one of several different
   techniques.
2 An *etching* is specific: it is a type of engraving, where a print is made from a design
   bitten into a metal plate by means of acid.
3 *Print* is an umbrella word for any reproduction of a work of art by any process
   (including a *print* from a film negative).
● RECOMMENDATION
When in doubt, follow the tendency in the art world, which is to use *print* for any
kind of engraving or reproduction.

enough / sufficient / adequate
● RECOMMENDATIONS
1 Use the simple Old English word *enough* in preference to the Old French word
   sufficient.
2 *Adequate* carries with it the suggestion of 'just about enough' or 'just about good
   enough': 'one bottle of wine is *adequate* for four people' doesn't make it sound
   lavish; 'the wine is *adequate*' is hardly enthusiastic.
● CAUTION
There's no need to use *adequate* because it seems more polite than *enough*. It is
perfectly in order even for the best people 'to have had enough'.

enquire / inquire / enquiry / inquiry

● RECOMMENDATIONS

1 Use *enquire* and *enquiry* about obtaining information.

2 Use *inquire* and *inquiry* about an investigation in some depth.

$ *Inquire* and *inquiry* are preferred for all meanings.

ensemble (pronunciation)

● RECOMMENDATION

Make the last syllable rhyme with the last syllable of 'resem*ble*' ('ahnSAHMbul').

NOTE An *ensemble* is a collection of parts taken as a whole. It's used in English mostly about different items of women's clothes designed to be worn together, and in the artistic sense of a small group of musicians or actors performing together.

ensure / insure / assure

See **assure** . . .

enthral / enthrall

● RULE

Enthral (one *l*).

$ Usually *enthrall* (two *l*s).

envelope (pronunciation)

● OPTION

The pronunciation 'AHNvelope', still often used, is an echo from the time when the word was self-consciously French. BBC announcers are asked to say 'ENNvelope'✓.

enviable / envious

● RULE

People are *envious* because the qualities, possessions or achievements of another person are *enviable*: 'her success is enviable'; 'he is envious of her success'.

● CAUTION

Enviably and *enviously* are particularly easy to confuse: we look at someone *enviously* because they do something *enviably* well.

environment / ecology

See **ecology** . . .

ephemeral (pronunciation)

● OPTION

PRON 'ifFEMMeral'✓ or 'ifFEEMeral'.

The word means something that passes quickly, not lasting: 'an ephemeral pleasure'.

episcopalian / Anglican

See **Anglican** . . .

epoch

● CAUTION

An *epoch* is an event of such magnitude that things are never the same again. As with other portentous words, *epoch* is trivialised in journalism and advertising ('a new epoch in women's hairstyles'). This is even more true of *epoch-making*. Not many discoveries are as epoch-making as headlines would have us believe. They may be notable, important, significant, breath-taking, without being momentous and world-shattering, which is what *epoch-making* suggests.

epoch-making

See **epoch**

equally as

See **as** (RECOMMENDATION 3)

era / period / age

See **age** . . .

-erous / -rous

● RULE

The usual ending is *-erous*: boister*ous*; murder*ous*; slander*ous*. *Disast**rous*** and *wond**rous*** are the most common exceptions ('disast*erous*' and 'wond*erous*' are not alternative spellings).

Erse / Irish

See **Irish** . . .

ESP / parapsychology

See **parapsychology** . . .

especially / specially

● RECOMMENDATION

Make a distinction between *especially* and *specially*. Use *especially* to suggest something outstanding ('this is especially good'), or for something singled out (see example below under CAUTION). Use *specially* for something designed for a purpose: 'specially designed for handicapped people'.

● CAUTION

More especially uses two words when one does the job: 'there are problems with the company, more especially with the chairman'. Leave out 'more' and nothing is lost.

Esq

● RECOMMENDATION

Long ago, *Esquire* was a title of rank. Then it became a standard form of address on an envelope for any man. It is now long past its use-by date, and should be replaced by plain 'Mr' or just nothing: Mr John Brown or simply John Brown.

● CAUTION

It is wrong to use 'Mr' *and* 'Esq' ('Mr John Brown Esq').

-ess forms

● CAUTION

With animals, *-ess* forms are taken for granted, and no one feels that a lioness or a tigress is a substandard lion or tiger. But with humans, it is different. Many women feel that to be a something-or-other-*ess* is to sound like a second-class substitute for the male counterpart.

● RECOMMENDATIONS

1   Whenever possible, avoid *-ess* forms. After all, some have never existed, and we've managed without them: director; doctor; surgeon; solicitor; barrister; conductor (of an orchestra); prime minister.

2   **Actor** is standard in the theatre for both sexes, and *authoress, poetess, sculptress* are old-fashioned. Heads of departments in business are *managers*, whatever their sex, and no one ever goes to see their bank *manageress*.

3   Where it is necessary to identify sex, it is often preferable to refer to a 'woman director'; 'woman doctor'; 'woman barrister'. When such forms are used, refer in the same text to 'men doctors'; 'men barristers', to avoid any suggestion that a man in those occupations is the norm.

See also **feminine forms; -person / -man; unisex grammar.**

etc

Etc is the abbreviation for the Latin phrase *et cetera*, meaning 'and the other (things)'.

● RECOMMENDATIONS

1   In a list of items separated by commas, include a final comma before *etc*: 'the room was furnished with tables, chairs, bookshelves, etc'.

2   Even when there is only one item, still use a comma before *etc*: chairs, etc. (RECOMMENDATIONS 1 and 2 are not standard practice but the extra comma makes it easier for readers.)

3   The alternative *&c.* is old-fashioned and pointless.

4   Although *etc*, without a stop, looks wrong to some people, the prevailing practice is to omit it: 'there are tables, chairs, bookshelves, etc in the room'.

● CAUTIONS

1   It seems offhand to follow a list of *people* with *etc* (bishops, archdeacons, canons, etc), and preferable to use a phrase, such as 'and others (of the same kind)'.

2   Avoid using *etc* unnecessarily. Sometimes there's a case for giving a more or less

complete list of items, or a phrase that adds a further meaning: 'the room was furnished with tables, chairs, bookshelves and everything else required in a reading-room'.

3 When speaking, it's careless to slip into 'ex**SET**era', instead of 'et**SET**era'.

etching / print / engraving

See **engraving** . . .

ethics *is / are*

● RULE

As a branch of philosophy, *ethics* is *singular*. As a quality that someone manifests, or as a code of conduct, it is *plural*: 'their ethics *are* different from ours'. See also **-ics.**

EU / EC / EEC (European Union)

● RULES

1 On the basis of the Maastricht Treaty, the names *EC* (European Community) and *EEC* (European Economic Community) are superseded by *EU* (European Union), which is now the official name for the political and economic alliance of European countries.

2 *EC* remains as the abbreviation for the European Commission in Brussels, the executive body of the European Union.

Euro / Euro- / euro

● RECOMMENDATIONS

1 Most *Euro* combinations need not be hyphenated, and a number can begin with a small *e*: *eurobond* (a bond in eurocurrency); *eurocrat* (a member of the administration of the European Union); *eurocheque*; *eurocurrency*.

2 When the next word begins with a *vowel*, retain the hyphen: *euro-ad* (an advertisement designed to be used in all countries in the EU); *euro-economics*.

3 Use a hyphen and a capital *E* for *Euro-sceptic* (someone who is opposed to Britain forming closer links with the EU). The following also take a capital *E* (but no hyphen), because they are official names: *Eurostar* (the passenger train between Britain and mainland Europe); *Eurotunnel*; *Eurovision*.

Europe / the Continent

● CAUTION

If you talk about going to *the Continent*, every time you make the three-hour train journey from Waterloo Station to the Gare du Nord in Paris, you will sound like a Colonel Blimp. *Mainland Europe* is the usual way now to distinguish between the rest of Europe and the British Isles.

● RECOMMENDATION

Although *European* is still used as a descriptive word for anyone or anything belonging to the continent of Europe, excluding Britain, it is advisable now to reserve *European* as the political and economic term relating to the European Union.

NOTE The quaint expression '*continental* breakfast' lives on in British hotels – but it's only coffee and rolls.

European Community

See **EU** . . .

even

● RULE

The word *even* must be placed *immediately before* the word it refers to, because this affects the meaning. Take these three sentences:

i   I did not *even* see Mary yesterday.

ii   I did not see *even* Mary yesterday.

iii   I did not see Mary *even* yesterday.

The first suggests that although I had expected to have a conversation with Mary yesterday, I did not manage to see her at all. The second suggests that I saw no one yesterday, although normally I would have expected to see at least Mary. The third suggests that yesterday was the usual day when I expect to see Mary, but for some reason didn't see her.

● CAUTION

In *speaking*, the meaning can be conveyed by stressing the appropriate word: 'I did not even see Mary yesterday' could have any one of the above three meanings, depending on whether the stress is placed on *see*, *Mary*, or *yesterday*. But in *writing*, the difference of meaning is achieved only by placing *even* in the right place.

-ever

● RECOMMENDATION

There is a grammatical subtlety that keeps *ever* separate from a *wh-* word when it is part of a question ('Where ever did you find it?'), but it is better to follow the tendency now, which is to write *wherever*, *whatever*, *whoever*, etc as *one* word in every context. See also **forever** . . . .

-ever so

● CAUTION

Using *ever so* as an alternative to 'very', in order to stress a point, strikes a downmarket note. No matter how grateful you are, leave it at 'Thank you so much' rather than '. . . ever so much'; no matter how nice he is, stop at 'He's so nice', rather than '. . . ever so nice'.

every

● RULE

The verb after *every* should always be *singular*, even when a *plural* noun follows on: 'every one of the women *has* the right to vote'.

everybody

See **unisex grammar**

everyday / every day

● RULE

Every day as *two* words relates to a *verb* describing the regularity with which something happens. *Everyday* as *one* word comes before a *noun*, describing something that is unremarkable or routine. Milk is delivered *every day*, which makes it an *everyday* occurrence. See also **everyday / ordinary.**

everyday / ordinary

● RECOMMENDATION

The two words are similar in meaning. But an *ordinary* dress, *ordinary* wine, etc writes off the dress and the wine as dull and uninteresting. An *everyday* dress, an *everyday* wine does not dismiss them in the same way: it suggests that the dress or the wine may be quite pleasant, all right for those times when something special is not called for.

everyone / every one

● RULES

1 *Everyone* (*one* word) is for *people* in general: 'everyone turned up'.

2 Use *every one* (*two* words) for *a number of specific people*: 'every one of the bishops turned up'.

3 *Every one* (*two* words) is for *things*: 'every one of the glasses was broken'.

4 When required, should *everyone* be followed by 'his' or 'his or her'? For RECOMMENDATIONS, see **unisex grammar.**

ex- / late / former

● RULE

Before he died, Richard Nixon was an *ex*-president, or a *former* president of the United States. Now he's dead, he will be the *late* president for a few years, for *late* is used about someone who has died more or less recently.

● CAUTIONS

1 An *ex*- or a *former* whatever-it-is remains that for life. We cannot say, of John Major for example, he *was* a former foreign secretary. Even though he became prime minister, he *is* a former foreign secretary. Only after he is dead, can we say 'When he became prime minister, he *was* a former foreign secretary.'

2   When a woman or a man is talking about a husband or a wife who is no longer alive, no matter how long they have been dead, they remain 'my *late* husband' or '*late* wife' (*former* or *ex*-husband implies they are divorced).

except / excepting

● RULE

Excepting is used only in negative constructions: 'all the cabinet ministers were there, *not excepting* the Prime Minister'. This means the Prime Minister *was* present, otherwise it would be '. . . *except* the Prime Minister'.

● CAUTION

Not excepting phrases are awkward, and people can hesitate for a moment to be sure of the meaning. In the above example, '. . . including the Prime Minister', or '. . . even the Prime Minister' lays it clearly on the line.

● RECOMMENDATION

With the exception of has twice as many syllables as *except for*, so why use it?

exceptionable / exceptional / unexceptionable / unexceptional

● CAUTIONS

1   Surprisingly often something outstanding is described as *exception**able*** instead of *exception**al***. *Exceptionable* means something that can be objected to, that we can take exception to. But *exceptionable* should be used with care, since some people would misunderstand it and take 'this is exception**able**' (that is, we should object to it) to mean 'this is exceptional' (meaning 'outstanding').

2   The negative forms can also be confusing. *Unexception**able*** means there is nothing that can be criticised: *unexception**al*** means ordinary or unremarkable: 'the statement is unexception**able**' is praising it, because it means there's nothing wrong with it. But 'the statement is unexception**al**' is dismissing it as commonplace.

excitable / exciting

● RULES

1   *Exciting* describes someone or something that arouses excitement in others: 'the fight was exciting and had everyone on the edge of their seats'.

2   *Excitable* can be used only about *people* or *animals*, since it means easily becoming excited: 'she is excitable, so be careful how you speak to her'.

exclamation mark (!)

● RULES

1   Use an exclamation mark after a command, a fervent appeal, or an interjection: Stop!; Come here!; Help!

2   Use an exclamation mark after a word or short phrase said with strong emotion: Great!; How good this is!; I love you!

3   An exclamation mark is justified to show surprise or anger when this would not

obviously follow from the words themselves: 'He said *that* to you!'; 'It doesn't matter what you say!'

● CAUTIONS

1   At times it can be as wrong to omit an exclamation mark as to leave out a question mark after a question.

2   Avoid using an exclamation mark to show superiority, or as a heavy-handed way of telling a reader 'That's a joke, see?': 'He went to the Ritz in a T-shirt and jeans!'; 'A funny thing happened to me on the way to the opera!' The words in such statements work on their own, and an exclamation mark labours the point.

3   Using double (!!) or treble (!!!) exclamation marks is always over the top.

4   When there's a case for an exclamation mark, use one – but not often or they lose their impact.

$ The usual term for an exclamation mark is exclamation *point*.

exhausting / exhaustive

● RULES

1   *Exhausting* describes an activity that leaves you exhausted: 'the long journey was exhausting'.

2   *Exhaustive* describes a treatment of a subject that is thorough, detailed and comprehensive: 'he wrote an exhaustive account of what he had seen'.

exorbitant

● CAUTION

Look out for an intrusive *h* that can creep into this word ('ex*h*orbitant'), probably because of a mistaken association with 'exhort'. (Even *The Times* has commented on 'ex*h*orbitant interest charges'.)

expatriate / expatriot

● CAUTION

The word for someone who lives abroad is *expatri**ate***. (*Expatri**ot*** is not found in dictionaries, and could only mean someone who is no longer prepared to support or defend their country.)

expect / anticipate

See **anticipate** . . .

exquisite (pronunciation)

● OPTION

Stress on the *first* syllable ('EXquisite')✓ or the *second* syllable ('exQUIsite') is acceptable.

extasy / ecstasy

See **ecstasy** . . .

extended / extensive

● RULE

Extended is for something drawn out or added to, whereas *extensive* is long, wide-ranging, far-reaching: 'It was an extended assignment because the work was so much more extensive than anticipated.'

extension / extention

● CAUTION

There is no such word as 'extention': it is a spelling mistake. Remember 'extensive' and there should be no problem.

extensive / extended

See **extended** . . .

extention / extension

See **extension** . . .

exterior / external

● RECOMMENDATION

Exterior is appropriate where there is clearly a corresponding interior. *External* simply means outside. The *exterior* door, for example, could mean there is a double door, an inner door as well as an outer one; an *external* door is simply any outside door.

extraordinary

● CAUTION

The word has *five* syllables (not six), so the first *a* should not be pronounced: 'ekSTRAWdinery' (not 'eksTRA-AWdinary').

NOTE Placed *after* a noun, *extraordinary* may be used in diplomatic affairs for someone with a special assignment, such as an *envoy extraordinary*. It has also come to be used in that position, sometimes (but not necessarily) hyphenated, to imply exceptional distinction: Nelson Mandela, before his release, was referred to as a 'prisoner-extraordinary'.

F

façade / facade
● OPTION

The cedilla under the *c* is now optional in English: *façade* ✓ or *facade*. It indicates that the *c* has an *s* sound: 'faSAHD'.

face / confront
See **confront** . . .

facile
● CAUTION

Although *facile* means easy and without effort, it always carries with it the negative meaning of superficial and without real value: a facile argument is one that has not been thought out. Do not use *facile* in a complimentary sense.

factitious / fictitious
● RULES

1 Anything *factitious*, although seemingly genuine, is deliberately contrived for an ulterior motive: spreading a rumour about a takeover bid could create a factitious demand for shares, which would push up the price.
2 *Fictitious* is imaginary or untrue: 'a fictitious demand for shares' means there was no demand at all.

faith / religion
Both words reflect a system of beliefs concerning the purpose of life. But the distinction is fundamental.

● RECOMMENDATIONS

1 *Religion* usually refers to an organised external structure, with institutions proclaiming and regulating doctrines and ceremony.
2 *Faith* is essentially personal, an inner belief, which may or may not be linked to an established religion.

faithfulness / fidelity
See **fidelity** . . .

fallacy / falsehood
● RULES

1 *Fallacy* and *fallacious* should carry with them the suggestion of a wrong inference:

'it is a fallacy that high inflation leads to high unemployment'; 'the argument that low interest rates always leads to high inflation is fallacious'.

2 *Falsehood* (and *false*) is a deliberate attempt to mislead.

● CAUTION

Fallacy is often wrongly used to mean a falsehood, or even a lie, as in 'she was sacked, and it is a fallacy to say she resigned'. The word there should be *falsehood*.

fallout / fall out

● RULES

1 *Fall out* (*two* words) is the *verb*: to fall out with someone is to have a row or disagree with them.

2 *Fallout* (*one* word) is the *noun* for airborne radioactive debris from a nuclear explosion or an accident in a nuclear reactor. *Fallout* is also used for any kind of side-effect, good or bad: the 'literary fallout' from the war would mean the books written about it.

falsehood / fallacy

See **fallacy** . . .

false illusion

See **delusion** . . . (CAUTION 2)

(the) family *is* / *are*

See **collective words**

fantasy / phantasy

● OPTION

These are still alternative spellings: *fantasy* ✓ or *phantasy,* although the spelling *phantasy* is becoming obsolete.

faraway / far away

● RULE

Keep *far away* as *two* words ('the place is *far away* from here'), except as a descriptive word in front of a noun ('*faraway* places').

farther / further

● OPTION

Either can be used about *distance*: 'London is *farther* (or *further* ✓) from Rome than it is from Brussels.'

● RULE

When it comes to time, something additional, or symbolic distance, only *further* should be used: 'until further notice'; 'a further payment on account'; 'can we take this further?'

fathers-in-law / father-in-laws

● RULE

Fathers-in-law.

fawn / buff / beige

See **beige** . . .

fearful / fearsome

● RECOMMENDATIONS

1 *Fearful* is the usual word, always followed by 'of' or 'that': 'he is fearful *of* being made redundant'; 'she is fearful *that* he will get hurt'.

2 *Fearsome* is a more literary word, more applicable to appearance: 'a fearsome sight'; 'a fearsome ogre'.

fearless / unafraid

● RECOMMENDATIONS

1 *Fearless* describes the quality of being brave, without fear in the face of danger: 'she will do what she believes to be right, fearless of the risks involved'.

2 To be *unafraid* is a right that belongs to living in a civilised society, to be able to go about our daily life without fear of oppression, unfair discrimination, or violence.

See also **courage / fearlessness.**

fearlessness / courage

See **courage** . . .

fearsome / fearful

See **fearful** . . .

February (pronunciation)

● CAUTION

It is easy to slip into the sloppy pronunciation 'FEB*y*oo-ery', instead of 'FEB*r*oo-ery'.

feet / foot

● RULES

1 Use *foot* when it is hyphenated as a unit of measurement: 'a six-foot man'; 'a three-foot rule'.

2   Use *foot* in measurements, such as 'two foot three'. But when 'inches' follows, use *feet* (to correspond to the plural 'inches'): 'two feet, three inches'.

fellow/fellow-

● RECOMMENDATIONS

1   Hyphenate: fellow-countryman; fellow-creature; fellow-feeling; fellow-officer.
2   Keep as separate words: fellow author; fellow passenger; fellow sufferer; fellow soldier.

NOTE *Fellow traveller* are separate words for two people travelling together; the hyphenated form *fellow-traveller* is the now outdated term for a person who secretly supports the Communist Party.

female/woman/lady

See **lady** . . .

feminine forms

● CAUTION

Many people feel that to define women because of their sex is as discriminatory as defining them because of colour, race or religion, that 'woman barrister', 'lady doctor', 'headmistress' are as invidious as 'black barrister', 'Asian doctor', Jewish teacher'. The argument is that separate classification for women implies the standard is male, which is as wrong as suggesting the standard is white or Christian. For specific examples of controversial forms, see: **actor/actress; chairman/chairperson/the chair; -ess forms; he/they; headteacher/headmaster/headmistress; humankind/mankind; maiden/single name; Ms/Miss; -person/-man; spinster; unisex grammar.**

feminism/sexism

● RULES

1   *Feminism* is the stand taken by women against any form of discrimination because they are women.
2   *Sexism* is a masculine attitude, sometimes conscious, sometimes unconscious, that women are an inferior species.

feminist/sexist

● RULES

1   A *feminist* is a woman who actively campaigns for feminism: a *sexist* is a man guilty of sexism (see **feminism/sexism**).
2   Both words are used to describe people and attitudes: 'that's a feminist point of view'; 'that's a sexist remark'.

fête / fete

● RECOMMENDATION

Although there is a tendency to drop the circumflex (*fete*), because of the pronunciation ('**fayt**') it seems better to keep it in place: fête.

fewer / less

● RULES

1 Use *fewer* about *numbers* and when the associated noun is *plural*: 'fewer than seven men'; 'fewer miles to the gallon'.

2 Use *less* about *quantity*, when the associated noun is *singular*: 'more work for less money'; 'less butter means fewer calories'.

3 An exception is '*less* than 20 miles away' since '20 miles' is taken as a distance, rather than separate miles.

fewest / least

● RULE

See RULES 1 and 2 under **fewer / less.**

● CAUTION

Least is often used wrongly: 'he had the least votes of all the candidates' should be '. . . *fewest* votes . . .'.

fiascos / fiascoes

● RULE

Fiascos.

$ *Fiascoes.*

fictional / fictitious

● RECOMMENDATIONS

1 *Fictional* describes the imaginary: a character, event, place, etc that exists only in a novel, play or film. (*Fictitious* can also be used for say an imaginary country in a novel, but the word often carries with it the pejorative sense described in RECOMMENDATION 2, which is why *fictional* is preferred.)

2 *Fictitious* describes something that is false or untrue: 'his fictitious excuse didn't convince anyone'.

fictitious / factitious

See **factitious . . .**

fidelity / faithfulness

● RECOMMENDATION

Prefer *fidelity* to *faithfulness* for someone who never has sexual affairs outside marriage or another committed relationship. *Faithfulness* has become an old-fashioned word in that context.

fifth (pronunciation)

● CAUTION

It is easy and wrong to drop the second *f* and say 'fith'.

figures / numbers / numerals

● RULES

1 *Numerals* refers to the actual symbol used to represent a number: arabic numerals; roman numerals.

2 *Numbers* relates to specific things: house numbers; telephone numbers; the numbers on lottery tickets; the number of people unemployed.

3 *Figures* is applicable to statistics and accounts: unemployment figures; sales figures; 'the figures in the accounts'.

4 In writing, numbers can be expressed as *figures* or in *words* (*2000* or *two thousand*). The golden rule is *consistency*: whatever guidelines are followed, keep to them throughout the same piece of writing.

● RECOMMENDATIONS FOR USING FIGURES OR WORDS

1 Use *figures* for:
   i *Numbers over ten*: 'there are 11 men in the room'; 'classes in schools should not be more than 30'.
   ii *Time and other measurements*: 4 o'clock; 8°C; 5 per cent (or 5%); 3 km. But time and distance are better expressed in *words* when the precise figure is not being stressed: 'let's meet about six'; 'the house is about fifteen miles away'.
   iii *-year-old*: a 4-year-old girl, but 'my daughter is four years old'.
   iv *House numbers and most street numbers*: 10 Downing Street; 42nd Street. But see **2ii** below.
   v *Years*: 1066; 1999. (The title of George Orwell's novel *Nineteen Eighty-Four* is a rare exception.)

2 Use *words* for:
   i *Numbers below 11*: 'there are nine men in the room'; 'we need another three directors on the board'.
   ii *Fifth Avenue, Third Avenue*, etc, where avenue numbers are distinguished from street numbers (42nd Street), as in New York.
   iii *Legal contexts:* It is usual for figures to be expressed in both *words and figures* to make doubly sure.
   iv *Beginning of sentences*: Use *words,* if the sentence cannot be turned round to avoid it: 'Seventeen guests came to dinner' looks better than '17 guests . . .'.

3 *A series of related quantities* When there are two items, it is easier to follow when you use *words* for one set and *figures* for the other (this supersedes RECOMMENDATIONS

1 i and 2 i above): 'There are eight groups of 5 men, fifteen groups of 7 men and twenty-five groups of 9 men.'

4 *Separating thousands* The old rule was to mark off thousands with a comma (3,000; 60,500 . . .). The tendency now is to leave out the comma on figures from 1000 to 9999, and reserve commas for figures over 9999: 7277; 70,277. In scientific and foreign-language contexts, *spaces* should be used instead of commas: 10 000, 1 700 300.

5 *Millions* 7 million or 7m.

6 *Ranges* When writing about a *range* of figures or dates, a dash can often be used: 'Rows 18–21 are at the back'; William Somerset Maugham (1874–1965). But note these exceptions:

   i *Between* should be followed by *and*: 'Queen Victoria reigned *between* 1837 *and* 1901' (not '. . . between 1837–1901').

   ii *From* should be followed by *to* or *until* : 'all ages are welcome, *from* 18 *to* 80' (not '. . . from 18–80'); 'the war lasted from 1914 *to* (or *until*) 1918' (not '. . . from 1914–1918').

See also **billion / trillion; money.**

Filipino / Philippino

● RULE

Philippine describes anything to do with the Philippine Islands and their people, but anyone who comes from those islands is a *Filipino*.

   NOTE There is a feminine form, *Filipina*, but it doesn't come in for much use, since *Filipino* is the usual unisex word.

films / cinema / pictures

● RECOMMENDATION

To say you're going to the *pictures* is elderly. To say you're going to the *cinema* is middle-aged. People now go to a *film*, just as the critics are called *film* critics, and directors, cameramen and other technicians say they're 'in films' or 'the film industry'. *Cinema* remains the usual word for the place where films are shown.

$ Americans go to a *movie-theater* to see a *movie*, or if they want to be really formal about it, they see a *motion picture*.

filmscript / screenplay / scenario

● RECOMMENDATIONS

1 Use *filmscript* ✓ or *screenplay* for the script of a film. *Scenario* (PRON 'se(r)NAHrio') is a dated term.

2 *Scenario* is a trendy and pointless substitute for 'situation', as in 'faced with this scenario, he had to resign'.

$ *Screenplay* is the usual term. *Scenario* is pronounced 'se(r)NAIRrio'.

finance (pronunciation)

● OPTION

Either 'FINEance'✓ (stress on the *first* syllable) or 'finn-ANCE' (stress on the *second* syllable).

$ 'finn-ANCE'.

financial / fiscal / monetary

● RECOMMENDATIONS

1 Use *financial* as the everyday word in commercial and personal contexts: people have financial problems.

2 Use *fiscal* as a governmental term relating to public expenditure and taxation: governments have fiscal policies.

3 Treat *monetary* more as a specialised term in the context of economic theory or politics (monetary union).

fiord / fjord

See **fjord** . . .

first / last

See **former / latter** (RULE)

first, second . . . / firstly, secondly . . .

● OPTION

No one seems to mind whether it's *first* ✓, *second* ✓, *third* ✓. . . , or *firstly*, *secondly*, *thirdly* . . . .

first name / *Christian* name / *forename*

● RECOMMENDATION

Use *first* name (it may be out of place to ask someone for their *Christian* name, when their first name happens to be Isaac or Mohammed). *Forename* is still heard, but sounds old-fashioned, even biblical.

$ *Given* name is used for names other than the family name.

fiscal / monetary / financial

See **financial** . . .

fjord / fiord

● OPTION

Both *fjord* ✓ and *fiord* (PRON 'fyawd') are current spellings in English for this word taken from Norwegian, for a narrow inlet of sea between precipitous cliffs.

flaccid (pronunciation)

● OPTION

Either 'FLAKsid'✓ or 'FLASSid'.

flagrant / blatant

See **blatant** . . .

flammable / flameproof / inflammable / inflammatory

● CAUTION

Because of the *in-* prefix, *inflammable*, which means liable to catch fire, can be taken as meaning the opposite, that is *not* able to burn.

● RECOMMENDATIONS

1 Use *flammable* (rather than *inflammable*) for material that catches fire easily.

2 Reserve *inflammable* for people who are easily excited or angered: 'it was dangerous to make that speech in front of such an inflammable audience'.

3 The clearest way to describe material that cannot burn is *flameproof*.

● RULE

Inflammatory cannot be used in the literal sense of easily set on fire, only in a symbolic way about words, actions or a situation: 'his speech was inflammatory and the audience shouted with anger'.

flat / apartment

● OPTION

Apartment, the American word for a *flat* ✓, has become common in Britain, especially in London, although mostly for large and expensive flats.

● CAUTION

If you live in a modest bedsitter, it's pretentious to call it an *apartment*.

flaunt / flout

● RULES

1 *Flaunt* means to show off something, and implies arrogance: 'he flaunts himself in a Rolls-Royce'.

2 *Flout* means to disregard something or somebody openly and contemptuously: 'by publicly supporting a different policy, the ministers are flouting the decision of the Prime Minister'.

flautist / flutist

● RULE

While *flute* is the name of the instrument, *flautist* (PRON 'FLAWtist') is the name of the player.

$ *Flutist* (PRON 'FLOOtist').

fleshly / fleshy

● RULES

1   *Fleshy* is about the physical flesh, whether human or otherwise. Hands can be *fleshy*, that is plump and fat, so can fruit when the texture reminds you of flesh.

2   *Fleshly* can be used only about worldly, sensual tastes of human beings: 'he is too concerned with fleshly satisfactions to give much thought to things of the spirit'.

flier / flyer

See **flyer** . . .

floor / storey

● RULES

1   A *two*-storey house has living-rooms on the *ground* floor and bedrooms upstairs on the *first* floor. A *three*-storey building has a *ground* floor, *first* floor and *second* floor.

2   It is usual to refer to a ten-*storey* building when it's commercial, and a ten-*floor* building when it's residential, and to have a flat or office on the tenth *floor*, rather than on the tenth *storey*.

\$ The terms are more logical: the *ground* floor becomes what it really is, the *first* floor, with the *second* floor (British *first* floor) above it, and so on. As a result, the *top* floor of a 30–*story* (the spelling used in America) building in Manhattan is the *30th* floor, whereas in London it would be the *29th* floor.

flout / flaunt

See **flaunt** . . .

flush / blush

See **blush** . . .

flutist / flautist

See **flautist** . . .

flyer / flier

● OPTION

Both *flyer* ✓ and *flier* are used in connection with aviation. But when it's someone on their way up to the top, it's usually *high-flier*.

fo'c'sle / forecastle

See **forecastle** . . .

focused / focussed

● OPTION

The other forms of the *verb* can take a *double ss* or a *single s*: *focused* ✓ or *focussed* [!], *focusing* ✓ or *focussing* [!].

● RULE

The *plural* of the *noun* never takes a double *ss*: one focus, two *focuses*.

● CAUTION

The alternative plural *foci* (PRON 'FOHsi') is so uncommon now that it might not be understood.

follows / follow

See **as follows** . . .

foot / feet

See **feet** . . .

foot / foot-

● RULE

Nearly always when *foot* is combined with another word, the compound has become *one* word and there is no hyphen: football; foothills; foothold; footlights; footbath; footbrake; footbridge; footprint; footstep; footnote. Some exceptions are a foot-fault in tennis; foot-rule; foot-soldier.

forbear / forebear

● RULES

1 *Forbear* (PRON 'forBEAR' with the stress on the *second* syllable) is the *verb* (*forbore* is the past form), meaning restrain, hold back from: 'please forbear from interrupting until I have finished'.

2 *Forebear* (PRON 'FORbear' with the stress on the *first* syllable) is the noun, meaning an ancestor: 'some of his forebears were parliamentarians'.

forceful / forcible

● RULE

Forceful is possessing force: *forcible* is using it physically. An argument or a person can be *forceful*, meaning powerfully persuasive, but it takes an *action* to be *forcible*. 'A *forceful* entry' is someone entering a room with presence and making an impact: 'a *forcible* entry' is breaking in (usually called a 'forced entry').

forecastle / fo'c'sle

● RECOMMENDATION

The spelling *fo'c'sle*, for the forward part of a ship, is best left to Horatio Hornblower. *Forecastle* is the standard spelling. Either way, the pronunciation is 'FOHKsl'.

forego / forgo

See **forgo** . . .

forehead (pronunciation)

● OPTION

'FORRid'✓ or 'FOREhead'.

forename / Christian name / *first* name

See *first* name . . .

forever / for ever

● RECOMMENDATION

Treat *for ever* as *two* words when it means for all time: 'I will love you for ever.' Treat it as *one* word when it means persistently: 'he's forever saying that'.

$ *Forever* is always *one* word.

foreword / preface / introduction

● RECOMMENDATIONS

1 Use *foreword* when it's a short note, written by someone other than the author, at the beginning of a book.

2 Use *preface* when the introductory note is written by the author of the book.

3 Use *introduction* for a longer and more detailed essay at the beginning of a book, written with the purpose of helping readers to approach the book in the way the author intended.

● CAUTION

Don't mix up *foreword* with *forward* (*foreword* clearly describes *words* that come *before*).

forgo / forego

● RULES

1 As a *verb*, the word is *forgo*, meaning to do without something: 'he will forgo a holiday this year'. (The alternative spelling *forego* is more or less obsolete.)

2 The spelling *forego-* is found mostly in the descriptive words *foregoing* and *foregone*: 'a foregone conclusion' is a result that can be seen in advance.

former / late / ex-

See **ex-** . . .

former / latter

● RECOMMENDATION

Resist the temptation to overuse *former* and *latter* to save yourself trouble. They oblige readers to look back to see which is the *former* and which is the *latter*. In *speech*, keep in mind that listeners have to remember which is which, while the speaker goes on talking.

● RULE

Former and *latter* can only be used for one of *two* things previously mentioned. If there are three or more, *first* or *last* are required.

formidable (pronunciation)

● OPTION

Stress the *first* syllable ('FORmidable')✓ or the *second* ('forMIDable'). [!]

formulae / formulas

● OPTION

Mathematicians and scientists are more likely to say *formulae* (PRON 'FORmulee') for more than one formula. Otherwise it is more usual to say *formulas* ✓.

forte

● RULE

Forte (PRON 'FAWtay') is an all-purpose word for anything a person is good at: 'his forte is his ability to think clearly in a crisis'.

forthwith / straightaway / immediately

See **immediately** . . .

forward / forwards

● RECOMMENDATIONS

1   When there is a physical movement, use *forwards*: 'the car moved slowly forwards'.
2   Look *forward* to something, bring *forward* a date, and use *forward* as a descriptive word in front of a noun: 'forward price' (a price fixed for buying or selling at a future date).
3   When it comes to *forward* as a *verb*, it is commercial jargon to *forward* anything to anyone, unless it means redirect it to a new address. Otherwise, just *send* it.

for / in years

● OPTION

Either will do: 'she hasn't seen him *for* ✓ years (or *in* years)'.

$ *In* years.

four-letter words

These words are a deep-seated sociolinguistic fetish, loaded with double standards. They are given full frontal exposure in dictionaries, many books, in most newspapers, and on radio and television. Eric Partridge, a respected lexicographer, considered that some of these words 'belong to the aristocracy of the language'. Yet alongside all that, a lot of people regard such words as offensive.

● OPTION

We have to decide for ourselves when we should avoid these words altogether, when to cast a coy typographical veil of dots or asterisks over them (f . . . k; c***), or when we should use the language that belongs to us in ways that are natural and appropriate to the situation and context.

● CAUTION

Four-letter words can still give great offence, so even when the context justifies spelling them out in full, look out for the shock waves.

fraction / percentage / proportion

● RECOMMENDATIONS

1   A *fraction* of something could logically be a *small* or a *large* part, although it would usually be taken to mean a *small* part. But when that is intended, make it extra clear by preceding *fraction* by 'only': 'only a fraction of the debt has been repaid'.

2   A *percentage* of something is so vague as to be almost useless. If the precise figure cannot be given, at least it should be defined as a 'small' or 'large' percentage. See also **per cent / percentage.**

3   *Proportion* properly relates a quantity to the whole: '£3000 a year for rent is too high a proportion out of an income of £12,000'.

framework / setting / context

See **context** . . .

freelance / freelancer

● OPTION

The orthodox form is *freelance* ✓ but so many people have come to add an -*r* , that current dictionaries now show *freelancer* as an alternative.

French names ending in -s and -x

● RECOMMENDATION

For the possessive form in English of French names ending in -*s* or -*x*, add 's in writing, but do not pronounce the final *s*. For example, write Alexandre Duma*s's* novels; Delacroi*x's* paintings; but say 'DJOOmaz' novels; 'DELLer-crwahz' paintings.

French words ending in -eau

● OPTION

In English, the plural of *gateau; plateau;* etc, can be formed by adding -*s* (*gateaus; plateaus*), or in the French way with an -*x* (*gateaux; plateaux*)✓.

PRON Either way, the words are pronounced with a final *z* sound ('GATohz'; 'PLATohz').

fresh / renewed / new

See new . . .

frisson

● RULE

To refer to a 'slight' *frisson* is wrong. A *frisson* (PRON 'FREEsonn') is always slight, a tremor of nervous excitement that someone or a group of people experience.

-ful (plural forms)

● RULE

Spoonfuls, handfuls, roomfuls (not 'spoonsful', 'handsful', 'roomsful').

fulfil / fulfill

● RULE

Fulfil, fulfilled, fulfilling, fulfilment.

$ Fulfi**ll**, fulfi**ll**ment.

full stop / period / stop

See stop / full stop . . .

furore (pronunciation)

● RULE

A *furore* (meaning an uproar) has *three* syllables: 'fewRAWree'.

$ The spelling is *furor* (PRON 'fewRAW').

further / farther

See farther . . .

future

● CAUTIONS

1   *Future* has a way of creeping in when it's not wanted: 'he would not reveal his future intentions'; 'what are their future prospects?'; 'their future plan is to live in New Zealand'. Leave out the word *future* from those sentences and the meanings remain unaltered.

2   'In the near future' and even worse, 'in the not too distant future' are pompous officialese, which should be replaced by 'soon' and 'before very long' respectively.

G

Gaelic/Gallic/Celtic/Celt
See **Celt** . . .

gage/gauge
See **gauge** . . .

gainsay
● CAUTION

Gainsay means to go against or deny. But the trouble is that if you write or say something 'cannot be *gainsaid*', a lot of people will be uncertain what you mean. It's safer to write or say 'it cannot be denied' or 'we cannot go against that'.

gale/cyclone/hurricane/tornado/typhoon/blizzard
See **blizzard** . . .

galleys/proofs
See **proofs** . . .

Gallic/Gaelic/Celtic/Celt
See **Celt** . . .

gambit
● RECOMMENDATIONS

1   An opening move in chess where you sacrifice a piece to secure an advantage is a *gambit*. A calculated move in any situation, that makes things go your way, can be called a clever or shrewd gambit.
2   Use 'an opening gambit' (even though it is argued that 'opening' is unnecessary, since a *gambit* is an opening move) for a preliminary comment calculated to win support.
3   Do not use *gambit* for any clever remark: *gambit* should be related to an attempt to secure an advantage.

gaol/jail/prison
See **prison** . . .

garage (pronunciation)

● RECOMMENDATION

    PRON 'G**Ar**ahj' ('GArij', the alternative pronunciation shown in some dictionaries, is considered sloppy by many people).

$ Stress on the *second* syllable: 'gaRAHJ'.

gâteau / gateau

● OPTIONS

1 While no one could say that a circumflex (*â*) is wrong, Oxford dictionaries now show the word as *gateau* ✓, without a circumflex in sight.

2 The plural can be either *gateaux* ✓ or *gateaus* (either way PRON 'GATohz'). See also **French words ending in -*eau.***

gauge / gage

● RULE

    As a *noun* for a measuring instrument, or a *verb* meaning to measure or calculate, the spelling is *gauge*. (*Gage* is a rarely used word for something deposited as a security.)

$ Usually *gage*.

gay / lesbian

● RECOMMENDATIONS

1 *Gay* is the standard noun and descriptive word for a homosexual.

2 Although the expression 'gay women' is heard, *gay* is primarily associated with men, and *lesbian* remains the usual word for women.

gender / sex

● RECOMMENDATIONS

1 *Sex* should be used for the physical and statutory aspects of differences between women and men: 'sex is shown on birth certificates'; 'students of either sex can be admitted'.

2 When the word *sex* seems out of place, *gender* is an alternative word, especially for social and psychological differences: 'Margaret Thatcher's gender did not diminish her authority as Prime Minister.'

3 *Gender* can be useful when *sex* could have a double meaning: 'As chairperson, her gender caused resentment among the other directors.'

4 See whether 'woman' or 'man' fits in better than either *sex* or *gender*: 'she finds that being a woman makes the other directors listen to her more sympathetically' (instead of 'she finds that her sex makes the other directors . . .').

5 Guard against using *gender* as a coy or prudish alternative to *sex*: 'she enjoys the company of someone of the opposite gender'. When in doubt over which word to use, *sex* is usually preferable.

General American

This is the term used in linguistics that corresponds to *standard English* in Britain (see **British English / standard English**). See also **American English / Americanisms**.

genetic / hereditary / congenital

See **congenital** . . .

genius

● CAUTION

Be careful about using the word *genius* for mere aptitude or talent, as in 'she has a genius for making soufflés'. If we use it that way, what word do we have left for a Mozart or an Einstein? See also **great.**

gentleman / man

See **man** . . .

genuine / real / authentic

See **authentic** . . .

geo-

Geo- relates to the earth, which is a useful guide to the meaning of some words: *geobotany* (the distribution of plants throughout the earth); *geophysics* (the study of physical forces relating to the earth, which includes meteorology and oceanography); geopolitics (the effect of the features of the earth's surface on politics).

● CAUTION

Give the prefix *geo- two* syllables: it is 'jeeOGraphy' (not 'JOGraphy'); 'jeeOMetry' (not 'JOMetry').

geographic / geographical

● OPTION

Geographic and *geographical* ✓ have the same meaning.

geometric / geometrical

● OPTION

Although both spellings are possible, architects and designers usually refer to *geometric* ✓ features and *geometric* patterns, rather than *geometrical.*

germ / microbe / bacteria / virus

● RECOMMENDATIONS

1	In ordinary non-medical use, it is reasonable to use *germ* or *microbe* about micro-organisms that cause diseases, with the reservation that *germ* is also used for harmless living seeds that contribute to good health, such as *wheatgerm.*

2 *Bacteria* should be kept as a general-purpose word for all micro-organisms, specifying when necessary whether they are dangerous or harmless.

3 *Virus* needs to be used more cautiously by people without medical knowledge. It is used mostly in relation to certain epidemic diseases.

● RULES

1 To call the disease itself a *virus* ('he is suffering from a virus') is the wrong use of the word.

2 *Bacteria* is the plural of *bacterium*, the singular form, and should always be followed by the *plural* form of the verb: 'the bacteria in the water *are* dangerous'.

gibe / jibe / gybe

● OPTION

Gibe ✓ and *jibe* are alternative spellings both for the *verb*, meaning to jeer or taunt, or the *noun*, meaning a provocative taunting remark.

● RULE

Gybe is the spelling for the term meaning a change of tack when the wind is behind the centre line of the boat, catching the sail on the wrong side and making it jump across.

$ *Gibe* is the only spelling for all the above meanings. (*Jibe* is another word, a conversational word meaning to fit in or agree with something: 'Your information jibes with what I've heard.')

gift (verb)

● CAUTION

Gift should be used as a *verb* only when it covers a formal gift of money or property for tax reasons or other statutory purposes. In other contexts, it is pointless to use *gift* as an alternative to the usual verb *give*.

gigantic / huge / vast / colossal

See **colossal** . . .

girl

● CAUTION

Although it is a long-established custom to talk about *women* as *girls*, there are many women who find this sexist. They argue that we would not usually call a man over 18 a *boy*, so why call a woman a *girl*, with its belittling implication of immaturity and lack of importance. In the 1990s, about 17 is the age that separates a *girl* from a *woman*.

girlfriend / partner / boyfriend

See **boyfriend** . . .

girlish / boyish

See **boyish** . . .

given name

See *first* name . . . ($)

glueing / gluing

● OPTION

Dictionaries allow both *glueing* ✓ and *gluing*.

God / god

● RULES

1   In religious services or prayers, *God* is always spelt with a capital G. This also applies
    when God refers to the supreme being of monotheistic religions: Thank God!; God
    knows; God forbid!; God bless you!
2   When *god* is used in other ways, or refers to a number of gods, a small *g* is
    appropriate: 'money is his god'; 'she treats him like a god'; 'Thou shalt have no other
    gods before me!'

goddaughter

● RULE

Double *d*, no hyphen: *goddaughter*.

gold / golden

● RULES

1   It's *gold* when it describes an object made of the yellow metal: a gold coin; a gold
    ring.
2   It's *golden* when it is used for the colour or quality of gold, or in a symbolic sense:
    golden age; golden moment; golden hair.

got

● RECOMMENDATION

'I haven't got it in stock' is more down-to-earth; 'I don't have it in stock' is more
formal. With that difference in mind, use *got* whenever it suits you.

$ 'I haven't got . . .' is rare, as it's usually 'I don't have . . .'. *Gotten* is retained in the
sense of 'obtain': 'I have gotten it for you.'

gourmand / gourmet

● RULE

A *gourmand* (PRON 'GOORmahn(d)') eats like a pig: a *gourmet* (PRON 'GOORmay')
also enjoys food, but eats with discrimination.

● CAUTION

It may be considered a compliment to call someone a *gourmet*, but it's always an insult to call them a *gourmand*.

Government / government
● RECOMMENDATION

Except in formal contexts or the phrase 'Her Majesty's Government', use a small *g*.

● CAUTION

The relaxed attitude in the above recommendation should not affect the pronunciation, and it's careless not to sound the *n* in the second syllable: 'GUVer**n**ment'.

(the) **government** *is / are*
● RULE

Usually *government* is treated as *singular* (the government *is* . . .), as a collective body making laws.

graffiti *is / are*
● RULE

Graffiti (PRON 'graFEEtee') is *plural*: 'the graffiti *are* . . .'. (The singular form *graffito* is not often used in English.)

gram / gramme

See **metric measurements**

grammatical terms
● RULES

It is useful to be clear about what are referred to as the eight *parts of speech*, for one of these terms applies to nearly every word we use, and they provide a useful basis for talking about language.

1 A *noun* is a word for a person, an object, a place, an action, a concept: *woman*; *book*; *town*; *walking*; *imagination*. (See also **nouns**.)
2 A *verb* is a word for action or doing: *walk*; *talk*; *think*; *love*.
3 An *adjective* is a descriptive word: *good*; *bad*; *large*; *small*; *beautiful*.
4 An *adverb* is to a verb what an adjective is to a noun, that is it describes an *action*: to walk *slowly*; to think *quickly*; to do *well*.
5 A *pronoun* takes the place of a noun. The most common ones are *she*, *he*, *it*: 'I saw the woman as *she* left the house'; 'the train was late but *it* arrived eventually'. (See also **pronouns**.)
6 A *preposition* is a word expressing the relationship between two other parts of speech: 'she went *into* the house'; 'he stood *before* her'; 'wine goes well *with* cheese'. (See also **prepositions at *end* of sentences**.)

7 A *conjunction* links two words or two groups of words together. The most common one is *and*: 'Jack *and* Jill went up the hill'; 'Jack is clever *but* Jill is beautiful'; 'Do you want tea *or* coffee?' (See also **and**.)

8 An *interjection* is anything from a howl (*Ouch!*), to a greeting (*Hello!*), to any word used to express irritation, frustration or any other emotion (*Oh dear!*; *Ha! Ha!*). A more logical term is *exclamation*, since interjections are always followed by *exclamation marks*. (See also **exclamation mark**.)

grandad / granddad / granddaughter / grandmother . . .

● OPTION

Grandad ✓or *granddad*.

● RULES

Granddaughter and *goddaughter* retain the double *d* but do not require a hyphen.

PRON It's not necessary to make the effort to pronounce the *-d-* in *grandmother*; *grandfather*; *grandson*; *grandchild*: it's in order to say 'GRANmother'; 'GRANfather'; etc.

grass / dope / hashish / pot / marijuana / cannabis

See **cannabis** . . .

gratuitous

● RULES

1 There are *two* senses of the word, one is for something done without charge, the other for something altogether uncalled for.

2 *Gratuitous*, in the sense of uncalled for, is always used about unpleasant things. A *gratuitous remark* would be taken to mean an unnecessary insult or criticism; *gratuitous damage* to property and *gratuitous acts of violence* are without justification.

gravy / sauce

● RULES

1 *Gravy* applies only to meat: it is properly used for the juices coming from a joint of meat during cooking, usually thickened with flour.

2 *Sauce* implies that it has been prepared from various ingredients to add flavour to any dish – meat, fish, vegetables . . . , even sweet dishes.

● CAUTION

The use of *sauce* for impudence or cheek, and *saucy* for a sexual innuendo, both common at one time, are now dated.

gray / grey

See **grey** . . .

great

● RECOMMENDATION

As a descriptive word, *great* should be reserved for real giants: Shakespeare; Newton; Beethoven. It is too valuable a word to be squandered on someone of modest achievements. This applies less to *greats* as a plural *noun,* as in 'the Hollywood greats'. See also **genius.**

Great Britain / United Kingdom / British Isles / Britain

See **Britain** . . .

Greek / Grecian / Hellenic

● RULES

1 *Greek* is the usual word for the people, language, food, wine, islands.

2 *Grecian* is retained for architectural elements (Grecian columns); archaeological finds (Grecian urns); facial features (Grecian noses) and a few other specialised uses.

3 *Hellenic* (PRON 'heLENNik') is the word related to *Hellenism* (PRON 'HELLinizm'), the spirit and culture of ancient Greek civilisation: a tour of the archaeological sites in Greece can be called a *Hellenic* tour, a cruise round the Aegean, focused on history and art, a *Hellenic* cruise.

grey / gray

● RULE

The accepted spelling now is *grey*.

$ *Gray*.

grill / grille

● RULES

1 *Grill* is the only possible spelling for the appliance or part of a cooker that grills meat, fish, etc.

2 *Grille* is the usual spelling for the latticed metal screen erected for security.

grisly / grizzly

● RULES

1 *Grisly* means gruesome and ghastly: 'a grisly apparition'.

2 *Grizzly* is grey-haired, now used more about bears than people.

ground / grounds

● OPTION

We can have *grounds* ✓ or *ground* for complaint, *grounds* ✓ or *ground* for suspicion, *grounds* ✓ or *ground* for satisfaction.

(the) **group** *is / are*

See **collective words**

growth

● RECOMMENDATION

Growth has to be something getting *bigger*. The expression 'negative growth' is turning the word upside down. There are good alternatives, such as 'reduction', or those simple words 'drop' and 'fall'.

guarantee / guaranty

● RECOMMENDATION

Use the spelling *guarantee* both as a *noun* and a *verb*.

guesstimate / guestimate

● RECOMMENDATION

Spell it with *-ss-* to make it look more like a *guess* than an estimate.

gunwale / gunnel

The *gunwale* (or *gunnel*) is the top edge of the side of a ship (the word relates to its use at one time to support guns).

● OPTION

Sailors usually prefer the spelling *gunwale* ✓, but *gunnel* is an accepted alternative. PRON 'GUNNe(r)l' (whatever the spelling).

gutsy

● CAUTION

This conversational word has two meanings: gluttonous and greedy, or full of courage. Make sure the context makes it perfectly clear which is intended.

gybe / jibe / gibe

See **gibe** . . .

gymnastics *is / are*

See **-ics**

gynaecologist / obstetrician

● RULES

1 A *gynaecologist* treats diseases and malfunctions of the breasts and genital organs of women.

2 An *obstetrician* does not necessarily deal with diseases, but looks after a woman during pregnancy and childbirth.

NOTE Although *obstetrician* is in common use in hospitals, it is a term that has become less familiar to many people, and *gynaecologist* is the name often preferred for a specialist who looks after the functioning of women, whether or not they are pregnant.

$ The spelling is *gynecologist*.

gypsy / gipsy

● OPTION

Both *gypsy* ✓ and *gipsy* are accepted spellings.

● RULE

When the people or their language is meant, a capital *G* is appropriate, but not when the word is used in a figurative way, as in 'a gypsy way of life'.

H

haggle / wrangle

● RULES

1 *Haggle* involves money, when someone argues over the price and tries to get it reduced. Although it exists as a *noun*, it is more likely to be used as a *verb*: 'although they had agreed the price, they haggled over the bill'.

2 *Wrangle* is any kind of argument or dispute. Although it exists as a *verb*, it is more likely to be used as a *noun*: 'there was a long wrangle about whether a man or a woman should be appointed'.

half

● OPTIONS

1 Which is correct: 'three metres and a half' or 'three and a half metres'; 'a year and a half' or 'one and a half years'? In such cases either will do, but 'three and a half metres'✓; 'one and a half years'✓ are easier to take in.

2 It can be 'half a dozen'✓ or 'a half-dozen'.

● RULE

When there is 'one and a half' of anything, the *noun* is in the *plural* but the *verb* in the *singular*: 'one and a half weeks *is* long enough'; 'one and a half litres *is* all that's left'.

● CAUTION

Watch out for an unnecessary *a* creeping in before 'half a(n)': 'it will take *a* half an hour'; 'it weighs *a* half a ton'. The *a(n)* before *half* has no place in such sentences: 'it will take half an hour'.

For combining *half* with other nouns, see **half / half-**.

half / half-

● RECOMMENDATIONS

Halfback; half-baked; half-blue (for sports at Oxford and Cambridge); half-brother and half-sister; half cock but half-cocked; half-dozen; half-hearted; half-hour; half-light; half-mast; half measures; half moon; half-past seven, etc; *half-price* before a noun, *half price* after a noun (a half-price ticket, but a ticket for half price); half-term; half-time; half-tone; half-truth; halfway; halfwit.

half-caste / mulatto / Creole

● CAUTIONS

1 *Half-caste* is considered racist. (It was used mostly by the British Raj in India about a child of a European father and an Indian mother.)

2 Although *mulatto*, for a child of black and white parents, is not derogatory, it is not generally liked. In the highly sensitive area of racist words, 'of mixed parentage' is a more acceptable alternative.

3 *Creole* (not always with a capital) is used about people in confusing ways. In general, it is safer to use *Creole* (spelt with a capital) for someone of European (usually Spanish) descent, born in the West Indies or Central or South America. For the linguistic meaning of *Creole*, see **pidgin / Creole.**

hallelujah / alleluia

See **alleluia** . . .

hallmark / benchmark

See **benchmark** . . .

hallo / hullo / hello

See **hello** . . .

hamlet / village

See **village** . . .

(*at / on / to*) **hand**

● RULES

1 *To hand* is used after the verb *come*: 'he used it because it came to hand'.

2 *At hand* is used about an event, meaning that it is about to happen: 'victory is at hand'.

3 *At hand* or *on hand* are used about a person: 'she is *at* (or *on*) hand'.

4 *Hands-on* is the fashionable descriptive term for being actively involved: 'the chairman is adopting a hands-on approach to the problem'.

handbook / manual

● RECOMMENDATIONS

1 *Manual* is the usual word for instruction books for operating a machine: cars and computers are supplied with manuals.

2 *Handbook* is the usual word for a reference book of displayed information on a particular subject: *The Writer's Handbook*, for example, gives lists of publishers, newspapers, magazines, etc.

handfuls / handsful

See **-ful**

handkerchiefs / handkerchieves

● OPTION

Some dictionaries show *handkerchiefs* ✓ and *handkerchieves* as alternative plural forms.

PRON The last syllable is 'chiffs' (whatever the spelling).

hanged / hung

● RULES

You *hang* a picture or wallpaper, *hang* your coat up, and an executioner can *hang* a person. If it happened yesterday, the picture and the coat were *hung*, the person was *hanged.*

hang-up / inhibition / block

See **block** . . .

harass (pronunciation)

● OPTION

Dictionaries now show stress on the *first* or *second* syllables as alternatives: 'HARass'✓ or 'haRASS'. [!] The same applies to *harassment*: 'HARassment' ✓ or 'haRASSment'. [!]

$ Stress on the *second* syllable: 'haRASS'; 'haRASSment'.

hardly / scarcely / barely

See **barely** . . .

hashish / pot / dope / grass / marijuana / cannabis

See **cannabis** . . .

haven't

See **contracted forms**

he or she

● RECOMMENDATION

The phrase *he or she* becomes laboured when it is used too often in contexts where a statement applies to either sex. If it is used more than once in a paragraph, at least keep the balance by occasionally changing the order to *she or he.* See **he / they**, and for further RECOMMENDATIONS, see **unisex grammar.**

he / they

● CAUTION

A problem arises in a sentence such as 'No one expects you, does *he* (or do *they*)?' The trouble with *he* is it could seem to exclude women: the problem with *they* is it is plural following the singular 'no one'. For RECOMMENDATIONS, see **unisex grammar**.

headmaster / headmistress / headteacher

See **headteacher** . . .

headquarters *are / is*

● OPTION

We can choose between headquarters *are* ✓ or *is*.

headteacher / headmaster / headmistress

● RECOMMENDATION

Use *head**teacher*** for the heads of most schools, but retain *head**master*** and *head**mistress*** for the heads of famous public schools (headmaster of Eton; headmistress of Benenden).

heart attack / stroke / coronary

See **coronary** . . .

heath / moor

As topographical words, there is nothing much to distinguish between a *heath* and a *moor*, as both are rough uncultivated uplands, usually covered with rough grass and shrubs.

● RECOMMENDATION

Heath is the more general word, while moor is particularly associated with Yorkshire and Scotland, as well as being the word for shooting reserves (*grouse moors*, for example).

heaved / hove

● RULES

Heavy objects are *heaved* about, and sighs are *heaved*. It is different at sea, where 'the boat was *hove* to' (brought to a standstill) or another ship '*hove* into sight'. But even at sea, anchors are *heaved* overboard.

Heaven / heaven

● RULE

When *heaven* is another word for God, use a capital: for **H**eaven's sake; in **H**eaven's name. But not otherwise: move **h**eaven and earth.

he'd

See **contracted forms**

he'd *have* / she'd *have* / you'd *have* / I'd *have*

See **I'd *have*** . . .

Hellenic / Grecian / Greek

See **Greek** . . .

hello / hallo / hullo

● OPTIONS

No one should make a fuss if you write *hello* ✓, *hallo* or *hullo*, or if you say 'he(r)LOH'✓, 'haLOH' or 'huLOH'.

hemi- / semi- / demi-

See **demi-** . . .

here- words

● RECOMMENDATION

Herein, hereof, hereto, hereunder, herewith and so on are heavy-going words and should be avoided in everyday writing and speaking. (These words sometimes have a place in formal or legal contexts.)

hereditary / genetic / congenital

See **congenital** . . .

hero / heroine

● RECOMMENDATION

Use *hero* for both sexes. [!]

● RULE

The plural is *heroes* (not 'heros').

Herr / Frau / Fräulein

When Germans are in Britain, do we introduce them as *Herr* Schmidt, *Frau* Brandt, etc, or *Mr* Schmidt, *Mrs* (or *Ms*) Brandt?

For RECOMMENDATIONS, see **Mr, Mrs . . . / Monsieur, Frau** . . .

hers / her's

● RULE

Her's is *always* wrong, since *hers* is already a possessive word.

hiccup / hiccough

● RECOMMENDATION

Even though some dictionaries show *hiccough* as an alternative spelling, there is no point in spelling it any other way than *hiccup*.

hide / conceal
See **conceal** . . .

highjack / hijack
See **hijack** . . .

highlight / accentuate / accent
See **accent** . . .

high seas / deep sea
See **deep sea** . . .

hijack / highjack
● RULE

Hijack has become the standard spelling.

Hindi / Hindu / Hindustani / Asian / Indian
See **Indian** . . .

historic / historical
● RULES
1 Something that makes history is *historic*: 'that was a historic event'.
2 Something that belongs to history is *historical*: 'here's a historical account of the event'.
    NOTE The financial world refers to '*historic* cost' (the cost of an item at the time it was produced), an incorrect use which is accepted, you could say, for *historical* reasons, since the usage belongs to history.

hitherto
● CAUTION

There is a trap in using this word: it means up to *this* time, not up to *that* time. That is, it should be used only about the *present*: 'we must deal with this using a hitherto untried approach' (that is, untried up to the present time). It should not be used about the *past*, so it would be wrong to write 'ten years ago we dealt with this using a hitherto untried approach'. That should be 'a previously untried approach' or 'an approach untried at that time'.

hoard / horde
● RULES
1 *Hoard* is to accumulate things or the accumulation itself: a miser hoards money, and his money is a hoard.
2 *Horde*, at one time a word for hostile nomadic tribes, now means a disorderly crowd: 'a horde of football hooligans'.

hodgepodge / hotchpotch

See **hotchpotch** . . .

Holland / The Netherlands

● RULE

The Netherlands is the official name for the whole country, with *Holland* as the name only for the NW region, comprising *North Holland* (which includes Amsterdam) and *South Holland* (which includes The Hague).

● RECOMMENDATION

Most people are more at home using *Holland* for any part of the country, or for the country as a whole, which is generally acceptable outside official contexts.

homo- words

● RULE

The prefix *homo-* (or *homeo-*), which comes from the Greek word for 'same', is a guide to the meaning of a number of words. Examples: *homogeneous* (of the same kind – see **homogeneous / homogenous**); *homographs* (words spelt the same); *homophones* (words with the same sound); *homeopathy* (treating like with like); *homosexual* (someone who prefers sexual relations with someone of the same sex – see also **gay / lesbian**).

● RECOMMENDATION

PRON The first syllable of *homo-* words should rhyme with 'Tom', rather than with 'tome'. An exception now is *homosexual*: the pronunciation has shifted from the correct '**hommo**SEXual' to '**hohmo**SEXual', now generally preferred.

homogeneous / homogenous

● RULES

1 *Homogen**eous*** is used for different things composed of similar or identical elements, or about something of a uniform and consistent composition: homogeneous materials (such as different kinds of plastics); 'Conservative members of parliament are not homogeneous in their lifestyles.'

2 *Homogen**ous*** is restricted to biology, describing the similarity of organisms because of common descent and ancestry.

● CAUTIONS

1 Because the meanings of the two words have something in common, *homogen**ous*** is often wrongly used for *homogen**eous***. The correct use of *homogen**ous*** is very limited, and nearly always the word you want is *homogen**eous***.

2 It is *-**eous*** not *-**i**ous: homogeneous.*

PRON The words are pronounced differently. *Homogen**eous*** has stress on the *third* syllable, and the last three syllables rhyme with 'genius': 'hommo-JEENious'. *Homogen**ous*** has the stress on the *second* syllable: 'he(r)MODGE-e(r)ne(r)s'.

homonym / antonym / synonym

See **synonym** . . .

homosexual

See **gay / lesbian;** *homo-* **words**

hooves / hoofs

● OPTION

Horses can have *hooves* ✓ or *hoofs*.

hopefully

● RECOMMENDATION

The original meaning of *hopefully* is 'full of hope': 'To travel hopefully is a better thing than to arrive.' (Robert Louis Stevenson). But the time has come to forget about the fuss over using *hopefully* to mean 'it is hoped', as in 'hopefully the train will be on time'. This alternative use of *hopefully* is so useful that most people now accept it. [!]

● CAUTION

There is an occasional risk of confusion: 'we'll set off hopefully tomorrow' could mean 'we'll set off full of hope', or 'we hope to set off tomorrow'. Where there is this risk, substitute 'we hope to' or 'full of hope', to make the meaning clear.

horde / hoard

See **hoard** . . .

horrible / horrid / horrific / horrifying

● CAUTION

These were strong words once, but the first two have had the guts taken out of them because they are used in such trivial ways: 'a horrible meal'; 'horrid weather'. *Horrific* and *horrifying* still retain power and their full meaning, and should only be used about something that is truly bloodcurdling: 'a *horrific* (or *horrifying*) crime'.

horsey / horsy

● OPTION

Both spellings are used: *horsey* ✓ or *horsy*.

● CAUTION

Whichever way you spell it, *horsey* is usually an uncomplimentary word, used mostly about women to suggest they're unfeminine and galumphing.

hospitable (pronunciation)

● OPTION

Stress on the *first* syllable ('HOSpitable')✓ keeps the word in line with 'hospital', although stress on the *second* syllable ('hosPITable') [!] is shown in many dictionaries as an alternative.

hospitalise

● RECOMMENDATION

This is one of the *-ise / -ize* formations that many people dislike. But we should accept it now, as all current dictionaries do, as the standard term for 'admit to hospital'.

host (verb)

● RECOMMENDATION

To *host* a dinner-party, meaning 'to be the host at', is not a usage that everyone finds comfortable. All current dictionaries accept it, so by now we should feel free to use *host* as a *verb*.

hotchpotch / hodgepodge

● OPTION

A disorderly mix-up of things can be a *hotchpotch* ✓ or a *hodgepodge*.

$ *Hodgepodge.*

hove / heaved

See **heaved** . . .

however

● RECOMMENDATION

Avoid using *however* as a stuffy extra word to insert for no good reason: 'We must consider, however, another point of view'; 'You should remember, however, that he is her husband.' In many sentences, especially where *however* has a comma on either side of it, the sentence is more direct when *however* is left out: 'We must consider another point of view.' If required, the effect of *however* can be obtained by beginning the sentence with *But*: 'But we must consider . . .'.

huge / vast / gigantic / colossal

See **colossal** . . .

hullo / hallo / hello

See **hello** . . .

humankind / mankind

● RECOMMENDATION

*Human*kind is preferable, since many women object to *man*kind. Some people find *humankind* awkward. But there are many examples of modifying words to avoid sexism (not that there is anything new about *humankind,* as it is recorded as far back as the mid-17th century).

human / civil rights

See *civil* rights . . .

hung / hanged

See hanged . . .

hurricane / cyclone / gale / tornado / typhoon / blizzard

See blizzard . . .

hyper- / hypo-

● RULE

These two prefixes, which derive from Greek, are used medically and in some other contexts to describe contrary conditions. *Hyper-* means over, above or excessive, while *hypo-* is below and lacking: *hyper*tension is high blood pressure; *hypo*tension is low blood pressure.

hyphens

Even the best dictionaries disagree in many cases over whether a hyphen should go in or not.

● RECOMMENDATIONS

1 Hyphens should be used (or omitted) with the reader in mind, that is to avoid confusion: '*three-inch* nails' is one thing, 'three *inch-nails*' is something else; 'extra marital sex' is ambiguous, whereas '*extra-marital* sex' (sex outside marriage) or 'extra *marital-sex*' (more sex within marriage) lays it on the line.

2 You can usually drop the hyphen when a compound word becomes familiar, and write it as one word. *Week-end* had become *weekend* by the 1960s, and there are many other examples of words that are now fused together: *airstrip*; *breakthrough*; *bypass*; *teapot*; *subcommittee*; *takeover* (as a noun). But with some combinations, the hyphen lingers on: *coffee-pot.*

3 Where both hyphenated and one-word forms exist, you can usually assume that it's a matter of time before the hyphen fades out: *healthfood, lifeforce, marketplace, shopwindow* are examples of words hyphenated in some dictionaries but shown as one word in others. In this free-for-all situation it is not always necessary to wait for your dictionary to catch up, as they often lag behind general usage when it comes to hyphens.

4 Use hyphens in most compounds coming *before a noun*, as they combine separate elements into one descriptive word, making it easier for readers to take in quickly: 'the figures have been brought up to date', but 'the up-to-date figures'; 'we must investigate this in depth', but an 'in-depth investigation'.

5 When verbs plus linking words are used as *nouns*, hyphens are necessary to help readers. We *run through* a procedure and the result is a *run-through*; when things are *mixed up* they become a *mix-up*; burglars *break in* and a *break-in* occurs.

6 *Re-* words: The hyphen is now usually left out, even when the resulting word looks odd: *redo, reread, rerun, restructure.* But when the following word begins with an *e*, the hyphen is retained to help with pronunciation: *re-elect, re-educate, re-entry, re-establish.* A hyphen is also useful to separate some *re- verbs* from corresponding *nouns*: we *re-count* the votes because a *recount* has been called for. And there are a few cases where *hyphenated* and *one-word* forms of *re-*words have different meanings: *reserve* and *re-serve, recover* and *re-cover*: 'when the umbrella was *recovered*, it had to be *re-covered*'.

   See also **after / after-; co / co-; Euro / Euro-; fellow / fellow-; foot / foot-; half / half-; inter / inter-; less / -less; like / -like; mini / mini-; multi / multi-; neo-; night / night-; non / non-; odd; off / off-; one / one-; out / out-; over / over-; psycho- words; quasi; self / self-; tele / tele-; trans / trans-; under / under-; video / video-; well / well-; -wise.**

7 Breaking words with a hyphen at the end of a line: see **division of words.**

● RULE

   The golden rule is *be consistent*. If a hyphen is used (or not used) in a compound, the die is cast. The same form must be used whenever that compound recurs in the same text.

hypo- / hyper-

See **hyper-** . . .

I

I/me

● RULE

No matter how often you hear 'between you and *I*', 'for you and *I*', 'from you and *I*', it is ungrammatical. Prepositions (short words, such as *to*, *for*, *after*, *from*) are followed by *me*: between you and *me*, for you and *me*, from you and *me*.

● RECOMMENDATION

When *I* or *me* stands alone, they should strictly take the same form as when the verb is present: 'Who did this?' – '*I*.' (That is, 'I did.') To avoid sounding pedantic, in everyday conversation it's natural to slip into: 'Who did this?' – '*Me*.' If you prefer to avoid this dilemma, follow *I* by the appropriate verb: 'Who will light the fire?' – 'I will.' (instead of *Me*).

-ible / -able

See **-able / -ible**

-ics

This ending (derived through French or Latin from a Greek suffix) forms many nouns for arts, sciences or other fields of activity: athletics; classics; dynamics; electronics; gymnastics; linguistics; physics; statistics. The problem is whether to treat these words as *singular* or *plural*.

● RECOMMENDATIONS

1 Treat the words as *singular* when they are followed by a *singular* noun: 'gymnastics *is* her favourite *sport*'; 'statistics *is* an important *part* of the course'; 'linguistics *is* a *subject* every student should study'.

2 When these words are used about different aspects of the subject, they are usually better treated as *plural*: 'gymnastics *cover* many different forms of exercise'; 'the statistics relating to this question *are* difficult to follow'.

● CAUTION

While an *-ics* word can be treated as *singular* or *plural* within the same text, depending on the context, you have to be consistent within the same *sentence*: 'Gymnastics *is* an important subject that *covers* many different forms of exercise.'
See also **economics *is/are*; ethics *is/are*; politics *is/are*.**

I'd

See **contracted forms**

I'd *have* / she'd *have* / you'd *have* / we'd *have*

● RULE

When *I'd*, *you'd*, *she'd*, *we'd* . . . are short for 'I had', 'you had', 'she had', 'we had' . . . , it is a mistake to add *have* after the contraction. 'If I'd *have* known you were coming'; 'if you'd *have* seen this' are in effect saying 'If I *had have* . . .', etc. The correct forms are 'If I'd known . . .'; 'If you'd seen . . .'.

identify / discover

See **discover** . . .

ie / eg

See **eg** . . .

ie / viz

● OPTIONS

1   These Latin abbreviations can be used, in similar but slightly different ways. The abbreviation *ie* (for *id est*, meaning 'that is') leads on to expressing something in different words: 'There are three principles, *ie* guidelines to daily behaviour.' The abbreviation *viz* (for *videlicet*, meaning 'namely', *z* being an old Latin symbol for *et*) leads on to a list of items or a definition: 'There are three principles, *viz* faith, hope and charity'; 'My husband, *viz* the person I care most about . . .'.

2   ✓ We can substitute the phrase 'that is' for both *ie* and *viz*. Try this in the three examples above, and you'll see that nothing is lost in conveying the meaning.
    See also **eg / ie**.

if / providing / provided

See **provided** . . .

if / whether

● RECOMMENDATIONS

1   There is a difference between *whether* and *if*: 'please let me know *whether* you can come' means let me know one way or the other: 'please let me know *if* you can come' means let me know only if it is possible for you to come. But not enough people recognise this distinction any longer for it to be reliable. To avoid misunderstanding, it's better to be specific: 'let me know *whether or not* you can come' or '. . . *only if* you can come'.

2   In many statements, 'or not' after *whether* should be omitted as unnecessary: 'at this stage, we do not know *whether* the project will succeed' already means *whether or not*. In such statements, *whether* leaves the possibility evenly balanced, while *if* ('. . . if the project will succeed') suggests greater uncertainty.

if and when

See **as and when** . . .

if I *was* / if I *were* . . .

● OPTIONS

1   When *if* introduces a statement that is clearly not true or is unlikely or poses a
hypothesis, 'if I *were* . . .'; 'if she *were* . . .', etc are considered educated usage: 'If
she *were* married to someone else, she'd probably be happier.'; 'If I *were* you, I
wouldn't have another drink.' In grammar, this is the subjunctive form of the
verb.

2   ✓ Regard the subjunctive use of the verb as more or less obsolete, and use 'if I *was*
. . .'; 'if she *was* . . .' [!]: 'If she was married . . .'; 'If I was you . . .'. [!]

if you like

● RECOMMENDATION

If you like is useful to soften what could otherwise seem a dogmatic statement,
suggesting that it is a personal or particular point of view: 'many investments are, if
you like, just another form of gambling'.

ignorant *of* / *about*

● OPTION

We can be ignorant *of* ✓ or *about* something.

ilk

● RECOMMENDATION

Ilk is a Scottish word, used to mean 'of the same name' or 'of the place belonging to
that name': 'McTavish *of that ilk*' means 'McTavish of McTavish', confirming that
this is one of the authentic McTavishes, or of the McTavish estate. But south of the
Border, we can use *ilk* about anyone, simply to mean of the same kind: 'statisticians
and others of that ilk are always telling us what we think'.

● CAUTION

Only use *ilk,* as in the second example above, when you intend to be derogatory or
sardonic, because that's how it will usually be taken. (This does not apply to the
traditional use of *ilk* in Scotland, as in the first example above.)

I'll

See **contracted forms**

ill / sick

● RECOMMENDATIONS

1   Use *ill* for 'not well' ('she cannot come because she's ill'), and *sick* for vomiting ('I
was sick after the meal').

2   Use *sick* as the descriptive word to describe someone who is not well: a *sick* person (rather than 'an *ill* person').
3   To avoid misunderstanding, the separate meanings should always be retained after the verb 'feel': using 'I feel ill' suggests 'I'm not well', and 'I feel sick' suggests 'I might vomit'.
$ *Sick* usually means 'not well', although *sick* can also be used for vomiting.

illegal / illicit

● RECOMMENDATIONS

1   Use *illegal* about something that breaks the statutory law.
2   *Illicit* is less clearly defined. It could correspond to *illegal*, describing an act that is against the law (illicit dealings in shares, for example), but could also be used about something that breaks the rules of an organisation or a code of conduct. An *illicit* love affair, for example, might contravene the conventional moral code, but would not usually be breaking the law.

illegible / unreadable

● RULES

1   *Illegible* is a fact: something is impossible to read because, for example, the handwriting is so bad or the print is blurred.
2   *Unreadable* is a matter of opinion: something is too dull, technical or heavy-going to read.

illicit / illegal

See **illegal** . . .

ill-informed / misinformed / uninformed

● RECOMMENDATIONS

1   Use *ill-informed* to mean that the facts are not correct, without implying dishonesty: 'because the timetable was out of date, she was ill-informed about the times of the trains'.
2   Use *misinformed* to suggest that wrong information was given to mislead: 'she was misinformed about the time of the last train, because he wanted her to stay the night'.
3   Use *uninformed* simply to mean not knowing, not being in the picture: 'she had to telephone the station, because she was uninformed about the times of the trains'.

illness / disease

See **disease** . . .

illusion / delusion

See **delusion** . . .

I'm

See **contracted forms**

imaginative / creative

See **creative** . . .

imbue / infuse

● RULES

1 Someone or a group of people are *imbued* with a quality, such as confidence or a sense of purpose: 'the captain imbued the team with a determination to win'.

2 It is a *quality* that is *infused* into a person (not the *person* who is infused): 'the captain infused a determination to win into the team'.

● RECOMMENDATION

The best way to separate the two words is to follow *imbue* by the *person or people* who are affected, and *infuse* by the *quality* that is affecting them (as in the above examples).

immanent / imminent

● RULES

1 *Immanent* is a quality that is indwelling: 'sexual drive is immanent throughout nature'.

2 *Imminent* is something that is about to happen, and is always used about something that is threatening: 'he is in imminent danger of being made redundant'.

immediately / forthwith / straightaway

● RECOMMENDATIONS

1 While it's too soon to write off *forthwith* as obsolete, it is better to ask someone to do whatever it is *immediately* – or simply *now*.

2 *Straightaway* ✓ (or as two words, *straight away*) is useful to convey a heightened sense of urgency.

3 *Immediately* means 'at once', and is less appropriate when something else has to happen first: 'please send the order as soon as you have supplies' (rather than '. . . *immediately* you have supplies').

immigrant / emigrant

See **emigrant** . . .

imminent / immanent

See **immanent** . . .

immoral / amoral

See **amoral** . . .

immovable / unmovable / irremovable

● RULES

1 ***Im**movable* (also but less commonly spelt *immov**ea**ble*) is clearly something that cannot be moved, either because it is too heavy or is a permanent fixture. The word is extended for a person whose opinion or decision cannot be changed ('once he has made up his mind, he is immovable') or shows no emotion.

2 ***Un**movable* (also but less commonly spelt *unmov**ea**ble*) is used about *people* (in the senses described in **1** above) rather than objects: 'he was unmovable in spite of her tears'.

3 ***Irre**movable* ('irremov**ea**ble' is *not* an alternative spelling) is the only word to use for someone who cannot be forced out of office: 'since he owns most of the shares, the chairman is irremovable'.

impartial / neutral

● RULES

1 *Impartial* describes feelings that are genuinely unprejudiced: 'we are impartial in this dispute, ready to listen to both parties'.

2 *Neutral* is not allowing a bias to affect an attitude: 'although we have definite feelings about who is in the right, we have decided to remain neutral, not supporting either side'.

impasse (pronunciation)

● OPTION

Both a French and an anglicised pronunciation for the first syllable are acceptable: '**am**PASSE'✓ or '**im**PASSE'.

impassive / dispassionate / poker-faced / deadpan

See **deadpan** . . .

impel / compel

See **compel** . . .

imply / infer

● RULES

1 A speaker or a writer *implies* when they suggest or hint at something.

2 When we read or listen, we *infer*, that is we read between the lines and pick up the intended meaning, even though it is not spelt out.

● CAUTION

'Do you *infer* that I am wrong?' is a common mistake. It should be 'Do you *imply* . . . ?' Remember someone *infers* from what someone else *implies*.

important / importantly

● OPTION

There are grammatical arguments for writing or saying both *more important* ✓ and *more importantly*.

NOTE A lot of important people make a point of saying *more importantly*, and the day may come when *more important* will be written off as ungrammatical. Until then, many writers agree with the preference marked above.

impracticable / impractical / unpractical

● OPTIONS

1 If you are no good at doing the everyday things in life, you are **im***practical* or **un***practical*.

2 If something isn't worth doing because, for example, it's too complicated or not worth the expense, that is also *impractical* or **un***practical*.

● RECOMMENDATION

Although the words mean the same, **im***practical* is better for *ideas* and *things*, with **un***practical* better for *people*: 'it's an impractical idea' but 'she's an unpractical woman'.

● RULE

Something is **im***practicable* when it cannot be done, or is an idea that could not possibly be carried out for one reason or another: 'the plan is impracticable because there is no way in which it could be given the go-ahead'.

See also **practicable / practical.**

impresario / impressario

● CAUTION

'Impressario' may look right to some people, but the correct spelling is *impresario*.

in / into / in to

● RULES

1 *In* is for location: 'she was in the room'; 'dinner is in the oven'.

2 Although *in* can be used where *movement* is involved ('she went in the room'), *into* is preferable: 'she went into the room'.

3 When a *noun* follows, *into* is *one* word: 'we went into the theatre'; 'she put it into the box'.

4 When a *verb* follows, the *to* is part of the following verb, so *in to* are *two* words: 'she went in *to see* the play'; 'she took it in *to give* to him'.

● CAUTION

A common mistake is to write *into* as *one* word, when it should be *two* (see RULE 4 above).

NOTE There is also the trendy conversational use of *into* (as *one* word) to mean caught up with or enthusiastic about: 'she's into Japanese flower arrangement'.

See also **onto / on to.**

in / on

● RULES

1 The British live *in* streets, Americans *on* streets. Saks, the famous department store in New York, is *on* Fifth Avenue. Selfridges, one of London's famous department stores, is *in* Oxford Street. The British are usually *in* town, while Americans tend to be *on* the town.

2 Others may sail *on* a ship, but the Royal Navy sails and serves *in* ships.

$ See RULE 1 above.

in- / un- / non-

● CAUTIONS

1 There is no reliable set of rules to tell us whether it is **undetectable** or **indetectable**, **inexperienced** or **unexperienced** (**undetectable** and **inexperienced** are correct). When in doubt over *in-* or *un-*, check with a dictionary.

2 *Non-* is not always an alternative prefix to *in-* or *un-*: it can sometimes carry a different meaning. In front of certain words, *non-* means no more than something is not so, without any suggestion of criticism, while *in-* and *un-* could carry a pejorative meaning: **non**-*scientific*, for example, means not connected with science, but **un**scientific can mean slipshod or misguided, because science has not been taken into account.

3 Some words have been coined using *non-* as a contemptuous way of writing off someone or something: a *non-event*, for example, is an event that was inconsequential and disappointing.

● OPTION

There are a few words that take either *in-* or *un-*. Five common ones are: **in**advisable ✓ or **un**advisable (**un**advisable can have the alternative meaning for a person who will not listen to advice); **in**decipherable ✓ or **un**decipherable; **in**disciplined or **un**disciplined ✓; **in**essential ✓ or **un**essential; **in**escapable ✓ or **un**escapable.

in / under the circumstances

See **circumstances**

inability / disability

See **disability** . . .

inadvisable / unadvisable

See **in-** . . . (OPTION)

in an hour / *within the* hour

● RULES

1 To arrive '*in an* hour' is to arrive in 60 minutes, that is if it's 7.30pm, to arrive at 8.30pm.

2   To arrive '*within the* hour', if it's say 7.30pm, is to arrive sometime before 8pm, that
    is within the same hour.

inasmuch as / *insofar* as / *insomuch* as
● RECOMMENDATION

These long-winded expressions, which mean more or less the same as each other,
have some purpose when they mean 'to the extent that': 'the sales figures are
acceptable but only *inasmuch as* (or *insofar as* or *insomuch as*) they are no worse than
the figures last year'. But generally all three expressions are best left to formal texts,
and can often be replaced simply by 'in that'.

in *between times* / in *the interim* / in *the meantime*
See **in *the meantime* . . .**

incidentally
● CAUTION

Incidentally is so often pronounced with *four* syllables ('in-ci-DENT-ly') instead of
'in-ci-DENT-**e(r)**-ly', that it is easy to slip into the wrong spelling 'incidently'.

● RECOMMENDATION

Incidentally has some use in speech as a buffer word to create a pause before an aside
(even then, 'by the way' or 'in passing' serve just as well). But in writing it can get in
the way of the flow of a sentence: 'incidentally, we should also consider . . .';
'incidentally, there is another way of . . .'. It's worthwhile omitting *incidentally* to see
if the sentence is better without it.

incline
● CAUTION

To be *inclined* to think or do something is valid where a final decision has not been
made: 'I am inclined to buy a new computer, but need more advice first.' Otherwise
it is pointless shilly-shallying, and is better replaced by the honest word 'want':
compare 'I am *inclined* to have another drink' with 'I *want* to have . . .'.

include / consist / comprise / compose
See **compose . . .**

incomparable (pronunciation)
● RECOMMENDATION

Stress the *second* syllable: 'inCOMparable'. (Although some dictionaries show
'incomPARable' [!], with stress on the *third* syllable as an option, this is usually
considered wrong.)

in / *by* comparison
See **comparison**

in connection with / in this connection
● RECOMMENDATION

In connection with and *in this connection* do have a place occasionally, but often they are just long-winded ways of saying 'about': 'I am writing in connection with . . .', instead of 'I am writing about . . .'.

incredible / incredulous / unbelievable
● RULES

1 *Incredible* and *unbelievable* ✓ mean the same, and it's a matter of preference which one you use to describe something that's beyond belief.

2 *Incredulous* can be used only about a *person*, or the way they look at someone or the tone of their voice, to indicate they do not believe something: 'he is always incredulous, and questions everything you say'.

independent / independant
● CAUTION

There is no such word as 'independant'. Unlike **dependant / dependent**, *independent* is the only form, and serves as both the noun and descriptive word: 'he is an independent, not attached to any political party'; 'she has an independent spirit'.

indexes / indices
● RECOMMENDATIONS

1 Use *indexes* as the plural form in general contexts, such as the indexes of books, or card indexes.

2 Reserve the alternative plural *indices* (PRON 'INDiseez') for mathematical and economic contexts: 'retail price indices'.

Indian / Asian / Hindi / Hindu / Hindustani
● RULES

1 *Indian* should be used only for and about a citizen of the Republic of India.

2 *Asian* is the correct generic name for someone whose ethnic origins belong to India, Pakistan, Bangladesh or Sri Lanka.

3 *Hindi* is the most well-known of the 15 official languages of the Indian Union.

4 *Hindu* is a follower of Hinduism, one of the world's great religions.

5 The name *Hindustani* has no place now, except in historical contexts. It was a northern Indian dialect made up of other dialects from all over the subcontinent, and is associated with the British Raj.

indict / indictment

When someone is *indicted*, they are formally charged with a crime: an *indictment* is the formal written accusation.

● CAUTION

Because the words are pronounced 'inDYTE' and 'inDYTEment', be on guard against spelling them wrongly as 'indite' and 'inditement'.

indirect / direct object

See *direct / indirect* object

indisciplined / undisciplined

● OPTION

Either *indisciplined* or *undisciplined* ✓ will do. See also **in- / un- / non-**.

indiscriminate / undiscriminating

● OPTION

Both *indiscriminate* and *undiscriminating* ✓ mean unable to distinguish between different things, usually between good and poor quality: 'many television viewers are *indiscriminate* (or *undiscriminating*) over the programmes they watch'.

● CAUTIONS

1 *Indiscriminating* is not an alternative word: it is not in any dictionary.

2 Only *indiscriminate* has the further meaning (not shared by *undiscriminating*) of random, without selection: 'an indiscriminate collection of books'; 'indiscriminate bombing'.

$ *Indiscriminate* is the usual form for all meanings.

individual

● RECOMMENDATION

Do not use *individual* simply as another word for a person ('he is a strange individual'; 'there were several individuals in the room'). Instead, reserve *individual* for contrasting one person with society or with a large group of people: 'The worth of a State, in the long run, is the worth of the individuals composing it.' (John Stuart Mill).

inedible / uneatable

● RECOMMENDATIONS

1 Use *inedible* as a statement of fact, to mean something should not be eaten because it is poisonous or not suitable in some other way for human consumption.

2 Use *uneatable* for an expression of opinion, to mean you cannot stand the taste.

● CAUTION

Not everyone understands this difference of meaning, and if you are warning that something is *inedible*, it is prudent to add 'because it's poisonous', or whatever reason applies.

See also **eatable / edible.**

inescapable / unescapable
● OPTION

A situation can be either *inescapable* ✓ or **unescapable**. See also **in- / un- / non-.**

inessential / unessential / non-essential
● OPTION

Something or someone can be either *inessential* ✓, **un**essential or **non**-essential. See also **in- / un- / non-.**

inevitable / inevitably
● RECOMMENDATION

Regard these words as absolute, describing something that is certain to follow. So it is unnecessary to write or say 'completely' *inevitable.* In the same way, 'must' *inevitably* ('this must inevitably cause problems') is not required, since *must* or *inevitably* is sufficient on its own: 'this must cause problems' or 'this inevitably causes problems'.

in excess of
● RECOMMENDATION

Why not simply 'more than'?

infamous / notorious
● RECOMMENDATIONS

1 Use *infamous* to stress the evil or shocking nature of a deed or person: an infamous event; an infamous criminal.

2 Use *notorious* to stress that the person, deed or event is well-known for evil qualities: 'a notorious crime that was on every front page'.

infectious / contagious

See **contagious** . . .

infer / imply

See **imply** . . .

infinitive
● RULE

The *infinitive* is a form of the verb which, as its name indicates, is not restricted to singular or plural, or past, present or future. The *infinitive* is usually the *to* form of the verb ('I want *to dance*'). See also **split infinitive.**

inflammable / flameproof / inflammatory / flammable
See **flammable** . . .

inflection / inflexion
● OPTION

Dictionaries allow both *inflection* ✓ and *inflexion*.

informal / slang / non-standard / colloquial
See **colloquial** . . .

informant / informer
● RULES

1   An *informant* is an innocent word for anyone who supplies information: 'we have a reliable informant to keep us up to date about prices charged by local restaurants'.

2   An *informer* gives the police information about suspects, and is known in the underworld as a *stool-pigeon*, *copper's nark* or *grass*.

infuse / imbue
See **imbue** . . .

ingenious / ingenuous
● RULES

1   *Ingenious* is always a positive word, meaning that someone or something is clever or resourceful.

2   Except when used about children, *ingenuous* is often a negative word, implying that someone or something is oversimple or lacking in worldliness.

● CAUTION

Disingenuous is not the straight opposite of *ingenuous*: it means appearing to be innocent and open, but in fact cunning and devious.

inherent / innate / intrinsic
All three words can be used about a quality in a person, a situation or certain things.

● RECOMMENDATIONS

1   *Inherent* means underlying, ever-present: 'the nobility of a human being, inherent in all Shakespeare's tragedies, always comes through at the end'.

2   *Innate* means interwoven, not easily eradicated, even if it is not always apparent: 'there is an innate nobility in Shakespeare's heroes that reveals itself in moments of crisis'.

3   *Intrinsic* describes something that is a basic or irreducible part of a larger scheme: 'the intrinsic nobility of Shakespeare's heroes is never diminished by the ebb and flow of their reactions to events'.

● OPTION

The *second* syllable of *inherent* can be pronounced as in 'h*er*itage'✓ or as in 'h*ere*'.

   NOTE   *Inherent value* can have two meanings: the basic measurable value of something, such as the melted-down value of the gold in a gold coin, or a less specific value based on a special interest or quality (a painting, for example, might have an intrinsic value because the artist gave it to his wife as a wedding present).

inherent value

See **inherent . . .** (NOTE)

inhibition / hang-up / block

See **block . . .**

initiate / initiation

● RULE

It is always *people* who are *initiated* at an *initiation* ceremony, into membership of a society, group or a body, such as the House of Lords, or as a disciple of a master. *Ideas* and *knowledge* are not *initiated* – they are instilled or inculcated: 'the secret knowledge was instilled into him before he was initiated into Freemasonry'.

● RECOMMENDATION

Business jargon *initiates* new sales campaigns, new schemes, new approaches. In such uses, *initiate* is a self-important word, usually better replaced by 'begin' or 'start'.

-in-law

● RULE

-in-law never takes an *-s*, so the plural forms are *sons-in-law; sisters-in-law*, etc.

innate / inherent / intrinsic

See **inherent . . .**

innovative / innovatory

● OPTION

Innovative ✓ and *innovatory* mean the same thing, and either word can be used about a person or proposals that introduce new approaches or new ways of thinking. PRON Both words stress the *first* syllable, with a light stress on the *third* syllable: 'INN-oh-*vay*-tive'; 'INN-oh-*vay*-tery'.

innuendo

● RULE

Innuendo always has a *derogatory* meaning: 'the remark contained an innuendo that he had bungled the matter'. We cannot write 'it was an innuendo that he had done well' (the word there is 'implication').

● OPTION

Dictionaries show two plural forms: *innuendoes* ✓ and *innuendos*.

inoculate / vaccinate

● RECOMMENDATION

Use *inoculate* for injecting a person or an animal with a serum or vaccine to give immunity against a disease, with the exception of protection against smallpox, where *vaccinate* is the better word.

● CAUTION

It is a common mistake to spell *inoculate* with a double *n*.

inquire / enquire / inquiry / enquiry

See **enquire** . . .

in respect of

See **respect of** . . .

insensitive / insensible

● RECOMMENDATIONS

1 Use *insensitive* to suggest a person is unable to feel anything about someone's feelings or suffering, or is unresponsive to beauty or culture.

2 Use *insensible* to suggest deliberate callousness.

NOTE *Insensible* also has the separate meaning of being physically unconscious: 'she was knocked insensible by the blow'.

insinuate

● RULE

Insinuate always means something bad, so we cannot insinuate anything good: 'What are you insinuating?' is asking what *nasty* thing is being suggested.

insofar as / *insomuch* as / *inasmuch* as

See *inasmuch* as . . .

in spite of / despite of / despite

See **despite** . . .

install / instal

● OPTION

Install ✓ or *instal*.

● RULE

Installed, installing, installation but *instalments*.

$ The same as above, except that it's always *install* and *installments*.

institute / institution

● OPTION

It's a matter of custom whether an organisation is called an *institute* or an *institution*. *Institute* is by far the most common term for professional bodies: Institute of Chartered Accountants; Institute of Actuaries; Institute of Chiropodists. Learned societies also usually prefer to be *institutes*: Institute of Historical Research; Institute of Zoology. But most engineering and allied societies prefer the dignity of *institution*: Institution of Civil Engineers; Royal Institution of Chartered Surveyors.

insurance / assurance

See **assurance** . . .

insure / ensure / assure

See **assure** . . .

intaglio / cameo

See **cameo** . . .

integral (pronunciation)

● OPTION

Stress can be on the *first* syllable ('INtegral')✓ or the *second* ('inTEGral').

inter / inter-

● RECOMMENDATION

Hyphens are no longer required in the many words formed using the Latin prefix *inter* (meaning 'between' or 'among'), even when the linked word begins with an *r*: *intercontinental*; *interpersonal*; *interplanetary*; *interrelate*.

inter alia

● RECOMMENDATION

In most contexts there's nothing to be said for using this Latin phrase (PRON 'inte(r)AYlia'). 'Among other things' is the exact English equivalent, has the same number of syllables – and everyone knows what it means.

intercourse

● CAUTION

Although there are dictionaries that still give the primary meaning of *intercourse* as 'communication between people, nations, etc', it can invite misunderstanding to use the word in that way, unless the context makes it clear. For *intercourse* has lost its innocence, and the first meaning that now comes to mind is *sexual* intercourse.

(in the) *interim* / in *between times* / in the *meantime*
See **in the *meantime*** . . .

intermezzi / intermezzos
● OPTION

The plural *intermezzos* is as much at home now in English as the Italian plural *intermezzi*. But as the word is used mostly about music (for a short composition performed between acts, or simply a short piece for a solo instrument), it is better to use *intermezzi* ✓ (musical terms usually take Italian plural forms).

international / cosmopolitan
See **cosmopolitan** . . .

interval / intermission
● RULE

Inter means 'between', and an *interval* is a period *between* things or events: 'three months was a long interval between sending a bill and receiving the cheque'. It is wrong to use *interval* just to mean a period of time, as in 'three months was a long interval to wait for a cheque'. (That should be '. . . a long *time* to wait . . .').

● RECOMMENDATION

Use *interval* for breaks in performances in the theatre, and *intermission* for breaks in television programmes.

$ *Intermission* for both the theatre and television.

inter-war / pre-war
See **pre-war** . . .

in the absence of
See **absence**

(*in* / *under* the) **circumstances**
See **circumstances**

in the event
● RECOMMENDATIONS

1 *In the event of* has a place for formal declarations: 'in the event of war'; 'in the event of the terms of this contract not being adhered to'.

2 In everyday contexts, *in the event that* is usually no more than five-syllable long-windedness for 'if': 'in the event that you are late'; 'in the event that the board agrees'; instead of 'if you are late'; 'if the board agrees'.

3   *In the event*, meaning 'as it turned out', is a valid use: 'In the event, they reached an agreement'.

in the *meantime* / in the *interim* / in *between times*

● RECOMMENDATIONS

1   While *interim* has its place as a descriptive word in official language for something that is provisional (an interim report; an interim dividend), in the *meantime* is more natural than in the *interim*: 'in the meantime, she had gone to live in Cornwall'.

2   In *between times* is useful for a longer intervening period than in the *meantime*: 'in between times, she married and had two children'.

in the neighbourhood of

● RECOMMENDATION

In the neighbourhood of is nothing more than a six-syllable substitute for the simple two-syllable word 'about': 'the cost will be in the neighbourhood of . . .' instead of 'the cost will be about . . .'.

in the wake of / afterwards / after

See **after** . . .

in the world / on earth

● RECOMMENDATION

On earth and *in the world* are often interchangeable: the greatest show *on earth* (or *in the world*). But *on earth* suggests an idea that is more transcendent and timeless: 'Mozart was the greatest composer on earth'. *In the world* is something more specific, more here and now: 'he is the greatest tennis player in the world'. See also **Earth / earth / world.**

in this connection / in connection with

See **in connection with** . . .

in to / into / in

See **in** . . .

intonation

Intonation conveys meaning by pitch and tone of the voice. Sometimes this can be indicated in written language.

● RECOMMENDATIONS

1   *Intonation* can be indicated by the choice of a *question mark* or an *exclamation mark*: for example, 'Really?' suggests a tone of doubt, whereas 'Really!' suggests shock or amazement; 'Yes?' suggests a rising tone, asking 'What do you want?', whereas 'Yes!' marks a sharp tone expressing emphatic agreement.

2   *Italics* (or underlining, when italics are not available) is another way of indicating *intonation*: for example, 'he said *that* to you' or 'he said that to *you*' tells the reader how those lines were spoken.

in toto

● **RECOMMENDATION**

In toto is Latin for *completely* or *entirely*, and there is no reason why it should not be replaced by one of those words: 'I reject the proposition *in toto* (or *completely* or *entirely*)'.

● **CAUTION**

Because *in toto* sounds like 'in total', it is often wrongly used to mean that: 'the profits of the group of companies *in toto* are a record' ('in total' is right there).

intricacy (pronunciation)

● **RULE**

The stress belongs on the *first* syllable: 'INtricacy'.

intrinsic / innate / inherent

See **inherent** . . .

introduction / preface / foreword

See **foreword** . . .

invalid (pronunciation)

● **RULES**

1   Whether it is a *noun* or a *verb* referring to a person who is weakened or incapacitated by illness, stress is on the *first* syllable: 'INvalid'. But when used as a *verb*, as in 'because of his injuries, we shall *invalid* him out of the service', the last syllable has a 'leed' sound: 'INva*leed*'.

2   As a descriptive word, meaning the opposite of 'valid', stress is on the *second* syllable: 'inVALid'.

invaluable / valuable / priceless

● **RECOMMENDATION**

Treat *invaluable* as more valuable than *valuable*: it suggests beyond value, the equivalent of *priceless*.

invariable / invariably

● **RULE**

Invariable should be used only to describe a factor that is a constant, something that *never* changes: 'as production costs go up and down, we adjust the selling price to maintain an invariable profit margin'.

● RECOMMENDATION

Strictly, the above RULE also applies to *invariably*, but no harm is done by the occasional relaxed use of *invariably* to mean 'nearly always': 'the train is invariably late'.

invent / discover

See **discover** . . .

inventory (pronunciation)

● RULE

Stress is on the *first* syllable ('INventory') and moving it forward to the *second* syllable ('inVENTory') is not an option. And *inventory* is pronounced with *three* syllables, rhyming with 'infantry'.

inverted commas / quotes / quotation marks

See **quotation marks** . . .

invoice / statement / bill / account

See **account** . . .

inward / inwards

● RULE

As a descriptive word *in front of a noun* it is *inward*: an inward direction.

● OPTION

In other uses either *inwards* ✓ or *inward* will do: 'the direction is *inwards*' (or *inward*); 'move it *inwards*' (or *inward*).

in / for years

See *for / in* years . . .

Ireland / Eire / Ulster / Northern Ireland / Southern Ireland

● RULES

1 The *Republic of Ireland* (as proclaimed 18 April 1949) replaced *Eire* as the official name, with the *Irish Republic* as the shorter form, leaving *Southern Ireland* as the everyday name.

2 *Northern Ireland* is the official name for the NE part of the country that remained with the United Kingdom after partition was proclaimed in 1921.

3 *Ulster* can have different meanings, but is accepted by most people as the everyday name for *Northern Ireland* (as defined in RULE 2 above).

● RECOMMENDATION

Northern Ireland and the *Republic of Ireland* (or the *Irish Republic*) should be used for the two parts of the country in formal writing or speaking. In general use, *Ulster* can be used for *Northern Ireland,* and *Southern Ireland* for the Irish Republic. (People living in Northern Ireland refer to their country as *Ulster*.)

Irish / Erse
● RULE

The usual name now for the language is *Irish*, which is what it is officially called in the Irish Republic. See also **Celt / Celtic / Gaelic / Gallic.**

ironic / ironical
● OPTION

Either *ironic* ✓ or *ironical* can be used to describe a situation or event that has irony.

● CAUTION

The words should be used only when there is a twist in what has happened, so that it's the wrong way round: 'it was *ironic* (or *ironical*) that as well as giving me a big order, he paid for dinner'. To use the words to mean no more than surprising or unexpected misses the point: 'it was ironic that the train was on time' would be true only if you had brought sandwiches and a book, expecting the train to be late.

irrefutable (pronunciation)

See **refutable**

irregardless / regardless

See **regardless . . .**

irreligious / nonreligious / unreligious / sacrilegious
● RULES

1 *Irreligious* is anti-religion: 'the vicar was outraged by their irreligious behaviour in church'.
2 *Nonreligious* is neutral, not taking religion into account: 'the Church should treat homosexuality as a nonreligious matter'.
3 *Sacrilegious* describes an irreligious deed, a condemnation for the violation of something sacred.

● RECOMMENDATION

Because *unreligious* covers *irreligious* and *nonreligious*, and can have either meaning, it is usually better avoided.

irremovable / unmovable / immovable

See **immovable . . .**

irreparable

See **repairable . . .**

irrevocable (pronunciation)

● RULE

As the word for something that cannot be cancelled or altered ('this decision is irrevocable'), stress on the *second* syllable is obligatory: 'irREVocable'. But in legal matters, where the word is used for an agreement or powers of appointment that may not be revoked ('once you sign this, it is irrevocable'), there is the OPTION of stressing the *third* syllable: 'irreVOCable' ✓.

-isation / -ization

See **-ise / -ize** (NOTE)

-isation nouns

● RECOMMENDATION

Many *-isation* nouns have their place, of course, but using too many of them is heavy-going. Often simple words or phrases are much easier to take in: compare 'the utilisation of the new equipment' with 'using the new equipment'; 'hospitalisation of patients' with 'admitting patients to hospital'.

-ise / -ize

● OPTION

In most (but not all) words *-ise / -ize* are alternative endings. Dictionaries usually follow this principle: where both *-ise* and *-ize* are correct, they show the *-ize* spelling first as the main one, followed by the alternative *-ise* spelling: realize / realise; vocalize / vocalise; hospitalize / hospitalise.

● RECOMMENDATION

Use *-ise* for *all* words with *-ise / -ize* endings. That can never be wrong (with the one exception of *capsize*). Nearly all British newspapers now follow that RECOMMENDATION.

NOTE The above OPTION and RECOMMENDATION also apply to *all* words ending in *-isation / -ization*: realisation✓ / realization; vocalisation✓ / vocalization; hospitalisation ✓ / hospitalization.

$ Where British dictionaries show -ize / -ise or -ization / -isation as alternative endings, only *-ize* and *-ization* are used in America. Where the *-ise* ending is obligatory in British English (advertise; devise; compromise), the *-ise* ending is also required in American English.

Islamic / Arabic / Arabian / Arab

See **Arab** . . .

-is **nouns**

● RULE

The plural of a number of nouns ending in *-is* is formed by changing the *-is* to *-es*

(PRON '-eez'). Here are some common ones: analysis (analys*es*); antithesis (antithes*es*); basis (bas*es*); crisis (cris*es*); hypothesis (hypothes*es*); metamorphosis (metamorphos*es*); oasis (oas*es*); parenthesis (parenthes*es*); synopsis (synops*es*); thesis (thes*es*).

PRON the plural forms: 'aNALi-*seez*'; 'anTITHe(r)-*seez*'; 'BAY-*seez*'.

NOTE The reason for forming the plural in this way is partly the Greek origin of the words and partly pronunciation, which can be demonstrated by trying to say 'synopsises' (instead of *synopses*).

isn't

See **contracted forms**

issue (pronunciation)

● OPTION

Two pronunciations are acceptable: 'I**SH**oo'✓ or 'I**SS**-yoo'.

$ Always 'I**SH**oo'.

italics

● CAUTION

Reference books, such as this one, have a special need for *italics* to help users pick out points quickly. Otherwise, *italics* should be used sparingly or they lose their effect and become an irritation.

● RECOMMENDATIONS

1   *Titles* of books, plays, films, operas, works of art, etc, should go into *italics* to single them out. The word *The* is sometimes a problem: if it is part of the title, it should also be in *italics*, but in the flow of a sentence it does no harm at times to leave out *The* altogether: 'Shakespeare's *Tempest* and *Merchant of Venice* were written at different periods' (instead of *The Tempest* and *The Merchant of Venice*).

2   *Newspapers and periodicals*: Some consider *The* part of the title and like it in *italics*. This applies more to the broadsheets (*The Times*; *The Independent*) than the tabloids (*Daily Mirror*; *Daily Express*). There is no reliable rule: *The Sun*, for example, keeps its *The*, and so does *The News of the World*, yet the *Financial Times* has dropped *The* from its title, and perversely, *The Observer* has taken to calling itself *the Observer* (with a small *t* for *the*). If you are writing about a newspaper or a magazine, it is a courtesy to look it up in a directory or to enquire whether *The* should be included as part of the title. But in some contexts, it's reasonable to leave out *The*, whatever the dictate: even *The Times* could hardly object to 'There was a *Times* on the doormat.'

3   *Stress in speech* can be marked by *italics* in print: 'Did he really say *that*?'; 'Marry *him*!' (See **intonation**.)

4   *To focus attention on a point*, it is helpful to pick out a particular word in *italics*, but it can be condescending to use *italics* to stress something unnecessarily. The dividing

line is a fine one: 'It is not grammatically *wrong* to begin a sentence with *And.*' (*Italics* for *And* are justified but are not required for 'wrong'.)

5   *Foreign words and phrases:* At one time nearly all of them were in *italics*. Even now dictionaries are inconsistent: ad infinitum but *ad hominem*; hors-d'oeuvre but *hors de combat*; à la carte but *à la russe*; ex officio but *ex cathedra* (the examples are from *The Concise Oxford Dictionary*). This is too arbitrary to make much sense, and *The Times* now prints *all* foreign words and expressions in standard roman type. This is a sensible rule in the linguistic internationalism of the 1990s.

its / it's

● RULE

Its is the possessive form ('a book has its title on the cover'): it*'s* is the contracted form of 'it is' ('it's a good title for a book').

I've

See **contracted forms**

-ization / -isation

See -ise / -ize

-ize / -ise

See -ise / -ize

J

jail (and jailer) / gaol (and gaoler)

See **prison** . . .

jam / conserve / preserve

● RECOMMENDATIONS

1 *Jam* is the usual word for what is spread on bread and butter for tea.

2 *Conserve* is hardly more than a grand name that some jam manufacturers like to put on their labels.

3 *Preserve* should be reserved for a jam that consists of chunks of fruit.

janitor / porter / doorman / doorkeeper

See **doorkeeper** . . .

Jap

● CAUTION

Although it is sometimes heard on the BBC and some Japanese seem to find it harmless, *Jap* could give offence, so it's better to use *Japanese*, both for the people and the descriptive word (a Japanese restaurant).

jargon

● CAUTION

Jargon properly used as expert-to-expert language saves a lot of time. But good jargon in one place becomes bad jargon when an expert is speaking to or writing for other people who do not understand it. The test for *good* jargon is to ask if it is useful shorthand that communicates quickly and clearly to the people at the receiving end. It fails that test if it uses complicated words, when simple ones will do ('residential structures' instead of 'houses and flats') or when the other person does not understand it easily. For example, 'low-dependency care' is effective communication between doctor and nurse, but confusing, even alarming, if it is used to the patient.

jeans / denims

See **denims** . . .

Jew / Jewish

● CAUTIONS

1 Some Jewish people are uncomfortable with the word *Jew* because of its associations, and prefer the descriptive word *Jewish* ('several Jewish people' rather than 'several

Jews'), as less rabbinical and nationalistic. But it must be added that others strongly reject any such distinction.

2 Be on guard against using *Jewish* unnecessarily as a defining term (a Jewish businessman; a Jewish MP). This could come across as racist, unless it is required by the context.

See also **Jewess.**

Jewess

● CAUTION

Although the most recent dictionaries include *Jewess* usually without comment, *Collins Cobuild Dictionary* warns that 'many people consider this to be an offensive word' for a Jewish woman. See also **-ess forms.**

jibe / gybe / gibe

See **gibe** . . .

join together

● RECOMMENDATION

Some people object to *join together*, because *join* on its own means *bringing together*. Yet the phrase can have a reassuring ring to it because of the marriage service in *The Book of Common Prayer*: 'Those whom God hath joined together let no man put asunder.' But use *join together* only in contexts where you want to stress the point, or add a note of solemnity. See also **link together.**

joint / common

See **common** . . .

Jones (plural form)

● RECOMMENDATION

When you need a plural form for *Jones*, it's preferable to have the *Joneses* to dinner, rather than the *Jones*. See also **names ending in -s, -ch, -sh.**

judge / adjudge / adjudicate

● RECOMMENDATIONS

1 *Judge* is the more general word: 'we *judge* a beauty contest', or '*judge* how long something might take'.

2 *Adjudge* is usually confined to courts of law: 'judges *judge* or *adjudge* a case' (it comes to the same thing). But when damages are awarded, these are *adjudged*.

3 *Adjudicate* is the usual word for tribunals: 'they *adjudicate* over a dispute or *adjudicate* a claim'.

    NOTE We cannot *adjudicate* a beauty contest – we adjudicate *at* or *over* it (which is the same as judging it).

judgement / judgment

● OPTION

Many lawyers prefer *judgment*, but in non-legal contexts, *judgement* ✓ is more usual.

jurist / juror

● RULE

'A *juror* is a member of a jury, while *jurist* is a rather academic word for a legal scholar.

$ As in British English, a *juror* is the usual word for a jury member, but *jurist* is much more of an everyday word for an expert in law or a judge.

just

● RECOMMENDATIONS

1 'We just had dinner'; 'the post just arrived' are acceptable in conversation, but formal writing requires: 'we *have* just had dinner'; 'the post *has* just arrived'.

2 If you want to make a question sharper, slip in *just* right at the beginning. The difference between 'What do you mean by that?' and '*Just* what do you mean by that?' is that the second question is more pointed and demands a clear answer.

● CAUTION

Just not and *not just* can be confusing, as they mean different things. 'She's just not experienced enough' suggests she has almost enough experience but not quite enough. *Not just* is the equivalent of 'not only'. To write or say 'she's not just experienced enough', requires a further positive comment: 'she's not just experienced enough, she's also available immediately'.

K

kerb / curb

See **curb** . . .

keyboard / keypad

● RECOMMENDATIONS

1 The standard word is *keyboard* for the panel holding the keys of a computer, the keys of a typewriter and the keys of a piano.

2 Use *keypad* for small adaptations of keyboards, particularly on hand-held equipment, and for the panel of buttons on telephones.

kilometre

A kilometre is 1000 metres, approx 0.62 miles.

● OPTION

Orthodox pronunciation puts the stress on the *first* syllable ('KILometre')✓, which keeps it in line with 'MILLimetre'; 'CENTimetre'; 'KILogram'. But 'kiLOMetre' [!] (stress on the *second* syllable) has become so common that recent dictionaries show it as an alternative.

● RULE

Do not add -*s* after the plural abbreviation: 1km; 100km (and no stop is needed).

$ 'kiLOMetre' (stress on the *second* syllable) is more or less standard.

kind / sort

● CAUTIONS

1 Both words are *singular*: '*this* kind of argument'; '*that* sort of person'. A common error is '*those* kind of arguments'; '*these* sort of people'.

2 There's no need to follow *a kind of* and *a sort of* by a second *a*: 'a kind of *a* dinner'; 'a sort of *a* novel'. 'A kind of dinner'; 'a sort of novel' is better.

3 In speaking, *kind of* too often degenerates into 'kinda'.

knelt / kneeled

● OPTION

Knelt ✓ is the more usual past form, although *kneeled* is an alternative.

$ *Kneeled* is the usual past form.

knight-

● RULE

The -*s* of the plural forms of *knight-* combinations is added to the word *knight*: knights bachelor; knights errant; Knights Templar.

knots

● CAUTION

Knots, the standard way of measuring the speed of ships, already means nautical miles *per hour*, so 'knots *per hour*' is a landlubber's error.

NOTE A nautical mile is 1852 metres, about 2025 yards.

know-how / savoir faire

● RECOMMENDATIONS

1 Although most dictionaries still label *know-how* as conversational English, it can now be used even in written language. Use *know-how* for a blend of knowledge, ability, experience and lessons learned by trial and error, particularly in practical, business and technical applications.

2 *Savoir faire* (French for 'to know how to do') should be used in a more sophisticated way for the ability to handle any social situation, from speaking to the Queen or an archbishop, to dealing with a lordly wine-waiter at the Ritz.

kudos

● RULE

Kudos is taken from a *singular* Greek word meaning fame or glory. So it is 'the kudos that *is* her due' (not '. . . *are* her due').

● OPTION

PRON 'KYOOdos'✓ or 'KOOdos'.

L

-l-/-ll-

See **appal . . . ; distil . . . ; fulfil . . . ; install; doubling final letter before -*ed* and -*ing***

laboratory (pronunciation)

● RULE

Stress on the *first* syllable has become obsolete, and the standard pronunciation now is 'le(r)BORatery'.

$ Stress is on the *first* syllable: 'LABe(r)tery'.

lady / female / woman

● RECOMMENDATIONS

1 Use *woman* as the standard word, particularly in professional contexts: a woman barrister; women executives; the woman of the year. But 'cleaning *ladies*' and 'tea *ladies*' are still the order of the day.

2 'An old *lady*' is more gracious than 'an old *woman*', which sounds disparaging.

3 It's better to restrict *female* to statistical use: 'the percentage of female buyers'; 'the number of female doctors'.

● RULES

The Queen has *ladies-in-waiting*, a woman MP is addressed in the House of Commons as the *honourable lady*, and at Wimbledon it's *ladies' singles*.

● CAUTIONS

1 Avoid using *woman* as a descriptive term in a way that could imply the male equivalent is the standard. For example, 'we consulted seven architects, including three women architects' is better expressed as 'we consulted four men and three women architects'.

2 As a noun, *female* may carry with it a derogatory implication, especially when used by a man: 'So I said to this female . . .'.

3 Treat the above recommendations as suggestions for steering round a sociolinguistic dilemma. As you hover between offending a 'lady' by calling her a *woman*, or sounding genteel by saying *lady*, you have to decide for yourself when the situation or context calls for *lady*, *female* or *woman*.

See also **girl; man / gentleman.**

$ The situation is much more relaxed, and the tendency is to use *lady* for a woman without uneasiness: 'a whole lot of crazy ladies are in charge'; 'when I rang the bell, a lady answered the door'.

lamentable (pronunciation)

● RULE

Stress on the *first* syllable ('LAMentable') is the only correct pronunciation.

languid / limpid

● RULES

1 *Languid* means feeble or limp: 'she raised a languid hand'.

2 *Limpid* is used mostly about water or eyes when they are clear: a pool can be limpid, so can innocent blue eyes.

lapse / elapse

See **elapse** . . .

last / first

See **former** . . . (RULE)

last / lastly

● RECOMMENDATION

Although some people believe *lastly* is the only correct form ('and lastly, I have this to say . . .'.), this is arguable. In fact, *last* is sharper and sounds more to the point: 'and last, I have this to say . . .'.

last / latest

● CAUTION

The meaning is usually clear when we use *last* to mean the most recent: 'the last time I saw Paris' doesn't mean you don't expect to go there again. But there are times when we should choose carefully between *last* and *latest* : 'this is my *last* word on the subject' suggests the subject is now closed, whereas 'this is my *latest* word on the subject' leaves the door open to a change of mind.

late / former / ex-

See **ex-** . . .

latest / last

See **last / latest**

latter / former

See **former** . . .

laudable / laudatory

● RULES

1 Someone or something that is *laudable* is praiseworthy: 'it was a laudable suggestion'.

2   Only a *form of words* expressing praise can be *laudatory* (PRON 'LAWDitery'): 'her laudatory speech singled out each of the members for praise'.

lawful / legal

● RECOMMENDATION

Treat *lawful* as a general word meaning in accordance with what is recognised by the law, and *legal* as a precise term for specific requirements of the law. A procedure, a request or an action is *lawful* if it is within the law, and *legal* arguments could be advanced to defend it.

lay / lie

● RULES

1   When these verbs are *not* followed by the person or object laid down, these are the correct forms: 'If you are tired, *lie* down' (present); 'yesterday she was tired and *lay* down' (past); 'he has *lain* in bed all day' (past form after *has* or *have*).

2   When the verbs *are* followed by the person or object laid down, these are the correct forms: 'it is fragile so please *lay it* down carefully'; 'she is injured, so be careful how you *lay her* down' (present); 'because it was fragile, he *laid it* down carefully' (past); 'he has already *laid it* down'; 'we have *laid the baby* down' (past form after *has* or *have*).

3   The ship *lay* (or *will lie*) at anchor for a week.

● CAUTION

The most common mistake is 'go and *lay* down'; 'tell her to *lay* down'. *Lie* is required in those sentences (see RULE 1 above).

leader / editorial

See **editorial** . . .

leading question

● CAUTION

Leading question is often used wrongly to describe a question that is awkward or embarrassing. It means a question that prompts you (or *leads* you on) to give the answer that is actually wanted: 'When you came home, he was already there, wasn't he?', instead of an open question: 'Was he there when you came home?'

leafs / leaves

● RULE

There are autumn *leaves* and the *leaves* of a book (nouns), but 'she *leafs* (verb) through the pages'.

leaned / leant
● OPTION

Both *leaned* ✓ and *leant* are correct for the past form of the verb *to lean*.

$ *Leaned* is the only past form.

leaped / leapt
● OPTION

Both *leaped* and *leapt* ✓ are correct for the past form of the verb *to leap*.

$ *Leaped* is the only past form.

learned / learnt
● OPTION

Both *learned* ✓ and *learnt* are correct for the past form of the verb *to learn*. For *learned* as a *descriptive word*, see **-ed.**

$ *Learned* is the only past form.

leave go / *let* go

See *let* **go** . . .

leaves / leafs

See **leafs** . . .

leeward / windward
● RULE

At sea *leeward* is pronounced 'LOOerd', but on dry land it is 'LEEwerd'. The **lee**ward side of a boat is the side sheltered from the wind, just as **wind**ward (PRON 'WINDwerd' both at sea and on land) is the side on which the wind is blowing.

● CAUTION

Both words are invariable, and the forms 'leeward*s*' and 'windward*s*' do not exist.

leftward / leftwards
● RECOMMENDATION

As a descriptive word, it is better as *leftward* ('he went off in a leftward direction'), with *leftwards* preferable when it indicates direction after a verb ('he moved leftwards').

legal / lawful

See **lawful** . . .

legend / myth
● RULES

1 A *legend* may stem from some historical truth ('the legend of Napoleon's invincibility').

2 A *myth* is entirely imaginary, and may even be a lie ('he was sacked, and it is a myth to say he resigned').

3 *Myth* is used about the stories of classical literature (Greek myths).

legible / readable

● RULES

1 *Legible* is a fact: it means it is possible to read something because, for example, the print is large enough or the handwriting decipherable.

2 *Readable* is a matter of opinion: a trite romantic novel is readable to some people, that is interesting for them to read, but not readable to others, who find it boring.

● CAUTION

A common mistake is to use *readable* about an inscription that has been partly worn away: 'the letters are hardly *readable*', instead of '. . . hardly *legible*'.

lend / loan

● RECOMMENDATION

Lend is the usual verb, with *loan* appropriate only where large sums of money are involved, particularly in official contexts: 'the government is loaning millions of pounds to finance further exploration for North Sea oil'.

$ *Loan* is the usual word for any sum of money.

length (pronunciation)

● CAUTION

Remember the word *long* and sound the *g* lightly in *leng*th (it's slipshod to say 'lenth').

length of sentences

See **sentences**

lengthy / long

● RECOMMENDATION

A *long* letter or a report is what it says, that is a text running into a number of pages, but a *lengthy* letter or report could imply that is *too* long, because it is boring and heavy-going.

● CAUTION

If you comment that something is *lengthy*, when you mean *long*, the writer of it could take offence.

lesbian / gay

See **gay . . .**

less / -less

● RECOMMENDATION

There is no need for a hyphen when *-less* is added to nouns, unless it results in *three* ls coming together: *childless*; *carless*; *husbandless*; *railless*; *soulless* . . . but *shell-less*; *smell-less*.

less / fewer

See **fewer** . . .

let go / *leave* go

● CAUTION

'*Leave* go of the rope'; '*leave* go of the dog', etc, are wrong. It is *let* go that means release, set at liberty.

letter / vowel / consonant

See **consonant** . . .

liable / apt

See **apt** . . .

libel / slander

● RULES

1 *Libel* is something *written* that is untrue, and damages a person's reputation. The evidence is the written or printed document. Since the Defamation Act 1952, something said on radio or television is regarded as publication, and is also subject to the law of *libel*.

2 *Slander* is *spoken*, and a witness is required to prove it.

library (pronunciation)

● CAUTION

Even when you're in a hurry, give it *three* syllables: 'LYB-rer-ree' (not 'LYBree').

libretti / librettos

● RECOMMENDATION

Librettos as the plural form of 'libretto' is fine for the text of musicals, but when it comes to operas, only *libretti* will do.

licence / license

● RULE

You may have a driving *licence* or a *licence* to sell wine. These mean that you are *licensed* to drive or *licensed* to sell wine in your *licensed* restaurant. That is, *licence* is the noun, *license* the verb, and *licensed* the descriptive word.

$ *License* is the only spelling for all uses.

lie / lay

See lay . . .

(in) **lieu (of)**

● RECOMMENDATION

It is difficult to think of any good reason why *in lieu of* (PRON 'lyoo'✓ or 'loo') should be used instead of 'in place of' or 'instead of', which are the obvious words.

lieutenant (pronunciation)

● RULE

In the army, you're a 'lefTENant', in the navy, a 'le(r)TENant'.

$ It's always 'looTENant'.

NOTE The spelling stays the same whatever the pronunciation.

life-size / life-sized

● OPTION

Either *life-size* ✓ or *life-sized* can be used.

lighted / lit

● RECOMMENDATIONS

1 Use *lit*, as in 'the fire was lit'; 'the torch was lit'.

2 Use *lighted* as the descriptive word before a noun: 'the lighted fire'; 'the lighted torch'.

lightening / lightning

● RULE

Lightning goes with thunder. *Lightening* is making lighter, either literally or metaphorically: 'lightening a dark area'; 'the lightening of a situation'.

like

● RECOMMENDATIONS

1 In spite of what some grammar books say, we are in good company when we use *like* to mean 'in the same way as': 'Some girls change their lovers like they change their clothes.' (Graham Greene); 'They didn't talk like other people talked.' (Martin Amis); 'Everything went wrong . . . like it does in dreams.' (Iris Murdoch).

2 To use *like* to mean 'as if' sounds ungrammatical, as in 'she spends money like there's no tomorrow'. [!] Change it to '*as if* there's no tomorrow'.

3 *Like* and *such as* are used interchangeably so often now, that it is generally acceptable: 'she enjoys games like tennis and squash'. [!]

● CAUTION

Look out for the risk of ambiguity when you follow RECOMMENDATION 3 above: *Take a Girl Like You* (title of a novel by Kingsley Amis) could mean 'like you, for example' *or* 'similar to you'. It is better to use *such as* to precede examples: 'the great squares in Paris, such as the Place de la Concorde and the Place des Vosges'. And use *like* when you mean 'similar to': 'there is no other square in the world *like* the Piazza San Marco in Venice'.

like / -like

Many words are formed by adding *-like*, and there is no rule about whether a hyphen should be used.

● RECOMMENDATIONS

1 With new or less familiar formations, a hyphen is appropriate: *boat-like*; *monk-like*; *priest-like*.

2 With established words, the hyphen can be dropped: *childlike*; *ladylike*; *lifelike*.

3 In the rare cases when adding *-like* results in three *l*s coming together, insert a hyphen: *bell-like*; *hell-like*.

likeable / likable

● OPTION

Likeable ✓ and *likable* are shown in most dictionaries as alternative spellings.

$ *Likable.*

likewise

Likewise is a short version of 'in like wise', meaning 'in the same way' or 'the same thing': 'if you like what she is doing, why not do likewise?'

● CAUTION

It is a vulgarism, heard quite often, to use *likewise* as a substitute for 'and', 'as well as', 'in addition to', etc: 'there are many problems – late delivery, higher prices, *likewise* a demand for immediate payment'. Any of the alternatives shown should be used, or simply 'plus' ('. . . plus a demand for . . .').

limited / constrained

See **constrained** . . .

limpid / languid

See **languid** . . .

linage / lineage

● RULES

1   *Linage* (PRON 'LYNE-idge' with *two* syllables) is the number of lines on a printed page or in a complete printed text.

2   *Lineage* (PRON 'LINN-ee-idge' with *three* syllables) is another word for ancestry, the line of descendants.

lingo

● CAUTION

At best, *lingo* is conversational rather than written English. But even then it's better avoided, as it has a hint of Colonel Blimp about it ('They were speaking some kind of funny lingo.').

linguistics *is* / *are*

See -**ics**

link / linkage

● RECOMMENDATION

Use *link* for a simple connection between things: 'there's a link between the items, since they are all bathroom fittings'. Prefer *linkage* for the leverage or effect that one thing has on another: 'there is a linkage between the takeover price and the value of the bonus that would be paid to shareholders'.

link together

● RECOMMENDATION

In the interests of brevity, the word *together* can usually be omitted, since it is impossible to link one thing to another, without linking them *together*. See also **join together**.

liquidise / liquefy

● RECOMMENDATION

Liquidise is the word used in the kitchen for reducing food to liquid state in a *liquidiser*. *Liquefy* means the same thing but belongs more to chemistry or technical processes.

lire / liras

● OPTION

Lira is the monetary unit of Italy. The plural in Italian is also the official plural form in English: *lire* ✓ (PRON 'LEEReh'), although the anglicised plural *liras* is also commonly used.

● CAUTION

What is clearly wrong is to use the singular *lira* for the *plural* form: 'we came home because we were running out of *lira*'. It has to be '. . . running out of *lire* (or *liras*)'.

lists of names or things

● RECOMMENDATIONS

1 *Commas* are the usual way to separate names or items in a list, with the comma omitted between the last but one item and the 'and' preceding it: 'in Oxford Street, there are many famous shops, including Selfridges, John Lewis and Marks & Spencer'.

2 There are times when a comma before the 'and' can help to make a list clearer, particularly when a second *and* follows: 'on the ground floor are the fashion, fabrics, and jewellery and accessories departments' (this shows that jewellery and accessories are *one* department).

3 In some lists, a *semicolon* is preferable to a comma, especially where items have additional comments: 'in Oxford Street, there are many famous shops, such as Selfridges, the first department store to be opened in Britain; John Lewis, part of the John Lewis Partnership; Marks & Spencer, perhaps the best loved of all stores; . . .'.

lit / lighted

See **lighted** . . .

literal / typo / misprint

See **misprint** . . .

literally

● RECOMMENDATION

Literally is using a word or expression in its true sense: if a knife is *literally* as sharp as a razor, it should be possible to shave with it. But *literally* is so often used to mean, not in reality but in a manner of speaking: 'dinner at that restaurant literally costs the earth'. This use of *literally* is far too common to make a fuss about it, but we might prefer to be careful ourselves to use *literally* only when we mean in reality: 'he is so rich that he could literally write out a cheque for £1,000,000'. After all, when we are exaggerating for effect, nothing is lost by leaving out *literally*: 'dinner in that restaurant costs the earth'.

lithograph (pronunciation)

● OPTION

The *first* syllable can be pronounced to rhyme with 'myth', or the *i* can have the same sound as 'eye': 'LITHe(r)graf'✓ or 'LYTHe(r)graf'.

loan / lend

See **lend** . . .

loath / loth / loathe

● OPTION

Loath ✓ and *loth* are alternative spellings of the word meaning reluctant to do something: 'she is *loath* (or *loth*) to give up her job'.

PRON Whichever spelling is used, it rhymes with 'both', not with 'clothe'.

● RULE

Loathe (which does rhyme with 'clothe') is another word altogether, meaning hate or detest: 'she loathes her job'. *Loathsome* keeps the same *th* sound as *loathe*.

loch / lough

● RULES

1   *Loch* Lomond is the largest lake in Scotland, for *loch* is the Scottish word for *lake*.

2   In Ireland, the river Erne flows across the border through *Lough* Erne, for *lough* is the equivalent Irish word.

PRON Both *loch* and *lough* are pronounced in the same way, with a final guttural sound. This can be arrived at by a gentle gargling. But to help out English people who cannot handle it, most dictionaries, as a concession, offer the alternative pronunciation 'lok'.

logo / trademark

● RULE

Trademark (abbreviated TM) is the legal term (*trademarks* can be registered with the Patent Office) for the emblem that represents a product. The name of the product itself is a *trademark*, particularly the style in which the name is displayed.

● RECOMMENDATION

Other than for legal purposes (see RULE above), *logo* is the term to use now for the trademark of a product or company. *Logo* is the fashionable term in business and industry for the graphic design that represents the corporate identity of an organisation.

-logue / -log

● RULE

This suffix derives from Greek 'logos' (word), and forms nouns connected with speech and reason. It should always be *-logue* in British English: *analogue*; *catalogue*; *dialogue*; *travelogue*.

● CAUTION

Although we are used to the simplified spelling *-log* in American English (*analog*; *catalog*; *dialog*; *travelog*), be careful not to use this spelling in British English. [!]

$ See above.

lone / *single* **parent**

● RECOMMENDATION

Because *single* parent could imply that a woman or a man bringing up a child on their own is unmarried, *lone* parent is preferred ('the problem of lone parent families').

long / lengthy

See **lengthy** . . .

lookout / look out

● RULE

It is *one* word as a *noun*, meaning someone whose job it is to keep watch, or in the phrase 'on the lookout for'. The *verb* is always *two* words: 'Look out for trouble!'

loose / lose

● RULES

1 *Loose* has several different meanings as a verb, all connected with releasing or setting free: a boat can be loosed from its moorings; dogs can be loosed when they are taken off their leads; a gun is loosed when it is fired.

2 *Lose* also has a number of meanings, mostly related in some way to no longer having something or to being deprived: we can lose money; lose our nerve; lose a game; lose ground.

PRON *Loose* rhymes with 'noose': *lose* rhymes with 'cruise'.

lorry / truck

● OPTION

Either *lorry* ✓ or *truck* can be used for a heavy motor vehicle transporting goods.

● RULE

On the railways, it is a *truck* that carries goods.

$ The word *lorry* does not exist – it's always a *truck*.

lose / loose

See **loose** . . .

lose no time

● CAUTION

Lose no time can mean two different things: 'lose no time doing this' could mean get started on it without delay, *or* it is a waste of time doing it. Where there could be any doubt, use alternatives: for example, 'do this right away' *or* 'don't waste time doing it'.

(a) lot / a lot of / lots of

● RECOMMENDATION

Lots of ('lots of money') is conversational, so there's a case for avoiding it in serious writing. But this cannot reasonably apply to *a lot* or *a lot of*: 'he paid a lot for it'; 'a lot of money'.

lough / loch

See **loch** . . .

lovable / loveable

● OPTION

Someone can be *lovable* ✓ or *loveable*.

$ Always *lovable*.

lover / mistress

● RECOMMENDATION

The word *mistress* seems dated, as *lover* is now used freely by both men and women about someone they are having an affair with.

Ltd / plc

● RULE

It is a statutory requirement to identify a public limited company quoted on the Stock Exchange by adding *plc* after the name. Private limited companies add *Ltd*. Although *plc* is written in small letters, by convention *Ltd* requires a capital *L*.

-ly / -ilily

The problem arises when descriptive words, such as *friendly, holy, silly*, etc, are used after verbs, and we are landed with the awkward forms *friendlily, holily, sillily*: 'she spoke holily'; 'he grinned sillily'.

● RECOMMENDATION

Nearly always it is better to rephrase the sentence or use another word: 'she spoke in a holy way'; 'he grinned stupidly'.

lyric / lyrical

● RECOMMENDATION

Lyric, as a descriptive word, is still mostly reserved for poetry, as in lyric poets; lyric drama. *Lyrical* can also mean poetic ('he described it in a lyrical way'), but more usually means being carried away by enthusiasm: 'he was lyrical about his holiday on a Greek island'.

NOTE *Lyric* is for the words of pop songs: refer to the *words* of operatic arias and songs such as lieder.

M

Mac-/Mc-/Mack-

These prefixes to Scottish and Irish family names are variants of the Gaelic word for 'son'. Whether it is *Mac-*, *Mc-* or *Mack-* depends on what is customary for a particular family, and there is no rule to help the uninitiated, except to ask. The family name usually begins with a capital (McArthur; McDonald), but after *Mac* or *Mack*, this does not always apply (Macauley; Mactavish).

● RECOMMENDATION

When it comes to *alphabetical order*, follow the standard practice used in directories: treat all three prefixes as *Mac*, with the *next* letter in the name determining alphabetical order: McArthur; Mackbride; McHuish; Macmillan; McVicar. The alphabetical order follows on as if the last *Mac-*, *Mc-* or *Mack-* name was spelt *Mac-*: McVicar; Maddox; Madgwick.

machismo/macho

Both words describe heavy-going masculinity. The Spanish word *macho* ('male') can also be a noun in English for a man who is showing off his *machismo*.

● RECOMMENDATION

The preferred pronunciation is 'me(r)TCHIZmoh' and 'MATCHoh', which are nearer to the Spanish sound than the alternative pronunciations 'me(r)KISmoh' and 'MAKoh'.

● CAUTION

Neither word is generally complimentary.

Mack-/Mc-/Mac-

See **Mac-** . . .

macro/macro-

This prefix, derived from the Greek word for 'large', is used in some technical and academic terms, such as *macromolecule* (a molecule that consists of great numbers of atoms); *macrolinguistics* (the study of overall patterns in the use of language).

● RECOMMENDATION

A hyphen is not necessary to link *macro-* to the word it is joined to, even when that begins with a vowel: *macroeconomics* (the study of the aggregation of all economic factors).

See also **micro/micro-**.

Madame / Mademoiselle / Monsieur

For RECOMMENDATIONS concerning the use of foreign courtesy titles in an English context, see **Mr, Mrs . . . / Monsieur, Frau . . . .**

maestros / maestri

Maestro (PRON 'MYStro') is used mostly for great conductors, but is also extended to cover anyone who does almost anything in a masterly way.

● OPTION

It's the Italian word for 'master' and the Italian plural is *maestri*. That is one of the plural forms used in English but sounds affected to some people, who prefer *maestros* ✓.

Magdalen / Magdalene

● RULES

1 It is spelt with a final *-e* when it is St Mary Magdalene of Magdala in Galilee (Luke 8:2), or one of the churches named after her. The name is usually pronounced with *three* syllables ('MAGde(r)lin').

2 There is a final *-e* in Magdalen**e** College, Cambridge but not in Magdalen College, Oxford. The names of the colleges in both universities are pronounced with *two* syllables: 'MAWDlin'.

magisterial / magistral

● RULES

1 When the word is used to describe a person who speaks or bears themselves with great authority, it's *magis**terial*** (PRON 'madge-i-STEERial').

2 *Magis**tral*** (PRON 'maJIS-tre(r)l') is a descriptive word for someone who is a master with great knowledge.

　　NOTE Someone can be *magisterial* in manner but not necessarily *magistral*. Or the same person can be both.

maiden / single name

Even the most recent dictionaries still include *maiden name* as the term for a woman's family name before she was married. And many women still use that expression. At the same time, more and more women retain their single name after marriage, and would give you a funny look if you asked for their *maiden name*.

● RECOMMENDATION

Refer to a woman's *single name*.

mail / post

● OPTION

For the time being, we can still *post* ✓ or *mail* a letter, receive the *post* ✓ or the *mail*.
　　NOTE Post Office vans have *Royal Mail* on the side, advertisers have *direct mail*

campaigns, sending out tons of *junk mail*, so the choice between *mail* and *post* is shifting towards *mail*.

$ Americans never *post* letters – they *mail* them and receive *mail*.

Majorca / Mallorca

See **Mallorca** . . .

majority / bulk

See **bulk** . . .

majority / minority *is* / *are*

● RECOMMENDATION

Although *majority* and *minority* are singular words, they represent a number of people or things, and it usually sounds better to follow them by a *plural* verb: 'the majority of us *do* not agree'; 'a minority of MPs *have* voted against the motion'. See also *majority of* / *most of.*

majority of / most of

● RECOMMENDATIONS

1 *The majority of* should be used only when it is the larger number of two *measurable* things. When it is an indeterminate number or something that is unspecified, *most of* is appropriate: 'the *majority* of the members have agreed'; but 'she writes *most of* the letters'; 'he does *most of* the work'.

2 Avoid *the vast majority of:* it is more to the point to write or say 'nearly all'.
See also **majority / minority** *is / are.*

make / take a decision

See **decision**

male / masculine

● RECOMMENDATIONS

1 Use *male* in anatomical, biological, botanical or zoological contexts to denote the male species capable of fertilisation.

2 Use *masculine* about humans to describe qualities and characteristics that belong to men.

NOTE Some women now use *male* as a word of attack ('male prejudice'; 'male attitudes'), and *masculine* as a word of admiration.

malign / malignant

● RECOMMENDATIONS

1 Use *malign* about someone's influence, intention or the effect they have, to suggest

that it is evil or causing great harm. (*Malignant* can also be used in this sense, but is less common.)

2 Restrict *malig**nant*** more to pathological use, usually for a tumour or growth that is cancerous. (Although *malign* can also be used in this sense, doctors usually prefer *malignant*.)

NOTE *Malign* is also a *verb*, meaning to slander or defame.

Mallorca / Majorca

● OPTION

Mallorca ✓ (PRON 'maYORKa') is the Spanish spelling, which has more or less taken over, although there remain a number of people who stay with the English spelling *Majorca* (PRON 'maJORKa').

man / gentleman

● RULE

The term *gentleman* is kept alive by after-dinner speakers ('Ladies and gentle-men . . .'); MPs ('The honourable gentleman . . .'); signs outside lavatories in the more gracious hotels; waiters and the few surviving butlers; and a few titles, such as gentleman-at-arms (a member of the Queen's bodyguard).

● RECOMMENDATION

In many contexts *gentleman* seems out of place in the egalitarian 1990s, and is better replaced by *man*: 'all the directors are men'; 'there's a man waiting to see you'; 'I'm having dinner with a man'.

● CAUTION

In formal contexts *gentleman* is still obligatory, and older men in particular might object to a receptionist referring to them as a *man* ('There's a man here to see you.'). The rules are thin on the ground, and in most cases you have to decide for yourself whether the situation calls for *gentleman* or *man*, steering between sounding genteel on the one hand, or giving offence on the other.

See also **lady / female / woman**.

-man / -person

See **-person** . . .

manageress / manager

See **-ess forms** (RECOMMENDATION 2)

mandatory / obligatory

● RULES

1 When something is *mandatory* (PRON 'MANde(r)tery', not 'manDAYtery'), it is required by law or a command from a higher authority: 'it is mandatory to advertise vacancies to persons of either sex'.

2 *Obligatory* is a less legalistic word, which could apply to the rules of a club, for example ('it is obligatory for men to wear jackets and ties at dinner') and to moral obligations ('it's obligatory for me to visit my mother on Sundays'). *Mandatory* should not be used in those ways.

manifold

● RECOMMENDATIONS

1 The proper use of *manifold* is for things of different and various kinds, so a piece of equipment can make *manifold* savings of time and money, meaning a number of savings in different ways.

2 There's no point in using *manifold* in place of the simple words 'a lot' or 'many', as in 'there are manifold books on the subject'.

mankind / humankind

See **humankind** . . .

man-made / synthetic / artificial

See **artificial** . . .

manoeuvre

● CAUTION

It's easy to slip in an incorrect *e* for the *-ed* and *-ing* forms of the verb. The correct spellings are *manoeuvred* and *manoeuvring* (not 'manoeuvered'; 'manoeuvering').

$ *Maneuver, maneuvered, maneuvering.*

manqué

● RULE

Although the past form of the French verb 'manquer' has been used in English for a very long time, it still follows the French word-order and is placed *after* the noun: 'a cabinet minister manqué', meaning someone who might have become a cabinet minister but didn't.

● RECOMMENDATIONS

1 When *manqué* is used about a woman, it should, following French grammar, be the feminine form *manquée,* but this is not usually followed in English: 'she is a writer *manqué*'.

2 There is no English word that means quite the same, that is something a person might have achieved but didn't. The alternative is to rephrase the sentence: 'he might have been a cabinet minister'. But the flavour of *manqué* is caught better by hyphenating *might have been* and using it descriptively: 'a might-have-been cabinet minister'.

manual / handbook

See **handbook** . . .

manuscript

● RECOMMENDATION

Originally a *manuscript* was a text written by hand, but it is usual now to use *manuscript* for a typed text or a text printed out from a wordprocessor.

NOTE The abbreviations *MS* and *MSS*, for the singular and plural, are still in common use. But archivists are more likely to use the words *manuscript* and *manuscripts* in full, and only for texts actually written by hand.

many a . . . *is/are*

● RULE

Many a . . . is always followed by a *singular* verb: 'many a woman *has* to put up with . . .'.

marijuana / pot / grass / dope / hashish / cannabis

See **cannabis** . . .

marketplace

● RECOMMENDATION

The word is used less now for the open space in a town where markets are held than for the general world of buying and selling: that's the meaning of 'Let's try it out in the marketplace.'

masculine / male

See **male** . . .

massage (pronunciation)

● RULE

The *first* syllable is stressed: 'MASSage'.

$ The *second* syllable is stressed: 'massAGE'.

master / mistress (of colleges)

● RULE

Once a college has a *master*, it always has one, which is why Baroness Tessa Blackstone, for example, became *Master* of Birkbeck College, London.

masterful / masterly

● RECOMMENDATION

Accept that *masterful* and *masterly* are both used now to mean skilful and accomplished, in the manner of a master: 'he is *masterly* (or *masterful*) at handling difficult situations in the boardroom'. But *masterful* is the only word to use when we mean dictatorial: 'he is so masterful with her, always telling her what to do'.

mat / matt / matte
● OPTION

Mat ✓, *matt* and *matte* are variant spellings of the word describing a dull rather than a shiny finish.

$ *Matt* is the standard spelling.

material / relevant
● RECOMMENDATION

Treat *material* as the stronger word, implying that something is essential, of real significance, while *relevant* does not go beyond suggesting that whatever it is has some bearing on the matter: 'because the new information is material to the question, it must be taken into account'; 'although the new information is relevant, it is of no great importance'.

matt / matte / mat

See **mat** . . .

maximise / minimise
● CAUTION

Maximise and *minimise* mean to take something up to the top limit, or take it down to the lowest limit. No degree is involved, so we cannot 'greatly' maximise or minimise anything, even though these expressions are often heard.

maximum / minimum (plural forms)
● OPTION

Some authorities are strict about allowing only the Latin plurals: *maxima* and *minima*. At the same time, the anglicised plurals are very commonly used: *maximums* ✓ and *minimums* ✓.

may / can

See **can / may**

may / might
● RECOMMENDATIONS

1   In general, use *may* for the present, *might* for the past: 'it may happen any moment now'; 'it might never have happened'.

2   Use *may* in a direct statement in the present, *might* when something is reported: 'it may rain'; 'the weatherman said it might rain'.

3   After *if* statements, *might* should be used: 'if she had married someone else, she

might have been happier'. This applies generally to other statements of uncertainty: 'without her help, he might not succeed'.

4 Conversationally, *might* is a polite way of making a request, or alternatively a resentful complaint: 'While you're out, you might post these letters for me.'; 'You might help with the washing-up!'

maybe / may be

● RULE

One word when it is an alternative to 'perhaps': 'maybe it is true'. Otherwise it is *two* words: 'it may be true'.

mayoress

● CAUTION

Although some dictionaries tell you that a *mayoress* is a woman holding the office of a mayor, most women mayors rightly insist on being called *mayor*. And when a Lord Mayor is a woman, she is the *Lord* Mayor (not 'Lady' Mayor).

● RULE

Mayoress is properly used for the wife of a mayor.

Mc- / Mack- / Mac-

See **Mac-** . . .

mean / average

See **average** . . .

means *is / are*

● OPTION

Means, for the way in which something can be brought about, can be treated as *singular* or *plural*: '*this is* the means to an end' ✓ or '*these are* the means to an end'.

● RULE

When the word is used about someone's financial resources, it is always *plural*: 'now she is on her own, her means *are* reduced'.

● RECOMMENDATION

The use of *means*, as in the RULE above, is old-fashioned, and it's more natural to say '. . . she has less money'.

meantime / meanwhile

● OPTION

There is no discernible difference in the way these two words are used. We can do something 'in the *mean**time***' ✓ or 'in the *mean**while***'.

Mecca / mecca

● RULE

With a capital *M*, *Mecca* is the holy city of Islam.

● RECOMMENDATION

When the word is used in a general way for a place that people are drawn to, *mecca* (with a small *m*) is less offensive to Muslims: 'there is a shop in Milan that is the mecca of fashionable women'.

mechanics *is* / *are*

See -**ics**

media *is* / *are*

● RULES

1 *Media* is the *plural* form of the noun: 'the media *are* . . .'.

2 The singular form is *medium*: 'Which advertising medium *was* used?' (The answer to that could be 'All the *media*.')

meditative / reflective / contemplative

See **contemplative** . . .

mediums / media

● RULE

When the word *medium* is used for a spiritualist, someone who believes they can communicate with the dead, the plural form is *mediums*. For the plural form *media*, see **media** *is* / *are.*

meet *with* / meet *up with*

● RECOMMENDATION

Both expressions have an American ring and seem unnecessary in Britain, where the verb *meet* on its own is enough: 'boy meets girl'.

melancholy / melancholic

● RECOMMENDATION

Melancholy is the better word to describe a sad thoughtful state of mind, particularly when it is transient. *Melancholic* is better reserved for describing a permanent state of depression, and can also be a *noun* for someone in that state.

memo / memorandum

● RECOMMENDATION

Memo is now used so often, in writing as well as speech, that *memorandum* has become the formal word, only strictly necessary in official prose.

● OPTION

Memo has only one plural form: *memos*. The plural of *memorandum* can be either *memoranda* ✓ or *memorand**ums***.

-ment

● RULE

The suffix should be added to the *complete* verb, retaining any final *e*: abridge – *abridgement*; amaze – *amazement*; excite – *excitement*. Possible exceptions are *acknowledge* and *judge*, as *acknowledgment* and *judgment* are alternative spellings. But **acknowledgement** and **judgement** are taking over, so the above RULE holds good.

mental telepathy

● CAUTION

When some inexplicable communication occurs, people often say, 'it was mental telepathy'. But telepathy *is* mental, so 'it was telepathy' says it all.

metaphor / simile

● RULES

1 These are literary words for describing something by relating it to something else with which it has no realistic connection: 'his ideas are a *load of old rubbish*'; 'she made a *song and dance* about it'. Those examples are *metaphors*.

2 A *simile* works in the same way, but uses the word 'like' to link the comparison: 'she was dressed up like a dog's dinner'; 'he was like a bull in a china shop'.

● CAUTION

Mixed metaphors should be avoided as they easily become ridiculous: 'you must put your foot down with a firm hand'.

meter / metre

● RULE

Both spellings are used for different purposes. A *meter* is a gauge for measuring things: *barometer*; *speedometer*; *thermometer*. *Metre* is used in **metric measurements**: *metre*; *kilometre*.

$ *Meter* is the only spelling, whatever the meaning.

method / technique

● RECOMMENDATION

Method suggests a procedure that has been developed. *Technique* can be more of a surface word for a way of doing something quickly and efficiently. Compare 'he has worked out a method for assessing when to order new stock' with 'she has a technique for dealing with complaints'.

methodology

● RECOMMENDATION

The word is sometimes criticised as an unnecessary *-ology* word that means no more than 'method' (see **method / technique**). But *methodology* does add the suggestion of a detailed analysis of principles and a scientific approach: 'the methodology of statistical analysis'.

meticulous

● RECOMMENDATION

The proper meaning of *meticulous* is fussy and pernickety, an *over*-attention to detail. But dictionaries accept that *meticulous* is often used now in a good sense, to mean careful and detailed. As a result, *over-meticulous* has to be used for the original meaning.

metre / meter

See **meter** . . .

metric land measurements

See **acre**

metric measurements

● RECOMMENDATION

The stop after abbreviations km, cm, ml, etc, is unnecessary (see **abbreviations**).

● RULES

1   The abbreviations do not take an *-s* in the plural: 17km; 57ml.

2   *Gramme* is French for one-thousandth of a kilogram, but *gram* is the usual spelling in English (dictionaries show *gramme* as an alternative, but it looks wrong). The abbreviation in the *singular* and *plural* is *g*, not 'gm': lg; 50g.

mews

● CAUTION

Although *mews* is a plural noun, it is normally treated as *singular*, as if it were 'road' or 'street': 'Hays Mews *is* a couple of minutes' walk from Berkeley Square.'

micro / micro-

● RULE

This Greek prefix for 'small' is joined to words without a hyphen: *microsurgery* (complex surgical operations using miniature instruments); *microlinguistics* (a study of the detail of language, rather than the overall pattern). See also **macro / macro-.**

microbe / bacteria / virus / germ

See **germ** . . .

microchip / silicon chip

● OPTION

> In general use they come to the same thing. A **microchip** ✓ (a minute wafer processed to form an integrated circuit) is usually made from *silicon*, a semiconductive element, hence a **silicon** *chip*.

middle class

> See **class**

might / could

> See **could . . .**

might / may

> See **may / might**

militate / mitigate

● RULES

1 When something is *mitigated*, the bad effects are lessened: 'aid from the world community will mitigate the effect of the famine'.
2 *Militate* is connected with 'military' and means to go against something: 'his casual appearance militated against people taking him seriously'.

● CAUTION

> Never write or say *mitigate* against, as it is only possible to *militate* against something (see RULE 2 above).

millennium

● RULE

> A *millennium* is 1000 years, and that's the only possible *singular* form.

● OPTION

> *Millennia* ✓ and *millenniums* are alternative *plural* forms.

● CAUTIONS

1 It's a common mistake to use *millennia* as the *singular* form ('during the next millennia').
2 It's easy to slip up and spell *millennium* with one *-n-*.

mini / mini-

● RECOMMENDATION

> When a *mini* word is in everyday use, a hyphen is unnecessary: *minibus*; *minicab*; *miniskirt*. With less frequently used words, use a hyphen: *mini-break*; *mini-budget*; *mini-prospectus*.

minimise / maximise

See **maximise** . . .

minimum / maximum (plural forms)

See **maximum** . . .

miniscule / minuscule

See **minuscule** . . .

minister / parson / priest / rector / vicar

● RULES

1 *Minister* is short for *minister of religion*: it can refer to a Protestant clergyman who is authorised to administer sacraments and conduct religious services. It is also a convenient name for clergy of other denominations (a Methodist minister, for example), and can extend to the Jewish faith, where a rabbi can be called a *minister*.
2 *Priest* is one of the orders of ministry in the Anglican, Roman Catholic and Orthodox Churches. The term can also be used about a minister in other religions of the world: we can talk about a Tibetan priest or a Buddhist priest, for example, but not a Jewish priest.
3 At one time, in the Church of England, there was a distinction between a *rector* and a *vicar*. An echo of that remains in the names *rectory* and *vicarage* in particular parishes. But in general use now, *vicar* and *rector* are simply alternative titles.

● CAUTIONS

1 *Parson* is sometimes felt to be a disrespectful term (except in America, where it is used freely).
2 The above notes are a guide to everyday use, but within different churches there are complex ecclesiastical subtleties in the way titles are used.

minority / majority *is / are*

See **majority / minority** *is / are*

minuscule / miniscule

● CAUTION

Because of the pull of the prefix 'mini-', *minuscule* (PRON 'MINNe(r)skyool') is often misspelt 'min*iscule*'.

mis-

● RULE

Words formed with the prefix *mis-* never take a hyphen. There are no exceptions, and you can ignore older dictionaries that show hyphens in such words as 'mis-shape'. You can *mishandle* something, *misremember* your *misspent* youth, and make as many *misstatements* as you like – all without hyphens.

misinformed / uninformed / ill-informed

See ill-informed . . .

misprint / literal / typo

These are alternative words for a printing error.

● RECOMMENDATIONS

1 *Misprint* is the most common word, particularly for people not involved in publishing or printing.
2 *Literal* (short for 'literal error', that is a mistake in letters) is the word most in use by writers, publishers and proofreaders.
3 When dealing with printers, *typo* is the most usual term.

Miss / Ms

See **Mr / Mrs / Miss / Ms** (RECOMMENDATION 4)

mistakable / mistakeable

● RECOMMENDATION

As some current dictionaries have dropped *mistakeable* as an alternative spelling, always use *mistakable*.

mistress / master (of colleges)

See **master** . . .

mistrust / distrust

See **distrust** . . .

mitigate / militate

See **militate** . . .

modern / contemporary

See **contemporary** . . .

modern / contemporary architecture (definitions)

See **contemporary** . . . RECOMMENDATIONS 1 and 2

modern dance (definition)

See **contemporary** . . . RECOMMENDATION 2

modern English (definition)

See **contemporary** . . . RECOMMENDATION 2

Mohammedan / Moslem / Muslim

See **Muslim** . . .

mold / mould

See **mould** . . .

momentarily (pronunciation)

● OPTION

Some dictionaries accept stress on the *third* syllable ('momenTARily') [!] as an alternative to stressing the *first* syllable: 'MOmentarily'✓ .

monetary / fiscal / financial

See **financial** . . .

money (expressed in writing)

● RECOMMENDATIONS

1 Write even small amounts of money in *figures*: £3 (rather than *three pounds*).
2 When it is a round sum of £100 or £1000, this is preceded by *a* only if *words* are used: 'it costs *a* hundred pounds' but 'it costs £100'.
3 Express *millions* as *m* right up against the figure, or *million* with a space between: £100m or £100 million (rather than £100,000,000).
4 Express *billions* as *bn* right up against the figure: £100bn. For the definition of *billion*, see **billion / trillion.**

monologue / soliloquy

● RULES

1 *Monologue* is the word generally used when an actor talks directly to the audience. A play that consists of only one actor speaking is a *monologue.*
2 A *soliloquy* is a character thinking out loud, while the audience listen, almost as if by chance.

monopoly / cartel

See **cartel** . . .

monseigneur / monsignor

● RULES

1 *Monseigneur* (PRON 'monnsayNYER') is French, a title formerly used for princely ranks in the aristocracy, and now accorded to French bishops and certain other prelates.
2 *Monsignor* (PRON 'monSEENyer') is the Italian version of the title, which is accorded to certain senior Roman Catholic priests, as well as to some officers at the Vatican.

Monsieur / Madame / Mademoiselle

When French people are in Britain, do we introduce them as *Monsieur* Desbrosses, *Madame* Signoret, *Mademoiselle* Legrand, etc, or *Mr* Desbrosses, *Mrs* Signoret, *Miss* (or *Ms*) Legrand? For RECOMMENDATIONS, see **Mr, Mrs . . . / Monsieur, Frau . . . .**

montage / collage

See **collage . . .**

moonlight / moonlit

● RULE

Use *moon**light*** as the *noun*, *moon**lit*** as the *descriptive word*: 'we met by moonlight'; 'it was a moonlit night'.

moor / heath

See **heath . . .**

more / most

● RULES

1 *More* is for a comparison between *two* things: 'the students from the girls' school are more advanced than the students from the boys' school'.
2 *Most* is used when *more than two* things are involved: 'comparing the students from the three schools, these are the most advanced'.

● RECOMMENDATION

When it's a straight statement, rather than a comparison, there is often a choice between *more* and *most*: 'the *more* (or *most*) expensive wines on the list'. In that example, *more* suggests that there are a fair number of 'more expensive wines', while 'most expensive wines' suggests only a few high-priced wines are meant.

more especially

See **especially . . .**

more importantly

See **important . . .**

more or less

● RECOMMENDATION

More or less is a useful way of indicating that a statement may not be completely accurate, but is sufficiently so for it to be worth making: 'we have more or less agreed terms' suggests we have gone a long way towards agreeing them, but there remain a few minor points to be cleared up.

● CAUTION

More or less should really mean rather *more* than less, but that is no guarantee that someone might not use it to mean rather *less* than more.

more than one *is* / *are*

See **one** (RULE 4)

morgue / mortuary

● RULE

Both are places where dead bodies await identification, autopsies or burial. Hospitals have *mortuaries*, while municipal authorities have *morgues*.

mortgage (pronunciation)

● RULE

The *t* is not pronounced: 'MAWgidge'.

mortuary / morgue

See **morgue** . . .

Moslem / Muslim / Mohammedan

See **Muslim** . . .

mosquitoes / mosquitos

● OPTION

Mosquitoes ✓ and *mosquitos* are alternative plural forms.

most of / *majority* of

See *majority* of . . .

motivate / activate

See **activate** . . .

motley

● RECOMMENDATION

Use *motley* mostly as a descriptive word for a variety of colours: 'a dress of motley colours'.

● CAUTION

Motley can also be used for any ill-assorted combination of people or objects ('a motley crew'; 'a motley collection'), and in this sense it would usually be taken as a disparaging comment.

motorcade / cavalcade

See **cavalcade** . . .

mottoes / mottos

● OPTION

One *motto*, two or more *mottoes* ✓ or *mottos*.

mould / mold

● RULE

All meanings of the *noun*, whether it's a hollow shape used to create a form by pouring in liquid that sets, or a growth of fungus on food, topsoil, etc, are spelt *mould*. And the same spelling also applies to the *verb*: 'she has moulded his opinions'.

$ All uses of the *noun* and *verb* are spelt *mold*.

movable / moveable

● OPTION

Feasts and lots of other things can be *movable* ✓ or *moveable*.

Mr / Mrs / Miss / Ms

● RECOMMENDATIONS

1 When using people's names in full it is usually in order to leave out courtesy titles, but if they are much older than you are, or hold a position of particular importance, be careful: 'John Brown and Helen Forbes are working on this project.', but if you want to be safe, '*Mr* Henry Ford, the chairman, is dealing with this.'

2 A courtesy title seems out of place for someone of ill-repute, as in '*Mr* Phipps makes a living by mugging old ladies.'

3 It's downmarket to announce yourself on the telephone or to introduce yourself as '*Mr*': 'I'm John Brown.' is preferable to 'I'm *Mr* John Brown.'

4 Generally *Ms* should be used in preference to *Miss*. *Ms* (PRON 'mizz'✓ or 'merz') is the usual form for addressing a woman when you don't know her first name or whether she's married. *Ms* should also be used when you need to use a courtesy title for a married woman who retains her single name: '*Ms* Forbes's husband, Mr John Brown, has just arrived.'

5 Women who are no longer alive should be identified by their traditional courtesy titles as it would sound odd to change them: *Miss* Gertrude Stein; *Mrs* Virginia Woolf; *Mrs* Golda Meir; *Mrs* Patrick Campbell.

● CAUTION

The rules of the game are uncertain, and the above recommendations are offered as guidelines for keeping a balance between being overfamiliar to people who might not like it and sounding out of touch with the style of the 1990s.

Mr, Mrs . . . /Monsieur, Frau . . .

Which courtesy titles should be used in an English context when referring to foreigners?

● RECOMMENDATIONS

1 If we insist on the appropriate foreign titles, it can become awkward: 'Mr Brown welcomed Frau Brandt to the meeting, and they were later joined by Monsieur Dupont, Signor Fradeletto and Señorita Gonzàlez.' So apart from situations where protocol must be observed, it gives fewer difficulties to use English forms of address: 'Mr Brown welcomed Mrs Brandt to the meeting, and they were later joined by Mr Dupont, Mr Fradeletto and Miss Gonzàlez.'

2 With heads of state and other dignitaries, this dilemma can be avoided by using their titles: 'President Chirac is meeting Chancellor Kohl.'

● CAUTION

Be careful about using *Mademoiselle*, *Fräulein* and *Señorita*, particularly for older women, as those titles are not always used in the same way as *Miss*.

MS/MSS

See **manuscript**

Ms/Miss

See **Mr/Mrs/Miss/Ms** (RECOMMENDATION 4)

mulatto/Creole/half-caste

See **half-caste . . .**

multi/multi-

● RECOMMENDATION

Drop the hyphen in all *multi-* combinations, except *multi-storey*, where it insists on staying put: *multicultural*; *multidirectional*; *multiracial*.

municipal (pronunciation)

● RULE

Stress the *second* syllable not the *first*: 'mewNISSiple'.

Muslim/Moslem/Mohammedan

These are names for a follower of the faith of Islam.

● RECOMMENDATION

The only one to use is *Muslim* (with a capital *M*).

● CAUTION

Many Muslims find it patronising to be called *Mohammedans*, nor is *Moslem* liked.

● OPTION

Muslim can be pronounced 'MOOZlim' (the first syllable with the vowel sound of 'g*oo*d')✓ or 'Muzzlim'.

must (noun)

● RECOMMENDATION

To describe something as *a must*, meaning something we need, is commercial jargon, and covers too broad a band of meaning. It's better to indicate the level of importance: 'necessary'; 'important'; 'essential'; 'vital'; 'something we really cannot do without'.

mutual / common

See **common / mutual**

myself

● RECOMMENDATION

Myself is often used pretentiously when all that's needed is a simple 'I' or 'me': 'please contact *myself* over this'; 'my wife and *myself* will be glad to come to dinner'. Why not 'please contact me . . .'; 'my wife and I . . .'?

mystical / occult

● RECOMMENDATIONS

1 *Mystical* should suggest divine revelation (it derives from a Greek word for someone who is initiated).

2 *Occult* (PRON with stress on the *first* syllable: 'OCCult') suggests magic and mysterious, rather than spiritual, and is used particularly in such areas as spiritualism, clairvoyance and hypnotism. And while the word does not necessarily imply evil, it is also used about witchcraft and voodoo.

● CAUTION

There is a tendency for *mystics* to be thought of as *Eastern* spiritual teachers wearing Buddhist robes. But *mystical* touches the concept of anyone who has transcended this life to find another reality, wherever they are, whatever clothes they are wearing.

myth / legend

See **legend . . .**

N

'n/'n'

See **ampersand (&)**

naive/naïve

● OPTION

Naïve (with two dots over the *ï*) is still often retained to mark the separate pronunciation of *a* and *i*. But the latest dictionaries show *naive* (without dots)✓ as an alternative spelling. Either way, the pronunciation is 'nahEEV'.

● CAUTION

Naive can have the harmless meaning of innocent and childlike, but when used about adults or ideas it's more likely to mean simple-minded and guileless. So it's better to use the 'innocent' meaning only when referring to children.

NOTE As a term in art, *naive* is not pejorative. It corresponds to *primitive*, used about art that is free from self-consciousness and academic tradition.

names ending in *-s, -ch, -sh*

● RECOMMENDATION

Form the plural of names, such as *Jones, Birch, Fish*, etc, by adding *-es*: *Joneses, Charleses, Fishes* ('the Joneses are coming to dinner'). Retain the *-es* for the *possessive* of plural forms, with the apostrophe after the *-es*: the Joneses' house; the Birches' children; the Fishes' car.

napkin/serviette

● CAUTION

There's nothing wrong with either word for the piece of cloth or paper used to protect our clothes while eating. But for some perverse reason only the down-to-earth word *napkin* is considered socially acceptable, and the elegant word *serviette* is regarded by some people as vulgar.

nation *is/are*

● RULE

A nation must be regarded as a whole, and always treated as *singular*: 'the nation *is* ready for war'.

native

● CAUTION

The word has uncomfortable colonial associations ('the natives were friendly').

While no one should be upset at being called a native of East Cheam, for example, if that's where they come from, if *native* is used carelessly about inhabitants of former colonies, it could understandably give offence.

. . . nature . . .

● CAUTION

Nature is a word that slips in pointlessly at times: 'problems of this nature are difficult to overcome'; 'because of the sensitive nature of this information, it must be kept confidential'. Leave out *nature* and the sentences are more direct: 'problems like these . . .'; 'because this information is sensitive . . .'.

naught/zero/'oh'/nought

See **nought** . . .

nauseated/nauseous

● RULES

1 *Nauseous* has three meanings: it describes something that makes people sick, such as a nauseous gas; it describes a particularly unpleasant taste or smell; it describes something or someone that is disgusting ('his behaviour was nauseous').

2 *Nauseated* is used about a person who is feeling sick ('she was nauseated by the sight of so much blood'), or for someone who is disgusted ('she was nauseated by his behaviour').

● CAUTION

A common mistake is 'I feel nauseous.' We can **be** *nauseous*, that is disgusting, but we can only **feel** *nauseated*, that is sick.

nautical miles

See **knots**

nearby/near by

● RULE

When it comes *before a noun*, it is always *one* word: 'we stayed at a *nearby* hotel'.

● OPTION

When it comes *after a verb*, it can be *one* word or *two*: 'we stayed *nearby* ✓ (or *near by*)'.

near disaster

● CAUTION

A common mistake is 'we were saved from a *near disaster*'. You can *have* a near disaster, that is something that just stops short of being a disaster, but if you were saved in time, you were 'saved from a disaster', not a '*near* disaster'.

necessarily (pronunciation)

● OPTION

Current dictionaries offer the choice between stress on the *first* syllable ('NECessarily')✓ and stress on the *third* syllable ('necesSARily').

need / require

● RECOMMENDATIONS

1 *Need* is usually the more direct word ('we need more time'), *require* more formal.

2 *Require* is also a way of issuing a command: 'we need you to be present' means we need your advice or agreement, but 'we *require* you to be present' is giving an order.

needless to say / not to mention

● RECOMMENDATION

It is argued that if anything is preceded by *needless to say* or *not to mention*, why say it or mention it? But at times the phrases are justified: sometimes the obvious needs to be stated, in case it's not obvious to the other person.

negative / positive

● RECOMMENDATION

Negative and *positive* have become overused indeterminate words in everyday contexts: 'I have negative feelings about this' (instead of 'uneasy feelings'); 'it has received a lot of negative publicity' (instead of 'bad publicity'); 'we've made negative progress' (instead of 'no progress' or 'we've lost ground'). And usually there's a more informative word than *positive*: 'happy' or 'hopeful' feelings; 'encouraging' or 'good' progress (rather than 'positive feelings'; 'positive progress').

negligence / carelessness

See **carelessness . . .**

(in the) **neighbourhood of**

See **in the neighbourhood of**

neither (pronunciation)

● OPTION

Dictionaries show alternative pronunciations: 'NYEther'✓ and 'NEEther'.

$ Usually 'NEEther'.

neither *is / are*

● RULE

Neither is *singular*: 'neither of us *is* ready yet'; 'neither *costs* more than £10'. See also **neither . . . *nor*/neither . . . *or*** (RULE 2).

neither . . . *nor*/neither . . . *or*

● RULES

1   *Neither . . . nor* is correct: 'neither . . . *or*' is wrong.

2   The verb after *neither . . . nor* can be *singular* or *plural*. It takes its cue from the noun that follows *nor*: 'neither the solicitors nor their *client is* available'; 'neither Mary nor her *solicitors are* available'.

3   It is not true, as some books lay down, that *neither . . . nor* should be used about only *two* alternatives: you can say 'neither Mary, nor John, nor Harry, nor Susan was present'.

neo-

Neo- can be prefixed to ideas, styles of art and architecture, and to almost anything else to indicate a revival, or a revised or adapted version.

● RECOMMENDATION

The hyphen can be omitted unless the following word begins with a vowel or a capital letter: *neoclassical*; *neocolonial*; *neorealism*; but *neo-imperialism*; *neo-Nazis*; *neo-Marxism*.

nephew (pronunciation)

● OPTION

'NE*V*you'✓ or 'NE*F*you'.

nerve-racking/nerve-wracking

● RULE

Rack, in the sense of straining, can also be spelt *wrack*, but this is becoming rare. Hence *nerve-racking*, straining the nerves, is now the accepted spelling.

net/nett

● RULE

When it is to do with sums of money, after all deductions have been made, or to do with weight excluding packing materials, etc, *net* is now the standard spelling (*nett* is obsolete).

(The) Netherlands/Holland

See **Holland** . . .

neutral/impartial

See **impartial** . . .

nevertheless/nonetheless

● OPTION

There is no difference in meaning between **never***theless* and **none***theless* ✓. They are alternative one-word ways of saying 'in spite of all that'; 'no matter what the outcome'; 'taking everything into account'.

new/fresh/renewed

● RECOMMENDATIONS

1   *New* is the basic word: 'she is writing a new book'; 'a new war has broken out'; 'there's a new man in her life'.

2   Where something stops and then restarts, the journalistic word is *fresh* ('fresh fighting has broken out'; 'fresh talks are taking place'). But *renewed* is the more apt word: 'renewed fighting . . .'; 'renewed talks . . .'.

3   When newness is implied in the noun, *new* is unnecessary, as in 'a new discovery'; 'a new speed record'; 'a new breakthrough' (discoveries, records, breakthroughs are always *new*). At the same time this seemingly unnecessary use of *new* is reasonable when we want to stress the point.

New World

● RECOMMENDATION

The expression *New World* is not only ill-defined but belongs to the 19th century. The exception is *New World* as a general term for wines from America, Australia, New Zealand and South America. In that context *New World* is in contrast to the traditional 'Old World' wine regions of Europe.

next to/adjacent/adjoining

● RECOMMENDATION

1   Reserve *adjacent* for when it comes *before a noun*: 'the adjacent houses'. In most other contexts, prefer *next to* to *adjacent to*. It's simpler and means the same: 'her house is *next to* (or *adjacent to*) mine' suggests both houses are side by side or very near each other, although they could be separated.

2   Use *adjoining* to suggest actually touching: 'her house adjoins mine' suggests the houses are immediately next to each other in a terrace, or are semi-detached.

nice

● RECOMMENDATION

There's always a tendency to use this maid-of-all-work word too often, and it is usually more complimentary to take the trouble to choose a more descriptive word: 'it was a *delicious* dinner, a *fascinating* evening, and you wore an *attractive* dress'. But that doesn't mean we should never use *nice*: sometimes it is a nice day because someone has been nice to us.

night/night-

● RECOMMENDATIONS

1   Treat as *one* word: *nightcap*; *nightclothes*; *nightclub*; *nightdress*; *nightfall*; *nightspot*.

2   Treat as *two* words: *night nurse*; *night school*; *night shift*; *night watchman*.

3   Few *night* combinations need be hyphenated, other than: *night-light*; *night-long*; *night-time*.

nobody

● CAUTION

'Nobody has made up *his* mind yet' is all right if it is a group of indecisive men, but what if it includes women? For RECOMMENDATIONS, see **unisex grammar.**

non / non-

● OPTION

When *non* is joined to another word to provide a negative meaning, it is usually optional whether to use a hyphen or to write the combination as *one* word. Examples: *non-alcoholic* ✓ or *nonalcoholic*; *non-communicating* ✓ or *noncommunicating*; *non-delivery* ✓ or *nondelivery*; *non-effective* ✓ or *noneffective*; *non-fiction* ✓ or *nonfiction*; *non-slip* ✓ or *nonslip*; *non-stick* ✓ or *nonstick*.

● RULE

There are a few examples where *non* forms a word that has a separate meaning, and these are always *one* word: *committal* is the act of committing someone to prison or a mental institution, whereas *noncommittal* means not committed to an action or an opinion; the usual meaning of *conformist* describes someone who follows the conventional line, whereas *nonconformist* is not conforming to the doctrine of the established Church.

non- / un- / in-

See **in- / un- / non-**

none *is / are*

● OPTION

None can be treated as *singular* or *plural*. In some sentences the choice between *none* **is** and *none* **are** provides a useful distinction: 'none of the members *have* cast their votes yet' covers members of both sexes, whereas 'none of the members *has* cast her vote' indicates that all the members are women. But in most sentences there is no rule: 'none of the members *has* ✓ (or *have*) arrived yet'.

non-essential / unessential / inessential

See **inessential** . . .

nonetheless / nevertheless

See **nevertheless** . . .

nonreligious / unreligious / sacrilegious / irreligious

See **irreligious** . . .

non-standard / slang / informal / colloquial

See **colloquial / informal** . . .

non-white

● CAUTION

We refer to *white* people or *black* people, or *whites* or *blacks*. In some contexts, *non-white* is useful as a collective term covering blacks and Asians, but many people consider it racist, as it could imply that the standard is white. See also **black / coloured; White / white.**

no one / no-one / noone

● OPTION

It is tempting to write *noone* as one word, on the lines of 'everyone', but it looks wrong. You can use either the hyphenated form (*no-one*) or keep the words separate (*no one*)✓.

● CAUTION

One other point arises: 'no one has made up *his* mind yet' is all right when it is a group of dithering men, but what if it includes women? For RECOMMENDATIONS, see **unisex grammar.**

(there's) **no question**

● CAUTIONS

1 Be careful with *there's no question*, for the meaning may not be clear: 'there's no question we can give you a discount' could be taken to mean 'of course we can give you a discount' or 'there's no hope of a discount'. Add 'but that' ('there's no question *but that* we can give you a discount') or 'of giving' ('there's no question *of giving* you a discount') and everybody knows whether it's *yes* or *no*.

2 *There's no question about . . .* usually means 'it is certain', but in some contexts it could mean uncertain. When there's any doubt, replace *no question about . . .* by either 'there's no doubt about . . .' ('there's no doubt about our delivering on time') or 'there's no question of . . .' ('there's no question of our delivering on time'), depending once again on whether it's *yes* or *no*.

nor / or

● RULES

1 When *neither* or *either* is part of the sentence, there is no problem: *neither* is always followed by *nor*, *either* by *or*: '*neither* Mary *nor* Joan is available'; '*either* Mary *or* Joan could do it'.

2 For RULES on whether *neither . . . nor* and *either . . . or* are followed by a *singular* or *plural* verb, see **neither . . . nor** (RULE 2) and **either** (RULES 1 and 2).

3 When *not* or any other negative comes after a verb, *nor* must follow and be repeated before every one of the words to which it applies: 'it will not be ready by tomorrow, *nor* by next week, *nor* the week after, *nor* even by next month'.

● OPTION

In some negative statements, *neither* or *nor* is possible: 'I don't like it *neither* ✓ (or *nor*) does my friend'; 'it is not good value *neither* ✓ (or *nor*) is it good quality'.

Nordic / Scandinavian

● RULES

1 *Scandinavian* is used both about the people, the language and the way of life of Denmark, Norway, Sweden, Iceland, sometimes including Finland as well.

2 *Nordic* is usually reserved for the physical appearance of the people, tall and blond.

norm / normal

● CAUTION

When *norm* or *normal* has a clinical or technical meaning (normal temperature; normal dose; normal output; the norm for this kind of car), there is usually little room for argument. In other contexts, particularly in relation to social behaviour and psychological reactions, *norm* and *normal* can represent a standard that is imposed by society or a psychiatrist. In that sense, what is normal in one group may not be normal in another. *Norm* and *normal* are words to watch, particularly when they carry an implied claim to rightness or goodness that is rooted in questionable beliefs and attitudes.

Norman / Romanesque

Both words describe the style of architecture from about 900 to 1200, generally recognised by round arches and powerful vaulted roofs.

● RECOMMENDATIONS

1 *Norman* is the term used for cathedrals and churches of this style and period in Britain, notably Durham Cathedral, Ely Cathedral and the crypt of Canterbury Cathedral.

2 *Romanesque* is used for the same style when it is found in France and elsewhere in Europe.

   NOTE The tendency now is for art historians to prefer *Romanesque* wherever the style is found.

North / north . . .

● RULES

1 You can go *south*, face a *north* wind, watch the sun rise in the *east* and set in the *west*, journey from *north* to *west*, without using capitals.

2 Whenever a region or a political or social divide is indicated, use a capital: 'the ballet dancer, Mikhail Baryshnikov, now lives in the *West*'; 'house prices in the *South*'; 'trade barriers between *East* and *West*'.

3 When *north, south* . . . are used about cities, they take a small letter when direction is indicated (*w*est London; *n*orth Oxford), but a capital letter when it becomes the actual name of part of the city (the *W*est End of London; *E*ast Side, New York).

Northern / northern . . .

● RULES

1   When *northern*, *southern* . . . are general indeterminate terms, they are spelt without a capital: *n*orthern Europe; *s*outhern Spain.

2   The main exceptions to the above rule are *N*orthern Ireland, the *W*estern Isles, *W*estern Australia.

NOTE   The long-lasting genre of Hollywood films, with heroic cowboys riding off into Technicolor sunsets, is traditionally spelt with a small *w*: *westerns*.

See also **Eastern / eastern.**

Northern Ireland / Ulster / Southern Ireland / Eire

See **Ireland** . . .

northward / northwards / northerly . . .

● OPTION

Northward, northwards, northerly, and the corresponding forms for the other points of the compass, can all be used as descriptive words before a noun, or after a verb, to indicate direction: 'a *northward* (*northwards* or *northerly* ✓) journey'; 'they travelled *southward* (*southwards* ✓ or *southerly*)'.

● RECOMMENDATION

The *-ward* or *-ly* forms are usually better *before nouns* and the *-wards* form *after verbs*: 'an *eastward* (or *easterly*) direction', but 'she looked *westwards*'.

● RULE

Only *northerly, southerly, westerly* and *easterly* can be used as *nouns* for a wind: 'a cold northerly'; 'a strong easterly'.

nosey / nosy

● OPTION

Nosey ✓ and *nosy* are alternative spellings.

not

● CAUTIONS

1   Be careful not to slip in an extra *not* when there is already a negative: 'I *don't* know *nothing* about it' should be 'I know nothing about it'.

2   When *not* is linked to 'because', there is a problem of ambiguity. Take this sentence: 'I did not telephone her because she was ill.' Was the telephone call made, not because she was ill, but for another reason? Or was it *not* made because she was ill? To make the meaning clear, the sentence has to be rewritten: 'I telephoned her, not because she was ill, but because I needed to speak to her.' covers one meaning. 'Because she was ill, I did not telephone her.' covers the other.

notice / criticism / critique / review

See **review** . . .

not in- / not un-

● RECOMMENDATION

Combinations such as *not infrequent*, *not unhappy* . . . are useful to express *in-between* meanings: 'her visits to him are not infrequent' suggests that visits are not frequent, but nor are they rare; 'she's not unhappy in her job' suggests that she may not be rapturous about her work, but it more or less suits her.

● CAUTION

Not in- and *not un-* are ways of avoiding coming out into the open with a direct statement. At times it is justified because it avoids exaggeration: 'the matter is not unimportant'. At other times, it can be evasive: 'it would not be untruthful if I denied what he has just said' is a mealy-mouthed way of saying 'what he has just said is a lie'.

See also *-un* **words.**

notorious / infamous

See **infamous** . . .

not to mention

See **needless to say** . . .

not un- / not in-

See **not in-** . . .

nought / naught / zero / 'oh'

● RULE

Nought is the spelling when the word is used for *zero*. In America the spelling is *naught*. In both countries, hopes, expectations, promises, etc may come to *naught*, which is the spelling when the word means 'nothing'.

● OPTION

When reading out figures, such as telephone numbers, the figure *0* can be given as *oh* (7070 = 'seven-oh-seven-oh') or *zero* ('seven-zero-seven-zero'). *Zero* ✓ is taking over as the standard term.

$ See RULE above.

nouns

● RULES

Grammarians divide nouns into four categories:

1   *Proper nouns* are usually spelt with a capital letter because they are names of people, places, etc: Mary; Paris; the Derby.

2 *Common nouns* are ordinary nouns, usually spelt with a small letter: book; language; letter.

3 *Collective nouns* are groups of people, animals or objects: committee; herd; orchestra; family; collection. For dealing with the problem of whether to treat such nouns as *singular* or *plural*, see **collective words**.

4 *Abstract nouns* are words for qualities, actions, states, etc: doubt; fear; honesty.

nowhere

● CAUTION

Even people who are careful have been known to slip in an unnecessary negative before *nowhere*: 'wherever we looked, we couldn't find it *nowhere*' (instead of 'we could find it nowhere' or 'we couldn't find it anywhere'). See also **not** (CAUTION 1).

nuclear / atomic

See **atomic** . . .

number / quantity / amount

See **amount** . . .

number of . . . *is / are*

● RULES

1 '*A* number' is *plural*, followed by *are, have,* etc: '*a* number of women *are* coming tonight'.

2 '*The* number' is *singular*: '*the* number of women coming tonight *is* small'.

● CAUTIONS

1 It's easy to slip up when a sentence begins with 'There', and a word comes between *a* and *number*: 'There *was* a small number of women unable to be present' should be 'There *were* a small number . . .' (because '*a number*' is *plural* - see RULE 1 above).

2 When 'who' (or another word) comes in between, be extra careful. We have to write, for example, 'the number of women who *are* . . .', but RULE 2 above still holds, as a *singular* verb follows: 'the number of women who are coming tonight *is* small'.

See also **total of . . . *is / are.***

numbers / numerals / figures

See **figures** . . .

nutrition / dietetics

See **dietetics** . . .

O / Oh

● RULES

1 For an invocation or a prayer, it is *O*, not usually followed by a comma or an exclamation mark: 'O God our help . . .'.

2 When it is an exclamation of dismay or surprise, it is *Oh*, followed immediately by an exclamation mark, or with the exclamation mark at the end of the sentence: 'Oh! Do you really think so?'; 'Oh my God!'

3 When it is a lead-in to a comment that follows, it is *Oh*, followed by a comma: 'Oh, if it's going to rain, we'd better cancel the match.'

oasis (plural)

● RULE

The only plural form is *oases* (PRON 'ohAYseez').

object / objective

● OPTION

In the sense of purpose, aim or intention, *objective* is the fashionable word: 'our objective is to secure the film rights before anyone else does'; 'the objective is to achieve lower production costs'. *Object* ✓ is a perfectly satisfactory word in such sentences.

● RECOMMENDATION

There is no good reason to use that self-important cliché, *the object of the exercise*, instead of 'the intention'; 'the purpose'; or simply – 'the object'.

obligatory / mandatory

See **mandatory** . . .

oblige / obligate

● RECOMMENDATIONS

1 *Obligate* suggests a legal or moral duty: 'they are obligated by the lease to have the outside of the building painted every five years'.

2 *Oblige* is the everyday word for something that has to be done for any reason: 'she is obliged to visit her mother at least once a week'.

3 Why indulge in that old-worldly expression 'I am obliged (or much obliged) to you for . . .', when you can simply say 'Thank you for . . .'?

oblivious *of* / *to*

● RECOMMENDATIONS

1 When *oblivious* is used to mean forgetful, follow it by *of*: 'she continued reading, oblivious *of* her promise to meet his train'.

2 When it is used to mean unaware, follow it by *to*: 'she continued reading, oblivious *to* the knocking on the door'.

oboist / oboeist

● RULE

Oboist.

obscenity / blasphemy

See **blasphemy** . . .

obsolescent / obsolete

● RECOMMENDATIONS

1 Use *obso**lescent*** for a stage on the way to something becoming *obso**lete***. For example, a piece of equipment could be *obsolescent*, in that it is superseded by a new design that is more efficient. In the meantime, the obsolescent equipment may function perfectly well, with spare parts still available. When eventually it can no longer meet present-day needs or be properly maintained, it is *obsolete*.

2 *Obso**lescent*** should not be used about *language*. When a word or expression falls into disuse, it is *obsolete*. (After some time, the word or expression could be said to be 'archaic', implying that it belongs to the past, with few people left who have heard of it.)

obstetrician / gynaecologist

See **gynaecologist** . . .

obtain

● RECOMMENDATIONS

1 It is difficult to think of a good reason why anyone should say 'Can you obtain this for me?' instead of 'Can you get this for me?'

2 The other use of the verb *obtain*, to mean 'valid; in force; relevant', is useful in certain contexts: 'What are the conditions that obtain?' requires a more specific answer than 'What are present conditions?', which is more general.

occult / mystical

See **mystical** . . .

ocean / sea

● RULES

1 *Ocean* is used about one of the five expanses of water surrounding the continents: the Atlantic, Pacific, Arctic, Antarctic and Indian Oceans. In other contexts it can have a poetic exalted use ('A life on the ocean wave'). *Oceanic* is the corresponding descriptive word, as used, for example, in *oceanic climate*, that is a climate affected by an ocean.

2 *Sea* is the everyday word used for maritime traffic ('They that go down to the sea in ships, that do business in great waters', *Psalm 107*), and for the lesser expanses of water, such as the North Sea; China Sea.

o'clock

● RECOMMENDATION

Since this is short for 'of the clock', it should be a small *o*: Some style books recommend that *o'clock* should be written close up to the figure, but it is logical to leave a space: 7 o'clock.

oculist / ophthalmologist / optometrist / optician

See **optician** . . .

odd

● CAUTION

Compare these two sentences to see how a well-placed *hyphen* can avoid a possible misunderstanding: 'there were some 50 odd people present'; 'there were some 50-odd people present'.

-oes / -os

NOTE There is no consistent rule for forming the plural of nouns ending in *-o*: sometimes it is **-oes**, sometimes **-os**, sometimes either ending can be used: **mosquito(e)s; motto(e)s**. As guidelines, here are the usual plural forms of some common words ending in *-o*: *cargoes*; *commandos*; *concertos* (also *concerti* – see **concerto / sonata**); *curios*; *echoes*; *egos*; *frescos*; *heroes*; *medicos*; *potatoes*; *scenarios*; *tomatoes*; *zeros*.

oeuvre / work

● RECOMMENDATIONS

1 It is pretentious to use *oeuvre* for a painting, a book, a composition, etc. The general word to cover such things is *work*: 'this work by Beethoven was written in 1805'.

2 *Oeuvre* (PRON 'ERRvr') is useful for the complete works of a writer, artist, composer, etc, considered as a whole (it remains *oeuvre*, not 'oeuvres'). In this sense, *oeuvre* embraces more than 'works', and suggests a totality of style and achievement:

'the oeuvre of van Gogh became an enduring source of inspiration for generations of artists'.

of

● CAUTIONS

1 *Of* is out of order if a sequence starts with 'for' or 'to': 'the conditions *for* signing the contract, paying the balance due and *of* completing the sale'. That should read '. . . and *for* completing the sale'.

2 Unnecessary *ofs* are hiccups in a sentence: 'we are thinking *of* signing the contract, *of* paying the balance due and *of* completing the sale'. Leave out the second two *ofs*, and it flows better: '. . . signing the contract, paying the balance due and completing the sale'.

3 Omitting *of* when it is required can confuse the meaning: 'the prevention of completing the sale and signing the contract the next day caused many problems' could suggest that the contract was signed even though completion was prevented. 'The prevention of completing the sale and *of* signing the contract . . .' leaves no doubt that both were held up.

of all time

● CAUTION

We have long ago lost count of how many 'greatest films *of all time*' there have been. *Of all time* has a cosmic dimension, and there is a good case for using it very rarely indeed.

of course

● RECOMMENDATIONS

1 *Of course* is useful at times to avoid suggesting someone is ignorant or stupid, when you tell them something they ought to know but you're not sure: 'it is Washington, not New York, that is of course the capital of the United States'.

2 It was standard practice at one time to put a *comma* on either side of *of course*. Sometimes this is necessary, as in the second example under CAUTION below, but it is not always required.

● CAUTION

Be on guard against the devious use of *of course* to suggest something can be taken for granted, when it really should be looked into carefully: 'at this price, it is of course incredible value'; 'You know, of course, that I love you.'

off

See **off** *of*

off / off-

● RULE

When *off* combinations come *before a noun*, they are hyphenated (see **hyphens** RECOMMENDATION 4): off-peak fares; off-street parking; an off-white coat.

NOTE Otherwise, there is no RULE about whether an *off* combination is one word, hyphenated or two words. Here are the most common combinations: offbeat (see **offbeat / off-key**); off-Broadway (an experimental low-budget theatrical production in New York); off-centre; off chance; off colour; offcut; offhand; off-key (see **offbeat / off-key**); off-licence; off-load; off-putting; off-season; offset; offshoot; offshore; offside.

offbeat / off-key

● RECOMMENDATIONS

1 *Offbeat*, which musically means out of rhythm, describes anyone or anything, often interesting and amusing, that is not in line with the usual order of things. *Offbeat* can be used admiringly, or it can be derogatory.

2 *Off-key*, which in music is out of tune, is also used for something that is unexpected or out of line, but in an unpleasant jarring way. *Off-key* is usually derogatory.

3 Hyphenate *off-key*: treat *offbeat* as *one* word.

off of

● CAUTIONS

1 Do not take anything off *of* anything since the one word *off* is enough: 'she took it off the table'.

2 In restaurants, *off* can be ambiguous: 'the fish is *off*' may put you off the fish, or may simply be short for 'off the menu'.

often (pronunciation)

● OPTION

To pronounce the *t* (instead of letting it rhyme with 'soften') used to be considered vulgar. But 'OFten'✓ is heard so often now that the time is coming when 'offen' could sound old-fashioned. Current dictionaries show both pronunciations.

$ 'OFten'.

OK / OK? / okay

● RECOMMENDATIONS

1 *OK* changes its meaning with intonation. A falling tone expresses 'I agree'; 'all right'; 'if you insist'. A rising tone (*OK?*) asks 'Do you understand?'; 'Are you ready?'; 'Are you all right?'; 'How do I look?'

2 'It's OK by me', originally a New York Yiddishism, is at home now in Britain.

3 When used in writing as a descriptive expression to mean 'honest', 'good quality',

'competent', etc, *okay* is the usual form: an okay arrangement; an okay airline; an okay plumber.

4   In spite of its long history, *OK* and *okay* remain conversational, not considered suitable for serious prose.

old / elderly

See **elderly** . . .

olde / olden

● CAUTIONS

1   *Olde* is a 20th-century vulgar attempt to give the word 'old' a spurious Chaucerian flavour, and expressions such as 'olde worlde', should be avoided (except as a joke).

2   Although *olden* has genuine antiquity, phrases such as 'in olden times' are now both affected and vague, since they give no indication of the period referred to.

oldest / eldest / older / elder

See **elder** . . .

on / in

See **in / on**

on / upon

● OPTION

In most cases *on* ✓ and *upon* are interchangeable, with *upon* sounding more formal and dignified. But there are certain established phrases and place-names that usually keep to one form or the other. Here are some: **upon** *my word*; **on** *no account*; **on** *call*; **on** *hand*; *Burton-***upon**-*Trent*; *Henley-***on**-*Thames*; *Newcastle-***upon**-*Tyne*; *Southend-***on**-*Sea*; Shakespeare's birthplace has it both ways: *Stratford-***upon**-*Avon* ✓ or *Stratford-***on**-*Avon*.

on *behalf* of / on *the part* of

● RULES

1   *On behalf of* someone means in their interest or in their place: 'she is dealing with the matter on behalf of her husband'.

2   *On the part of* relates to a quality that is attached to a person: 'the matter went wrong because of incompetence on the part of the engineer'.

one

● RULES

1   Once you start using *one*, you are landed with it: '*One* feels that travelling to other countries enlarges *one's* experience and gives *one* a better understanding of *oneself*.'

It is wrong to change halfway: '*one* feels that travelling to other countries enlarges *our* experience . . .').

2　*One in . . .* is *singular*: 'one in five new businesses *fails* in the first year' (not '. . . *fail* in the first year'). The verb is controlled by *one*, not the figure that comes after.

3　*One of those* is *plural*, because the verb is controlled by *those*, not by *one*: 'she is one of those successful women who *are* now on the board' (not '. . . *is* now on the board').

4　*More than one* should logically be followed by a *plural* verb. But because of the influence of the word *one*, the usual way is to treat the phrase as *singular*: 'more than one woman *has* refused to attend the meeting'. Even when *more than one* stands on its own, it is still followed by a *singular* verb: 'more than one *has* refused . . .'.

● CAUTIONS

1　'*One of* the travellers has lost *his* baggage.' But what if the traveller turns out to be a woman? For RECOMMENDATIONS, see **unisex grammar**.

2　*One* can suggest a snobbish attitude: in a sentence such as '*one* wouldn't go to a place like that dressed in that way', *one* is another way of saying 'people like us'.

one / one-

● RULES

1　As *one* combinations are usually descriptive words coming in front of a noun, they are mostly hyphenated (see **hyphens** RECOMMENDATION 4): *one-horse* carriage; *one-man* show; *one-night* stand; *one-parent* family (see also **lone/single parent**); *one-time* minister; *one-way* road; *one-way* ticket.

2　*One-off* is hyphenated both as a noun ('it's a one-off') and a descriptive word ('a one-off experiment').

one another / each other

See **each other . . .**

on earth / in the world

See **in the world . . .**

one-sided / unilateral

● RULES

1　A *unilateral* decision is made by one party without reference to others who are involved, and such a decision could in certain circumstances be courageous.

2　*One-sided* is more down-to-earth, and usually suggests something done for a selfish advantage, disregarding other people.

only

There are purists who deny that 'we only live once' and insist 'we live only once'. *Only*, they say, must come *immediately* in front of the word it refers to.

- RECOMMENDATION

Everyone knows what we mean by 'I only want one glass of wine' (instead of '. . . only one glass . . .'). Many good writers, including Doris Lessing, Kingsley Amis, Graham Greene, Evelyn Waugh and George Orwell, are not at all fussed, placing *only* before the *verb*, which is its natural place, even though it refers to another word: 'The captain only appeared once at table' (Graham Greene), rather than '. . . appeared only once . . .'. The word order 'I want only one glass'; 'appeared only once at table' is justified *only* when we want to give the point extra strong emphasis (as in this last sentence).

on *the part* of / on *behalf* of

See on *behalf* of . . .

onto / on to

- RULE

When it is impossible to use *on* alone, *on to* should always be *two* words: 'please pass this on to her'; 'Keep right on to the end of the road.'

- OPTION

When the sense is *direction* or *placement*, *onto* ✓ or *on to* can be used: 'the children ran *onto* (or *on to*) the beach'; 'she climbed *onto* (or *on to*) the ship'.
See also in / into / in to.

onward / onwards

- RULES

1 As a word of encouragement or command, it is *onward*: 'Onward Christian soldiers'.
2 When it is an indication of *direction* or *time*, it is *onwards*: 'we must move onwards'; 'from the time of her marriage onwards'.

operator / operative

- RECOMMENDATIONS

1 *Operator* is the usual word for someone who operates a machine.
2 *Operative* should be used for a skilled worker in a particular field (there is, for example, a Federation of Building Trades Operatives).
$ Although it can also mean a skilled worker, as in British English, the first meaning of *operative* is a spy or secret agent.

ophthalmologist / oculist / optometrist / optician

See optician . . .

opinion / taste / attitude

See attitude . . .

opposite / converse / reverse / antithesis

● RECOMMENDATIONS

1   *Opposite* is the all-purpose word, usually the safest one to use.

2   **Converse** is more relevant to an action: 'she often cooks dinner, but the converse is also true, since there are many times when he cooks it'.

3   **Reverse** is a general word, more pointed than *opposite,* for something that is the other way round: 'it was not a case of carelessness but the reverse, an overattention to detail'. While *opposite* would work perfectly well in that sentence, *reverse* makes the point more sharply.

4   *Antithesis* is the strongest of all these words, since it represents the absolute opposite: 'the minister is hesitant and indecisive, and we need the antithesis, someone who can make strong forceful decisions'.

opposite *of / to / from*

● RECOMMENDATION

Of is preferable when *opposite* compares *two nouns*: 'Mary's attitude is the opposite of John's'; 'her attitude is the opposite of mine'.

● OPTION

To ✓ or *from* is required when *opposite* compares *directions* or *positions*: 'they left in the opposite direction *to* (or *from*) the one we were taking'; 'our house is on the opposite side of the road *to* (or *from*) theirs'.

optician / oculist / optometrist / ophthalmologist

● RULES

1   *Opticians* are not qualified doctors, and fall into two categories: an *ophthalmic optician* is qualified to test sight and supply spectacles, while a *dispensing optician* is limited to supplying spectacles against someone else's prescription.

2   *Oculist* is an obsolete term, replaced by *ophthalmologist* or *ophthalmic surgeon,* which are alternative terms for a medical specialist who deals with disorders of the eyes.

3   *Optometrist* (PRON 'opTOM-me(r)trist') is now the official name for an *ophthalmic optician* (see RULE 1 above).

● CAUTION

Because of 'optic', do not spell **oph**thalmic as 'opthalmic'. The pronunciation also needs to be watched: 'offTHALmic' (not 'opTHALmic').

optimum

● CAUTION

Optimum is often used wrongly to mean 'maximum'. *Optimum* does mean the most, but always taking into account other factors, which are usually specified. We refer to *optimum return,* for example, to mean not the highest possible return, but the highest return consistent with financial security, reasonable access to capital, or whatever other factors are mentioned.

optometrist / oculist / ophthalmologist / optician

See **optician** . . .

or

● RULES

1 When every item is *singular*, the verb should be *singular*: 'Susan or Mary or Helen *is* available to help'.

2 When every item is *plural*, the verb is *plural*: 'fifty men or three mechanical diggers *are* required'.

3 When items are a *combination of singular and plural*, the verb takes its cue from the *last noun* in the list: 'ten men or one mechanical digger *is* required'; 'one mechanical digger or ten men *are* required'.

-or / -our

See **-our** . . .

oral / verbal

See **verbal** . . .

(the) **orchestra** *is / are*

See **collective words**

ordeal (pronunciation)

● RULE

'orDEAL' (stress on the *second* syllable) is the only pronunciation considered correct.

ordinarily (pronunciation)

See **-arily**

ordinary / everyday

See **everyday / ordinary**

orient / orientate

● OPTION

Both words mean finding our bearings (originally facing or turning towards the East): if we are lost, we try to *orient* ✓ or *orient**ate*** ourselves.

NOTE The above meaning has become extended and the fashionable use of *orient* now is to say someone or something is biased in a particular direction: a new model of a car is claimed to be *oriented* towards safety or *safety-oriented*.

Or is it?

● RECOMMENDATION

Use *Or is it?*, *Or is she?*, *Or did he?* for a dramatic interjection of uncertainty into something that is being taken for granted. Keep this in mind when people are nodding too comfortably over something they should be thinking about: 'That's the end of the whole matter. Or is it?'; 'We all agree that this is a great painting. Or do we?'

-os / -oes

See **-oes** . . .

-our / -or

● CAUTIONS

1 British spellings are inconsistent, since when *-ous* or *-ious* is added, the *-u-* of *-our* is usually dropped, and the spelling follows the American pattern (see below): *glamour* – *glamorous*; *humour* – *humorous*; *labour* – *laborious*; *odour* – *odorous*. And there are other exceptions, such as *colourful* but *coloration*; *honourable* but *honorific*.

2 Where *-our* is correct, as it usually is, be careful to avoid the *-or* spelling which jars on many people.

$ The American lexicographer, Noah Webster, replaced the British *-our* by *-or* in most words: *color*; *humor*; *labor*; *odor*. One or two words slipped through the net, including *glamour*, often spelt that way in America, alongside *glamor*.

ours / our's

● RULE

Our's is always wrong.

ourselves / ourself

● RULE

Ourselves is the only form, as in 'we were pleased with ourselves'; 'we see ourselves as a new political party'.

out / out-

● RECOMMENDATION

When *out* is used as a prefix, in nearly every case it forms *one* word, without a hyphen: *outclass*; *outgoing*; *outpatient*; *outperform*; *outshoot*. But where the second word begins with a *-t*, a hyphen is preferable: *out-talk*; *out-top*; *out-tray*.

out / out of

See **out of** . . .

outcast / outcaste

● RULE

The two words have different meanings. An *outcast* is rejected by society or by a group: an *outcaste* is a person who does not belong to one of the four hereditary classes in Hindu society.

outcome

● RECOMMENDATION

It is worth being on guard against using *outcome* to make a simple sentence sound more important: 'the outcome of the delay was losing the business' is a roundabout way of saying 'the delay made us lose the business'. *Outcome* is more justifiable when it is applied to the result of a long and uncertain process: 'there were many problems to overcome, but the outcome made the effort worthwhile'.

outdoors / out of doors

● OPTION

There is no difference between *outdoors* ✓ and *out of doors*: 'the children are playing *outdoors* (or *out of doors*)'.

outline / summary / synopsis / résumé

● RECOMMENDATIONS

1 An *outline* is an indication of the overall form of a plan, a book, a project, sometimes prepared before the details have been worked out. The purpose is to convey the general idea, often to get approval in principle.

2 A *summary* is a short version of something, especially a report, that includes essential detail, and the purpose is to save a reader time and trouble, or to recapitulate the main points.

3 A *synopsis* can cover either an *outline* or a *summary*, and is more likely to be used for a shortened version of a piece of prose or of a complete book, rather than a report (see RECOMMENDATION 2 above). A *synopsis* usually conveys more detail than either an *outline* or a *summary*. Plural *synopses* (PRON 'siNOPPseez').

● OPTION

A *résumé* (PRON 'REZyou-may') is an alternative word for *summary* ✓.

● RULE

The corresponding *verbs* are *outline*, *summarise* and *synopsise* (there is no verb for *résumé*): 'please *outline* (*summarise*, *synopsise*) this'.

$ *Résumé* (with or without accents) is the word used for a **cv**.

out of / out

● OPTION

In conversation, *out of* ✓ and *out* have become interchangeable: 'she jumped *out* (*of*) the car and slammed the door'. In writing *out **of*** is preferable.

outside / outside of

● RECOMMENDATIONS

1   *Outside* is preferable when it relates to a place: 'there are important collections of art outside London'; 'while her application was being discussed, she waited outside the room'.

2   In the sense of 'apart from', *outside **of*** fits in better: 'he has other interests outside of politics'; 'there is a spirituality about her that seems outside of her religion'.

outstanding

● CAUTION

Look out for the two meanings of *outstanding* cutting across one another: 'there is an outstanding book we have to discuss before awarding the prize'. Is the book in question remarkable or is it the one book that still remains to be considered? When the second meaning is intended, uncertainty can be avoided by placing *outstanding after* the noun: 'there is a book outstanding that we have to discuss . . .'.

outward / outwards

● RECOMMENDATION

Outward in front of a noun, *outwards* after a noun or a verb: 'on the outward journey'; 'on the journey outwards'; 'while they journeyed outwards'.

over / over-

● RECOMMENDATION

Follow the tendency which is to drop the hyphen: *overanxious; overblown; overcapacity; overconfident; oversight; overwrite.* This applies even when the next word begins with an *r: overreach; overripe; overrun.*

over and above

See **each and every**

overall

● RECOMMENDATION

Overall has a place to indicate that a figure includes peripheral items: 'the overall length of a car would include bumpers'; 'the overall cost would include all extras'. In other cases, it is often unnecessary to use *overall*, instead of 'total' or 'complete', or even no qualifying word at all: 'total sales for this product' or simply 'sales for this product' rather than '*overall* sales'; 'the conclusion was', rather than 'the *overall* conclusion'.

overly

● RECOMMENDATION

Overly, before a descriptive word, is still distinctly American, and sentences such as 'this is not overly important' do not sound at home in Britain. The simple word *too* is often the best alternative. In other cases, the prefix *over-* can be suitable: 'she is too sensitive', or '. . . oversensitive' (instead of 'overly sensitive'). See also **over / over-**.

overtone / undertone

● RECOMMENDATIONS

1 *Overtone* suggests an unmistakable nuance: 'there was a threatening overtone in his speech to the workforce' (the suggestion is that threats were clearly implied, even if not openly expressed).

2 *Undertone* also means something not on the surface, but less obvious, more a general feeling that can be sensed: 'there was a confident undertone in the way the figures were presented' (presumably the figures were encouraging, which led to their being presented in an upbeat way).

overview

● RECOMMENDATION

Overview is vague, and is usually better replaced by a more explicit word, such as 'survey', 'outline', 'review', 'broad picture': 'an overview of marketing for the last year' is better as 'a *review* (or *broad picture*) of marketing . . .'.

owing to / due to

See *due* to . . .

P

pacemaker / pacesetter

● RULES

1   These are interchangeable words for someone who sets the pace for someone else to keep up with, usually in a race or in training, or for a person who takes the lead in an enterprise: 'the marketing director is the *pacesetter* (or *pacemaker*) in the export drive'.

2   Only *pacemaker* is used for the electronic device implanted surgically to regulate the heartbeat.

pacts (pronunciation)

● CAUTION

Retain a hint of the *t* sound, so that the pronunciation doesn't become 'pax'.

paean / peon

● RULES

1   *Paean* (from the name used for the Greek god Apollo in the Homeric hymn to his praise) is the word for a song of praise or a tribute to someone.

2   *Peon* is a Spanish word, used in English, for a farmworker, or sometimes for a poor peasant in Latin America.

PRON   Both words are pronounced exactly the same: 'PEE-e(r)n'.

painkiller / anodyne / analgesic

See **analgesic** . . .

pair / pairs

● RULE

In the *singular*, preceded by 'a', it is always *pair*: 'a pair of cuff-links'; 'a pair of socks'.

● OPTION

In the *plural*, *pairs* ✓ or *pair* can be used: 'two *pairs* (or *pair*) of cuff-links'; 'half a dozen *pairs* (or *pair*) of socks'.

See also **pair of *is/are.***

(a) pair of *is / are*

● OPTION

A *pair of* can often be seen as a unit or as two separate parts that come together: 'a pair of cuff-links *is* or *are* ✓. . .'; 'a pair of trousers *is* or *are* ✓. . .'.

● RULE
  A pair of scissors is always treated as *plural*.

pajamas / pyjamas
  See **pyjamas** . . .

pandit / pundit
● RECOMMENDATION
  Although these are variant spellings (PRON 'PUNdit' for both spellings) of the same word from Sanskrit, use *pandit* when it is the title given to a Hindu scholar, someone learned in Sanskrit, Indian philosophy or law, hence Pandit Nehru.

● CAUTION
  In Britain the spelling *pundit* is more often than not used in mock-seriousness about a so-called expert, who is either long-winded or lays down the law with more authority than they are entitled to.

para / para-
● RULE
  Words formed with the prefix *para-* are now treated as one word, without a hyphen. The key to their meaning is the word *parallel*, for Greek *para* means 'beside'. Examples: *paramedic* covers people who are not qualified doctors but have been trained to carry out certain treatments, usually in emergencies; *paramilitary* covers quasi-military movements, such as the IRA, which are organised like an army (hence *paramilitary uniforms*); *parapsychology* is the term for psychic phenomena such as telepathy and ESP (see **parapsychology / ESP**).

  NOTE   Alongside the Greek prefix, there is a Latin prefix *para-* with the different meaning of 'shelter' or 'ward off'. Hence words such as *parasol; parachute; parapet*.

paradox / contradiction
  See **contradiction** . . .

paragraphs
● RECOMMENDATIONS
1 As most people take in more information now from pictures than in any other way, they expect easy-going narrative, and long paragraphs can seem hard work. So the tendency is for shorter and shorter paragraphs in letters, newspapers and even in books.
2 But there is no need to give in all the time to the demands of living in the fast lanes of the 1990s. In some contexts longer paragraphs, like speaking more slowly, may be called for because of the seriousness and complexity of an argument.
3 As a general principle, when you start a different train of thought or a new subject,

and a full stop isn't a definite enough break from what has gone before, that's the time to start a new paragraph.

parallel
● RECOMMENDATION

A useful hint for remembering there are *two l*s in the middle is to think of *ll* being *parallel*.

parameter
● RECOMMENDATIONS

1 *Parameter* belongs to mathematical and technical contexts, representing a constant factor in one particular case, but subject to variation in others. The extended use has a place for limits controlled by a number of variations: 'an architect has to work within the parameters of the site, budget and purpose of the building'.

2 When boundaries are sharply defined, 'limits' or 'constraints' are better words: 'the architect has to work within the constraints of a fixed budget'.

paraphernalia *is / are*
● RECOMMENDATIONS

1 *Paraphernalia* is usually treated as *plural* when it concerns a list of items: 'you'll be surprised at all the paraphernalia that *are* required'.

2 When it is used conversationally to describe something that is long, drawn-out and complicated, it is treated as *singular*, for *paraphernalia* is the equivalent of 'procedure': 'The whole paraphernalia of getting a visa *goes* on for ever!'

parapsychology / ESP
● RULE

Parapsychology is the preferred scientific name for *ESP* (the abbreviation is used more than the words in full: *extrasensory perception*). Both are taken to include the following: telepathy, transference of thought from one person to another without any external means; precognition, foretelling an event that has not yet occurred; psychokinesis (PRON 'syekokiNEESis'), the movement of objects by mental concentration rather than physical means, such as making dice fall in a predetermined way.

parentheses
See **brackets**

parlous
● CAUTION

Although people still talk about a 'parlous journey', a roof in a 'parlous condition', or someone in a 'parlous state', the time has come to put the word on the shelf. Most current dictionaries label *parlous* as archaic or at best, humorous.

parson / priest / rector / vicar / minister

See **minister** . . .

partial to

● RECOMMENDATION

To be *partial to* a gin and tonic (or anything else) is perfectly in order, of course, but to express it in those words has a touch of old-fashioned gentility about it. What's wrong with 'liking a gin and tonic'?

partly / partially

● RECOMMENDATION

In most cases, *partly* is the word to use, and *partially* is unnecessary: 'the book is partly written'; 'the debt is partly repaid'; 'the decision was taken partly by the board, partly by the staff'. Some people prefer *partially* when it relates to a human state or faculty: 'his health is partially restored'; 'she was left partially handicapped by the accident'. But even in those examples, *partly* is perfectly satisfactory.

partner / girlfriend / boyfriend

See **boyfriend** . . .

parts of speech

See **grammatical terms**

passed / past

● RULES

1 *Passed* is a *verb*, the past form of *to pass*: 'he passed her window every day'; 'the years have passed'.

2 *Past* is a *descriptive word* and also a *noun*, both relating to direction or time: 'it happened in the past week' (time); 'he has just gone past her window' (direction); 'our love affair is long past' (time); 'it was all in the past' (noun).

passer-by

● RULE

When it is hyphenated, the plural is clearly *passers-by*. Although some recent dictionaries show it as *one* word, the plural remains *passersby*, which looks awkward and is an argument for retaining the hyphen.

passive / active voice

See *active* **voice** . . .

past / passed

See **passed** . . .

past experience / *past* history

● RECOMMENDATION

All experience is in the past, and there are no professors of *past* history, for all history belongs to the past. But both expressions are so common ('from past experience'; 'all that is past history'), that it is pedantic to fuss about them, especially when used in conversation. In writing, there is a case for thinking twice before inserting the unnecessary word *past*.

pathos / bathos

See **bathos** . . .

patois / dialect

See **dialect** . . .

peaceable / peaceful

● RECOMMENDATIONS

1 *Peaceful* describes freedom from disturbance, agitation or violence: 'the protest was peaceful and no one was arrested'; 'she looks peaceful sitting there, listening to music'.

2 *Peaceable* is more often applied to someone's attitude or manner, or to a way of acting: 'he is a peaceable man, not given to fits of anger'; 'we must follow a peaceable course of action'.

peal / carillon

See **carillon** . . .

pedantic / didactic

See **didactic** . . .

Peking / Beijing

See **Beijing** . . .

pendant / pendent

● RECOMMENDATIONS

1 *Pendant* is more common for the *noun* ('she wore a pendant round her neck').

2 *Pendent* is more usual for the *descriptive word* ('a pendent lamp').
   PRON (both spellings) 'PENde(r)nt'.

pending

● RECOMMENDATION

Pending remains a popular word in business letters, as in 'pending further information from you'. But it belongs to stuffy old-fashioned business English, and in many cases should be replaced by 'until': 'until we get further information from you'.

pension / annuity

See **annuity** . . .

Pentagon / pentagon

● RULE

A *pentagon* is any five-sided figure. The *Pentagon* is the pentagon-shaped headquarters of US defence forces.

NOTE The word Pentagon is also used for American military policy and opinion: 'The Pentagon view is . . .'.

peon / paean

See **paean** . . .

people / persons

● RECOMMENDATIONS

1 *People* is the usual word, the one to use in everyday contexts.
2 In formal or legal contexts, *persons* has a place because it strikes a more austere note: 'the persons responsible for this outrage must be brought to justice'.

people / race

See **race** . . .

per

The Latin word *per* is so common in English that it is easy to forget that in some expressions there are straightforward alternatives.

● RECOMMENDATIONS

1 In some *abbreviations*, *per* is indispensable: *pa* (per annum) and *mph* (miles per hour) are everyday examples. But when words are spelt in full, *per* is out of place: so much 'a year', so many miles 'an hour', for example, are preferable to *per year* (or *per annum*), *per hour*, etc.
2 *Per* is appropriate in Latin phrases, such as *per cent*, *per capita*, etc, and also occasionally helps to avoid an inconvenient repetition of *a*: 'school meals cost an average of £3 a day per child' ('a day a child' is not only awkward but is not as clear).

per annum / a year

See **a year** . . .; **per** (RECOMMENDATION 1)

per cent / percentage

● RECOMMENDATIONS

1 *Per cent* means 'in every hundred' and should usually be preceded by a figure: '55 per cent of the voters are women'.

2 *Percentage* is the corresponding noun, but *per cent* can also be used as a noun: 'What *percentage* (or *per cent*) of the . . .'.

3 Avoid using *percentage* without some qualification. If it is not possible to commit yourself to at least 'small' or 'low', or 'large' or 'high' percentage, simply use 'some' or 'part': 'some of the voters'; 'part of the costs' (rather than 'a percentage of the voters'; 'a percentage of the costs').

percentage / proportion / fraction

See **fraction** . . .

perchance

● RECOMMENDATION

Perchance belongs to poetry ('To sleep: perchance to dream', *Hamlet* Act III Sc i). It is affected in everyday use: 'If perchance you're going shopping, could you get me . . .'.

perfect

● RECOMMENDATION

Perfection is an absolute quality, so in principle something cannot be *quite perfect, absolutely perfect* or *very perfect*. But it does no harm to stress the point with an occasional *quite perfect*, although *very perfect* jars, and *absolutely perfect* seems over the top.

perhaps

● RECOMMENDATION

There's no need to follow the old convention of putting a comma on either side of *perhaps*, when it comes in the middle of a sentence. But sometimes it is valid as a way of emphasising uncertainty: 'whether we open up the market in France or in Germany is, perhaps, not as important as it seems'.

● CAUTION

The position of a *single* comma, one side or the other of *perhaps*, can in some contexts change the meaning altogether. 'She will go to Rome perhaps, with her lover' leaves open the possibility of her going to London, Madrid . . . . 'She will go to Paris, perhaps with her lover' leaves open the possibility of her going to Paris alone – or with someone other than her lover.

period / era / age

See **age** . . .

period / full stop / stop

See **stop / full stop** . . .

periodic / periodical

● RECOMMENDATION

Although both are interchangeable *descriptive words* ('this is a *periodic* (or *periodical*) problem'), the tendency now is to use *periodic* for the *descriptive word* ('a periodic event') and *periodical* as the *noun* for magazines that are published usually weekly or monthly.

persistent / consistent

See **consistent** . . .

-person / -man

● RECOMMENDATION

Where possible, use the unisex suffix *-person*: *chairperson; spokesperson* (in preference to *chairman, spokesman*), even when the person concerned is a man. See also **-ess forms; unisex grammar.**

persona / personality / character

See **character** . . .

personal / private / confidential / secret

See **confidential** . . .

personally

● RECOMMENDATIONS

1 *Personally* has an important use to make it clear that an action relates to someone *in person*: 'deliver this letter to him personally' (that is, do not give it to anyone else); 'I shall deal with this personally' (that is, it will not be delegated).

2 *Personally* is also useful for associating yourself with something, or making it clear that you are not involved: 'this is not just a job, I care about it personally'; 'I'll do what I can to help, although I am not personally affected'.

3 In many other contexts, *personally* can be a complacent intrusion: 'I personally believe . . .'; 'I don't personally enjoy . . .'; 'Personally, I would do this.' Remember that *I* is the most personal word in English, and does not often need propping up with *personally*.

persons / people

See **people / persons**

perspicacious / perspicuous

● RULES

1 *Perspicacious* (and *perspicacity*) can only be used about people: 'the financial director was *perspicacious* (or *showed perspicacity*)', that is he was shrewd.

2 *Perspicuous* (and *perspicuity*) relates to expressing something in words: 'the financial director made a *perspicuous* statement about policy' (or '*showed perspicuity* in his statement . . .'), that is clear and easily understood.

● RECOMMENDATION

There are simpler words available: 'shrewd', 'acute', and 'clever' in place of *perspicacious*; 'clear' and 'lucid' for *perspicuous*.

perverted / deviant

See **deviant** . . .

petite / small / compact

See **compact** . . .

phantasy / fantasy

See **fantasy** . . .

pharmacy / chemist

See **chemist** . . .

phenomenon / phenomena

● RULE

One *phenomenon*, two or more *phenomena*. (Some dictionaries show 'phenomenons' as an alternative plural form, but this is usually regarded as incorrect.)

● CAUTION

It is a common mistake to say 'a phenomen**a**', instead of 'a phenomen**on**'.

Philippino / Filipino

See **Filipino** . . .

philosophic / philosophical

● OPTION

There used to be some distinction between these two words, with *philosophic* related to the discipline of philosophy, and *philosophical* reflecting a calm acceptance of life. But now the words can be considered interchangeable in all contexts, with *philosophical* ✓ as the more usual form.

phone / telephone

● RECOMMENDATION

There is a curious reluctance to admit *phone* as standard English, with most dictionaries still labelling it 'colloquial' or 'informal'. Yet *phone* is the word we use most of the time, and words such as *answerphone, phone-in, phone-tapping, phonecard,* etc, are accepted as standard English. So there is no good reason why we should not use *phone* freely in writing as well as speaking, reserving, if we prefer to, **tele***phone* for really formal occasions.

physician / doctor

See **doctor** . . .

physics *is* / *are*

See **-ics**

pictures / cinema / films

See **films** . . .

pidgin / Creole

● RULES

1 A *pidgin* is a rudimentary second language made up from elements of other languages, and used for basic everyday communication between people who do not have any other language in common.

2 A *Creole* (PRON 'CREEohl') usually spelt with a capital, may have developed over a long period from a *pidgin* language, and has become an established first language, the mother tongue for people, even though it is closely linked to another language (most Creoles are related to English, French, Dutch or Portuguese).

● CAUTION

Pidgin, especially when used descriptively (*pidgin English,* for example) is a derogatory term for a crude adaptation of an established language.

pie / *bar* chart

See ***bar* / *pie* chart**

pilau / pilaff

● RECOMMENDATION

Various spellings occur for this rice dish. *Pilau* (PRON 'PEELow') is preferred, since it's closer to the original Turkish word than *pilaff.* And it's better to restrict *pilau* to Middle Eastern, Indian or Pakistani recipes.

piteous / pitiable / pitiful

● RECOMMENDATIONS

1 *Piteous* should not be used about people, but for things that make us feel pity: a piteous cry; a piteous sight.

2 *Pitiable* can be used for both people and for things that arouse pity: a pitiable beggar; a pitiable scene. It can also have the meaning of contemptuous: a pitiable offer; a pitiable effort.

3 *Pitiful* can stand in for *all* the above uses (a pitiful cry; a pitiful beggar; a pitiful offer), and is the easiest word to use in most contexts.

plain / clear (about language)

See **clear / plain**

plastic (pronunciation)

● RECOMMENDATION

The grand pronunciation used to be 'PLAHstic', which now sounds affected. The usual pronunciation makes it rhyme with 'fantastic'.

platform / podium / rostrum / dais

● RECOMMENDATIONS

1 By tradition, conductors of orchestras mount the *podium* (a *podium* is a small platform for one person).

2 *Rostrum* is the usual word for the platform used by a public speaker, and is also small.

3 Where a number of people are going to address an audience, they take their place on a *platform*, which can be as large as you like.

4 *Dais* (PRON 'DAYiss') is a less common word, and usually refers to a low platform.

plc / Ltd

See **Ltd** . . .

pleaded / pled (past form)

● RULE

The past form of *plead* is *pleaded*, except in Scotland, where *pled* is used in courts of law.

$ The usual past form is *pled*.

plebeian

● CAUTION

This is a notorious word for tripping people up over the spelling, because of the *e* after the *b*: *plebeian*.

pled / pleaded (past form)

> See **pleaded** . . .

plough / plow

● RULE

> *Plough* for the *noun* and *verb*.

$ *Plow*.

ploy

● CAUTION

> Do not use *ploy* to mean a useful idea, as in 'it was a good ploy to finish everything today'. *Ploy* always implies cunning, or at least a clever trick in order to take advantage of someone or a situation.

plural / singular

● RULE

> Everyone knows that a *singular* noun is followed by a *singular* form of the verb, a *plural* noun by the *plural* form. Rules of grammar are fine when the lines are clearly drawn but tricky in the no man's land in between.

● RECOMMENDATIONS

1 *Two nouns linked by 'and'* Usually these are followed by a *plural* verb: 'boys and girls *come* out to play'. But when they are clearly a single unit, use a *singular* verb: 'a gin and tonic *is* all I want'; 'roast beef and Yorkshire pudding *is* obligatory for Sunday lunch'.

2 There is a grey area with certain nouns linked by 'and', which can be regarded as either *singular* or *plural*: 'law and order *are* (or *is*) on the political agenda'; 'courage and determination *are* (or *is*) required'. In these cases, use the *plural* form.

3 *Two nouns linked by 'or'* There are three simple RULES set out under the entry for **or**.

4 *Plural nouns before a verb, followed by a singular noun after* The noun *before* the verb governs the form of the verb that follows: 'his wages *are* no more than a token'. (NOTE 'the wages of sin *is* death' in St Paul's Epistle to the Romans, is archaic usage.)

5 *Two nouns linked by 'plus'* It is a common mistake to treat *plus* as the equivalent of 'and', and requiring a *plural* verb (see **1** above). *Plus* is the equivalent of 'with', and should be followed by a *singular* verb: 'a man and his wife *have* arrived' but 'a man *plus* his wife *has* arrived'.

6 *Nouns ending in -ics* (*athletics; classics; statistics*) see under **-ics**; see also **economics *is / are*; ethics *is / are*; politics *is / are*.**

7 *Collective nouns* Group words, such as *government, orchestra, family*, also fall into a grey area. For guidance, see **collective words;** see also **data *is / are*;** and **media *is / are*.**

plus

● RULE

Should it be 'A plus B *is* or *are* . . .'? See **plural / singular** (RECOMMENDATION 5).

● RECOMMENDATION

The use of *plus* as a noun, to mean an advantage, is best left to advertising jargon ('the new model has five pluses'). It is better to choose a more specific word, such as 'benefits'; 'advantages'; 'improvements'.

podium / rostrum / dais / platform

See **platform** . . .

poetess

See **-ess forms** (RECOMMENDATION 2)

poker-faced / impassive / dispassionate / deadpan

See **deadpan** . . .

politic / political

● RULE

Politic is a neutral word describing a decision or an action that is wise and prudent, without the suggestion of self-interest.

● CAUTION

Political is a straightforward word when it is used about fields of study, such as *political anthropology* (the study of forms of leadership in primitive societies). But in many contexts, to say that something is *political*, suggests it is concerned with the narrow interests of a group or organisation (a *political decision*, for example, is not objective but partisan).

political correctness

● RECOMMENDATION

The English language is loaded with prejudices, built up over centuries. We have an obligation to avoid using words or expressions that disparage, even unintentionally, women, blacks, Jews, gays or any other group of people. At the same time, we should be on guard against fudging real issues by evasiveness, such as calling the *poor* 'the disadvantaged'. It is one thing to avoid giving offence, but something else to offend no one by blunting the edge of the truth as we see it.

● CAUTION

To say that something is *politically correct* is usually derogatory, suggesting that no matter where your heart is, it is important to be seen to be doing, and above all *saying* what is considered to be the right things.

politics *is* / *are*

● RULES

1   In many contexts, *politics* is treated as *singular*: 'politics *is* an uncertain business'.

2   When *politics* represents an attitude or preference for a political party or policy, it is treated as *plural*: 'What *are* his politics?'; 'Her politics on this issue *have* always been clear.'

portentous / portentious

● CAUTION

*Porten**tous*** (meaning 'of great moment') is sometimes wrongly spelt and pronounced *porten**tious***, because of a false association with 'pretentious'. (The word 'portentious' does not exist.)

porter / janitor / doorman / doorkeeper

See **doorkeeper** . . .

posh

● RECOMMENDATION

Dictionaries write down *posh* as slang or at best a conversational word. Yet it is useful in all kinds of contexts: *The Times* and the other broadsheets are sometimes called the *posh papers*, a Rolls Royce remains a *posh car*. But we should accept that *posh* is not appropriate in serious writing, so keep 'grand' or 'lordly' as standbys.

positive / negative

See **negative** . . .

positive discrimination

See **discrimination** (NOTE)

post / mail

See **mail** . . .

pot / grass / dope / hashish / marijuana / cannabis

See **cannabis** . . .

pound sterling

See **sterling**

practicable / practical

● RULES

1   *Practic**able*** is a neutral descriptive word meaning no more than that it is possible to

do something, but not implying it is either a good or a bad idea to do it: 'it's practicable but that's all you can say about it'.

2   *Practical* is always a term of praise, suggesting that something is suited in most respects for a particular purpose. When used about a person, it describes a down-to-earth problem-solving attitude: 'the scheme is practical and will overcome most of the problems'; 'she is a practical woman able to turn her hand to many things'.

   NOTE   For the distinction between the negative forms see **impracticable / impractical / unpractical.**

practice / practise

● RULE

   The *noun* is always *practice*, the *verb* always *practise*: 'practise the piano because practice makes perfect'; 'a doctor practises medicine in his practice'.

$ *Practice* is the standard spelling for both *noun* and *verb*.

prediction / prophecy / prophesy

● RECOMMENDATIONS

1   *Prediction* should imply a statement about the future based on knowledge and experience: 'from what she knew of his past, she made a prediction that his marriage would not last'.

2   *Prophecy* is crystal-gazing, divine revelation, or a hunch: 'although she knew nothing about him, for some reason she made a prophecy that his marriage would not last'.

● CAUTION

   Prophesy is the corresponding *verb*, often used wrongly for the noun: when we make a *prophecy*, we *prophesy* something will happen.

predominant / predominate

● RULE

   Predominant is the *descriptive word*, as in 'red is the predominant colour'. *Predominate* is the *verb*, as in 'red predominates in the colour scheme'.

● CAUTION

   Avoid using *predominate* as the *descriptive word*: 'the *predominate* colour' instead of 'the *predominant* colour'. (Although a few dictionaries accept that *predominate* can be used in that way, it is often considered a mistake.)

preface / introduction / foreword

   See **foreword** . . .

premiere (as a *verb*)

● RECOMMENDATIONS

1   The use of *premiere* (PRON 'PREMeeair') as a *verb* is now recorded in all current dictionaries, so we can accept it: 'the new opera will be premiered at Covent Garden'.

2   The grave accent (*première*), still insisted on by a few dictionaries, can be dropped, as it's on its way out.

prepositions at *end* of sentences

Prepositions are mostly short words that show how other words relate to each other: 'she went *to* the door . . . *into* the house . . . *up* the stairs'.

● RECOMMENDATION

Even the most cautious grammarian accepts that it is perfectly good English to *end* a sentence with a preposition, especially when that is the natural place for it: 'Which hotel are you staying *at*?'; 'Which box did you put it *into*?'; 'Where does it come *from*?'; 'Who's it going *to*?'

presently

● RECOMMENDATION

Presently is an uncertain word to use, because it can mean different things to different people. At best, it's a rather old-fashioned alternative to 'soon': 'the doctor will see you soon' is more direct than '. . . see you *presently*'.

preservation / conservation

See **conservation** . . .

preserve / conserve / jam

See **jam** . . .

presume / assume

See **assume** . . .

presumptuous / presumptious

● CAUTION

'Presump*tious*' is often written and said ('preZUMPshe[r]s'), but there is no such word. *Presumptuous* is the correct word, pronounced with *four* syllables: 'preZUMPchew-us'.

pretence / pretext

● RULES

1   *Pre**tence*** is to pretend something that is not true: 'they kept up the pretence of being happily married'.

2   A *pretext* has almost the same meaning, but adds the suggestion that the pretence is a dishonest deception in order to achieve something: 'she got into the security zone on the pretext that she worked there as a cleaner'.

pretty
● CAUTION

To use *pretty* in sentences, such as 'he is pretty well-off', 'this is pretty good', is normal in conversation, but out of place in writing.

prevaricate / procrastinate
● RULES

1 It is *procrastinate* when we put something off: 'she always procrastinates, never doing today what she can leave until tomorrow'.

2 *Prevaricate* is almost the same as lying. It implies evasiveness, not coming out in the open: 'she prevaricated instead of giving an honest answer'.

preventative / preventive
● OPTION

Both words exist with the same meaning. Although *preventative* is heard, *preventive* ✓ is taking over in expressions such as *preventive medicine*; *preventive dentistry*.

pre-war / inter-war
● CAUTION

Pre-war is an uncertain description of a period. For a few people it could mean before 1914, for others the period from the 1920s onwards, for others the 1930s. *Inter-war* is more precise, as it would usually be taken to cover the period from 1918 to 1939. But even then, in some countries *inter-war* might be linked to other wars than World Wars I and II. Whenever there's a doubt, be specific: 'the 1920s'; 'from the end of World War I to 1939'; 'between World War I and World War II'.

price / cost

See **cost / price**

priest / parson / rector / vicar / minister

See **minister . . .**

prima facie / a priori

See **a priori . . .**

primarily (pronunciation)
● OPTION

Stress on the *first* syllable ('PRImarily')✓ or the *second* syllable ('priMARily') is acceptable.

Prime Minister / prime minister

● RECOMMENDATION

Use initial capitals when referring to a particular holder of the office and small letters when referring to prime ministers in general: 'Margaret Thatcher, Prime Minister at the time, and two former prime ministers were present.'

primitive

● CAUTION

We should be sensitive about the use of *primitive*. In some fields, it is purely descriptive: in archaeology, *primitive* is used for simple non-literate societies, and *primitive art* is often an admiring term, sometimes used for native art unaffected by academic tradition. In other contexts, *primitive* can be derogatory: *primitive idea* or *primitive approach* suggests a crude simplistic attitude.

principal / principle

● RULES

1 *Principle* is always a *noun*: *principal* can be a *noun* or a *descriptive word* (see sentence in RULE 2 below).
2 The following sentence sets out the difference in meaning: 'The *principal* of the college believes in certain *principles* of teaching, which were the *principal* things he explained in his speech.'

print / etching / engraving

See **engraving** . . .

printout / galleys / proofs

See **proofs** . . .

prison / jail / gaol

● RULE

Prison is the standard word now and *jail* and *gaol* are archaic, as are *jailer* and *gaoler*, which have been replaced by *prison officer*.

privacy (pronunciation)

● OPTION

'PRIVasy' (first syllable rhyming with 'spiv')✔ or 'PRYVasy' (first syllable rhyming with 'dive').
$ 'PRYVasy'.

private / personal / secret / confidential

See **confidential** . . .

prognosis / diagnosis

See **diagnosis** . . .

program / programme

● RULES

1 The spelling *program* (with one *m*) is used for anything to do with computers. But the other forms, even in computer contexts, retain two *m*s: *programmer*, *programming*.

2 In all other contexts, the spelling *programme* is the only one to use: theatre programme; programme of studies.

\$ *Program* is used in *all* contexts: theatre program; program of studies. And one *m* is usually preferred in the other forms (although the double *m* form also appears): programer; programing.

progress (pronunciation)

● RULES

1 As a *noun* ('we are making progress'), stress is on the *first* syllable: 'PROgress'.

2 As a *verb* ('we progress a little every day'), stress is on the *second* syllable: 'proGRESS'.

● RECOMMENDATION

When a verb is followed directly by whatever is being progressed ('we must progress this matter'), put the stress back on the *first* syllable: 'PROgress'.

pronouns

Pronouns are those short words that save us repeating a noun: 'John looked up from John's book as John had finished reading' becomes 'John looked up from *his* book as *he* had finished reading'.

● CAUTIONS

1 Avoid using pronouns when they are too far away from the noun they refer to, so that readers or listeners lose track of who all the different *shes*, *hes* and *theys* are. When there could be any uncertainty, repeat the *noun*.

2 *Pronouns* are a focus of masculine bias in the English language: 'Will every passenger please take care of his own baggage' uses the pronoun *his* to include women, whether they like it or not. For RECOMMENDATIONS, see **unisex grammar.**

proofs / galleys / printout

The old typesetting terms *proofs* and *galleys* are still in use for a printout of a text used for making corrections.

● RECOMMENDATIONS

1 *Galleys* is archaic, an echo of typesetting in the 17th century, and *proofs* is preferred now as the standard term.

2 *Printout* is standard for a copy on paper of text on a computer, and is preferable to the alternative term 'hard copy'.

propellant / propellent

● RULE

Something that propels is a *propellant*, the correct spelling for the *noun*. *Propellent* is the *descriptive word*: 'a propellent force'.

prophecy / prophesy / prediction

See **prediction** . . .

proportion / percentage / fraction

See **fraction** . . .

pro rata

● RECOMMENDATION

It's usually unnecessary to use the Latin phrase *pro rata* ('according to the rate'): 'we can let you have further supplies pro rata'. Phrases, such as 'at the same price'; 'on the same terms', are good alternatives.

protagonist

● RULE

A *protagonist* is the *one* key person in a story or situation: 'the minister was the protagonist in the debate on European integration', that is the minister dominated it.

● CAUTIONS

1   No one can be 'one of the protagonists', because there is only one, and the expression 'leading protagonist' is also wrong, since a protagonist is the leading figure anyway.

2   *Protagonist* is often taken as the opposite of 'antagonist' (which it isn't), and used for someone who strongly supports a cause: 'the minister is a protagonist of European integration'. [!] This is so common that some recent dictionaries include it as one of the meanings. But it's better avoided, as this mistaken use is not always accepted.

protest *about / against / at*

● OPTION

We can protest *about*, *against* or *at* something, and it comes to the same thing: 'she protested *about* (or *against* ✓ or *at*) the court's decision'.

$ *Protest* is often used without the help of other words: 'she protested the court's decision'.

prototype / archetype

See **archetype** . . .

provable / proveable

● RULE

Provable is correct (*proveable* is not generally accepted as a variant spelling).

proved / proven (past form)

● OPTION

You can say that something has been *proved* ✓ or *proven*.

NOTE *Proven* is the standard form in Scotland.

PRON 'PROOVe(r)n', but in Scotland 'PR*OH*ve(r)n' is usual.

provided / providing / if

● OPTION

You can say: 'I can come *provided* (or *providing* or *if*) you can pay my fare.'
Provided ✓ and *providing* put a greater stress on the condition.

PS (postscript)

● RECOMMENDATIONS

1   *PS* seems a dated convention for an afterthought at the end of a letter. More often
    than not now, the afterthought is just added, without being preceded by *PS* (if it
    comes after the signature, what else could it be?).

2   Although *postscript* properly refers to something that is *written*, it is also useful in
    connection with speech: 'Having said all that, he then added a postscript before
    sitting down.'

psychic / pyschical

● RECOMMENDATION

Psychic is the usual descriptive word for a person who has paranormal powers, with
psychical as the descriptive word for the powers themselves, as in *psychical* research.

psycho- words

● RULE

Psycho- words, even new ones, are now formed without a hyphen: *psychoanalysis*;
psychoacoustics (psychological effects of sounds); *psychobiography* (biography that
focuses on the subject's psychological development); *psychometrics* (methods of
psychological testing); *psychosexual* (the psychological aspects of sex).

public / bank holiday

● RULE

Bank holiday is an outmoded term. The term found in most diaries, etc, for
Christmas Day, Boxing Day, Good Friday and so on, is *public holiday*.

(the) **public** *is / are*

● RECOMMENDATION

Generally *the public* evokes a collective image and is better followed by a *singular* verb: 'the public *is* entitled to know'. See also **collective words.**

pudding / dessert

See **desert / dessert**

punctuation

● RECOMMENDATION

The different stops (, ; : . ? !) are there to divide up the flow of words into units of meaning, and the only purpose is to help the reader to take in written language as easily as possible. Punctuation is an inexact science, more taste and common sense than RULES. See also **colon / semicolon; comma; exclamation mark; question mark; stop / fullstop / period.**

pundit / pandit

See **pandit . . .**

pyjamas / pajamas

● RULE

In Britain people sleep in *pyjamas* and call them 'pe(r)**DJAH**-me(r)s'.

\$ In America people sleep in *pajamas* and call them 'pe(r)**DJAMM**-e(r)s'.

Q

quantitative / quantitive

● OPTION

Both forms exist. There are linguistic arguments for preferring *quantitative*, but the awkward run of *t* sounds (and the multisyllables of *quantitatively*) has made the shorter variant *quantitive* ✓ (and *quantitively*) a recognised alternative.

quantity / number / amount

See **amount** . . .

quash / squash

● RULES

1 Rebellions are *quashed*, that is crushed or put down; arguments and legal judgements are *quashed*, that is destroyed or rejected.

2 Fruits are *squashed* into a pulp, and passengers are *squashed* into trains. When it comes to deflating a person by some crushing remark, they are *squashed* rather than *quashed*.

3 Only *squash* can be used as a noun for a crowd of people, or for a concentrated fruit drink diluted with water.

quasi

● RULE

Quasi, the Latin word for 'almost', can be attached, *always* with a hyphen, to other words to show that something is nearly something, but doesn't quite make it. A body can be quasi-governmental, quasi-official, quasi-political.

● OPTION

PRON 'KWAYzeye' ✓ or 'KWAHzee'.

Queen's English

● RECOMMENDATION

In general, the term *Queen's English* should be avoided, because for some people it has snobbish or imperialistic undertones. In any case, it doesn't make sense, since the Queen does not lay down standards for the language. **British English** is the most suitable term for the variety of more or less educated forms of the language used in the United Kingdom.

questionable / debatable

See **debatable** . . .

question mark (?)

In most cases there's no problem over using *question marks*, as they come at the end of a question. There are three things to look out for.

● RULES

1 When the question is indirect, a *question mark* at the end of the sentence is out of place: 'I am writing to ask if we can meet some time Thursday afternoon.' (no question mark).

2 If a question is used as a polite way of making a request, follow it by a question mark in the usual way: 'Would you meet me Thursday afternoon?' If you end the sentence with a full stop ('Would you meet me Thursday afternoon.'), it makes it nearer a command.

● CAUTION

In some cases, the choice between a *question mark* and an **exclamation mark** changes both the meaning and intonation: 'Really?' or 'Really!'; 'Never?' or 'Never!'; 'You did that?' or 'You did that!' See also **intonation** RECOMMENDATION 1.

queueing / queuing

● OPTION

Queueing ✓ and *queuing* are alternative spellings.

$ *Queuing.*

quick / quickly

● RECOMMENDATION

After a verb, *quickly* is grammatically correct: 'Please try to do it quickly.' But *quick* is acceptable conversational usage when it's a command: 'I don't care how it's done, but do it quick'; 'It's urgent, come quick!' In other contexts, and in writing, use *quickly*. See also **slow / slowly**.

quiet / quietness / quietude / quietism / silence

● RECOMMENDATIONS

1 *Quiet* is the everyday noun, meaning simply without noise or disturbance: 'they enjoyed a few minutes' quiet after all their visitors had left'.

2 *Quietness* has a little more content, suggesting a peaceful atmosphere: 'they enjoy the quietness of living in the country, far away from busy roads'.

3 *Quietude* is deeper still, for a quality that is reflective: 'there is a quietude in the cathedral that turns a visitor towards prayer'.

4 *Quietism* is a rarely used word. It is an inner quality in a person, a contemplative devotion, a surrender of ego that moves into mysticism: 'years of practising meditation had developed a quietism within her'.

5 *Silence* is not talking or making a noise: SILENCE is a notice in libraries; 'his silence on the subject suggested that he didn't want to commit himself'; 'Can we have silence please?' (meaning 'please do not talk').

quit / quitted

● OPTION

Quit ✓ and *quit**ted*** are alternative past forms of the verb: 'she *quit* (or *quitted*) the job last week'.

$ *Quit* is the usual past form.

quite

Quite can convey several different meanings, and is often meaningless in writing, as we need to hear the intonation to know where we stand.

● RECOMMENDATIONS

1 When the following word is a superlative, there is no ambiguity, for *quite* intensifies the superlative: *quite superb*; *quite marvellous*; *quite lovely*.

2 *Quite a* before a descriptive word means the same as 'moderately': 'quite a good wine'; 'quite a large flat'.

3 *Quite a* directly before a noun suggests admiration, although it is conversational rather than written English: 'she's quite a pianist'; 'this is quite a restaurant'.

● CAUTION

Quite and *quite so* are arguably the most noncommittal responses in the English language: they can mean almost anything from 'I agree' to 'So what?', or can be no more than a vague social comment filling a gap in the conversation. But if we add an **exclamation mark** it indicates emphatic agreement: 'This is a delicious wine.' – 'Quite so!'

quotation / citation

● RULES

1 In the sense of reproducing the words of a short passage from a text, **quo**tation is the proper word.

2 **Citation** is appropriate when a quotation is used to back up an argument: 'the minister used two citations from earlier speeches to demonstrate that government policy had not changed'.

3 A *quotation* or *citation* should follow word-for-word the original text. (This does not apply when using the verb *cite*: see **quote / cite**.) If some words are left out, or the quotation begins in the middle of a sentence, three dots in the appropriate place are the standard way to indicate that words have been omitted: '. . . we shall fight on the beaches, we shall fight on the landing grounds . . . we shall never surrender' (Winston Churchill).

quotation / quote

Dictionaries persist in labelling the abbreviation *quote*, for *quotation*, as colloquial or informal.

● RECOMMENDATION

Except in the most formal contexts, there's no need for misgivings about using *quote* or *quotes* in place of the longer word *quotation*: 'Here are some quotes from today's newspapers.'

quotation marks / quotes / inverted commas

All three terms mean the same, single (' ') or double (" ") commas above the line.

● RECOMMENDATION

Inverted commas is the older term, with *quotation marks* the usual one now. *Quotes* is the everyday abbreviation, as in 'Put that in quotes, please.'

NOTE *Quotation marks* are used in various ways, mostly to encase words to show they are the actual words written or spoken. Using them correctly in all cases is a daunting business, even for the most experienced writers. So the following RULES do require careful study, although they are set out as clearly as possible.

● RULES

1   *The position of punctuation marks relative to quotation marks*

   i   When a full stop, question mark or exclamation mark at the end of the quoted passage coincides with the end of the overall sentence, another full stop is *not* required: She said, 'I love you.' (not '. . . you.'.); She asked, 'Do you love me?' (not '. . . me?'.); She shouted, 'Go to hell!' (not '. . . hell!'.).

   ii When a quoted passage is incomplete and missing words are indicated by dots (see **quotation / citation** RULE 3), the stop comes *after* the closing quotation mark: '. . . my rule of life . . . smoking cigars and also the drinking of alcohol . . .'. (Winston Churchill)

   iii When the overall sentence continues after a quoted passage, include a *comma* within the quotation marks: 'I'd like you to meet my husband,' she said, introducing a dark good-looking man.

   iv When punctuation properly belongs to a quoted passage, it stays *within* the quotation marks: 'I wonder,' she said, 'do you know Jack?' When the punctuation does not relate to the quoted passage it goes *outside* the quotation marks: 'I wonder', she said, 'whether you know Jack.'

   v   When a quoted passage is a question, and is part of a longer sentence which is also a question, include *both* question marks, even though it looks awkward: 'Did you ask your husband "Why are you late for dinner?"?' But where possible avoid this by not using a direct quotation: 'Did you ask your husband why he was late for dinner?'

   vi When the quoted passage requires an exclamation mark, and is part of a longer sentence which is a question, include the exclamation mark *and* the question mark: 'Did he really say to her "Go to hell!"?'

2   *Writing what someone thinks* is not usually regarded as a direct quotation, so quotation marks are *not* required: I wonder whether I should believe him, she asked herself. (No quotation marks round: *I should believe him.*)

3   In print, *italics* are used for titles of books, operas, etc (see **italics**). When writing by hand, or when *italics* are not available, *quotation marks* can be used instead: 'The

Satanic Verses'; 'The Macmillan Good English Handbook'; 'Hamlet'. These are not required for *names of houses, pubs, hotels,* etc: The Old Rectory; Rose Cottage; the Bull and Bush. Nor should they be used for brand names: 'Do you believe Persil gives you a whiter wash?'

4   It is a snobbish mannerism to put *quotation marks* round words or expressions to show they are down-market or ill-educated: 'In *Coronation Street*, they eat "meat and two veg" at 1 o'clock for their Sunday "dinner".'

5   *Single* quotation marks are more usual now, with *double* ones used when there is a secondary quotation within the primary one: 'When is she going to say, "It's time to break for lunch."?'; 'After the orchestra plays the overture from "Don Giovanni", there will be a short interval.'

$ *Double* quotation marks are preferred, with *single* quotation marks for secondary quotations within the primary one.

quote / cite

● RULES

1   To *cite* a passage (or what someone has said), or to *cite* an example, is to submit it as evidence: 'I shall cite two authorities to prove what I have just said.'

2   *Cite* can also be used for presenting the factors in a situation: 'I shall *cite* all the reasons that led up to this decision.'

3   When you *cite* something from a book or other source, a paraphrase can be used instead of the actual words: 'she cited the minister as having said that Britain must play a central role in Europe'. But when the noun *citation* is used, the exact words should follow (see **quotation / citation** RULE 3).

4   We can *quote* something out of interest, not necessarily using it in an argument. Or we can *quote* a passage to make a point. But if the quotation is being used as evidence, *cite* is the better verb to use (see RULE 1 above).

5   The verb *quote* implies that the exact words in the original are used. This does not apply to *cite* (see RULE 3 above).
See also **quotation / citation.**

quote (noun)

See **quotation / quote**

quote / unquote

● RECOMMENDATIONS

1   *Quote* and *unquote* are occasionally useful when *reading aloud* or *dictating*, to indicate that certain words are between *quotation marks*: 'I was surprised when Mary said to me – *quote* – "I am truly so grateful for the help John has given me." – *unquote*, because he hasn't been kind to her.'

2   In ordinary conversation, this convention is clumsy, and there are other ways round it: 'She said to me – and these are her actual words –"I am truly so grateful. . .".'

NOTE The problem does not, of course, arise in writing, where *quotation marks* can be slipped in where necessary (see **quotation marks / quotes / inverted commas**).

quotes / inverted commas / quotation marks

See **quotation marks** . . .

qv / vide / see

See **see / vide** . . .

R

race / people

● CAUTION

Be careful over using *race* for one of the groups of the human species that can be defined by physical characteristics. No one is put out if we refer to the *human race*, because that brings in all of us, and *race* is often appropriate in anthropological and ethnic contexts. But in some contexts, *race* has become tainted with *racism*. When in doubt there is the simple alternative *people*: the Chinese people; the North African people.

racist words

See **black / coloured; dago; half-caste . . . ; non-white; race . . .**

rapport

● RECOMMENDATION

Do not say a '*good* rapport', since a '*bad* rapport' is not possible. For *rapport* already implies a good, harmonious or cooperative relationship: 'I have a rapport with him' means a 'good' rapport.

PRON As in French, the *t* is not sounded: 'raPAW'.

rapt / wrapped

● RULES

1 *Rapt* is the spelling when it means totally absorbed or carried away by an idea, a thought, a vision. We can listen with rapt attention; be rapt in thought; rapt in melancholy.

2 *Wrapped* is the past form of the verb *wrap*: parcels are wrapped. By extension and followed by 'up', *wrapped* can in some expressions have a similar meaning to *rapt*: 'she is wrapped up in her work', rather than 'rapt in her work'.

● CAUTION

Even good writers have been known to use *wrapped* in mistake for *rapt*, because the words have the same sound. Follow examples in RULE 1 above.

rather

● RECOMMENDATION

Rather is a way of avoiding being too outspoken: 'I'm rather hungry'; 'she's rather overdressed'; 'this is rather good'. Used in this way, *rather* seemingly softens the harshness of criticism, or modifies a comment – but it does sound *rather* wishy-washy.

re

● RECOMMENDATION

To use *re* instead of 'about' ('we are writing re your order') is old-fashioned business English. (This does not apply to the legal use, where *re* can be part of the formal title of briefs and other documents.)

re / re-

See **hyphens** (RECOMMENDATION 6)

-re / -er

● RULES

1 There is no sign of the American *-er* spelling (*center, fiber, theater*) being accepted in British English, where in most words *re-* remains the rule (*centre, fibre, theatre*).

2 The *-er* spelling should be retained, even in British English, for American institutions and buildings, such as the Kennedy Center, Washington DC; the World Trade Center, New York.

readable / legible

See **legible** . . .

real / genuine / authentic

See **authentic** . . .

rebut / refute / deny

See **deny** . . .

recess (pronunciation)

● RECOMMENDATION

Stress the *first* syllable for the *noun* ('REcess') and the *second* syllable for the *verb* ('reCESS'): 'the bookshelves fit into a "REcess" in the wall'; 'the bookshelves are "reCESSED" into the wall'.

recession / downturn / slump / depression

See **depression** . . .

recital / concert

See **concert** . . .

recourse / resource / resort

● RULES

1 When the word comes between the verb 'have' and the word 'to', it is *recourse* ✓ or

resort (not *resource*): 'if necessary you can have *recourse* (or *resort*) to extra funds that are available for the project'.

2   After the word *last*, *resort* ✓ or *resource* must be used (not *recourse*): 'in the *last resort* (or *resource*), there are extra funds available for the project'.

3   A *resource* is a means that is available for supplying needs ('the earth's resources' is a familiar environmental phrase), and can be used in general contexts in this sense, often in the plural: 'when the allocated funds are used up, there are no other *resources*'.

rector / vicar / parson / priest / minister
See **minister** . . .

rectory / vicarage
See **minister** . . . (RULE 3)

refer / allude
See **allude** . . .

referee / umpire
● RULES
1   The white-coated men presiding over a cricket match at Lord's are *umpires*. (Cricket also has *referees*, but their job is to settle disputes off the field.)
2   *Umpire* is the right word for tennis, and baseball has an *umpire*.
3   Boxing, football, hockey and rugby have *referees*.

(with) reference to
● RECOMMENDATION
There are hardly any examples in everyday communication, when 'about' isn't preferable to the stuffy phrase *with reference to*. An exception to that is quoting a reference number for an account, insurance policy, etc.

referenda / referendums
● OPTION
The Latinate plural of *referendum* is *referenda*, and this plural form is also used in English. Most dictionaries and the leader writers in *The Times* prefer *referendums* ✓.

reflective / meditative / contemplative
See **contemplative** . . .

refutable (pronunciation)
● RECOMMENDATION
Stress the *second* syllable: 'reFUTable', also in 'irreFUTable'.

refute / rebut / deny

See **deny** . . .

regardless / irregardless

● RULE

The suffix -*less* gives *regardless* its negative meaning 'without regard': 'we shall go ahead regardless of what people say'.

● CAUTION

There is no need for the prefix -*ir*: *irregardless* is a common error, and the word is not in dictionaries.

regime / régime

● RECOMMENDATION

Drop the acute accent over the *e*: *regime*.

● CAUTION

If you intend to use *regime* in a favourable way, make that clear, because the word is more often used about a government or social order regarded as bad: 'a corrupt regime'; 'a fascist regime'; 'overthrow the regime'.

(in the) region of

● RECOMMENDATION

'The price will be *in the region of* . . .' means nothing different from 'The price will be about . . .'. Why use *four* words when one simple word will do?

regretfully / regrettably

● RULE

People may be *regretful* (have feelings of regret), and what they do or not do may be *regrettable* (something to be regretted). '*Regretfully* he decided not to join us' means *he* felt sorry about it: '*regrettably*, he decided not to join us' means *we* felt sorry about it.

relatively / comparatively

See **comparatively** . . .

religion / faith

See **faith** . . .

Renaissance / renaissance

● RULES

1 With a capital *R*, the **Renaissance** (PRON 'reNAYse(r)ns') is the name of the great creative movement in Europe, starting in the 14th century, that heralded the modern world.

2 With a small *r*, **renaissance** is used in a more modest way for the 'rebirth' (which is

what the word means) or revival of ideas, beliefs or a fashion: '1991 saw the renaissance of the miniskirt'.

rendezvous

● RULE

The *singular* and *plural* forms are the same: one *rendezvous*, two *rendezvous*.
PRON 'RONdivoo' in the *singular*: 'RONdivooz' in the *plural*.

● RECOMMENDATION

Unlike the word in modern French, *rendezvous* in English is also a *verb*. But the only form that sounds natural is 'Let us *rendezvous* at the Café Royal.' When you get into *rendezvouses, rendezvoused, rendezvousing*, it is stretching the word too far (although those forms are listed in some dictionaries). It's easier to say 'she has a rendezvous'; 'they are having a rendezvous' (instead of 'she rendezvouses'; 'they are rendezvousing').

renege (pronunciation)

When someone goes back on a deal, they *renege* on the agreement.

● OPTION

PRON 'reNEEG' (to rhyme with 'league')✓ or 'reNAYG' (to rhyme with 'vague').

renewed/fresh/new

See **new** . . .

renunciation/renouncement

● OPTION

Both forms exist. *Renunciation* ✓ is so much more usual that some people might think you've made a mistake if you write or say *renouncement*.

repairable/reparable

● RULES

1 Shoes and other objects that are worn out or damaged, and can be repaired, are *repairable*. If it's not possible, such things 'cannot be repaired' (the word 'irrepairable' does not exist).
2 Mistakes, losses, broken hearts and other non-material things are *reparable*, that is put right again. If that's not possible they are *irreparable*.

PRON *repairable* is stressed on the *second* syllable ('rePAIRable'): *reparable* and *irreparable* are stressed on the *rep syllable* ('REParable' and 'irREParable').

repel/repulse

● RULES

1 *Repulse* is to drive back ('repulsing an attack'), or to rebuff someone by coldness or unkindness: 'she was repulsed by his unfriendliness'.

2 *Repel* means to drive away: 'a spray to repel insects'. It can also mean to disgust someone: 'she was *repelled* by him' means 'she found him repulsive'.

● CAUTION

A common mistake is 'Go away – you repulse me!' That should be 'Go away – you repel me!' or 'Go away – you're repulsive!' (see RULES above).

repertoire / repertory

● RULES

1 *Repertory* is used almost exclusively about the theatre, for a group of plays in rehearsal and ready for a performance during a particular period.

2 *Repertoire* is confined mostly to musicians and orchestras for the list of compositions they are able to perform. It has become extended to other items that are, so to speak, at the ready, such as a repertoire of dishes a cook can turn out to order.

repetitious / repetitive

● RULE

Both words mean something is repeated, but the implication is different. *Repetitious* implies that the repetition is unnecessary and boring: *repetitive* is merely descriptive, stating the fact without criticism: 'Ravel's *Boléro* has a strong repetitive theme which some people could find repetitious.'

reply / retort

● RULE

Reply is a neutral word. *Retort* suggests that the reply is sharp, witty, angry or to the point. This applies to both words as *nouns* or *verbs*: 'she replied thoughtfully to his question'; 'he was surprised at her angry retort' (even if 'angry' were deleted, *retort* would still suggest a sharp or curt reply).

repository / depository / depositary

See **depository** . . .

representative / senator / congresswoman / congressman

See **congressman** . . .

representative / symptomatic / characteristic

See **characteristic** . . .

repulse / repel

See **repel** . . .

reputable (pronunciation)
● RULE

> *Repute* is stressed on the *second* syllable ('rePUTE'), but with *reputable* the stress is on the *first* syllable 'REPutable'.

require / need

> See **need** . . .

research (pronunciation)
● OPTION

> While stress on the *second* syllable ('reSEARCH')✓ is the standard pronunciation, some dictionaries now allow stress on the *first* syllable ('REEsearch'). [!]

$ Stress on the *first* syllable is more usual, although both pronunciations are heard.

resolve / solve
● RECOMMENDATION

> Although in some contexts either word can be used, *resolve* is useful to stress finding a practical way of dealing with a difficulty or a problem: 'we must resolve the dispute that is holding up production'. *Solve* suggests finding an explanation of a mystery: 'we must solve the mystery of the missing components'.

resort / resource / recourse

> See **recourse** . . .

respective / respectively
● RECOMMENDATIONS

1 More often than not *respective* is there for no good reason: 'Mary, John and Helen have returned to their respective homes.' Omit *respective* and there's still no doubt about which homes they returned to.

2 *Respectively* can be a clumsy way of explaining what or who goes with which: 'Mary, John and Helen live in London, Oxford and Cambridge respectively.' That's the kind of sentence that makes us look back to see who lives where. It could be laid on the line without using any extra words: 'Mary lives in London, John in Oxford, Helen in Cambridge.'

3 In more complicated sentences, these words can avoid unnecessary repetition: 'Mary, John and Helen are married to people who work in law, teaching and politics respectively.'

(in) respect of / with respect to
● RECOMMENDATION

> Unless a formal style is necessary, it is usually better to replace either phrase by the simple word 'about': '*in respect of / with respect to* the decision made by the committee . . .' says nothing more than 'about the decision . . .'.

responsible / accountable

See **accountable** . . .

restaurant (pronunciation)

● OPTION

The word *restaurant* is as English as Yorkshire pudding, which is why many people say 'RESteront'. Some recent dictionaries give their blessing to the final *t* sound, while others insist on 'REStora(h)n'✓.

restaurant / café

See **café** . . .

restive / restless

● RECOMMENDATIONS

1 *Restive* should imply a refusal or inability to accept order or control: children are restive when they won't sit still; people at a public demonstration are restive when they look as if they might turn violent; a horse is restive when it jibs at the bridle.

2 *Restless* is better for describing agitation or nervousness: we are *restless*, rather than *restive*, when we toss and turn in bed; children may be restless when they have a fever; when a horse rears up in a paddock, it's a sign that it is restless.

résumé / synopsis / summary / outline

See **outline** . . . See also **cv** ($)

retain / consult / engage / appoint

See **appoint** . . .

retort / reply

See **reply** . . .

retreat / withdraw

● RECOMMENDATION

We *withdraw* in order to fight again another day: we *retreat* when we are defeated.

reveal / disclose

See **disclose** . . .

reverse / converse / antithesis / opposite

See **opposite** . . .

review / criticism / critique / notice

● RECOMMENDATIONS

1 *Review* is the best all-round word, for it can cover a book, play, film, anything from a pop concert to a tone poem.

2   A *critique* is an analysis, without any suggestion of praise or disapproval, but it can
    sound pretentious (except in the academic context of philosophy).
3   *Notice* is used more about *plays*, rather than films, books, art or music: 'the play has
    good notices'.
● CAUTION
    The problem with *criticism* is that it could imply pointing out the bad things: 'Have
    you read the criticism of the play?' could suggest a condemnation of it, although the
    criticism might have said it was marvellous.
$ *Critique* is used more often than in British English, even as a *verb* ('he has critiqued
    the play').

review / revue
● RULE
    Review is the right spelling in all contexts except one: the French form *revue* is used
    for a theatrical show composed of satirical sketches and songs.

revolutionary
● RECOMMENDATION
    Revolutionary is a strong word that describes turning upside down ideas, order,
    beliefs. Casual use about trivial changes ('the revolutionary hemline from Paris')
    should not be allowed to dilute the value of *revolutionary* for events and discoveries
    that change the world. In ordinary contexts, 'new' is a perfectly adequate alternative.

revue / review
    See **review** . . .

rhythmic / rhythmical
● OPTION
    Both *rhythmic* ✓ and *rhythmical* can be used for anything in sound or movement
    that has a steady rhythm.

ridiculous / absurd
    See **absurd** . . .

right / rightly
● RECOMMENDATIONS
1   *Right* is the normal form in conversation when it comes *after* the verb: 'make sure
    you do it right'; 'Did I pronounce it right?'; 'he guessed right about her age'. (*Rightly*
    is of course correct in such sentences but it would sound as if you were on your best
    grammatical behaviour.)
2   Even in writing, *right* is often acceptable in place of *rightly*, unless the context is
    particularly formal.

3   When it comes *before* the verb, *rightly* is required: 'it is rightly said that . . .'; 'he rightly decided to . . .'.

4   *Rightly* also belongs in the combination *rightly or wrongly*, whether it comes before or after the verb: 'Rightly or wrongly I have decided . . .'; 'She felt, rightly or wrongly, that . . .'. See also **wrong / wrongly.**

rightward / rightwards

See **leftward** . . .

risqué / suggestive

See **suggestive** . . .

role / rôle

See **accents** (RECOMMENDATION)

Roman / roman

● RULES

1   A capital *R* in connection with ancient or modern Rome: **R**oman law; a **R**oman road.

2   A capital *R* for a **R**oman nose (a nose with a high bridge).

3   A capital *R* for the **R**oman alphabet, the alphabet evolved (from a much older alphabet) by the ancient Romans for Latin, and used in most of the languages of Western Europe.

4   A small *r* for **r**oman letters, the standard upright type (as against sloping *italics*).

● OPTION

It can be either *Roman* numerals or *roman* ✓ numerals (see also **arabic / roman numerals**).

romance (pronunciation)

● RECOMMENDATION

Stress the *second* syllable: 'roMANCE'.

Romanesque / Norman

See **Norman** . . .

roofs / rooves

● OPTION

Both *roofs* ✓ and *rooves* can be used for the plural of *roof*.

rostrum / dais / podium / platform

See **platform** . . .

rouble / ruble

● RULE

Rouble is the standard spelling.

\$ *Ruble.*

PRON Either way 'ROObe(r)l'.

round / around / about

See **about** . . .

-rous / -erous

See **-erous** . . .

rouse / arouse

See **arouse** . . .

ruble / rouble

See **rouble** . . .

Rugby / rugby

● RECOMMENDATION

The game of rugby football is supposed to have originated at Rugby School. The connection is too tenuous and the game too widespread to warrant *Rugby*, so nearly all sports writers use *rugby*.

Russia / Russian

● RECOMMENDATION

Russia and *Russian* are no longer convenient umbrella names for the whole of the former Soviet Union and its people. We should not run that linguistic steamroller over the identities of individual nations that were submerged by the old regime. Armenia, Azerbaijan, Ukraine and the others, as well as the Baltic States, are independent countries with their own nationalities and their own languages. *Russia* should be applied now only to the Russian Federation, the constituent republic that was the main part of the former USSR.

● CAUTION

It is in order, of course, to use *Russian* for the people of the Russian Federation, since they are the main ethnic group. But it's a mistake to use *Russian* in connection with the new republics (unless it's about the Russians who form the largest minority groups within some of those countries).

Russian / Cyrillic

See **Cyrillic** . . .

S

s' / s's

See **apostrophe** (RULE 1i)

saccharin / saccharine

● RULES

1 *Saccharin* (PRON 'SAKerin') is the *noun*, white crystalline tablets or powder used as a substitute for sugar.

2 *Saccharine* (PRON 'SAKereen') is the *descriptive word*, used to describe a sickly sweet taste, or by extension anything that is cloying: a saccharine manner; a saccharine smile.

sacrilegious / nonreligious / unreligious / irreligious

See **irreligious** . . .

Saint / saint / St / Ste

● RULES

1 When it's someone who has been canonised, it is always a capital S: *Saint* (usually abbreviated to *St*): St George; St Paul.

2 When the word is used more generally, a capital is not appropriate: 'she's a saint, as she's kind to everyone'.

3 There is no capital in 'saint's day'.

4 A stop is usually omitted now after *St* (St John's Wood; St Paul's Cathedral). See **abbreviations.**

5 *Ste* is not used in English: it is the abbreviation for *Sainte*, the feminine form in French, which is always linked (as is *St* in French) to the name with a hyphen: Ste-Anne; Ste-Marie; St-Paul.

(for) . . . sake

● RULES

1 When it is for the sake of someone or something, and the name is used, *'s* follows: for Henry's sake; for the school's sake.

2 *'s* or an apostrophe on its own follows an ordinary noun (depending on whether it is singular or plural): for the chairman's sake; for the neighbours' sake (more than one neighbour).

3 When it's an abstract noun ending in an *s* sound, an *'s* isn't necessary: for goodness sake.

See also **apostrophe** (RULE 1).

saleable / salable

● RECOMMENDATION

Although dictionaries show these as alternative spellings, *saleable* is so much the rule that *salable* looks wrong, especially as most dictionaries show only *one* spelling for *unsaleable*.

$ *Salable* and *unsalable* are the usual spellings.

salvoes / salvos

● OPTION

Dictionaries allow ships to fire *salvoes* or *salvos* but the Royal Navy prefers its ships to fire *salvoes* ✓.

same

● RECOMMENDATION

It is stuffy commercial jargon to use *same* as a substitute for 'it': 'an extra charge will be involved and we shall advise you of *same*'; 'we enclose our statement and would ask you to settle *same*'; '. . . we shall advise you of it' and '. . . would ask you to settle it' are more to the point.

sanatorium / sanitarium

● RULE

Sanatorium.

$ *Sanitarium.*

sanction

● RULE

A *sanction* can be imposed as a penalty or as a way of enforcing a law. As a *verb*, *sanction* is a formal way of giving permission: 'the governing body will sanction his leave of absence'.

● CAUTION

Avoid using *sanction* as a verb to mean imposing sanctions or a penalty ('he was sanctioned for his absence'): the *verb* can only be used for giving approval.

sang / sung

● RULE

The two past forms are: 'I *sang* a song' and 'a song was *sung*'.

sank / sunk / sunken

● RULES

1 'The ship *sank*', but 'the ship was *sunk*'.

2 The older form *sunken* survives as a descriptive word before a noun: a sunken garden; a sunken road.

sari / saree

● OPTION

Saree is an alternative spelling shown in dictionaries, but *sari* ✓ is closer to the Hindi word.

sauce / gravy

See **gravy** . . .

savoir faire / know-how

See **know-how** . . .

sawed / sawn

● OPTION

'I have *sawed* ✓ the wood' or 'I have *sawn* . . .'.

● RULE

When it precedes a noun, it is *sawn*: 'the sawn planks of wood'.

scan

● CAUTION

Scan can mean to look at something intently. But it can also mean the opposite – to look through something quickly ('she scanned the property ads looking for a flat'). Be on guard against a possible misunderstanding: 'Would you scan that report?' could mean go through it carefully, but for some people it would mean take a quick look at it.

Scandinavian / Nordic

See **Nordic** . . .

scarcely / hardly / barely

See **barely** . . .

scarves / scarfs

● OPTION

Scarves ✓ and *scarfs* are alternative plural forms of scarf.

scenario / screenplay / filmscript

See **filmscript** . . .

scenery / setting / set

See **set** . . .

sceptic (pronunciation)

● RULE

Sceptic and its associated words are the only ones beginning with *sce-*, where the *c* is sounded: 'SKEPtic'.

$ The spelling is *skeptic*.

schedule (pronunciation)

● OPTION

Most dictionaries show 'SHEDjool'✓ and 'SKEDjool'[!] as alternative pronunciations.

$ 'SKEDjool'.

school / university / college

See **college** . . .

science / technology / technics

● RECOMMENDATIONS

1 Other than in schools, *science* tends to be used now mostly for research and in academic contexts.

2 *Technology* has become the standard word for *applied science*, for scientific developments with practical use in industry.

3 *Technics* is an alternative word for *technology*, but also an alternative word for 'techniques', which is a case for not using it often.

scissors

● RULE

The word *scissors* is *plural*: 'the scissors *are* on the table'. A *pair of scissors* is the only *singular* form.

Scottish / Scots / Scotch

● RECOMMENDATION

Refer to a *Scotsman*, a *Scotswoman* and *the Scots*. In most other contexts, when in doubt, use *Scottish*: Scottish scenery; Scottish hotels; Scottish nationalism; 'she is Scottish'. Some exceptions are: Scotch whisky; Scotch egg (a hard-boiled egg wrapped in sausage meat); Scotch mist (the fog-like drizzle in the Highlands).

screenplay / scenario / filmscript

See **filmscript** . . .

(*close*) scrutiny

See *close* **scrutiny**

sculpted / sculptured

● RECOMMENDATIONS

1 Use *sculpted* as the verb for the work of a sculptor: 'she sculpted his likeness in marble'.

2 *Sculptured* is better for something that has the appearance of sculpture: 'the sand dunes were sculptured by the wind'.

sculptor / sculptress

● RECOMMENDATION

Sculptor for both sexes. See also **-ess forms** (RECOMMENDATION 2).

sea / ocean

See **ocean** . . .

seasonable / seasonal

● RECOMMENDATIONS

1 Use *seasonable* when it refers to something natural and suitable for that season of the year: 'we're having seasonable weather' means that the weather is appropriate to the time of the year, warm days in summer, snow in winter, etc.

2 *Seasonal* applies not so much to natural phenomena, such as the weather, but to other events that occur at a particular time or season: 'seasonal unemployment', for example, is unemployment that usually occurs in a particular season or time of the year, such as soon after Christmas.

3 The above RECOMMENDATIONS apply equally to **unseasonable** and **unseasonal**. *Unseasonable* is for natural phenomena: weather is unseasonable when it is out of place for the time of the year, snow in June, for example. *Unseasonal* describes an inappropriate time or period when something other than a natural phenomenon is happening: to have a blazing log fire in July is unseasonal.

secret / personal / private / confidential

See **confidential** . . .

security / collateral

● RECOMMENDATION

The standard term is *security*, for a deposit of assets as a guarantee of payment or of carrying out an obligation. *Collateral* means exactly the same but is less commonly used.

$ *Collateral* is the more usual term, with *collateral security* for a security pledged by a third party, not by the person involved.

see / vide / qv

● RULE

See, vide and *qv* can all be used to refer a reader to a reference in a different book or another part of the same book. The Latin verb *vide* (PRON 'VEEday') simply means 'see'. The abbreviation *qv* stands for *quod vide* (PRON 'kwodVEEday') meaning 'which see'.

● RECOMMENDATION

There is no good reason for using *vide*, except academic formality, as *see . . .* serves the same purpose. And the expression *qv* can often be replaced by 'refer to . . .', which everyone will understand.

see above / see below

● RECOMMENDATION

In a letter or other text it's all right to use *as above, see above* to refer to something higher up the page, and *see below* for something lower down. But these expressions are sometimes also used to refer to a statement on a previous or following page, or even two, three or more pages earlier or later in the book. That is making unreasonable demands on the reader. It is more considerate to write 'see the previous page' or 'see page . . .'. Better still, if at all possible, summarise whatever it is (in brackets, if you like), to save readers turning back or forwards to other pages.

self / self-

● RULE

Self can be prefixed to many words and nearly always a *hyphen* should be used: self-catering; self-composed; self-conscious; self-contained; self-drive; self-fulfilling; self-pity; self-rule; self-sufficient.

selling

● RECOMMENDATION

Selling goods has always been with us. But now we *sell* ideas, *sell* policies, *sell* ourselves. *Selling* has become an overworked word covering any act of persuasion. It is worth taking some of the load off it: instead of *selling* someone on an idea, we could 'convince' them; instead of prime ministers *selling* the nation on a policy, they could 'explain' it to them; instead of *selling* ourselves, we could 'make a good impression'. And there are other words we can use from time to time, to take the strain off *selling*: persuade; convince; win over.

semicolon (;)

See **colon** . . .

Semitic

● RULE

Although *anti-Semitic* is confined to discrimination against Jews, *Semitic* can be used for other peoples, Arabs and Phoenicians, for example. *Semitic languages* are the family of languages that includes Arabic, Assyrian, Ethiopian, among others, as well as Hebrew.

● CAUTION

Semitic has become so associated with the Jewish people that there is sometimes a misunderstanding when it's used in other contexts. When there could be any doubt about what is intended, it's better to spell it out.

senator / representative / congresswoman / congressman

See **congressman . . .**

Señor / Señora / Señorita

When Spaniards are in Britain, do we introduce them as *Señor* Gonzalez, *Señorita* Fernandez, or *Mr* Gonzalez, *Miss* (or *Ms*) Fernandez? For RECOMMENDATIONS, see **Mr, Mrs . . . / Monsieur, Frau . . . .**

sensitiveness / sensitivity / sensibility

● RECOMMENDATIONS

1 We are likely to talk about the *sensitiveness* of an injured part of the body, such as the sensitiveness of a leg after an operation.

2 When it's a question of say a hand or fingers being responsive, *sensitivity* is the more appropriate word, as in the sensitivity of a pianist's fingers.

3 *Sensitivity* and *sensitive* are the better words for someone's feelings, or about a musical performance, a situation, or for the reaction of something, such as film, to light, heat, etc.

4 *Sensibility* is not used often. It can apply to the ability to feel either physically or emotionally: if a finger is badly injured, it could lose its *sensibility*, that is sense of touch. When Jane Austin contrasted *Sense and Sensibility*, in the title of her novel, she was distinguishing between good sense and responsive feelings and emotions.

sensual / sensuous

● RECOMMENDATIONS

1 *Sensual* is usually pejorative, implying lustful indulgence in sex or excessive pleasure from food: 'she was embarrassed by the sensual way he looked at her'.

2 *Sensuous* is a harmless word for enjoying something with one's senses: 'she loved the sensuous pleasure of swimming in a warm sea'.

(length of) **sentences**

● RECOMMENDATIONS

1 More than 30 words is a *long* sentence (the National Consumer Council recommends lawyers to keep sentences to less than 25 words).

2 In creative writing the *length of sentences* is a matter of style. Short sentences go with action: long sentences can have the sonority of organ music. Functional communication is something else: long sentences embodying a number of ideas can be hard work for readers. They can get lost halfway and lose contact with the sequence of thought. If a long sentence is really necessary, at least try to put the focal thought as near the beginning as possible. Then readers know from the start where the sentence is leading.

3 *Length of sentences* should vary. It is a relief to a reader when several long sentences are followed by a very short one, or for that matter, a succession of short sentences is slowed down by a longer one. It makes more impact on a reader or listener to *end* a passage with a *short* sentence.

sentiment / sentimentality

● RULES

1 *Sentiment* is usually considered a true expression of feeling, that is sympathy, compassion, awareness of the human situation.

2 *Sentimentality* is always a pejorative word, suggesting a facile expression of emotion.

sergeant / serjeant

● RULES

1 *Sergeant* is the spelling in the army and the police.

2 *Serjeant* survives only as the *Common Serjeant*, a judicial officer of the City of London, and *serjeant-at-arms* who performs ceremonial duties in parliament.

serviette / napkin

See **napkin** . . .

set / setting / scenery

● RECOMMENDATIONS

1 *Set* is the standard word used in the theatre for the design on the stage against which a play takes place. And *set* is also the word for designs of interior scenes of films.

2 *Setting* is used more outside the theatre to describe the general background against which anything in real life or fiction takes place: 'the setting of *Hiroshima, mon amour* was the port in SW Japan after the explosion of the first atomic bomb'.

3 *Scenery* belongs more to the general aspect of a landscape or the countryside. It is old-fashioned to use *scenery* for a stage set.

settee / sofa / couch

See **couch** . . .

setting / framework / context

See **context** . . .

setting / scenery / set

See **set** . . .

sewed / sewn

● RULE

The past forms are: 'she *sewed* it well'; 'she has *sewn* (or *sewed*) it well'; 'it is well *sewn* (or *sewed*)'.

● RECOMMENDATION

Where *sewn* and *sewed* are alternatives, prefer *sewn*.

● CAUTION

Do not confuse *sew* with the verb *sow*, for planting seeds or doubts in someone's mind (see **sown / sowed**).

sex / gender

See **gender** . . .

sexism / feminism

See **feminism** . . .

sexist / feminist

See **feminist** . . .

sexist language

See **-ess forms; feminine forms; -person / -man; unisex grammar**

sexual (pronunciation)

● OPTION

The sound in the middle can be either *y* ('SEX-**y**oo-e(r)l')✓ or *sh* ('SEX-**sh**oo-e(r)l').

Shakespearean / Shakespearian

● OPTION

Both spellings are accepted for describing either the writings and genius of Shakespeare, or someone who is an authority on his work. *Shakespearean* ✓ is the spelling favoured by most literary scholars.

shall / will

● OPTIONS

1   Keep to the copybook rules, which are:

    i   I / we *shall* and you / he / she / it *will* are used for the simple future: 'I *shall* be leaving tomorrow'; 'I hope it *will* be ready on time'; 'she *will* arrive next week'.

    ii   I / we *will* and you / he, etc, *shall* express intention or determination: 'We *will* pay the bill by the end of the month'; 'I *will* succeed whatever happens'; 'You *shall* do it, whatever you say.'

2   ✓ Follow the tendency now, which is for *will* to replace *shall* in all cases, especially in spoken English, but also in the written language: 'I *will* be leaving soon'; 'We *will* arrive next week.'

3   In conversation, you can often sidestep the problem with *I'll, she'll* . . . (see **contracted forms**).

sharp / sharply

● RULES

1   *Time* 'He came sharp on time'; '7 o'clock sharp'; 'Look sharp about it!'

2   *Direction* 'Turn sharp right at the church.'

3   *Music* 'You sang that note sharp.'

4   In most other contexts, it is *sharply*: we speak sharply, move sharply, pull something sharply (but 'pull up *sharp*').

shaved / shaven

● RULE

The old past form *shaven* is obsolete except as a descriptive form, where it remains an OPTION: 'he had shaved before breakfast', but 'he was clean-*shaved* ✓ (or clean-*shaven*)'.

she or he

See **he or she**

she'd

See **contracted forms**

she'd *have*

See **I'd *have* . . .**

sheik / sheikh

● OPTION

Both spellings are used: sheik**h** ✓ and sheik. PRON 'shayk'.

\$ PRON 'sheek'.

she's

See **contracted forms**

shined / shone

● OPTION

Either past form, *shined* or *shone* ✓ can be used when it's about a light: 'the lamp *shone* (or *shined*) to light up the passage'.

● RECOMMENDATION

Shone is the customary past form referring to the sun: 'the sun *shone* that day', with *shined* more usual for the moon: 'the moon *shined* bright'.

● RULE

When it's the past form of the verb *shine*, meaning polish, only *shone* will do: 'she *shone* the silver cup'.

ship / boat / vessel

See **boat** . . .

shortfall / deficit

See **deficit** . . .

should / would

● RECOMMENDATION

Although there is (or used to be) a rule about *should* and *would*, it has fallen into disuse, and *should* and *would* are now used more or less interchangeably, with *would* generally preferred: 'we *would* (or *should*) like to accept your offer'. The exception is the use of *should* to mean 'ought to': 'you should leave early to avoid the rush hour'.

showed / shown

● OPTION

Showed and *shown* ✓ are alternative past forms (after 'has' or 'have') of the verb *show*: 'they have *shown* (or *showed*) us some beautiful materials'.

sick / ill

See **ill** . . .

side-effect / spin-off

● RECOMMENDATIONS

1 A *side-effect* is nearly always an unwanted and undesirable resultant effect: 'a side-effect of the National Lottery is that people have less to spend in shops'.

2 Use *spin-off* for a good by-product or secondary benefit, often unexpected, derived from something planned for a different purpose: 'the children's television series makes even more money from the spin-off of toys being sold, based on characters in the programmes'.

Signor / Signora / Signorina

When Italians are in Britain, do we introduce them as *Signor* Clemente, *Signorina* Boldoni, etc, or *Mr* Clemente, *Miss* (or *Ms*) Boldoni? For RECOMMENDATIONS, see **Mr, Mrs . . . / Monsieur, Frau . . . .**

silence / quietude / quietness / quietism / quiet

See **quiet . . .**

simile / metaphor

See **metaphor . . .**

simple / elementary

See **elementary . . .**

single / lone parent

See *lone / single* **parent . . .**

sixth

● CAUTION

Keep a hint of the second -s- sound: 'siksth' (rather than 'sikth').

sizeable / sizable

● OPTION

Most dictionaries show these as alternative spellings, but *sizeable* ✓ is so much more usual that *sizable* could look like a spelling mistake.

$ *Sizable* is the standard spelling.

ski

● RULE

The *present* form of the verb after 'he' and 'she' is *skis*: 'she skis down the slope'. The -*ing* form is *skiing* (a hyphen isn't necessary, in spite of the double *i*): 'she is skiing down the slope'.

● OPTION

The *past* form is either *skied* ✓ or *ski'd*: 'she *skied* (or *ski'd*) down the slope'.

slander / libel

See **libel . . .**

slang / informal / non-standard / colloquial

See **colloquial / informal . . .**

slow / slowly

● RECOMMENDATION

Slow can sometimes replace *slowly*, which is the correct form to describe the action of a *verb*. Markings on roads read SLOW, rather than SLOWLY, and workers decide on to go-*slow* as a form of industrial action. In commands or very short sentences, especially following the verb 'go', *slow* is often the usual form: 'be careful and go slow'. In most other contexts, especially in writing or in longer sentences, *slowly* is the correct form: 'she drove slowly through the village'; 'let's go slowly until we see how things work out'. See also **quick / quickly.**

slump / downturn / recession / depression

See **depression** . . .

small / petite / compact

See **compact** . . .

smelt / smelled

● OPTION

Both past forms are used, *smelt* ✓ or *smelled*: 'she *smelt* (or *smelled*) the posy of flowers'.

$ *Smelled*.

smoky / smokey

● RULE

You see *smokey* in print sometimes but it is a mistake for *smoky*, the only form shown in dictionaries.

snooze / doze

See **doze** . . .

so-called

● RECOMMENDATIONS

1 In speech, *so-called* is a way of putting a word or a phrase in quotation marks, to indicate that it is not the speaker's choice but an expression that is used: 'the so-called feel-good factor'. This is less clumsy than saying 'the – in quotation marks – feel-good factor'.

2 In writing, *so-called* can be used in the same way, or quotation marks can be used instead: 'the so-called feel-good factor' or 'the "feel-good" factor'. But don't use both ('the so-called "feel-good" factor').

3 *So-called* is also a way of indicating doubt about whether someone or something is genuine: 'I don't think much of this so-called burgundy.'

sociable / social / sociological

● RECOMMENDATIONS

1 A person can be *sociable*, that is they enjoy being with other people.

2 An organisation, principle, problem, etc, can be *social*, that is relating to people and society: social club; social worker.

3 *Sociological* is a more scientific word describing anything related to **sociology**, the study of how societies function. But *social sciences* is the term for sciences that involve human society, such as sociology, anthropology, economics.

sociology (pronunciation)

● OPTION

The *second* syllable of *sociology* (and its related words, *sociological*, *sociologists*) can begin with an *-s-* or a *-sh-* sound: 'soh-**s**eeOLojee'✓ or 'soh-**sh**eeOLojee'.

sofa / settee / couch

See **couch** . . .

solar / solar-

● RULE

At present the rule is *not* to hyphenate compound terms formed with *solar* (from Latin *solaris*, meaning 'of the sun'): *solar cell* (a unit that converts solar radiation into electricity); *solar panels* (panels that use *solar energy* for heating); *solar satellite* (a satellite that converts solar energy into electrical energy and transmits it to Earth).

soliloquy / monologue

See **monologue** . . .

solve / resolve

See **resolve** . . .

some

● RECOMMENDATION

When *some* is followed by a figure, it is an alternative word for 'about', not for 'precisely', and is usually followed by a round number: 'we live some $21\frac{1}{2}$ miles from London' sounds wrong, and is better as '. . . some 20 miles' or '. . . some 20 miles or so'.

somebody / someone

● CAUTION

A problem arises in sentences such as 'somebody has left *his* briefcase behind'. For what if the briefcase belongs to a *woman*? For RECOMMENDATIONS, see **unisex grammar**.

someday / some day

● RECOMMENDATION

Some recent dictionaries show *someday* (as *one* word) to mean some time in the future, usually a long way off: 'we'll meet again someday, who knows when?' As *two* words, *some day* is more precise: 'before we part, we'll fix some day for our next meeting'.

someplace / somewhere

See **somewhere** . . .

sometime / some time

● RECOMMENDATION

As *one* word it means 'at any time': 'I'll arrive sometime on Monday'. It is better as *two* words when it means an unspecified *period* of time: 'it is some time since she has seen him'.

somewhat

● CAUTION

Somewhat means 'to some extent', which is open-ended, so no one is quite sure what is meant: 'he is somewhat drunk' could mean a little drunk or very drunk. To lay it on the line, we'd have to say 'he is more than somewhat drunk'. There's no doubt that means the man is outrageously drunk.

somewhere / someplace

● RECOMMENDATION

Someplace is often thought of as American English. But it has caught on in Britain, although *someplace* is more conversational here. *Somewhere* is the better word to use in writing.

$ *Somewhere* is used but *someplace* is heard more often.

sonata / concerto

See **concerto** . . .

sons-in-law / son-in-laws

● RULE

Sons-in-law.

sort / kind

See **kind** . . .

South / south

See **North / north** . . .

Southern / southern

See **Northern / northern** . . .

Southern Ireland / Eire / Northern Ireland / Ulster

See **Ireland** . . .

southward / southwards / southerly

See **northward** . . .

southwester / sou'wester

● RULE

A *southwester* (pronounced in full, as it's spelt) is a wind blowing from the south-west: a *sou'wester* (PRON 'sowWESTER') is a waterproof hat, the kind traditionally worn by seamen because it has a flap at the back to keep water off the neck.

sown / sowed

● OPTION

The verb *sow*, for planting seeds or a thought in someone's mind, has alternative past forms: 'she has *sown* ✓ (or *sowed*) a doubt in his mind'.

spaceman / cosmonaut / astronaut

See **astronaut** . . .

-speak / -babble / -spiel

● RECOMMENDATIONS

1 We can attach *speak*, usually without a hyphen, to many words to describe a particular jargon: Eurocrats converse in *Eurospeak*; wine experts talk *winespeak*. Used as a suffix in this way, *-speak* need not be derogatory: it simply describes a specialised vocabulary used by a group of people who understand it.

2 When we change the suffix to *-babble*, it suggests incomprehensible chit-chat: *psychobabble*, for example, describes half-baked psychological jargon that is almost incomprehensible.

3 Another derogatory suffix is *-spiel* (PRON 'shpeel'). This gives the resulting word the suggestion of glibness: *Eurospiel*, for example, suggests double-talk in Brussels.

specially / especially

See **especially** . . .

spelt / spelled

● OPTION

Spelt ✓ and *spelled* are alternative past forms.

$ *Spelled*.

-spiel / -babble / -speak

See **-speak** . . .

spilt / spilled

● OPTION

We can cry over *spilt* ✓ or *spilled* milk.

$ *Spilled*.

spin-off / side-effect

See **side-effect** . . .

spinster

● CAUTION

Unlike 'bachelor', the equivalent word for a man, *spinster* has for some people a derogatory ring to it. If we must have a term, 'single woman' is the most acceptable.

spire / steeple

● RULE

Steeple is used only for churches, but *spire* can be used for a tall pointed structure on any building, as in Matthew Arnold's description of Oxford: 'That sweet city with her dreaming spires.'

split infinitive

An *infinitive* is 'to' followed by a verb: 'to walk'; 'to consider'; 'to love': when another word comes between 'to' and the verb ('to carefully consider'; 'to passionately love'), that is a *split infinitive*. [!]

● RECOMMENDATION

If you don't want to upset anyone, you will avoid *split infinitives*. If you care more about writing good clear English, you will be prepared *to fearlessly split* an infinitive to allow words to fall in their natural place. But there's no need to split infinitives just for the sake of it: 'to' and its following verb belong to each other, and should be separated only when good sense and the natural flow of words require it.

spoilt / spoiled

● OPTION

Spoilt ✓ and *spoiled* are alternative past forms.

$ *Spoiled*.

spokesman / spokeswoman / spokesperson

See **-person** . . .

spoonfuls / spoonsful

See **-ful**

sprang / sprung

● OPTION

Although both past forms are acceptable, we're more likely to say a boat *sprang* ✓ a leak and 'he *sprang* to her help'. After 'have', *sprung* is the only form: 'it has *sprung* a leak'.

$ *Sprung* is the only past form.

square brackets [ ]

See **brackets**

squash / quash

See **quash** . . .

St / Ste / saint / Saint

See **Saint** . . .

stadia / stadiums

● RECOMMENDATION

The usual forms now are one *stadium*, two or more *stadiums*. (*Stadia* is a pedantic plural form.)

standard English / *British* English

See *British* **English** . . .

star / asterisk (*)

See **asterisk** . . .

starlight / starlit

● OPTION

Starlight and *starlit* ✓ are alternative descriptive words for a scene lit by stars.

start / commence

See **commence** . . .

State / state

● RULE

Always a capital S when *State* refers to a nation or a political entity: the State of Israel. A small *s* is appropriate when it is about states in general, or describes a general condition: 'New York State (specific) is one of 50 states (general) in the USA.' Other examples are the **S**tate opening of parliament, a **S**tate occasion – but the **s**tate of the economy.

statement / invoice / bill / account

See **account** . . .

state-of-the-art

● RECOMMENDATION

State-of-the-art is overused advertising jargon. Resist it in favour of 'the most advanced'.

(the) **States / US / USA / America**

See **America** . . .

stationary / stationery

● RULE

Stationery is paper, pens, envelopes, etc, while *stationary* is not moving.

statistics *is / are*

See **-ics**

steeple / spire

See **spire** . . .

sterile / aseptic / antiseptic

See **antiseptic** . . .

sterling

● RULE

Pound sterling for British currency is officially superseded by the international currency code *GBP* (**G**reat **B**ritain **p**ound). GBP should be used in transactions with other countries. In general use within Britain the old term, *pound sterling* is still commonly used, even in banking circles. Other than that, *sterling* survives now mainly in *sterling silver* (which must have 92.5% purity) and in phrases such as *sterling worth*, *sterling value* – echoes of faraway days when the unvarying *pound sterling* was the measure of all currencies.

still lifes / still lives

● RULE

A cat has nine *lives* but in the art world the plural of *still life* is *still lifes*.

stomach / belly

See **belly** . . .

stop / cease / discontinue / terminate

● RECOMMENDATIONS

1 *Stop* is the most general word and certainly the most urgent, which is why it's often followed by an exclamation mark: 'Stop!'

2 *Cease* has a finality about it: when, for example, production in a factory *stops*, the implication is usually that it will start up again at some time. But if production *ceases*, that sounds more final, as if the factory is closing down.

3 *Discontinue* suggests breaking-off something that has been going on for a period: 'after six months, she discontinued the treatment'. It is also the standard term in production for ceasing to manufacture a particular product: a line is discontinued because it is superseded by a new design.

4 *Terminate* belongs to medical, legal or scientific contexts: pregnancies and contracts are terminated. *Terminate* is out of place in everyday use. Admittedly, rail travellers hear 'We're now arriving at . . . station, where this train will now *terminate*.' But why not '. . . where this journey ends'?

stop / full stop / period (.)

● RECOMMENDATIONS

1 *Full stop* is the formal name for this punctuation mark but the everyday term is simply *stop*.

2 Stops mark the end of sentences, and the style now is to use fewer commas (see **comma**) and more *stops*, as sentences become shorter in keeping with the faster pace of life. No one should lay down a rule about this. It is a matter of style, and the principle must always be to make a piece of writing comfortable to read and intelligible to readers. See in particular (length of) **sentences**. For other uses of *stops*, see **abbreviations; stops in titles.**

$ The term *period* is preferred.

stops in titles

● RULE

Full stops should not be used at the *end* of titles and headings, and the only punctuation marks that belong at the end are *question marks* or *exclamation marks*. *For Whom the Bell Tolls; The Satanic Verses; How Green Was My Valley?; Winner Take Nothing!*

straightaway / forthwith / immediately

See **immediately** . . .

strategy / tactics

● RULE

Strategy is broad policy, medium to long-term planning. *Tactics* are day-to-day ways of achieving the long-term plan. *Strategy* is where you are going, while *tactics* are how you get there: 'Our strategy is to increase the overall size of the market, and to achieve that, our tactics are to have local promotions in as many different regions as possible.'

strength (pronunciation)

● OPTION

To give the *g* a light *k* sound ('stren**k**th') is all right, according to some recent dictionaries, although it's better to hint at the *g* ✓ sound.

● CAUTION

'Strenth' (with no *g* or *k* sound) is not an OPTION.

stricken / struck

See **struck** . . .

stroke / heart attack / coronary

See **coronary** . . .

struck / stricken

● RULES

1 The past form of *strike* is *struck*, whatever the meaning: 'she struck him as hard as she could'; 'he was struck by her beauty'; 'the clock has struck 7'.

2 *Stricken* is an archaic past form, which survives in one or two phrases, notably 'stricken with grief'; 'stricken with remorse'.

subconscious / unconscious

See **unconscious** . . .

subjunctive

See **if I *was*** . . .

subnormal / abnormal

See **abnormal** . . .

subtitle / caption

See **caption** . . .

such as / like

See **like** (CAUTION)

sufficient / adequate / enough

See **enough** . . .

suggestive / risqué

● RECOMMENDATIONS

1 *Risqué* (French for risky and hazardous) is a tut-tut of a word for a story or remark that is mildly sexual. PRON 'REESkay'.

2 *Suggestive* is used more for a story or remark that hints at a sexual meaning without coming out into the open.

summary / synopsis / résumé / outline

See **outline** . . .

sung / sang

See **sang** . . .

sunk / sunken / sank

See **sank** . . .

supersede / supercede

● RULE

The only correct spelling is *supersede* (no dictionary allows *supercede*).

surgery / consulting room

See **consulting room** . . .

swam / swum

● RULE

It is this way round: 'I *swam* yesterday'; 'I have *swum* a long way'.

● CAUTION

'I *swum* yesterday' is a common mistake.

swap / swop

● OPTION

Swap can be swapped with *swop*, as dictionaries show *swap* ✓ and *swop* as alternative spellings.

swum / swam

See **swam** . . .

sympathy / empathy

See **empathy** . . .

symptomatic / representative / characteristic

See **characteristic** . . .

synonym / antonym / homonym

● RULES

1 **Syn**onyms are words that have almost the same meaning: *peer* and *equal*; *referee* and *umpire*; *speed* and *velocity*. There are very few perfect *synonyms*, and an effort to find the *synonym* that has the right shade of meaning penetrates more deeply into a thought.

2 **Ant**onyms are words that have opposite meanings: *good* and *bad*; *hot* and *cold*; *quick* and *slow*.

2 A **hom**onym is a word with the same sound, sometimes also with the same spelling as another word but with a different meaning: *maid* and *made*; *May* (month) and *may* (verb). *Homograph* can be used for words with the same spelling but different meanings, *homophone* for words with the same sound. *Homonym* covers both.

synopsis / summary / résumé / outline

See **outline** . . .

synthetic / man-made / artificial

See **artificial** . . .

T

tactics / strategy
   See **strategy** . . .

tactics *is* / *are*
   See **-ics**

***take* / *make* a decision**
   See **decision**

taste / opinion / attitude
   See **attitude** . . .

(the) team *is* / *are*
   See **collective words**

teaspoonfuls / teaspoonsful
   See **-ful**

technical / technological

● CAUTION

   Because *technological* is a fashionable word, it is often used when *technical* is more appropriate.

● RECOMMENDATIONS

1   *Technical* is more practical, related to a specific mechanical or other technique, or to a skill. There may be technical problems with a piece of machinery, an artist or musician can have technical difficulties over brushwork or the fingering of an instrument.

2   *Technological* is more scientific, relating to the study and development of engineering and applied sciences. A *technical* problem is something a technician can often deal with on the spot, a *technological* problem usually requires research.

technics / technology / science
   See **science** . . .

technique / method
   See **method** . . .

technological / technical

See **technical** . . .

technology / technics / science

See **science** . . .

tele / tele-

● RULE

Even *tele-* words coined within the last few years are treated as *one* word without a hyphen: telebooking; telecommuting; teleconference; telemarketing; teleprompt; teleworker.

telecast / broadcast

See **broadcast** . . .

telephone / phone

See **phone** . . .

televise / televize

● RULE

Always *televise*, as it is a verb formed from 'television'.

temporarily (pronunciation)

● RULE

It may be easier to stress the *third* syllable, but dictionaries insist on 'TEMporarily' as the correct pronunciation.

$ The *third* syllable is stressed: 'temporRARily'.

terminate / discontinue / cease / stop

See **stop / cease** . . .

text

● RECOMMENDATION

Text has become an all-embracing term for poems, plays, novels, essays. But while *text* is appropriate to information technology, it can sound too clinical to refer to the *text* of *The Waste Land; Under Milk Wood; The Power and the Glory*. And it's often unnecessary: 'when we study the text of *The Waste Land*' could just as well be 'when we study *The Waste Land*'.

than *I* / *me*, etc

● OPTION

There are many examples of good writers and speakers using *than **me**, than **him***, etc, and Eric Partridge, a conservative scholar, came out in favour of *than **me***. Other grammarians insist on *than **I**, than **he***.

● RECOMMENDATION

Use whichever comes naturally. For most of us that will be *than **me**, than **him***: 'she is taller than *me*'; 'she arrived earlier than *him*'. If you prefer *than **I***, etc, it is better to complete the sentence: 'she is taller than *I am*'; 'she arrived earlier than *he did*'. Otherwise it can sound stilted.

● CAUTION

In some sentences, look out for possible confusion: 'she loves him more than *me*' could mean 'she loves him more than she loves me' or 'she loves him more than I love him'. In such cases, say what you mean.

that

● RECOMMENDATION

When *that* is unnecessary for the sense or the sound, it can often be omitted. Take this sentence: 'I believe *that* the book *that* she has written is *that* one'. The first two *thats* could be deleted and the sentence remains good English, perfectly clear: 'I believe the book she has written is *that* one'.

that / which / who

● RULE

Who is for *people*, *which* for *things*: 'the woman *who* is here'; 'the book *which* won the prize'.

● OPTION

That can be used for *people* or *things*: 'the women *who* ✓ (or *that*) came late'.

   NOTE Some grammarians believe there is a subtle difference between *who* and *that* (for people) and *which* and *that* (for things), but so very few people recognise this that it's better to follow the RULE and OPTION above.

● RECOMMENDATION

That (rather than *who* or *which*) is preferable for animals: 'the dog that died'.

theirs / their's

● RULE

Their's is *always* wrong.

there-

● RECOMMENDATION

Thereabouts, thereby, therefore and one or two other *there-* combinations have a place, but most of the others, such as *thereafter, therein, thereinafter, thereof, theretofore, therewith*, should be used very sparingly, as they strike a stuffy legalistic note.

therefore

● RECOMMENDATION

Therefore is at best a rather heavy-going word (see **there-**). At one time, it was always preceded and followed by a comma: 'I consider, therefore, that . . .'. If there are occasions when you have to use *therefore*, the commas can at least be omitted these days in most sentences.

there's no question

See **no question**

they'd *have*

See **I'd *have* . . .**

they're

See **contracted forms**

though / albeit / although

See **although . . .**

through

● CAUTION

The American use of *through* to mean 'up to and including' has not caught on in Britain, although it is used. It would be useful: for example, '7th *through* 27th January' makes it clear that the *27th* is included, whereas '7th to 27th' leaves it uncertain, and we need to say '. . . up to and including 27th'.

$ See above.

throw / cast

● RECOMMENDATIONS

1 *Throw* is the word used in most everyday contexts. In fact, where *throw* can be used, *cast* often sounds pompous: 'she cast his letter into the fire'.

2 *Cast* is now restricted mostly to technical and particular applications: moulds are cast; actors are cast for roles; votes are cast and so are fishing lines and anchors.

tilde (~)

See **accents**

till / until

See **until . . .**

tin / can

See **can / tin**

tissue (pronunciation)
- OPTION
  'TISHyou'✓ or 'TISSyou'.

titles of people
See **ambassador; clergy**

to
- RECOMMENDATION
  There is no need to be hesitant about ending a sentence with the word *to* ('Who is it going to?'). See **prepositions at *end* of sentences.**

to a degree
See **degree**

together with
- RULE
  If someone is *together with* another person, it is followed by a *singular* verb: 'my friend, together with her husband, *is* coming to dinner'.

ton / tonne
- RULES
1 *Ton* represents various units of weight, the most common of which in Britain is 20 hundredweight (2240 pounds or approx 1016 kilograms).
2 *Tonne* is a metric measurement and equals 1000 kilograms (approx 2205 pounds).
3 Both *ton* and *tonne* are pronounced 'tun', and if you need to indicate in speech which is which, refer to *tons* (or *British tons*) or *metric tonnes*.

tornado / cyclone / gale / hurricane / typhoon / blizzard
See **blizzard** . . .

tortuous / torturous
- RULES
1 *Tortuous* is winding and twisted: a tortuous route; a tortuous mind.
2 *Torturous* is something that inflicts torture: a torturous experience; torturous agony.
      NOTE At times they link up, for driving along a *tortuous road*, particularly when it is icy, can be *torturous*.

Tory / Conservative
See **Conservative / Tory**

total of . . . *is* / *are*

● RULES

1 'A total' is *plural*, followed by *are*, *have*, etc: 'a total of 20 women *were* at the meeting'.

2 '*The* total' is *singular*: 'the total number of women at the meeting *is* unknown'.

● CAUTIONS

1 It's easy to slip up when a sentence begins with 'There': 'There *was* a total of nine women unable to be present' should be 'There *were* a total of . . .' (because '*a total*' is *plural* – see RULE 1 above).

2 When 'who' (or another word) comes in between, be extra careful. We have to write, for example, 'the total number of women who *are* . . .', but RULE 2 above still holds, as a *singular* verb follows: 'the total number of women who are coming tonight *is* small'.

See also **number of . . . *is* / *are*.**

toward / towards

● OPTION

You can go *toward* or *towards* ✓ someone.

$ Usually *toward*.

town / city

See **city . . .**

trade / business

See **business . . .**

trademark / logo

See **logo . . .**

trade union / trades union

● OPTION

Both forms exist but trade union ✓ (plural *trade unions*) is usual now, except in Trades Union Congress (where *trades union* is used as the plural form).

trait (pronunciation)

● OPTION

Dictionaries show two pronunciations: 'tray' (with final *t* not sounded)✓ or 'trayt'.

trans / trans-

● RULE

Nearly all *trans* words now appear as *one* word (without a hyphen), even when it results in a double *s*: transcontinental; transnational; transoceanic; transsexual. This is the usual form, even when the second word is the name of an ocean or a country: transatlantic; transpacific (rather than 'trans-Atlantic'; 'trans-Pacific'). (One exception is the name of the longest railway in the world, the Trans-Siberian Railway.)

transcendent / transcendental
● RECOMMENDATIONS

1 Apart from philosophical contexts, use *transcendental* to connote something beyond ordinary human consciousness, a surpassing of the ego and attachment to this life: 'a transcendental experience'.

2 *Transcendent* has a similar meaning but can be used in non-mystical contexts to mean far beyond what is usual, as in 'transcendent importance'; 'transcendent ability'.

transfer / assign
See **assign** . . .

transferable (pronunciation)
● RECOMMENDATION

Most dictionaries now show only one pronunciation: 'transFERable' (stress on the *second* syllable).

translate / transliterate
● RULES

1 *Translate* is straightforward: it is expressing words in one language in another.

2 *Transliterate* (PRON 'transLITerayte') is representing the letters of a word in one alphabet as closely as possible using the letters of another. Russian and Greek, for example, which have their own alphabets, are usually shown in English using letters of the Roman alphabet, with an attempt to imitate the sound.

● CAUTION

Because *transliteration* can only be approximate, the adaptation of letters from one alphabet to another can vary in different texts. So there is sometimes disagreement over how Russian names, for example, are spelt in English.

transparency / colour negative / diapositive
See **colour negative** . . .

treble / triple
● OPTION

Other than as musical terms (where *treble* and *triple* are used in different ways), *treble* and *triple* ✓ can be used interchangeably: 'it is *treble* (or *triple*) the price it was ten years ago'.

trendy

● RECOMMENDATION

Dictionaries may consider *trendy* informal and not quite literary, but it is on its way to becoming standard English, available for use, even in serious writing.

● CAUTION

Trendy sometimes has a derogatory undertone, suggesting a self-conscious adoption of a style or manner.

trillion / billion

See **billion** . . .

triple / treble

See **treble** . . .

triumphal / triumphant

● RECOMMENDATIONS

1 *Triumph**ant*** is for people, their gestures, tone of voice and their deeds: players are triumphant when they win an important game; Oxford or Cambridge crews make triumphant gestures after winning the Boat Race; a successful take-over bid is triumphant.

2 *Triumph**al*** is more for objects or symbols celebrating a triumph: the Arc de Triomphe in Paris is a triumphal arch.

trooper / trouper

● RULES

1 *Troo**per*** is military, used for a soldier in a cavalry regiment.

2 *Trou**per*** is theatrical, for a member of a theatrical company, and by extension for a member of a team of people working together ('he's a good trouper').

$ *Troo**per*** is a member of the state police.

trousers *is / are*

● RULE

The word *trousers* is plural: 'the trousers *are* folded'. *A pair of trousers* is the only *singular* form.

truck / lorry

See **lorry** . . .

try *and / to*

● RECOMMENDATION

Try *and* is all right in speech, but less so in formal writing, where try *to* is preferable.

tsar / czar

● OPTION

> *Tsar* ✓ and *czar* are alternative spellings.
> PRON 'zahr' (for both spellings).

Turco- / Turko-

● RULE

> *Turco-* is the correct prefix relating to Turkey: a Turco-French agreement. (*Turko-* is never used.)

turquoise (pronunciation)

● OPTIONS

> 'TERkwoyze'✓, 'TERkwuzz' (last syllable rhymes with 'buzz'), or 'TERkwahz'.

typhoon / cyclone / gale / hurricane / tornado / blizzard

> See blizzard . . .

typo / literal / misprint

> See misprint . . .

U

Ulster / Northern Ireland / Eire / Southern Ireland

See **Ireland** . . .

ultimate

● RECOMMENDATION

Ultimate has a place in philosophy and theology, but in everyday contexts, such as 'the hotel is the ultimate in luxury', *ultimate* is an advertising cliché. Consider these alternatives: foremost, supreme, unequalled, or even 'the last word'.

umlaut / diaeresis

See **accents**

umpire / referee

See **referee** . . .

un- / non- / in-

See **in-** . . .

un- words

● RECOMMENDATION

So many *un-* words have accumulated, that no dictionary can list all of them. If you think of a useful *un-* word, and cannot find it in a dictionary, that's no reason for not using it. Kingsley Amis, for example, described a woman with *unabundant* brown hair; the *New Statesman* used *unpublicity* about something that had been completely ignored by the media.

● CAUTION

With some *un-* words, watch out for an occasional risk of confusion between two possible meanings: 'she's undressed', for example, could mean she has just taken her clothes off, or she has not dressed yet.

See also **not in- / not un-**.

unadvisable / inadvisable

See **in-** (OPTION)

unafraid / fearless

See **fearless** . . .

unbelievable / incredulous / incredible

See incredible . . .

unconditional / categorical

See categorical . . .

unconditional / unconditioned

● RECOMMENDATIONS

1   Use *unconditional* to mean 'without conditions', as in 'an unconditional surrender'.

2   Use *unconditioned* to mean a natural, unfettered open response, free from the clutter of associations, influences and unquestioned handed-down beliefs: 'if you look at this in an unconditioned way, you will see new solutions'.

unconscious / subconscious

● OPTION

Although Freudian psychologists may distinguish between these two words, in general use both *un*conscious ✓ and *sub*conscious refer to that part of the mind we are not usually aware of, which influences behaviour and manifests itself in dreams.

under / under-

● RULE

Nearly all *under-* formations are treated as *one* word (without a hyphen): underachieve; underact; undercarriage; undercover; undercut; underexpose; undermanned; undersexed. But with *titles*, a hyphen is used: under-secretary; under-sheriff.

under / in the circumstances

See circumstances

underdeveloped / developing country

See *developing* country . . .

undertone / overtone

See overtone . . .

undisciplined / indisciplined

See indisciplined . . .

undiscriminating / indiscriminate

See indiscriminate . . .

undue / unduly

● RECOMMENDATION

Undue means 'excessive for the circumstances', but it is often a word slipped in to sound important: 'there is no cause for undue alarm'; 'it does not require undue intelligence'. There's no need to use *undue* unless it is really necessary, which will not be often: 'too much' is a straightforward alternative. And *unduly* can usually be replaced by 'over-': 'we need not be overanxious' (rather than '. . . unduly anxious').

uneatable / inedible

See **inedible** . . .

uneconomic / uneconomical

See **economic** . . . (NOTE)

unequivocable / unequivocal

● RULE

*Unequivoc**al*** means there is no doubt, that something is altogether clear: 'we have to accept this unequivocal decision'. *Unequivoc**able*** is not in any dictionary.

unexceptionable / unexceptional

See **exceptionable** . . .

unilateral / one-sided

See **one-sided** . . .

uninformed / misinformed / ill-informed

See **ill-informed** . . .

uninterested / disinterested

See **disinterested** . . .

unique

● RULE

Unique means the only one of its kind and is an absolute word, like 'true'. We should avoid '*very* unique' or '*quite* unique', because there are no degrees of uniqueness.

● RECOMMENDATION

Almost unique is perhaps acceptable because it suggests that there are very few like it. But even so, 'rare' or 'extremely rare' is preferable.

unisex / unisexual

● CAUTION

The two words mean the opposite to each other. *Unisex**ual*** is used in biology or botany about an organism or a plant that has the characteristics of only *one* sex. *Unisex* is a descriptive word for something suitable or applicable to *both* sexes (unisex hairdressers cater for men and women).

unisex grammar

Everybody, everyone, nobody, someone and similar words are *singular*: 'everybody *is* . . .'. Such words were traditionally followed by *he, him, his,* blandly assuming that *he, him, his,* include women: 'nobody has taken *his* seat yet'. This is no longer acceptable to many people. We wear our readers out writing and saying **he or she** all the time. *S / he* is clumsy and awkward to say aloud.

More and more writers see the best resolution as using *they, them, their* as unisex pronouns: 'nobody has taken *their* seat yet'. [!] The grammatical objection is that the singular *nobody* conflicts with the plural *their*. In spite of this, *they* and *their* are taking on a *plural* or *singular* sense as required: 'Whoever is elected will take *their* seat in the House of Commons the next day.' (BBC News); Kazuo Ishiguro, in *The Remains of the Day* (winner of the 1989 Booker Prize), wrote '. . . some fellow professional . . . would be accompanying *their* employer'.

● RECOMMENDATIONS

1 *He, him, his* should no longer be used to include women.

2 When it seems appropriate, *he or she, him or her,* etc (varied with *she or he,* etc) can be used, but not repeatedly in the same text, or it becomes laboured.

3 Where it is neither awkward nor misleading, a sentence can be rewritten to sidestep the problem: 'nobody has taken his seat yet' could be recast as 'people have not taken their seats yet' (although the meaning is not quite the same).

4 In all other cases, use the plural forms *they, them, their* as singular unisex words, accepting with regret that some readers will shake their heads reproachfully. But you will be in good company: 'Nobody prevents you do *they*?' (Thackeray); 'No one would ever marry if *they* thought it over.' (Bernard Shaw).

United Kingdom / Great Britain / British Isles / Britain

See **Britain** . . .

United States / US / USA / America

See **America** . . .

university / school / college

See **college** . . .

unmistakable / unmistakeable

● RULE

Unmistakable.

unmovable / irremovable / immovable

See **immovable** . . .

unparalleled

For an easy way to remember how many *l*s there are, see **parallel**.

unpractical / impractical / impracticable

See **impracticable** . . .

unprecedented (pronunciation)

● RULE

'unPRESSedented', (not 'unPREESedented').

unquote / quote

For the use of this convention in speech, see **quote / unquote**.

unreadable / illegible

See **illegible** . . .

unreligious / nonreligious / sacrilegious / irreligious

See **irreligious** . . .

unsatisfied / dissatisfied

See **dissatisfied** . . .

unseasonable / unseasonal

See **seasonable** . . . (RECOMMENDATION 3)

unshakeable / unshakable

● RULE

Unshakeable.

unsociable / unsocial / antisocial

See **antisocial** . . .

until / till

● OPTION

In many contexts, there is nothing to choose between *till* or **until**: 'I will love you *till* (or *until*) I die.' In formal contexts, **until** is preferable, and **until** usually sounds better when it's the *first* word of a sentence: 'Until I die, I will love you.'

upon / on

See **on / upon**

upper class

See **class**

up to / *down* to

See *down* to . . .

up to date / up-to-date

● RULE

Use hyphens when it comes *before* a noun ('an up-to-date costing'): keep the words separate when they come *after* a noun ('a costing that is up to date'). See **hyphens** (RECOMMENDATION 4).

upward / upwards

● RECOMMENDATIONS

1   When attached to a *verb*, use *upwards*: look upwards; move upwards.
2   When attached to a *noun*, use *upward*: an upward look; an upward movement.
$ *Upward* is more usual in all contexts.

upwards of

● RECOMMENDATION

There is no good reason why *upwards of* ('upwards of ten people are waiting') should be used instead of 'more than' ('more than ten people . . .'), which is more direct.

US / USA / the States / America

See **America** . . .

us / we

● CAUTION

In some sentences, *us* is occasionally slipped in, when it should be *we*: 'we were not as tolerant as *us* English are supposed to be'. The way to avoid this mistake is to try the sentence leaving out the word or words between *us* and the verb: in the above example, clearly it has to be 'as *we* . . . are supposed to be'.

usage / use

● RECOMMENDATION

The *use* of anything is simply its being made use of, while *usage* is the customary or regular way in which something is used: 'the use of English all over the world is increasing all the time'; 'the usage of English is becoming less and less grammatical'.

● CAUTION

The most common error is for *usage* to become an official-sounding alternative to *use*: 'the usage of public libraries is increasing'. The proper word there is *use*.

used to

Even experienced writers have to stop and think about the different forms of *used to*. There is no problem when it's a straightforward statement: 'I used to walk to work.' The problems start when it is negative or a question.

● RULES

1 There are two *negative* forms. The strictly correct one is 'he used not to walk to work'. The more relaxed form is 'he did not (or didn't) use to walk to work'.

2 When asking a question, the strictly correct sequences are 'Used he to walk to work?'; 'Used he not to walk to work?' The relaxed forms are 'Did he use to walk to work?'; 'Didn't he use to walk to work?'

3 The correct *contracted forms* are: *usedn't to* and *didn't use to*. 'Usen't to' and 'didn't used to' are errors. Admittedly, when those incorrect forms are *spoken* they sound the same, and the contracted forms are not often used in writing.

● RECOMMENDATION

Except in very formal contexts, use the relaxed forms in RULES 1 and 2 above.

utmost / uttermost

● RECOMMENDATION

It could be that **uttermost** goes just a bit further than **ut***most*: 'the *uttermost* limits', for example, may be a whisker beyond 'the *utmost* limits'.

U-turn

● RECOMMENDATION

U-turn has been adapted for any complete change of mind or policy. But *U-turn* comes over as derogatory, implying a backdown. There's no need to fall in with that, for in life, as on the roads, it could be better at times to make a *U-turn* than continue in the wrong direction. To avoid a negative suggestion, use another expression, such as 'a re-evaluation'; 'a reconsideration'; 'a prudent reversal of direction'.

V

vaccinate / inoculate

See inoculate . . .

valuable / priceless / invaluable

See invaluable . . .

vast / huge / gigantic / colossal

See colossal . . .

verbal / oral

● CAUTION

All agreements using *words*, whether in speech or writing, are *verbal* agreements, because *verbal* relates to the use of words. But the misuse of *verbal* for *oral* (that is for something *spoken*, rather than written) is so widespread that for most people 'a *verbal* agreement' means a spoken agreement, not in writing. Because there is this misunderstanding over what *verbal* means, it's safer now to distinguish between 'a spoken agreement' and 'a written agreement'.

verbs

See **grammatical terms**

verify / cross-check

See **cross-check** . . .

very

● RECOMMENDATIONS

1   There is a grammatical principle that *very* belongs with *descriptive words* ('very hot'; 'very big'), and should not be used with -*ed* forms of *verbs*. We should say, for example, 'much used' rather than 'very used', to mean used a great deal. In fact, *very* does not sound right in front of the -*ed* form of many verbs, and where there's a doubt, use 'much' instead: 'this is a much debated question'; 'a much corrected version'; 'a much travelled woman'. At the same time, some -*ed* words, such as *pleased, tired, exaggerated*, are felt to be descriptive words, rather than verbs, so there's no reason to avoid, for example, 'very pleased'; 'very tired'; 'very exaggerated'.

2   *Very* is overused, so it's often worth finding an alternative word ('extremely grateful'; 'most kind'), which does not mean we can never be '*very* angry' or '*very* much in love'.

vessel / ship / boat

See **boat** . . .

via (pronunciation)

● RULE

'**VYE**-e(r)' (rather than '**VEE**er').

vicar / rector / parson / priest / minister

See **minister** . . .

vicarage / rectory

See **minister** . . . (RULE 3)

vide / qv / see

See **see / vide** . . .

video / video-

● RECOMMENDATION

A number of *video* combinations are fused into one word: *videoconference*; *videographics*; *videophone*; *videotape*; *videotext*. Dictionaries disagree over some words, but it is likely that compounds that are still separate words (*video game*; *video recorder*; *video signal*) will soon become one-word terms. So when in doubt, it's reasonable to treat most *video-* combinations as *one* word.

village / hamlet

● RECOMMENDATION

Hamlet might be used for any small cluster of houses, but there is no general agreement over when a *hamlet* becomes a *village*. If in doubt, call a place a *village*, which is by far the more usual word. For guidance on when a *village* becomes a *town*, see **city / town.**

virtuosi / virtuosos

● OPTION

Virtuosi is the plural in Italian. In English *virtuosos* ✓ is an alternative plural form.

virus / microbe / bacteria / germ

See **germ** . . .

vis-à-vis

● RECOMMENDATION

Vis-à-vis (PRON 'veez-ah-VEE') is French (short for 'visage-à-visage' – face to face). In English, the most usual meaning is 'concerning or relating to': 'the situation vis-à-vis our office in Birmingham'. In most cases *vis-à-vis* can be, and should be, replaced by 'concerning' or 'regarding', since there is little point in using a French expression unnecessarily.

vitamin (pronunciation)

● OPTION

You can choose whether you take 'V**I**TT-amins'✓ or 'V**Y**TE-amins'.

viz / ie

See **ie / viz**

voluntarily (pronunciation)

● RULE

'V**O**Luntarily' (stress on the *first* syllable) is more difficult to say because of the long flight of unaccented syllables, but it is considered the correct British pronunciation.

\$ 'volunT**A**Rily'.

vowel / letter / consonant

See **consonant** . . .

vulgar / common / coarse

See **coarse** . . .

waive / wave

● RULES

1 We *waive* our legal rights or a claim on someone, or an opportunity to do something, that is we give them up, or at least do not insist upon them: 'she waived her right to an allowance from him'.

2 We *wave* goodbye.

wake / awake

See **awake** . . .

want / wish / desire

See **desire** . . .

(if I) *was / were*

See **if I *was*** . . .

wastage / waste

● RULES

1 *Waste* is when something is consumed uselessly: dripping taps are a waste of water.

2 *Wastage* is loss through legitimate use or natural causes: in hot weather there is a wastage of water from reservoirs caused by evaporation.

3 The same distinction can apply to people. It is a *waste* of well-qualified people when an organisation does not make proper use of their talents: the expression 'natural *wastage*' is the loss of employees through retirement, resignation, death or for any other reasons than dismissal.

wave / waive

See **waive** . . .

we / us

See **us / we**

we'd

See **contracted forms**

we'd *have*

See **I'd *have*** . . .

well / well-

● RULES

1 When *well* compounds come *before a noun*, they should nearly always be hyphenated: a well-worn carpet; a well-thought-of book; a well-matched couple; a well-informed expert (see **hyphens** RECOMMENDATION 4).

2 When *well* compounds come *after a verb*, hyphens are not usually necessary: 'the carpet is well worn'; 'the book is well thought of'; 'the expert is well informed'.

3 There are some exceptions: *well-off* is easier to take in when it's hyphenated, wherever it comes in the sentence; *well-spoken* is hyphenated when it describes the way someone speaks, ('her secretary is well-spoken'), but kept as separate words when it refers to someone being praised ('she is well spoken of').

(if I) *were / was*

See **if I** *was* . . .

West / west

See **North / north** . . .

Western / western

See **Northern / northern** . . .

westward / westwards / westerly

See **northward** . . .

wh- (pronunciation)

● RECOMMENDATION

The advice of the best linguistic authorities is to forget about the *hw* sound and pronounce *whether* the same as 'weather', *which* the same as 'witch', and *what, when* as 'wot', 'wen'.

NOTE It is usual in Scotland and Ireland to stress the *h* in *wh-* words, and to pronounce *what, when, whether* as '**h**wat', '**h**wen', '**h**wether'. BBC announcers also seem keen on this.

wharves / wharfs

● OPTION

Wharves ✓ and *wharfs* are alternative plural forms of *wharf.*

what *is / are*

● RULE

When the word attached to *what* is *singular*, the verb must clearly also be *singular*: 'what we need is a faster delivery service'.

- **OPTION**

  When the word relating to *what* is *plural*, either a *singular* or *plural* form of the verb can follow: 'what we need *are* ✓ (or *is*) more houses'.

whatever / what ever

See -ever

whenever / when ever

See -ever

whereabouts *is* / *are*

- **OPTION**

  Whereabouts as a noun can be treated as *singular* or *plural*: 'her whereabouts at the time *were* ✓ (or *was*) unknown'.

wherever / where ever

See -ever

whether / if

See **if / whether**

which / who / that

See **that / which . . .**

which / whose

See **whose . . .**

whichever / which ever

See -ever

which *is* / *are*

- **RULE**

  'Which of the five books *are* best?' means which two, three or four of the books are best: 'Which of the five books *is* best?' means which *one* of them is best.

while / awhile

See **awhile . . .**

while / whilst

- **OPTION**

  While ✓ and *whilst* are interchangeable, with *whilst* having a more literary ring to it. Both words properly relate to time: 'she phoned *while* (or *whilst*) you were out'. Both words are also used as an alternative to 'although': '*while* (or *whilst*) I understand your problem, I don't think it is serious'.

● CAUTION

Look out for confusion in certain contexts: 'while she knows nothing about it, I expect she'll cope quite well' could suggest that if she knew more, she'd make a hash of it. If that's not the intended meaning, use 'although' instead ('although she knows nothing about it, . . .').

whisky / whiskey

● RULES

In Scotland, it's *whisky*. In Ireland, it's *whiskey*. In the US, it's *whiskey* (those in the know use the spelling *whisky*, when it comes from Scotland, and *whiskey* when it's made in the US). In Canada, it's *whisky*, wherever it's made.

White / white

● RULE

We should refer to *white* people or *whites*, without a capital *W*. See also **black / coloured; non-white**.

who / which / that

See **that / which** . . .

who / whom

● OPTIONS

1   Follow the orthodox grammatical rules, and here is a useful guide which works in most sentences. Divide the sentence into two parts and see whether you use 'he' or 'him' (or 'she' or 'her') in the *second* part. If it's 'him' or 'her', use *whom* in the original sentence, otherwise use *who*. Examples:
    i   The man *whom* I saw yesterday: The man. I saw *him* yesterday. (*Whom* is correct.)
    ii The man *who* I think was here yesterday: The man. I think *he* was here yesterday. (*Who* is correct.)
    iii The woman *whom* I'm going to marry: The woman. I'm going to marry *her*. (*Whom* is correct.)
    iv The woman *who* is going to marry me: The woman. *She* is going to marry me. (*Who* is correct.)
2   ✓ Write and say *whom* when it comes *immediately* after a preposition (short relating words, such as *to, for, at, from*): to *whom*, from *whom*, for *whom*, with *whom*, among *whom*. Everywhere else, use *who*. [!] You may be picked on for this, but the tide is going your way.

● CAUTIONS

    If you take OPTION 1 above:

1 Be on guard against forcing in *whom* where it doesn't belong: 'Her husband, *whom* she thinks is working late, is really having an affair.' Divide that sentence into two (see advice in OPTION 1 above): Her husband. She thinks *he* is working late. (*Who* is correct: 'Her husband, *who* she thinks . . .').

2 Avoid sounding stuffy: '*Whom* shall I send it to?', for example, although grammatically correct, can seem pedantic in informal writing and downright pompous in speech, since '*Who* shall I send it to?' is normal everyday language.

whoever / who ever

    See **-ever**

whoever / whomever

● RECOMMENDATION

    No matter how careful you are over using **who / whom** correctly, think twice before writing or saying *whomever*. One of the editors of the *Oxford English Dictionary*, no less, advises that *whomever* is stilted, and that *whoever* should now be used right across the board.

whom / who

    See **who / whom**

whomever / whoever

    See **whoever . . .**

whose / which

● RULE

    Whose can be used for *things* as well as people, so there is no need for such stilted sentences as 'the car of which the seats are made of leather'; 'the play the actors of which are all women'. We can write 'the car *whose* seats are made of leather'; 'the play *whose* actors are all women'.

wide / broad

    See **broad . . .**

will / shall

    See **shall . . .**

windfall / bonus

    See **bonus . . .**

windward / leeward

See **leeward** . . .

(names of) **wines**

● OPTION

Traditionally, regional names of French, German and Italian wines bear initial capital letters: we drink **B**ordeaux, **B**urgundy, **S**ancerre, **M**oselle, **C**hianti. With the present trend to use fewer **capital letters**, some wine writers are dropping capitals from the names of wines. Now it's a matter of taste (like the wines themselves) whether you drink **B**urgundy, **V**ouvray, **S**auternes, **C**hianti or **b**urgundy✓, **v**ouvray✓, **s**auternes✓, **c**hianti✓. But 'saint' names, such as St Emilion and Saint Amour, look wrong without capitals. And capitals are required when a *region* is used as a descriptive term: **B**eaujolais wines; **L**oire wines.

-wise

● RECOMMENDATIONS

1   If you use the suffix *-wise* too often, it becomes a trendy cliché, but occasionally -wise added to a word says something quickly and effectively: *careerwise* is neater than 'in relation to my career'; *moneywise* more direct than 'as far as money is concerned'; and Iris Murdoch lamented the end of the season for Cox's orange pippins by being 'in mourning *applewise*'.

2   When *wise* is tacked on to a word, the tendency is *not* to use a hyphen (as in the above examples).

wish / want / desire

See **desire** . . .

. . . with . . .

● RULE

When *with* links two nouns together, it is the noun that comes *first* which dictates whether the following verb is *singular* or *plural*: 'the *teacher* together with the children *has* arrived', but 'the *children* together with their teacher *have* arrived'.

withdraw / retreat

See **retreat** . . .

within the hour / *in an* hour

See *in an* **hour** . . .

with respect to

See (in) **respect of** . . .

with the exception of

See **except . . .** (RECOMMENDATION)

woman / female / lady

See **lady . . .**

wondrous / wonderous

● RULE

Wondrous (see **-erous / -rous**).

won't

See **contracted forms**

wordprocessor / word processor

● RECOMMENDATION

Most dictionaries continue to show the term as *two* words, but it is beginning to show up as *one* word, which makes sense, for who writes 'type writer'?

work / oeuvre

See **oeuvre . . .**

working class

See **class**

world / earth / Earth

See **Earth . . .**

worsen / deteriorate

See **deteriorate . . .**

worth / worthwhile / worth while

● RECOMMENDATIONS

1 When it comes *before a noun*, *worthwhile* should be *one* word: a worthwhile journey; a worthwhile charity.

2 When it comes *after a verb*, *worth while* is better as *two* words: 'the journey was worth while'; 'the charity is worth while'.

3 *Worth* is the word to modify a *verb*: 'if something is worth doing, it is worth doing well' (rather than '*worthwhile* doing').

worthwhile / worthy

● RECOMMENDATION

Worthy can be slightly patronising: 'a worthy young couple' could suggest they are dull and uninteresting. *Worthwhile* is more wholehearted: 'a worthwhile young couple' implies that you like and admire them.

would / should
See **should** . . .

wrangle / haggle
See **haggle** . . .

wrapped / rapt
See **rapt** . . .

writer / author
● RECOMMENDATION

The tendency now is for *authors* to call themselves *writers*. But 19th-century institutions retain *authors* (The Society of Authors; Authors' Club). And when the curtain falls on the first night of a play, it is still traditional for the audience to call out *Author! Author!*

wrong / wrongly
● RECOMMENDATIONS

1 *Wrong* is the usual form *after* verbs: 'you did it wrong'; 'she guessed wrong about his age'. (No one could say *wrongly* is incorrect in such sentences, but it is less natural.)
2 When it comes *before* verbs, *wrongly* is required: 'it is wrongly said that . . .'; 'he wrongly decided to . . .'.
3 *Wrongly* also belongs in the combination *rightly or wrongly*, whether it comes before or after the verb: 'she felt, rightly or wrongly, that . . .'. See also **right / rightly.**

X Y Z

Xmas / Christmas
    See **Christmas** . . .

(a) year / per annum
    See **per** (RECOMMENDATION 1); **a year** . . .

yeses / yesses
● RULE
    'When the vote was taken, there were many more *yeses* than nos' (not *yesses*).

yoghurt / yogurt / yoghourt
● OPTION
    *Yog**hurt*** ✓ is the usual spelling, with *yog**urt*** as a variation, and *yog**hourt*** is also
    possible. PRON 'YOGGert', whichever way it's spelt.
$ The same variations in spelling. PRON 'YOHgert'.

(between) you and *me* / *I*
    See **I / me** (RULE)

you'd
    See **contracted forms**

you'd *have*
    See **I'd *have*** . . .

you'll
    See **contracted forms**

young people / youths / youngsters
● RECOMMENDATIONS
    To some people, *youngster* can sound slightly patronising. *Youths* is more associated
    with men than with women, and *youths* often features in news items about unrest
    and violence, so the word has taken on that colouring. *Young people* is the most
    satisfactory term, and it clearly covers men and women.

you're

See **contracted forms**

yours / your's

● RULE

Your's is always wrong.

youths / youngsters / young people

See **young people** . . .

-yse / -yze

● RULE

-yse is the only accepted spelling for words such as *paralyse*; *analyse*.

\$ *-yze* is the standard spelling: *analyze*; *paralyze*.

-z / -zz

● RULE

Buzz, fizz, frizz, but *quiz*.

● OPTION

Whiz ✓ or *whizz*.

zero / 'oh' / naught / nought

See **nought** . . .

zoom *up / down*

● RECOMMENDATION

It's better to use *zoom* for an *upwards* direction, and to use 'swoop' or 'dive' for *downwards*: 'the aircraft zoomed up' but 'the eagle swooped down'. But as we all know, cars can zoom *round* a track, and camera lenses zoom *in* and zoom *out*.

Wilhelm von Humboldt (1767–1835)
related language to the continuous evolution
of humanity. These lines, from a translation of
one of his essays, are a reminder that the last word
on good English usage can never be written:

*There can never be a moment when language
truly stands still, any more than there is a pause
in the ever-blazing thoughts in the human mind.*